Peace Out, Dawg!

TALES FROM GROUND ZERO

Recent Doonesbury Books by G.B. Trudeau

Read My Lips, Make My Day, Eat Quiche and Die!
Give Those Nymphs Some Hooters!
You're Smokin' Now, Mr. Butts!
I'd Go With the Helmet, Ray
Welcome to Club Scud!
What Is It, Tink, Is Pan in Trouble?
Quality Time on Highway 1
Washed Out Bridges and Other Disasters
In Search of Cigarette Holder Man
Doonesbury Nation
Virtual Doonesbury
Planet Doonesbury
Buck Wild Doonesbury
Duke 2000: Whatever It Takes
The Revolt of the English Majors

Special Collections

The Doonesbury Chronicles
Doonesbury's Greatest Hits
The People's Doonesbury
Doonesbury Dossier: The Reagan Years
Doonesbury Deluxe: Selected Glances Askance
Recycled Doonesbury: Second Thoughts on a Gilded Age
Action Figure!
The Portable Doonesbury
Flashbacks: Twenty-five Years of Doonesbury
The Bundled Doonesbury

A DOONESBURY BOOK

Peace Out, Dawg!

TALES FROM GROUND ZERO

BY G. B. TRUDEAU

Andrews McMeel
Publishing

Kansas City

DOONESBURY is distributed internationally by Universal Press Syndicate.

Peace Out, Dawg! copyright © 2002 by G.B. Trudeau. All rights reserved. Printed in the United States of America. No part of this book may be used or reproduced in any manner whatsoever without written permission except in the case of reprints in the context of reviews. For information, write Andrews McMeel Publishing, an Andrews McMeel Universal company, 4520 Main Street, Kansas City, Missouri 64111.

www.andrewsmcmeel.com

ISBN: 0-7407-2677-3

Library of Congress Catalog Card Number: 2002107476

DOONESBURY may be viewed on the Internet at:
www.uComics.com and www.doonesbury.com

"All in all, it's been a fabulous year for Laura and me."

—George W. Bush, Dec. 12, 2001

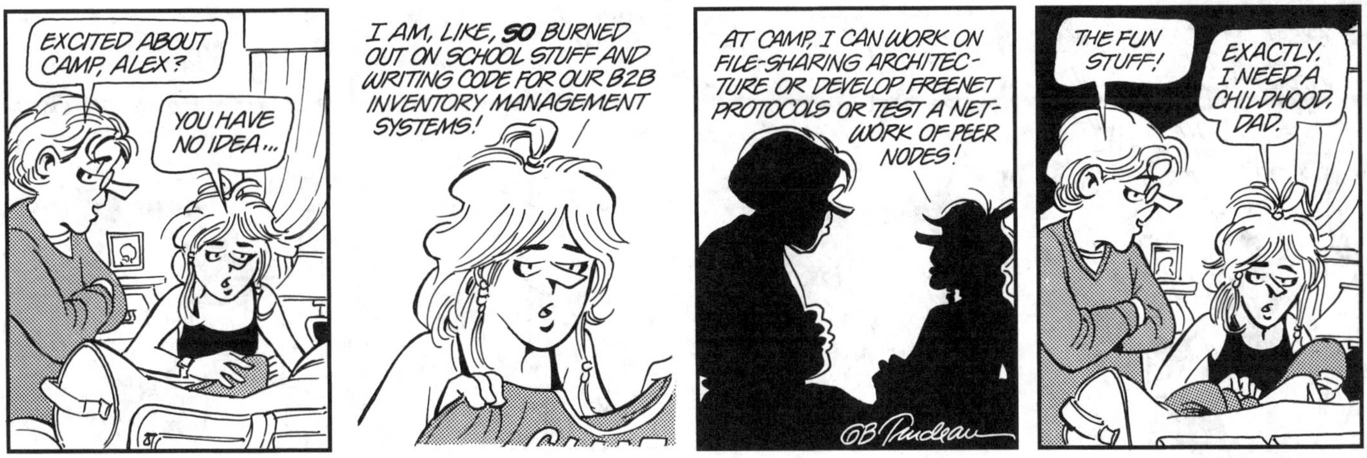
EXCITED ABOUT CAMP, ALEX?
YOU HAVE NO IDEA...
I AM, LIKE, **SO** BURNED OUT ON SCHOOL STUFF AND WRITING CODE FOR OUR B2B INVENTORY MANAGEMENT SYSTEMS!
AT CAMP, I CAN WORK ON FILE-SHARING ARCHITECTURE OR DEVELOP FREENET PROTOCOLS OR TEST A NETWORK OF PEER NODES!
THE FUN STUFF!
EXACTLY. I NEED A CHILDHOOD, DAD.

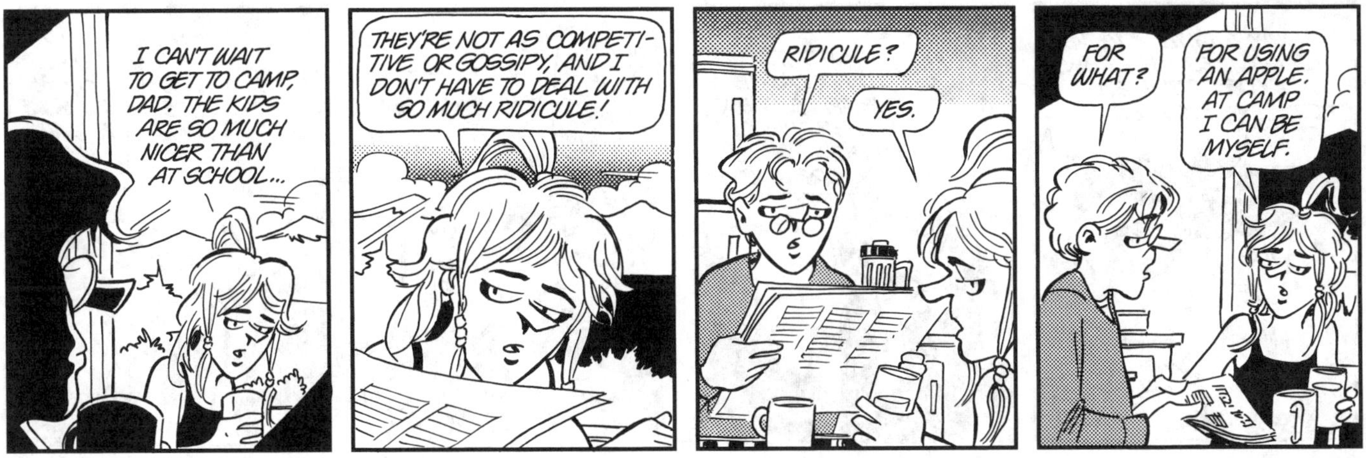
I CAN'T WAIT TO GET TO CAMP, DAD. THE KIDS ARE SO MUCH NICER THAN AT SCHOOL...
THEY'RE NOT AS COMPETITIVE OR GOSSIPY, AND I DON'T HAVE TO DEAL WITH SO MUCH RIDICULE!
RIDICULE?
YES.
FOR WHAT?
FOR USING AN APPLE. AT CAMP I CAN BE MYSELF.

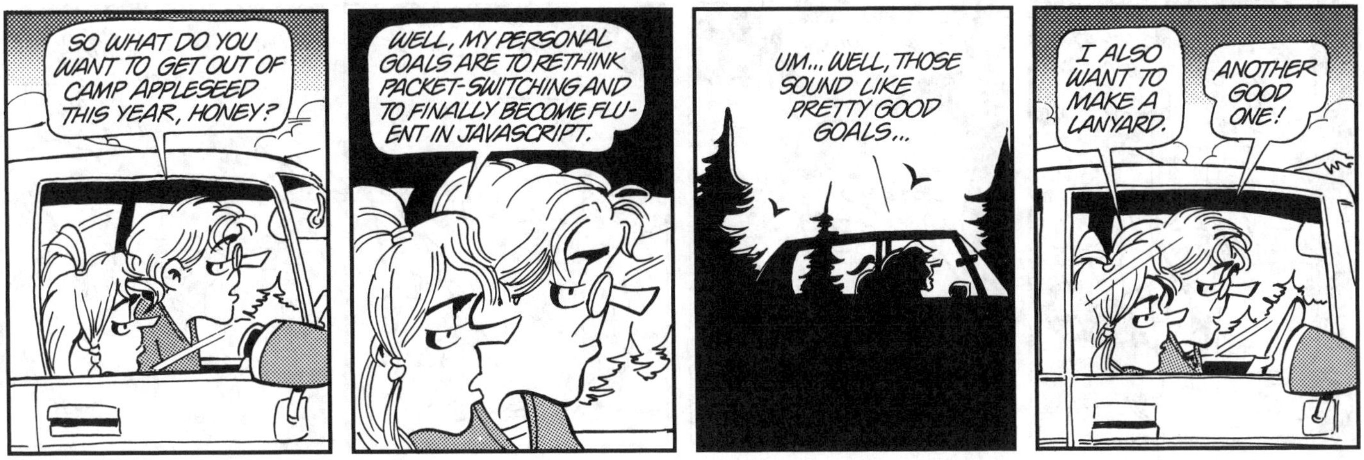
SO WHAT DO YOU WANT TO GET OUT OF CAMP APPLESEED THIS YEAR, HONEY?
WELL, MY PERSONAL GOALS ARE TO RETHINK PACKET-SWITCHING AND TO FINALLY BECOME FLUENT IN JAVASCRIPT.
UM... WELL, THOSE SOUND LIKE PRETTY GOOD GOALS...
I ALSO WANT TO MAKE A LANYARD.
ANOTHER GOOD ONE!

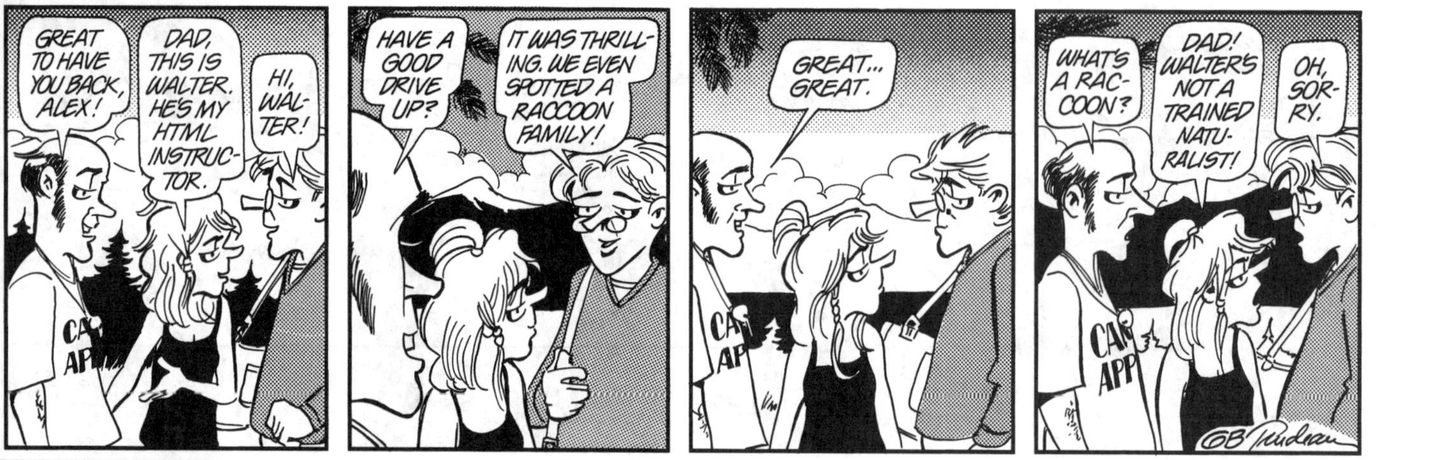
GREAT TO HAVE YOU BACK, ALEX!
DAD, THIS IS WALTER. HE'S MY HTML INSTRUCTOR.
HI, WALTER!
HAVE A GOOD DRIVE UP?
IT WAS THRILLING. WE EVEN SPOTTED A RACCOON FAMILY!
GREAT... GREAT.
WHAT'S A RACCOON?
DAD! WALTER'S NOT A TRAINED NATURALIST!
OH, SORRY.
©B Trudeau

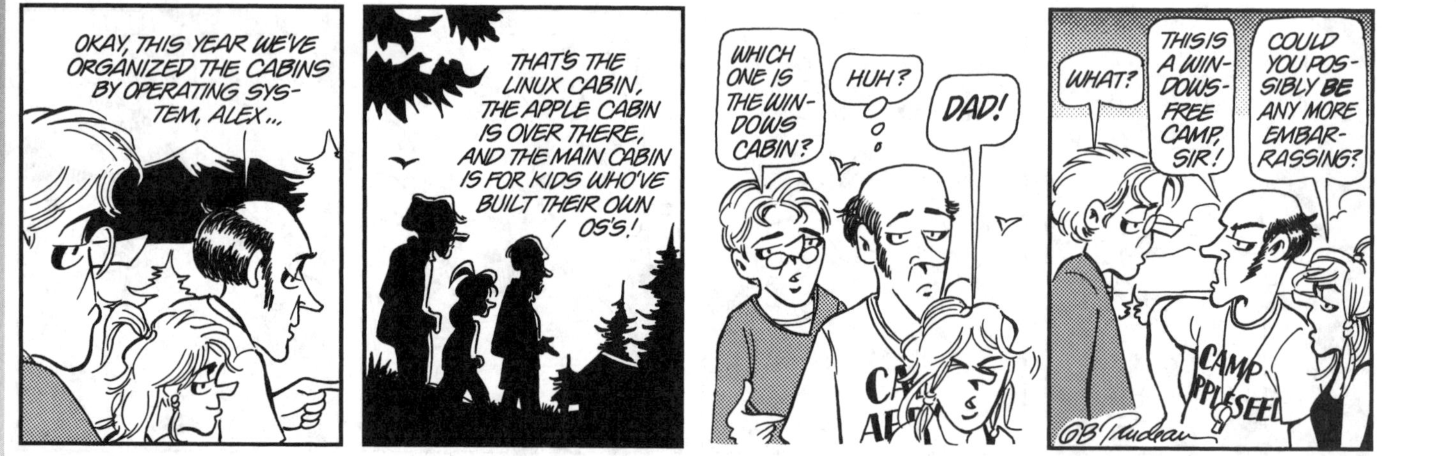
OKAY, THIS YEAR WE'VE ORGANIZED THE CABINS BY OPERATING SYSTEM, ALEX...
THAT'S THE LINUX CABIN, THE APPLE CABIN IS OVER THERE, AND THE MAIN CABIN IS FOR KIDS WHO'VE BUILT THEIR OWN OS'S!
WHICH ONE IS THE WINDOWS CABIN?
HUH?
DAD!
WHAT?
THIS IS A WINDOWS-FREE CAMP, SIR!
COULD YOU POSSIBLY BE ANY MORE EMBARRASSING?
CAMP APPLESEED
©B Trudeau

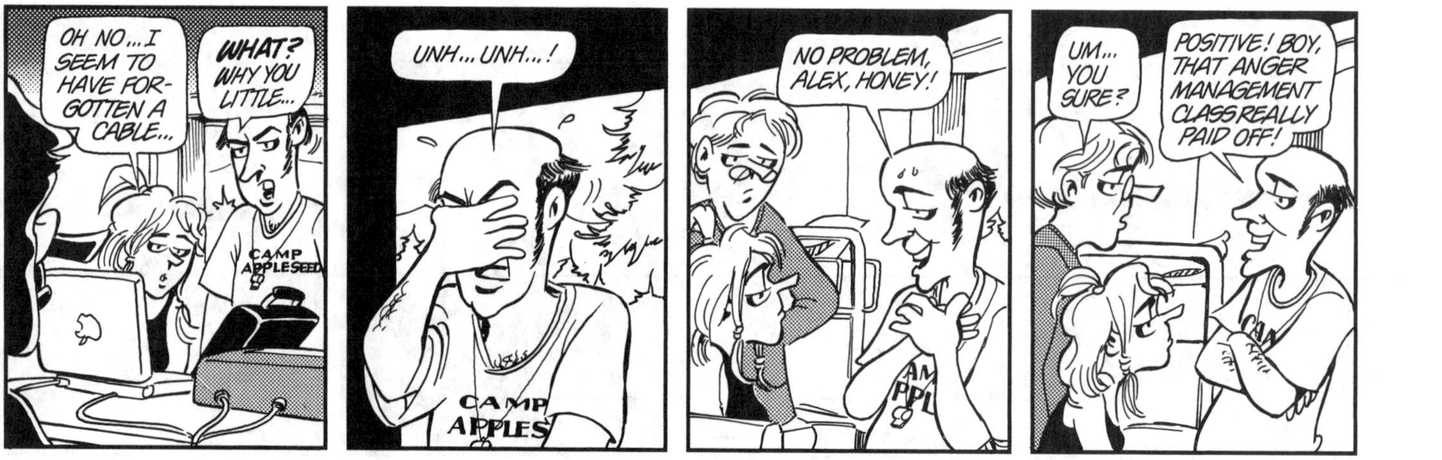
OH NO... I SEEM TO HAVE FORGOTTEN A CABLE...
WHAT? WHY YOU LITTLE...
CAMP APPLESEED
UNH... UNH...!
NO PROBLEM, ALEX, HONEY!
UM... YOU SURE?
POSITIVE! BOY, THAT ANGER MANAGEMENT CLASS REALLY PAID OFF!

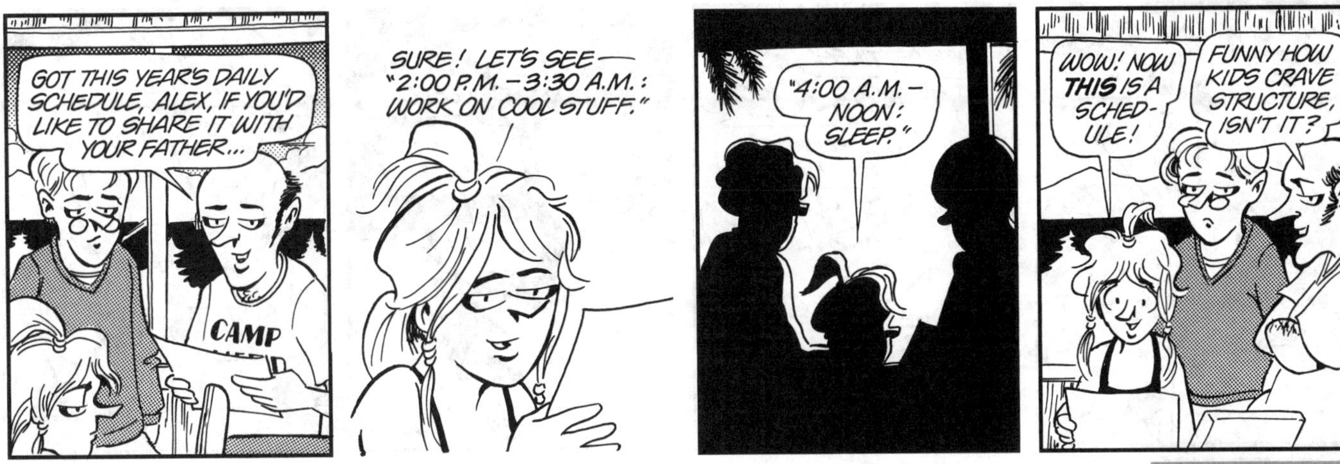
GOT THIS YEAR'S DAILY SCHEDULE, ALEX, IF YOU'D LIKE TO SHARE IT WITH YOUR FATHER...
SURE! LET'S SEE— "2:00 P.M. – 3:30 A.M.: WORK ON COOL STUFF."
"4:00 A.M. – NOON: SLEEP."
WOW! NOW **THIS** IS A SCHED-ULE!
FUNNY HOW KIDS CRAVE STRUCTURE, ISN'T IT?

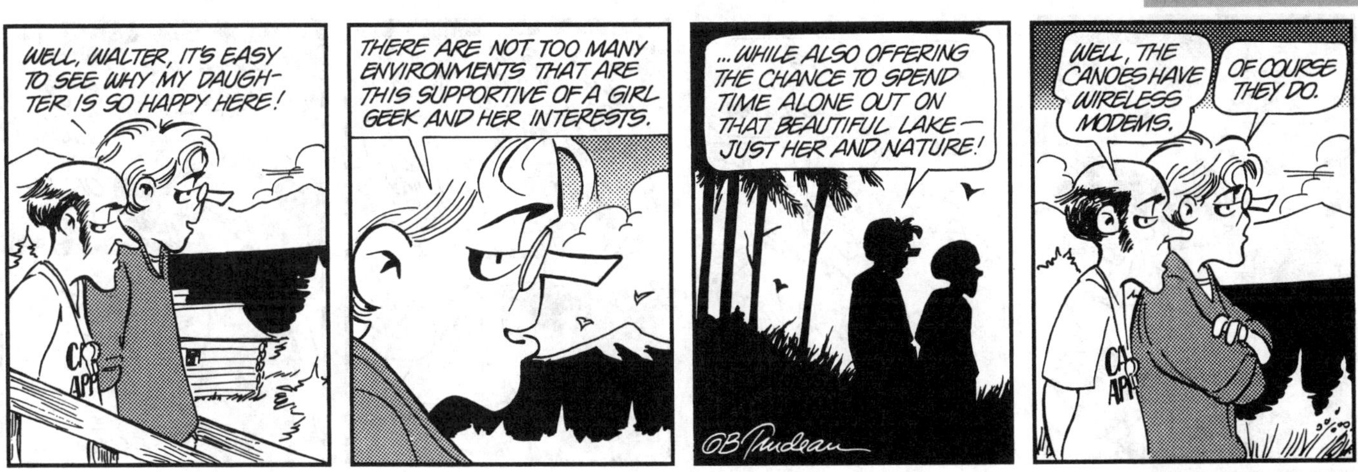
WELL, WALTER, IT'S EASY TO SEE WHY MY DAUGH-TER IS SO HAPPY HERE!
THERE ARE NOT TOO MANY ENVIRONMENTS THAT ARE THIS SUPPORTIVE OF A GIRL GEEK AND HER INTERESTS.
...WHILE ALSO OFFERING THE CHANCE TO SPEND TIME ALONE OUT ON THAT BEAUTIFUL LAKE— JUST HER AND NATURE!
WELL, THE CANOES HAVE WIRELESS MODEMS.
OF COURSE THEY DO.

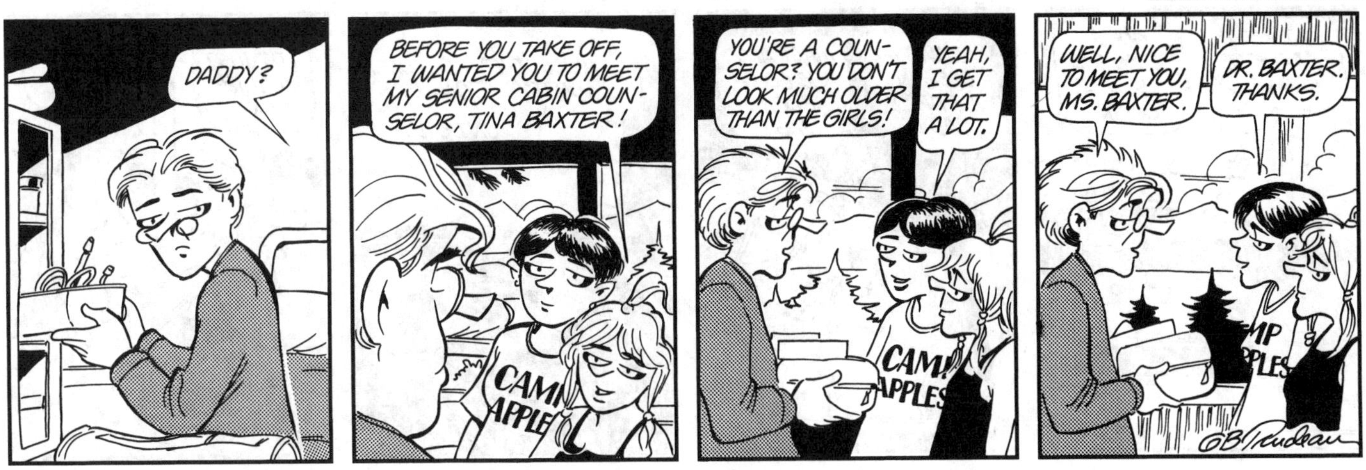
DADDY?
BEFORE YOU TAKE OFF, I WANTED YOU TO MEET MY SENIOR CABIN COUN-SELOR, TINA BAXTER!
YOU'RE A COUN-SELOR? YOU DON'T LOOK MUCH OLDER THAN THE GIRLS!
YEAH, I GET THAT A LOT.
WELL, NICE TO MEET YOU, MS. BAXTER.
DR. BAXTER. THANKS.

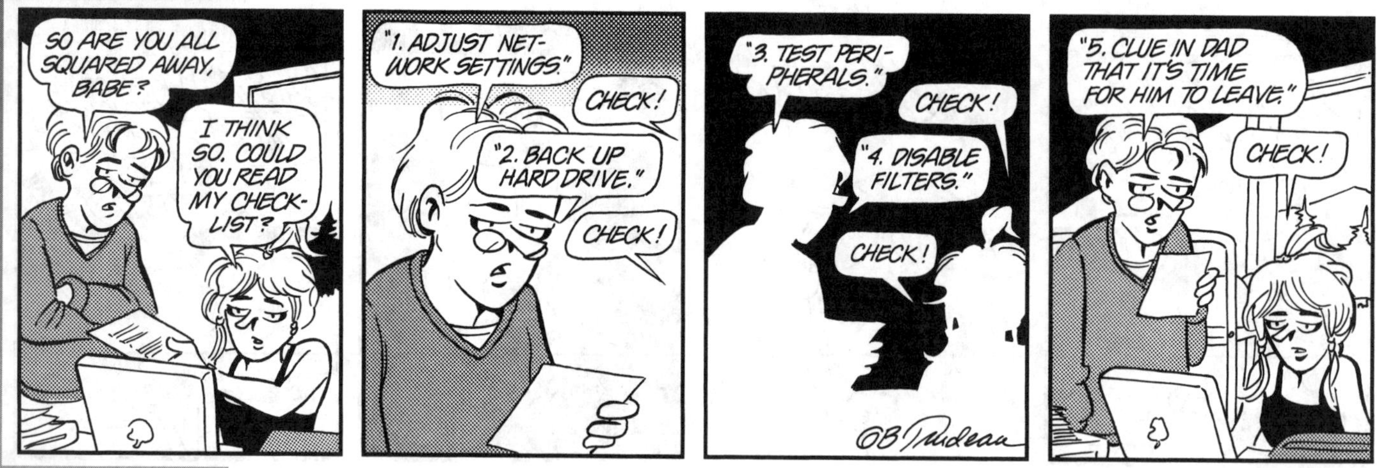
SO ARE YOU ALL SQUARED AWAY, BABE?
I THINK SO. COULD YOU READ MY CHECK-LIST?
"1. ADJUST NET-WORK SETTINGS."
CHECK!
"2. BACK UP HARD DRIVE."
CHECK!
"3. TEST PERI-PHERALS."
CHECK!
"4. DISABLE FILTERS."
CHECK!
"5. CLUE IN DAD THAT IT'S TIME FOR HIM TO LEAVE."
CHECK!
GB Trudeau

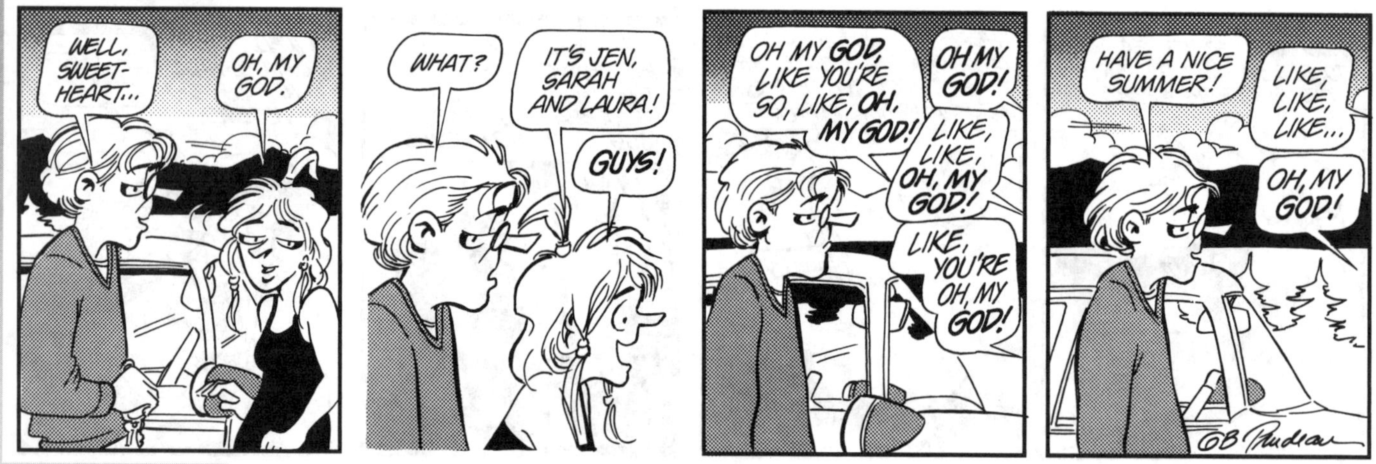
WELL, SWEET-HEART...
OH, MY GOD.
WHAT?
IT'S JEN, SARAH AND LAURA!
GUYS!
OH MY GOD, LIKE YOU'RE SO, LIKE, OH, MY GOD!
OH MY GOD!
LIKE, LIKE, OH, MY GOD!
LIKE, YOU'RE OH, MY GOD!
HAVE A NICE SUMMER!
LIKE, LIKE, LIKE...
OH, MY GOD!
GB Trudeau

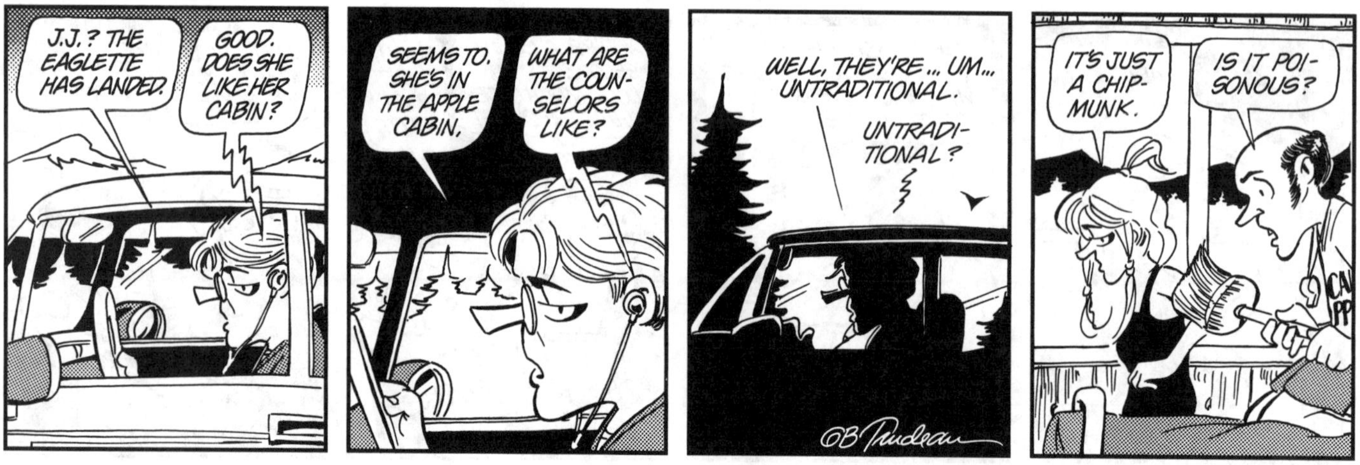
J.J.? THE EAGLETTE HAS LANDED.
GOOD. DOES SHE LIKE HER CABIN?
SEEMS TO. SHE'S IN THE APPLE CABIN.
WHAT ARE THE COUN-SELORS LIKE?
WELL, THEY'RE ... UM... UNTRADITIONAL.
UNTRADI-TIONAL?
GB Trudeau
IT'S JUST A CHIP-MUNK.
IS IT POI-SONOUS?

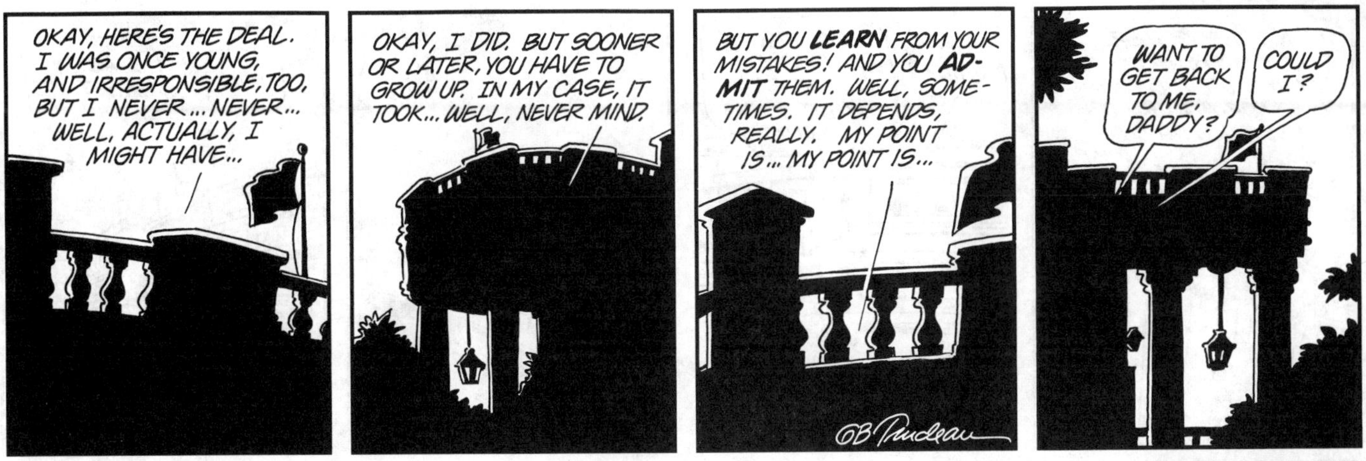
OKAY, HERE'S THE DEAL. I WAS ONCE YOUNG, AND IRRESPONSIBLE, TOO, BUT I NEVER... NEVER... WELL, ACTUALLY, I MIGHT HAVE...
OKAY, I DID. BUT SOONER OR LATER, YOU HAVE TO GROW UP. IN MY CASE, IT TOOK... WELL, NEVER MIND.
BUT YOU **LEARN** FROM YOUR MISTAKES! AND YOU **AD-MIT** THEM. WELL, SOME-TIMES. IT DEPENDS, REALLY. MY POINT IS... MY POINT IS...
WANT TO GET BACK TO ME, DADDY?
COULD I?

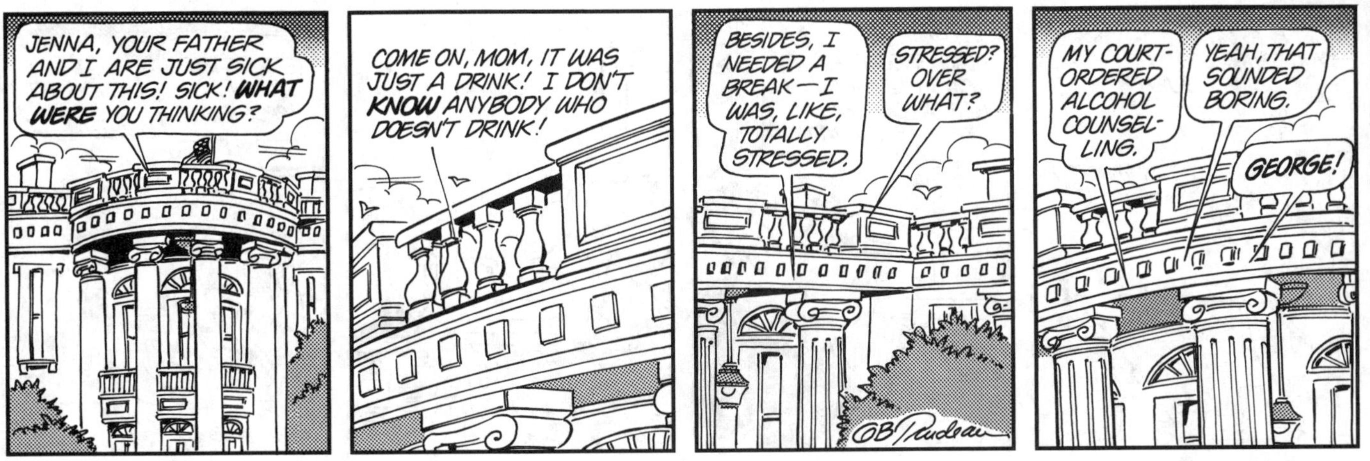
JENNA, YOUR FATHER AND I ARE JUST SICK ABOUT THIS! SICK! **WHAT WERE** YOU THINKING?
COME ON, MOM, IT WAS JUST A DRINK! I DON'T **KNOW** ANYBODY WHO DOESN'T DRINK!
BESIDES, I NEEDED A BREAK—I WAS, LIKE, TOTALLY STRESSED.
STRESSED? OVER WHAT?
MY COURT-ORDERED ALCOHOL COUNSEL-LING.
YEAH, THAT SOUNDED BORING.
GEORGE!

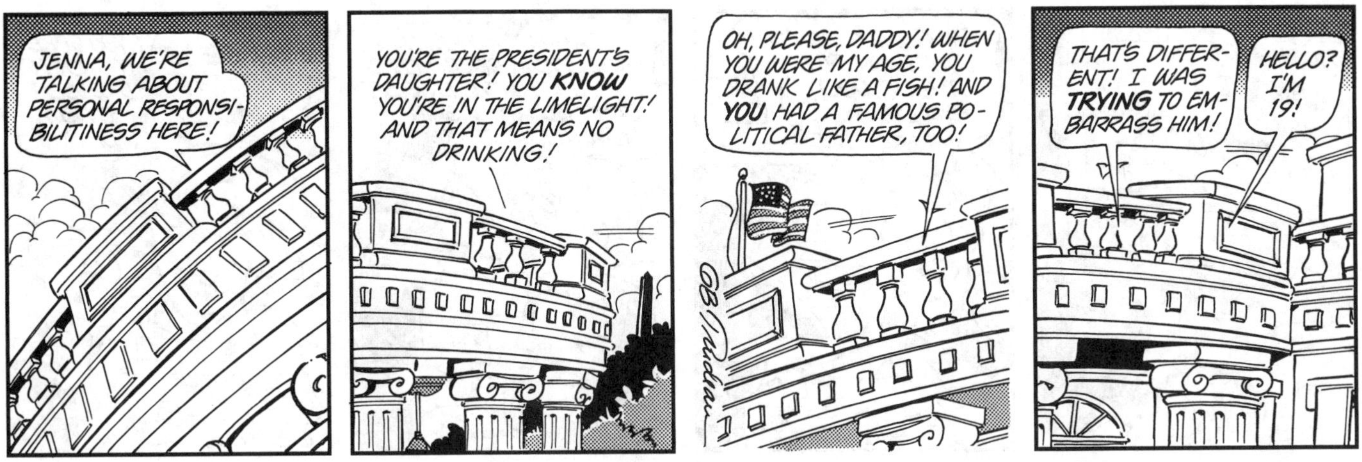
JENNA, WE'RE TALKING ABOUT PERSONAL RESPONSI-BILITINESS HERE!
YOU'RE THE PRESIDENT'S DAUGHTER! YOU **KNOW** YOU'RE IN THE LIMELIGHT! AND THAT MEANS NO DRINKING!
OH, PLEASE, DADDY! WHEN YOU WERE MY AGE, YOU DRANK LIKE A FISH! AND **YOU** HAD A FAMOUS PO-LITICAL FATHER, TOO!
THAT'S DIFFER-ENT! I WAS **TRYING** TO EM-BARRASS HIM!
HELLO? I'M 19!

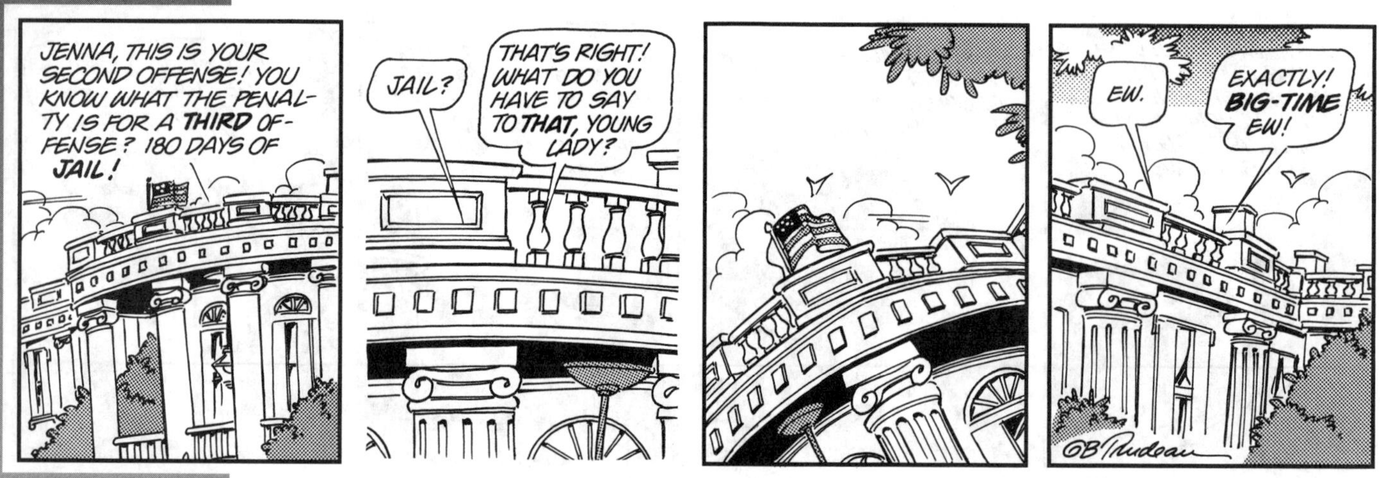
JENNA, THIS IS YOUR SECOND OFFENSE! YOU KNOW WHAT THE PENALTY IS FOR A **THIRD** OFFENSE? 180 DAYS OF **JAIL!**
JAIL?
THAT'S RIGHT! WHAT DO YOU HAVE TO SAY TO **THAT,** YOUNG LADY?
EW.
EXACTLY! **BIG-TIME** EW!
GB Trudeau

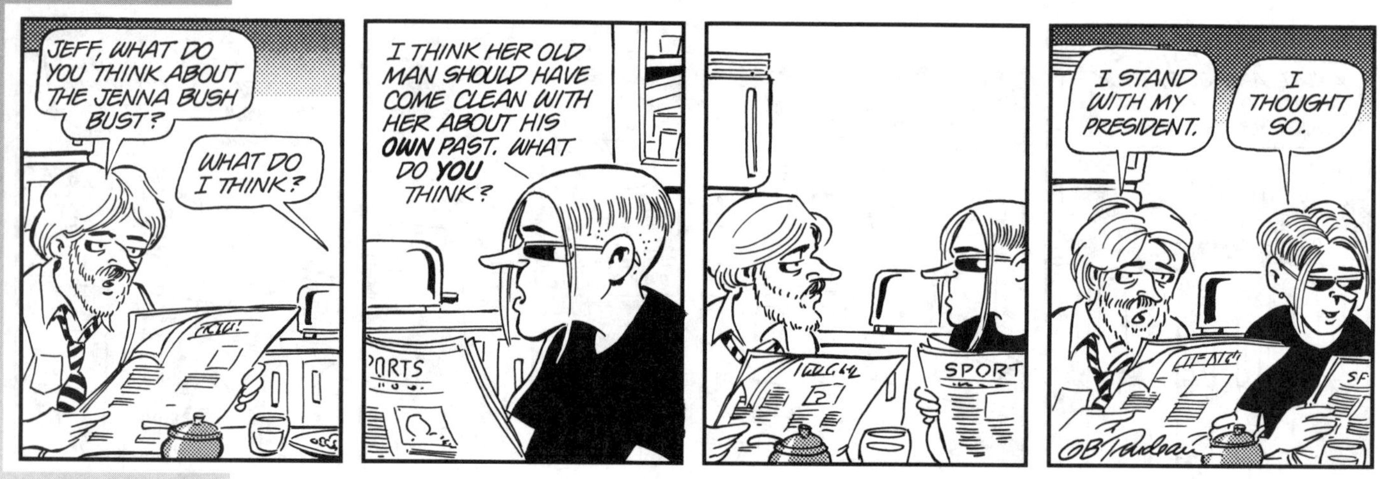
JEFF, WHAT DO YOU THINK ABOUT THE JENNA BUSH BUST?
WHAT DO I THINK?
I THINK HER OLD MAN SHOULD HAVE COME CLEAN WITH HER ABOUT HIS **OWN** PAST. WHAT DO **YOU** THINK?
SPORT
I STAND WITH MY PRESIDENT.
I THOUGHT SO.
GB Trudeau

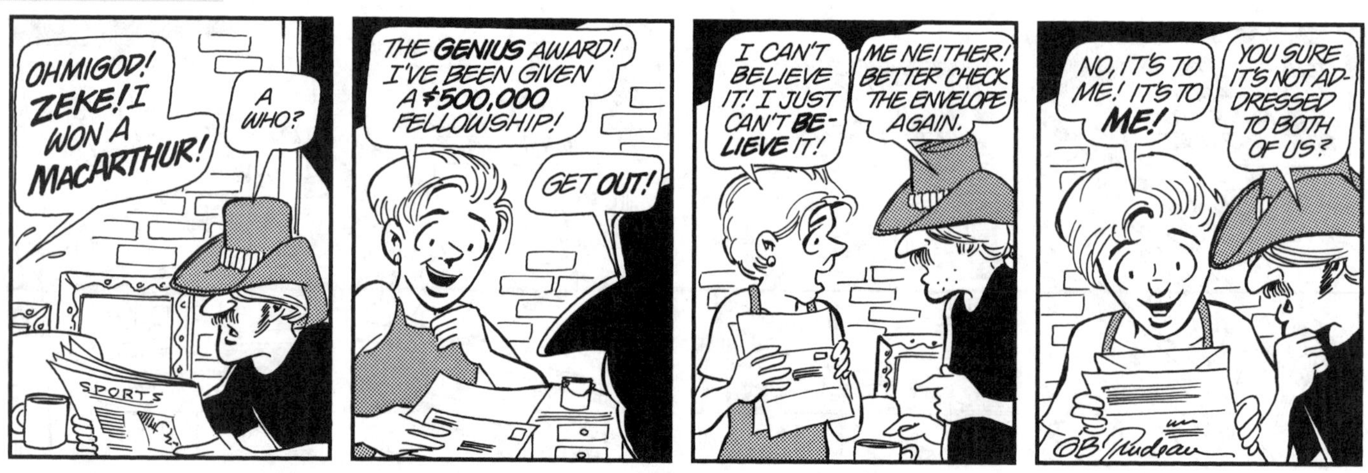
OHMIGOD! **ZEKE!** I WON A **MACARTHUR!**
A WHO?
SPORTS
THE **GENIUS** AWARD! I'VE BEEN GIVEN A **$500,000** FELLOWSHIP!
GET **OUT!**
I CAN'T BELIEVE IT! I JUST CAN'T **BELIEVE** IT!
ME NEITHER! BETTER CHECK THE ENVELOPE AGAIN.
NO, IT'S TO ME! IT'S TO **ME!**
YOU SURE IT'S NOT ADDRESSED TO BOTH OF US?
GB Trudeau

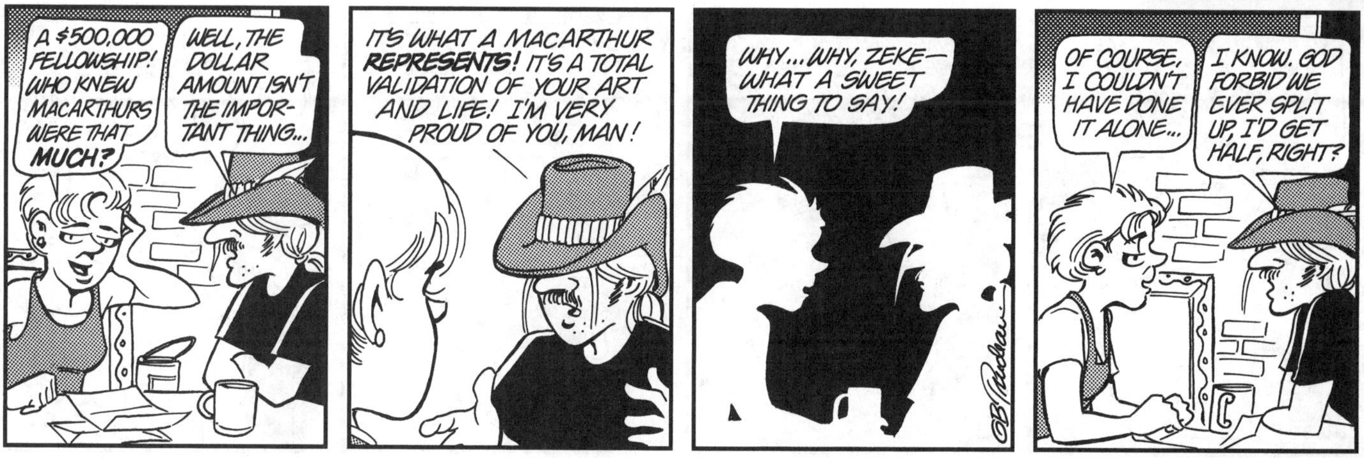
A $500,000 FELLOWSHIP! WHO KNEW MacARTHURS WERE THAT **MUCH?**
WELL, THE DOLLAR AMOUNT ISN'T THE IMPORTANT THING...
IT'S WHAT A MacARTHUR **REPRESENTS!** IT'S A TOTAL VALIDATION OF YOUR ART AND LIFE! I'M VERY PROUD OF YOU, MAN!
WHY... WHY, ZEKE— WHAT A SWEET THING TO SAY!
©B Trudeau
OF COURSE, I COULDN'T HAVE DONE IT ALONE...
I KNOW. GOD FORBID WE EVER SPLIT UP, I'D GET HALF, RIGHT?

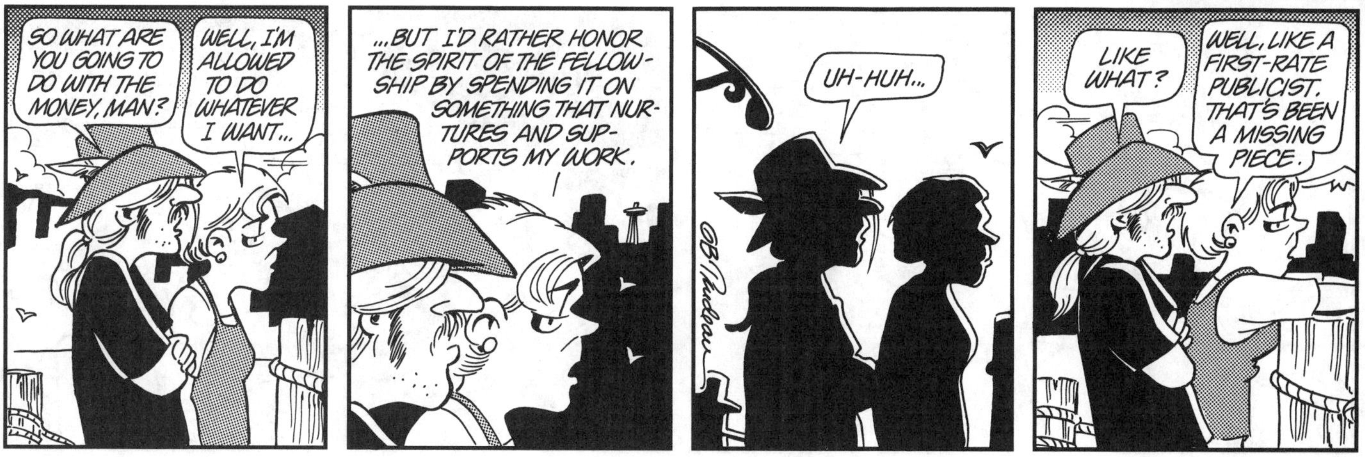
SO WHAT ARE YOU GOING TO DO WITH THE MONEY, MAN?
WELL, I'M ALLOWED TO DO WHATEVER I WANT...
...BUT I'D RATHER HONOR THE SPIRIT OF THE FELLOWSHIP BY SPENDING IT ON SOMETHING THAT NURTURES AND SUPPORTS MY WORK.
UH-HUH...
©B Trudeau
LIKE WHAT?
WELL, LIKE A FIRST-RATE PUBLICIST. THAT'S BEEN A MISSING PIECE.

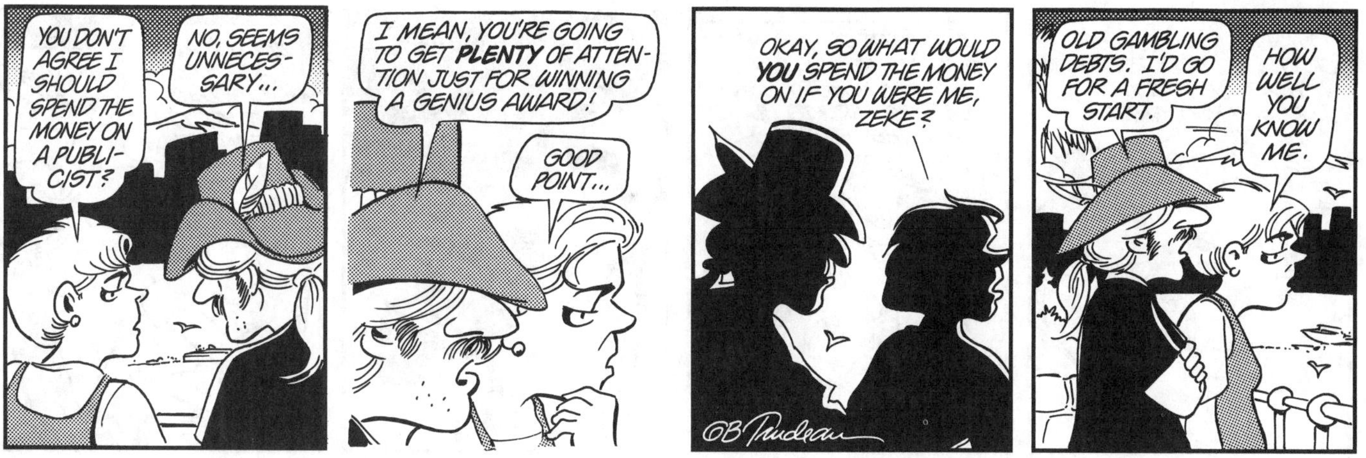
YOU DON'T AGREE I SHOULD SPEND THE MONEY ON A PUBLICIST?
NO, SEEMS UNNECESSARY...
I MEAN, YOU'RE GOING TO GET **PLENTY** OF ATTENTION JUST FOR WINNING A GENIUS AWARD!
GOOD POINT...
OKAY, SO WHAT WOULD **YOU** SPEND THE MONEY ON IF YOU WERE ME, ZEKE?
©B Trudeau
OLD GAMBLING DEBTS. I'D GO FOR A FRESH START.
HOW WELL YOU KNOW ME.

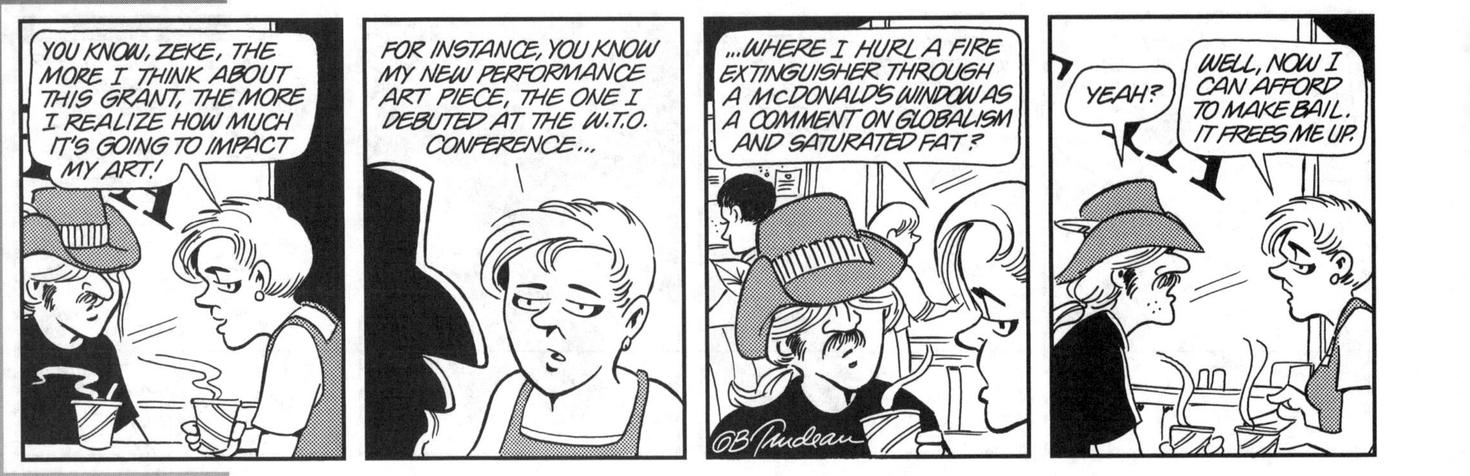
YOU KNOW, ZEKE, THE MORE I THINK ABOUT THIS GRANT, THE MORE I REALIZE HOW MUCH IT'S GOING TO IMPACT MY ART!
FOR INSTANCE, YOU KNOW MY NEW PERFORMANCE ART PIECE, THE ONE I DEBUTED AT THE W.T.O. CONFERENCE...
...WHERE I HURL A FIRE EXTINGUISHER THROUGH A McDONALD'S WINDOW AS A COMMENT ON GLOBALISM AND SATURATED FAT?
YEAH?
WELL, NOW I CAN AFFORD TO MAKE BAIL. IT FREES ME UP.
GB Trudeau

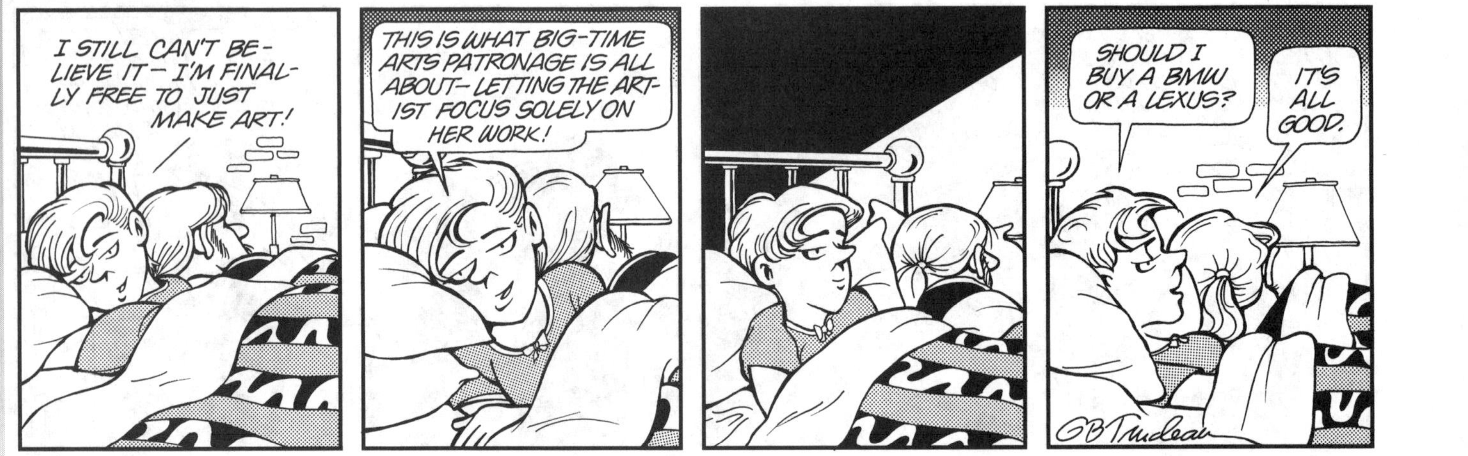
I STILL CAN'T BE-LIEVE IT – I'M FINAL-LY FREE TO JUST MAKE ART!
THIS IS WHAT BIG-TIME ARTS PATRONAGE IS ALL ABOUT – LETTING THE ART-IST FOCUS SOLELY ON HER WORK!
SHOULD I BUY A BMW OR A LEXUS?
IT'S ALL GOOD.
GB Trudeau

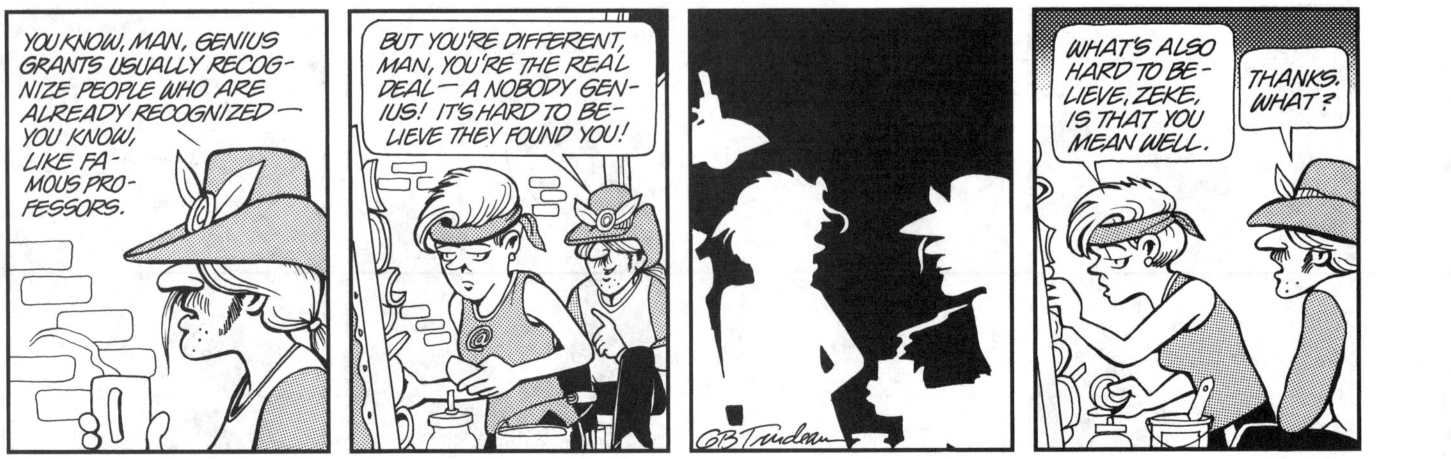
YOU KNOW, MAN, GENIUS GRANTS USUALLY RECOG-NIZE PEOPLE WHO ARE ALREADY RECOGNIZED – YOU KNOW, LIKE FA-MOUS PRO-FESSORS.
BUT YOU'RE DIFFERENT, MAN, YOU'RE THE REAL DEAL – A NOBODY GEN-IUS! IT'S HARD TO BE-LIEVE THEY FOUND YOU!
GB Trudeau
WHAT'S ALSO HARD TO BE-LIEVE, ZEKE, IS THAT YOU MEAN WELL.
THANKS. WHAT?

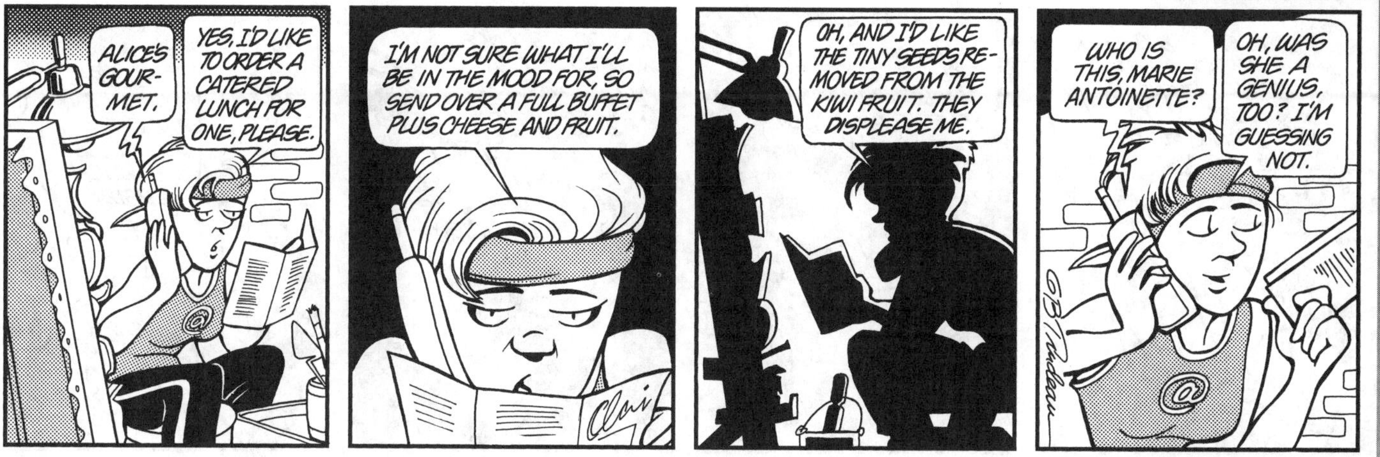
ALICE'S GOURMET.
YES, I'D LIKE TO ORDER A CATERED LUNCH FOR ONE, PLEASE.
I'M NOT SURE WHAT I'LL BE IN THE MOOD FOR, SO SEND OVER A FULL BUFFET PLUS CHEESE AND FRUIT.
OH, AND I'D LIKE THE TINY SEEDS REMOVED FROM THE KIWI FRUIT. THEY DISPLEASE ME.
WHO IS THIS, MARIE ANTOINETTE?
OH, WAS SHE A GENIUS, TOO? I'M GUESSING NOT.

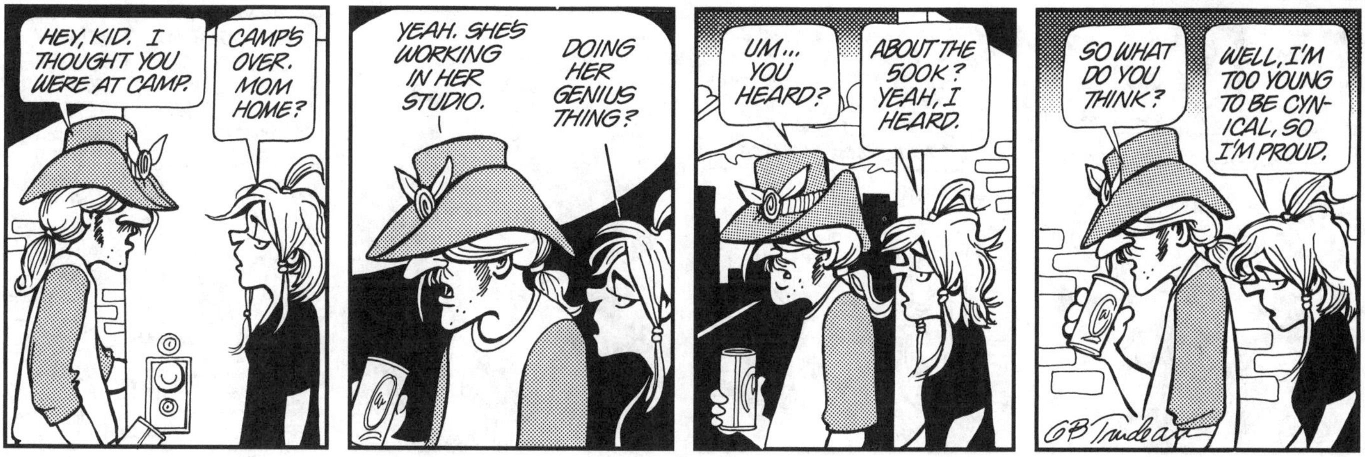
HEY, KID. I THOUGHT YOU WERE AT CAMP.
CAMP'S OVER. MOM HOME?
YEAH. SHE'S WORKING IN HER STUDIO.
DOING HER GENIUS THING?
UM... YOU HEARD?
ABOUT THE 500K? YEAH, I HEARD.
SO WHAT DO YOU THINK?
WELL, I'M TOO YOUNG TO BE CYNICAL, SO I'M PROUD.

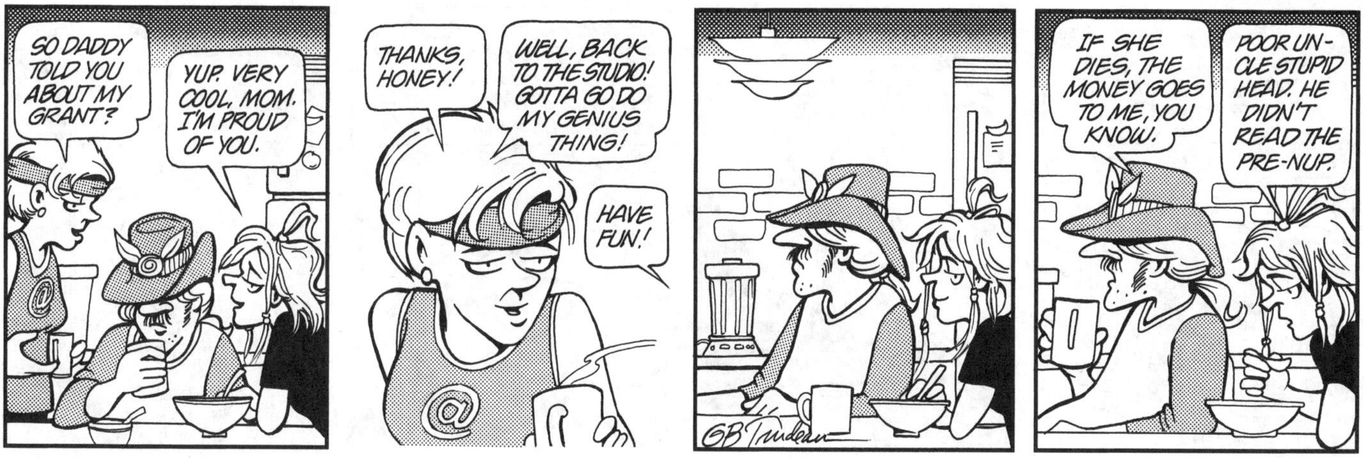
SO DADDY TOLD YOU ABOUT MY GRANT?
YUP. VERY COOL, MOM. I'M PROUD OF YOU.
THANKS, HONEY!
WELL, BACK TO THE STUDIO! GOTTA GO DO MY GENIUS THING!
HAVE FUN!
IF SHE DIES, THE MONEY GOES TO ME, YOU KNOW.
POOR UNCLE STUPID HEAD. HE DIDN'T READ THE PRE-NUP.

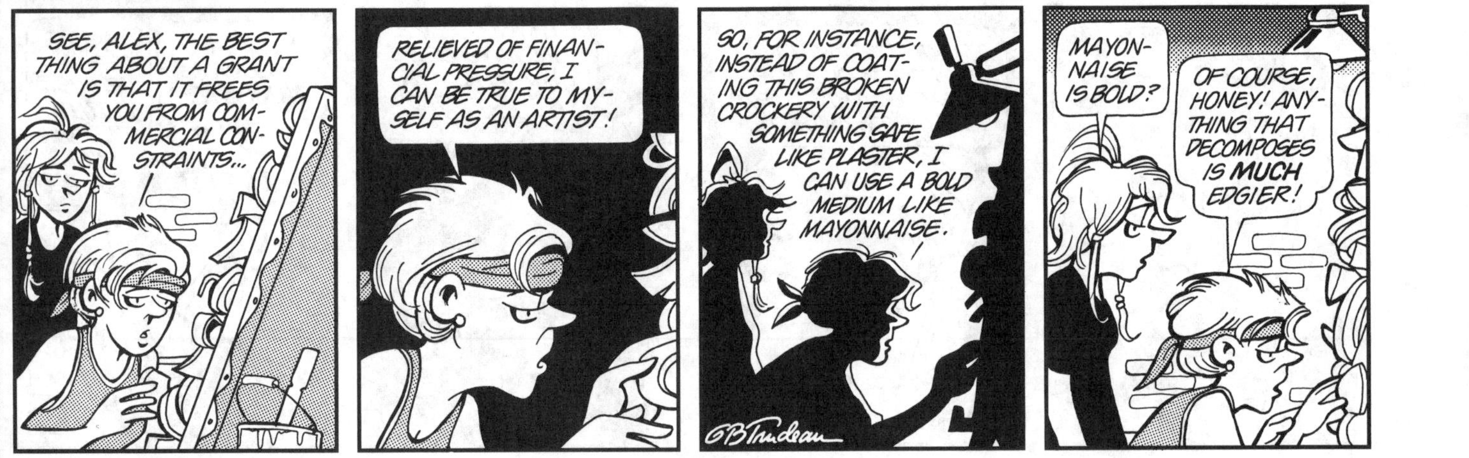
SEE, ALEX, THE BEST THING ABOUT A GRANT IS THAT IT FREES YOU FROM COMMERCIAL CONSTRAINTS...
RELIEVED OF FINANCIAL PRESSURE, I CAN BE TRUE TO MYSELF AS AN ARTIST!
SO, FOR INSTANCE, INSTEAD OF COATING THIS BROKEN CROCKERY WITH SOMETHING SAFE LIKE PLASTER, I CAN USE A BOLD MEDIUM LIKE MAYONNAISE.
!
MAYONNAISE IS BOLD?
OF COURSE, HONEY! ANYTHING THAT DECOMPOSES IS **MUCH** EDGIER!
GBTrudeau

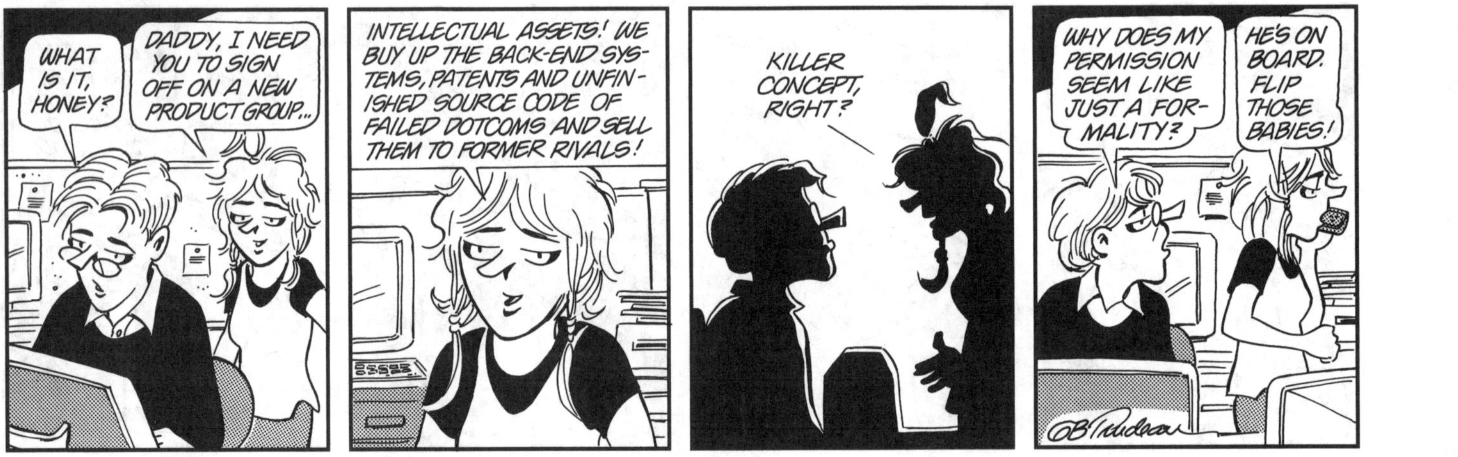
WHAT IS IT, HONEY?
DADDY, I NEED YOU TO SIGN OFF ON A NEW PRODUCT GROUP...
INTELLECTUAL ASSETS! WE BUY UP THE BACK-END SYSTEMS, PATENTS AND UNFINISHED SOURCE CODE OF FAILED DOTCOMS AND SELL THEM TO FORMER RIVALS!
KILLER CONCEPT, RIGHT?
WHY DOES MY PERMISSION SEEM LIKE JUST A FORMALITY?
HE'S ON BOARD. FLIP THOSE BABIES!
GBTrudeau

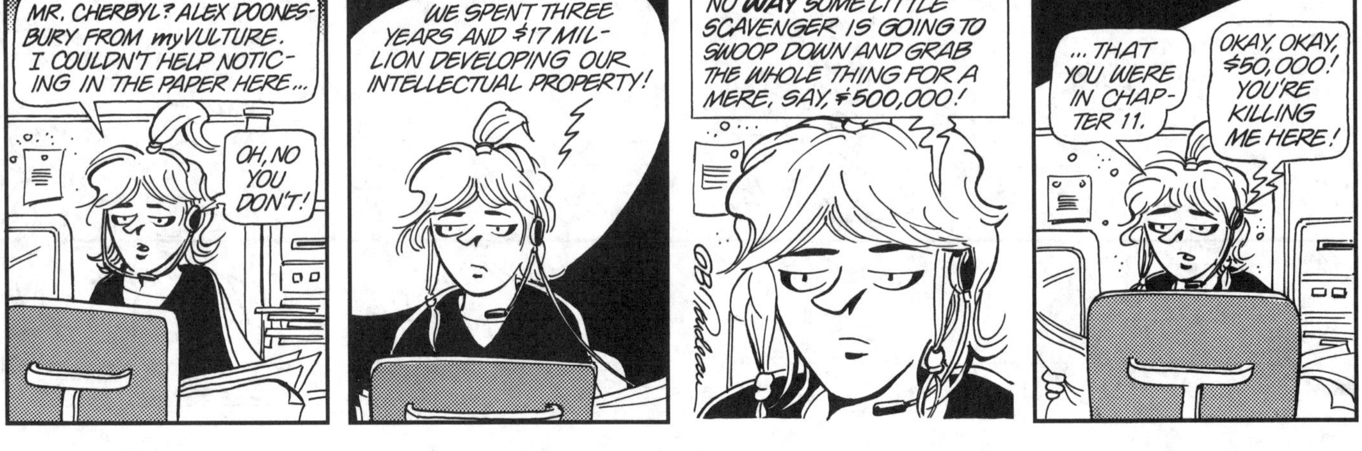
MR. CHERBYL? ALEX DOONESBURY FROM myVULTURE. I COULDN'T HELP NOTICING IN THE PAPER HERE...
OH, NO YOU DON'T!
WE SPENT THREE YEARS AND $17 MILLION DEVELOPING OUR INTELLECTUAL PROPERTY!
NO **WAY** SOME LITTLE SCAVENGER IS GOING TO SWOOP DOWN AND GRAB THE WHOLE THING FOR A MERE, SAY, $500,000!
GBTrudeau
...THAT YOU WERE IN CHAPTER 11.
OKAY, OKAY, $50,000! YOU'RE KILLING ME HERE!

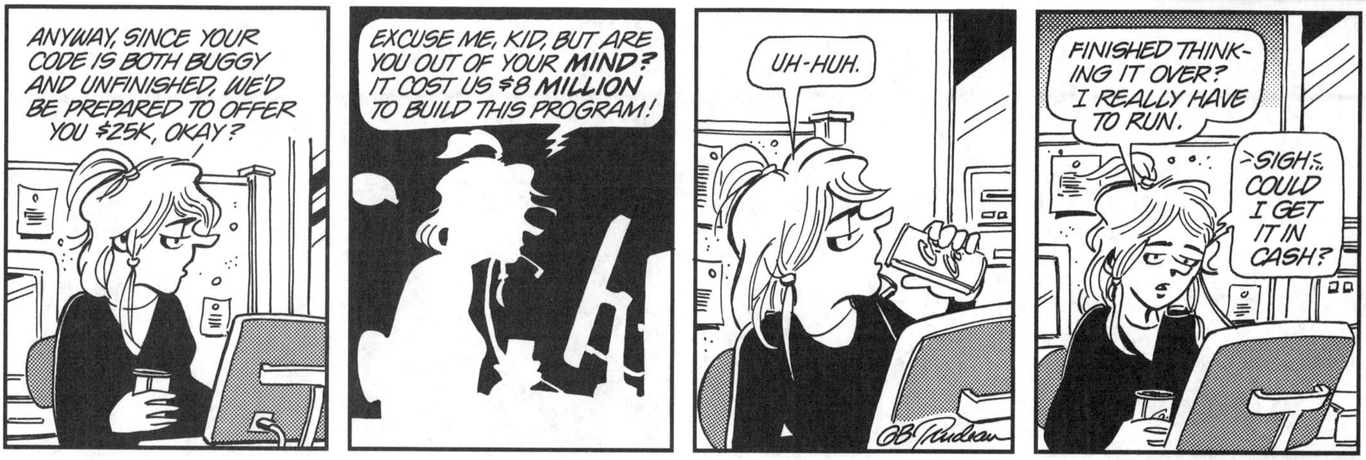
ANYWAY, SINCE YOUR CODE IS BOTH BUGGY AND UNFINISHED, WE'D BE PREPARED TO OFFER YOU $25K, OKAY?
EXCUSE ME, KID, BUT ARE YOU OUT OF YOUR MIND? IT COST US $8 MILLION TO BUILD THIS PROGRAM!
UH-HUH.
FINISHED THINKING IT OVER? I REALLY HAVE TO RUN.
>SIGH<... COULD I GET IT IN CASH?

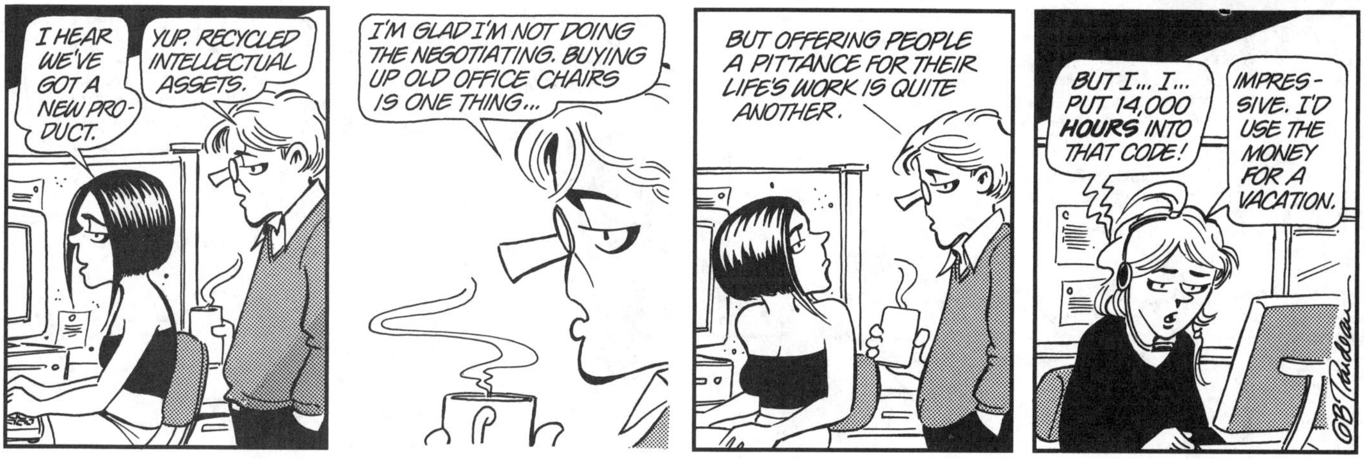
I HEAR WE'VE GOT A NEW PRODUCT.
YUP. RECYCLED INTELLECTUAL ASSETS.
I'M GLAD I'M NOT DOING THE NEGOTIATING. BUYING UP OLD OFFICE CHAIRS IS ONE THING...
BUT OFFERING PEOPLE A PITTANCE FOR THEIR LIFE'S WORK IS QUITE ANOTHER.
BUT I... I... PUT 14,000 HOURS INTO THAT CODE!
IMPRESSIVE. I'D USE THE MONEY FOR A VACATION.

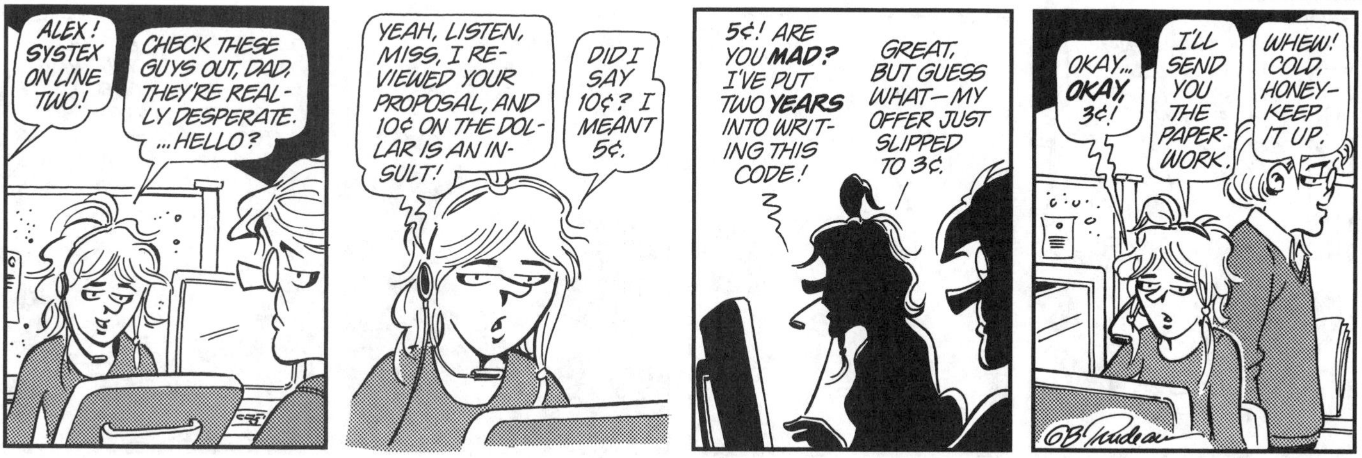
ALEX! SYSTEX ON LINE TWO!
CHECK THESE GUYS OUT, DAD. THEY'RE REALLY DESPERATE. ...HELLO?
YEAH, LISTEN, MISS, I REVIEWED YOUR PROPOSAL, AND 10¢ ON THE DOLLAR IS AN INSULT!
DID I SAY 10¢? I MEANT 5¢.
5¢! ARE YOU MAD? I'VE PUT TWO YEARS INTO WRITING THIS CODE!
GREAT, BUT GUESS WHAT— MY OFFER JUST SLIPPED TO 3¢.
OKAY... OKAY, 3¢!
I'LL SEND YOU THE PAPERWORK.
WHEW! COLD, HONEY— KEEP IT UP.

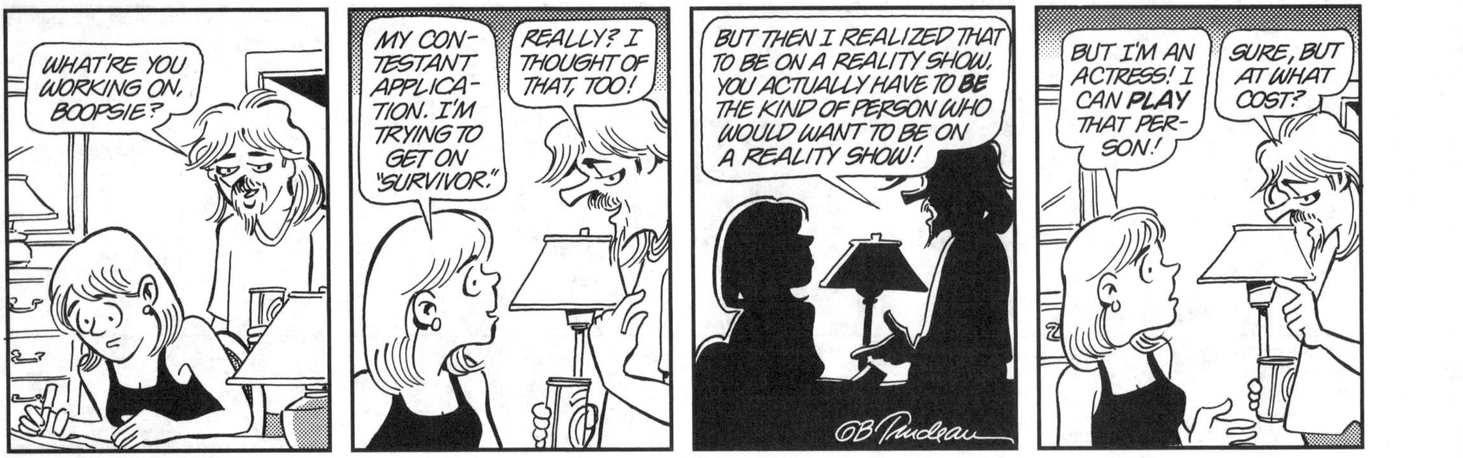
WHAT'RE YOU WORKING ON, BOOPSIE?
MY CON-TESTANT APPLICA-TION. I'M TRYING TO GET ON "SURVIVOR."
REALLY? I THOUGHT OF THAT, TOO!
BUT THEN I REALIZED THAT TO BE ON A REALITY SHOW, YOU ACTUALLY HAVE TO **BE** THE KIND OF PERSON WHO WOULD WANT TO BE ON A REALITY SHOW!
BUT I'M AN ACTRESS! I CAN **PLAY** THAT PER-SON!
SURE, BUT AT WHAT COST?

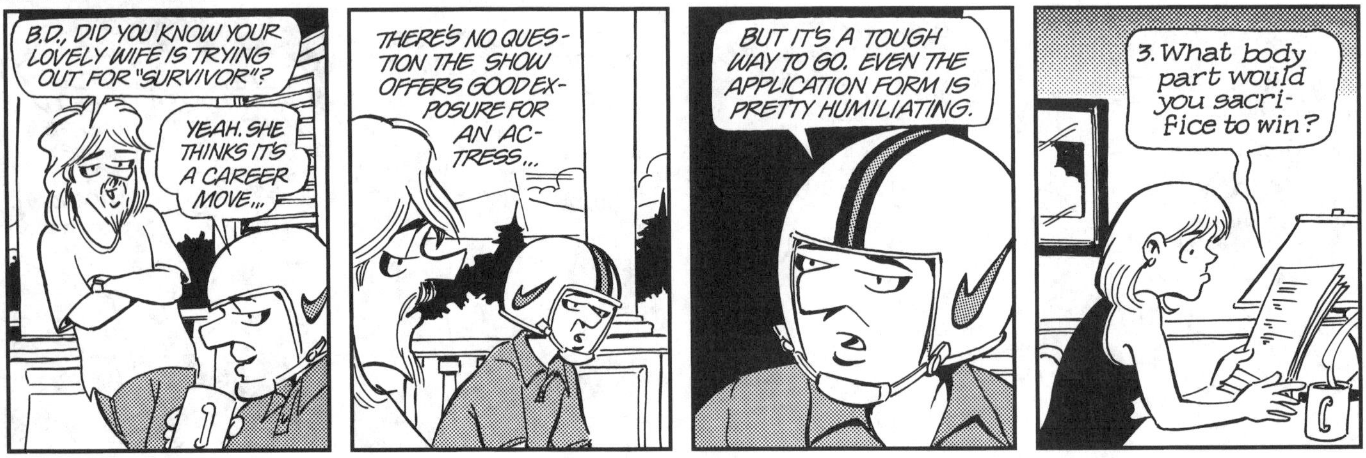
B.D., DID YOU KNOW YOUR LOVELY WIFE IS TRYING OUT FOR "SURVIVOR"?
YEAH. SHE THINKS IT'S A CAREER MOVE...
THERE'S NO QUES-TION THE SHOW OFFERS GOOD EX-POSURE FOR AN AC-TRESS...
BUT IT'S A TOUGH WAY TO GO. EVEN THE APPLICATION FORM IS PRETTY HUMILIATING.
3. What body part would you sacri-fice to win?

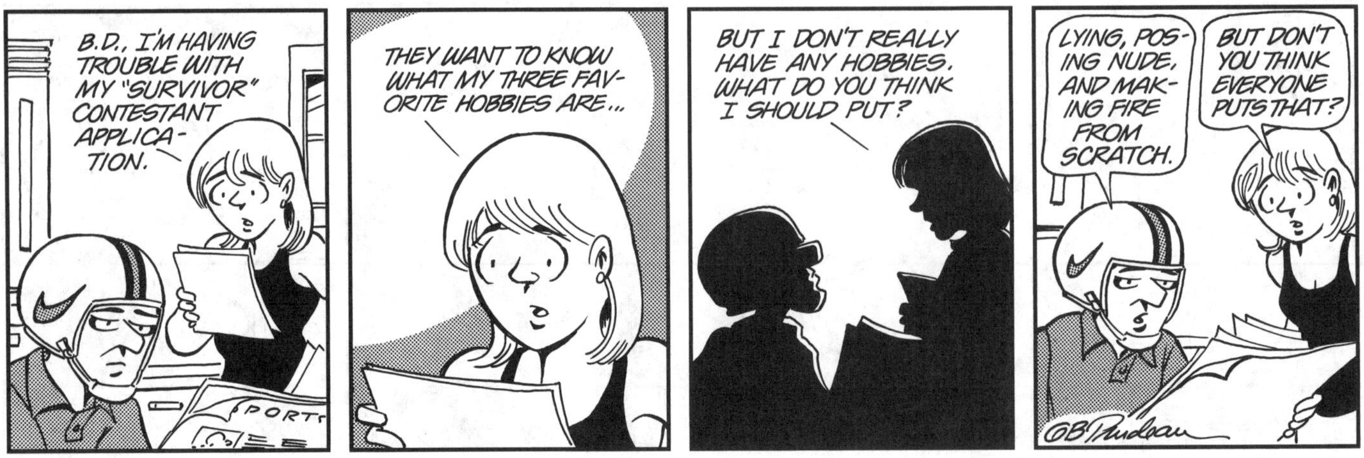
B.D., I'M HAVING TROUBLE WITH MY "SURVIVOR" CONTESTANT APPLICA-TION.
THEY WANT TO KNOW WHAT MY THREE FAV-ORITE HOBBIES ARE...
BUT I DON'T REALLY HAVE ANY HOBBIES. WHAT DO YOU THINK I SHOULD PUT?
LYING, POS-ING NUDE, AND MAK-ING FIRE FROM SCRATCH.
BUT DON'T YOU THINK EVERYONE PUTS THAT?

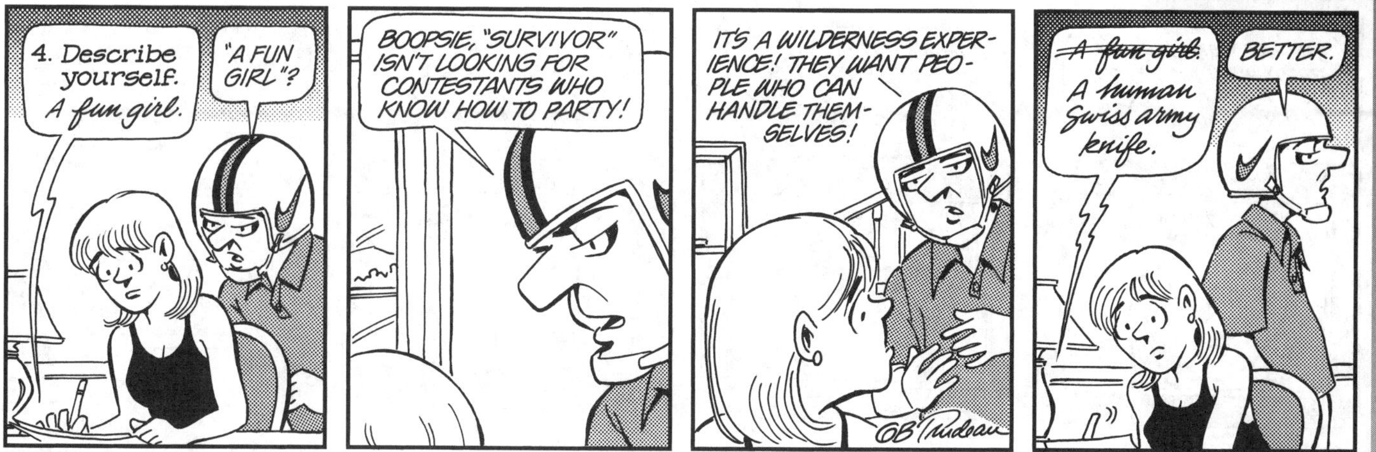
4. Describe yourself. A fun girl.
"A FUN GIRL"?
BOOPSIE, "SURVIVOR" ISN'T LOOKING FOR CONTESTANTS WHO KNOW HOW TO PARTY!
IT'S A WILDERNESS EXPERIENCE! THEY WANT PEOPLE WHO CAN HANDLE THEMSELVES!
~~A fun girl.~~ A human Swiss army knife.
BETTER.

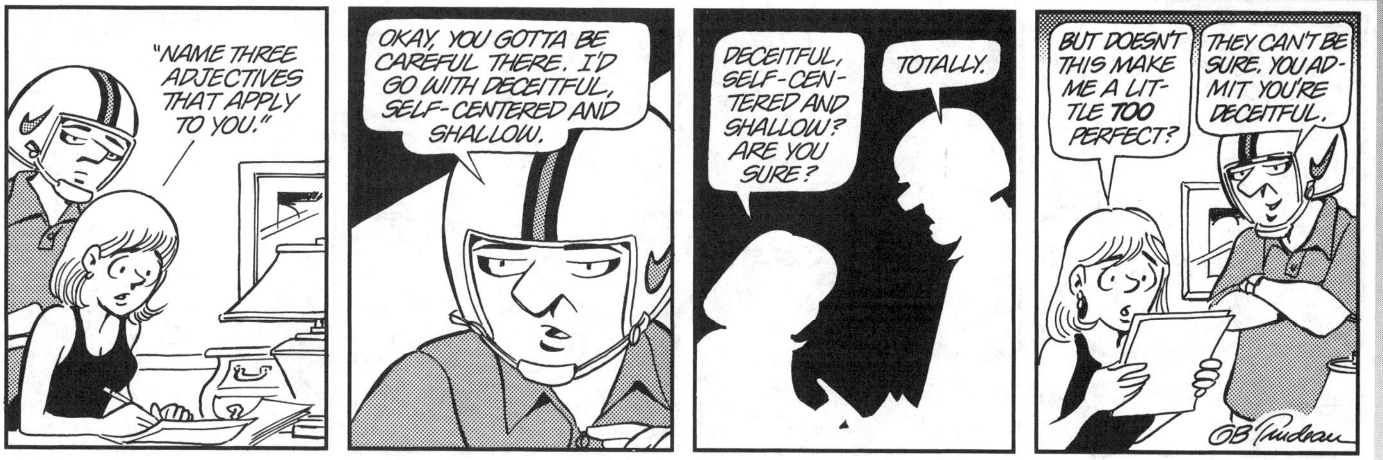
"NAME THREE ADJECTIVES THAT APPLY TO YOU."
OKAY, YOU GOTTA BE CAREFUL THERE. I'D GO WITH DECEITFUL, SELF-CENTERED AND SHALLOW.
DECEITFUL, SELF-CENTERED AND SHALLOW? ARE YOU SURE?
TOTALLY.
BUT DOESN'T THIS MAKE ME A LITTLE TOO PERFECT?
THEY CAN'T BE SURE. YOU ADMIT YOU'RE DECEITFUL.

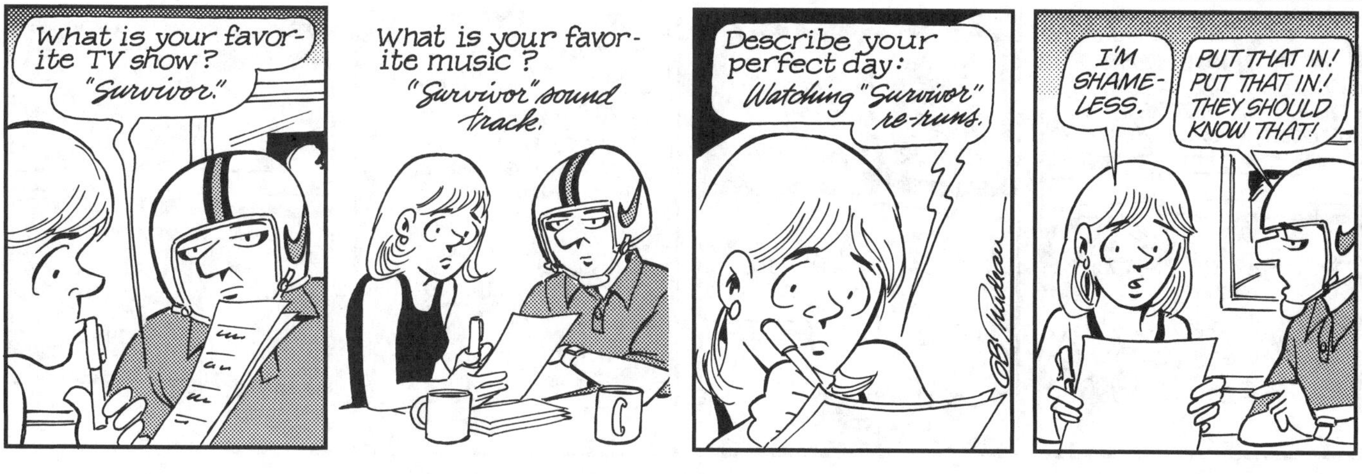
What is your favorite TV show? "Survivor."
What is your favorite music? "Survivor" sound track.
Describe your perfect day: Watching "Survivor" re-runs.
I'M SHAMELESS.
PUT THAT IN! PUT THAT IN! THEY SHOULD KNOW THAT!

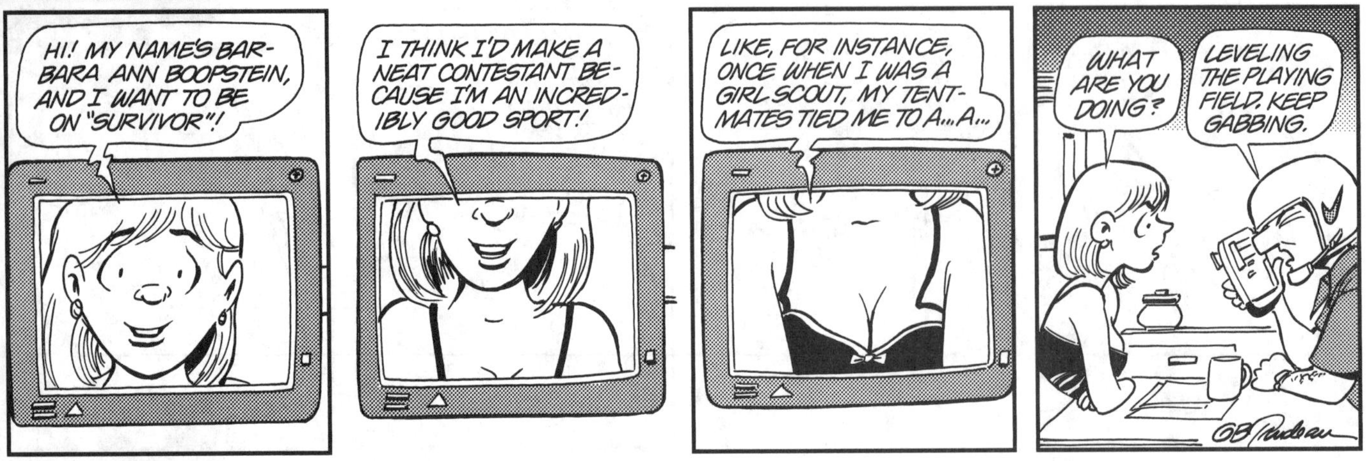
HI! MY NAME'S BARBARA ANN BOOPSTEIN, AND I WANT TO BE ON "SURVIVOR"!
I THINK I'D MAKE A NEAT CONTESTANT BECAUSE I'M AN INCREDIBLY GOOD SPORT!
LIKE, FOR INSTANCE, ONCE WHEN I WAS A GIRL SCOUT, MY TENTMATES TIED ME TO A...A...
WHAT ARE YOU DOING?
LEVELING THE PLAYING FIELD. KEEP GABBING.

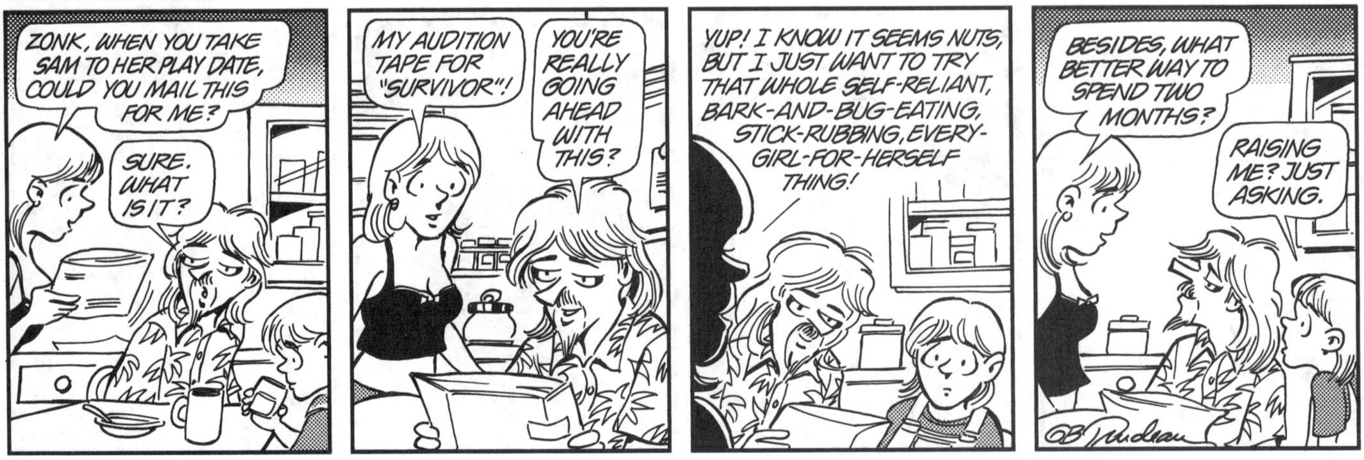
ZONK, WHEN YOU TAKE SAM TO HER PLAY DATE, COULD YOU MAIL THIS FOR ME?
SURE. WHAT IS IT?
MY AUDITION TAPE FOR "SURVIVOR"!
YOU'RE REALLY GOING AHEAD WITH THIS?
YUP! I KNOW IT SEEMS NUTS, BUT I JUST WANT TO TRY THAT WHOLE SELF-RELIANT, BARK-AND-BUG-EATING, STICK-RUBBING, EVERY-GIRL-FOR-HERSELF THING!
BESIDES, WHAT BETTER WAY TO SPEND TWO MONTHS?
RAISING ME? JUST ASKING.

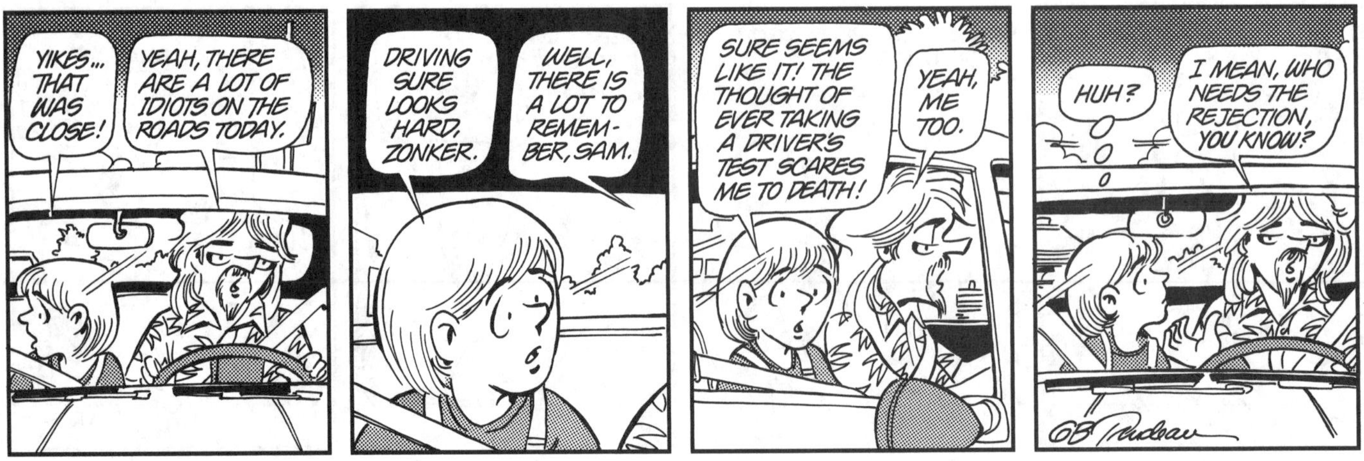
YIKES... THAT WAS CLOSE!
YEAH, THERE ARE A LOT OF IDIOTS ON THE ROADS TODAY.
DRIVING SURE LOOKS HARD, ZONKER.
WELL, THERE IS A LOT TO REMEMBER, SAM.
SURE SEEMS LIKE IT! THE THOUGHT OF EVER TAKING A DRIVER'S TEST SCARES ME TO DEATH!
YEAH, ME TOO.
HUH?
I MEAN, WHO NEEDS THE REJECTION, YOU KNOW?

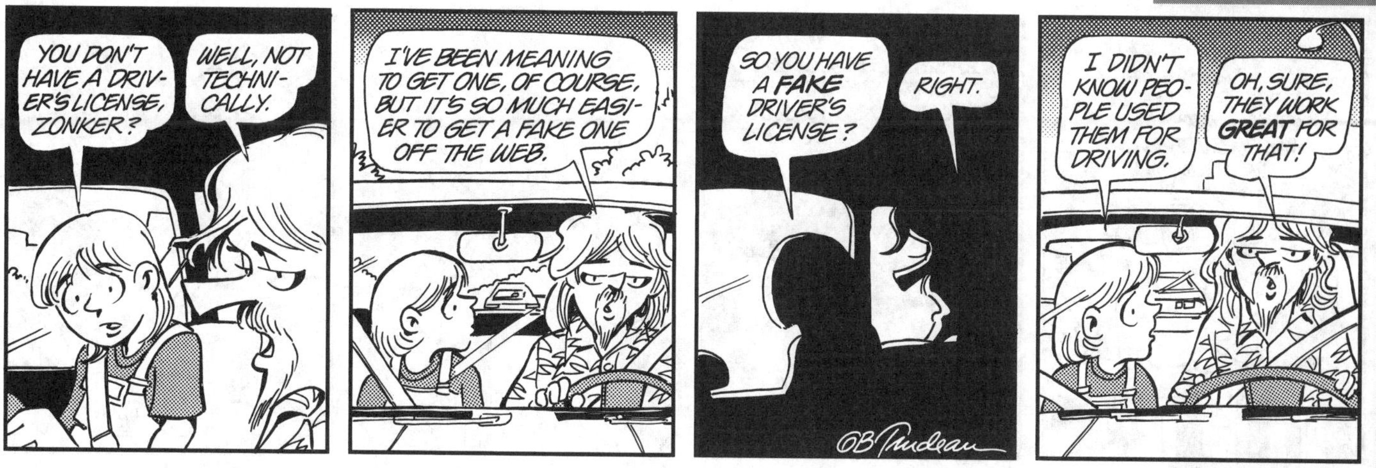
YOU DON'T HAVE A DRIVER'S LICENSE, ZONKER?
WELL, NOT TECHNICALLY.
I'VE BEEN MEANING TO GET ONE, OF COURSE, BUT IT'S SO MUCH EASIER TO GET A FAKE ONE OFF THE WEB.
SO YOU HAVE A **FAKE** DRIVER'S LICENSE?
RIGHT.
I DIDN'T KNOW PEOPLE USED THEM FOR DRIVING.
OH, SURE, THEY WORK **GREAT** FOR THAT!

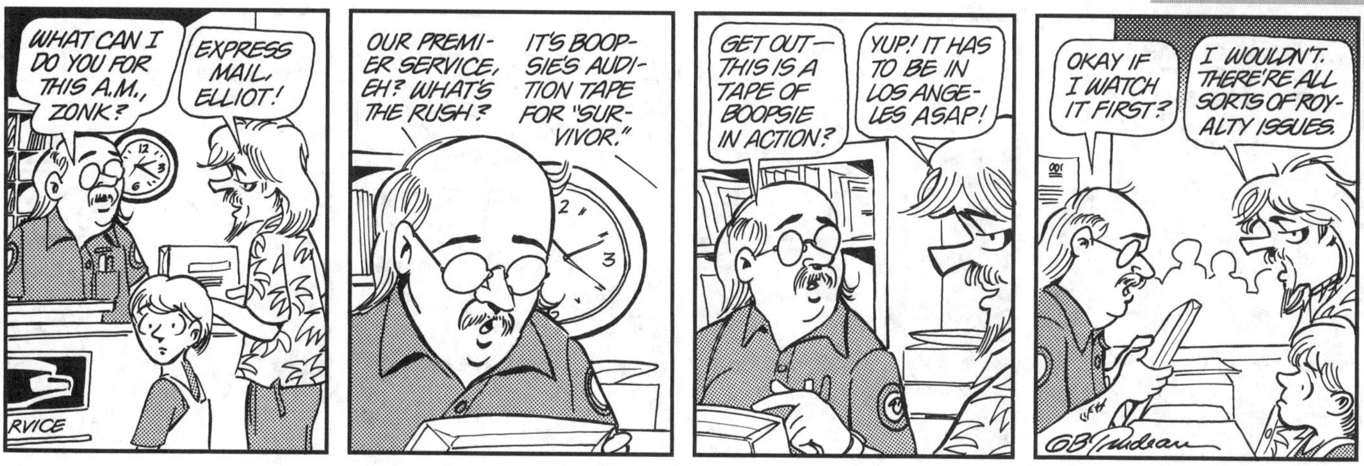
WHAT CAN I DO YOU FOR THIS A.M., ZONK?
EXPRESS MAIL, ELLIOT!
RVICE
OUR PREMIER SERVICE, EH? WHAT'S THE RUSH?
IT'S BOOPSIE'S AUDITION TAPE FOR "SURVIVOR."
GET OUT—THIS IS A TAPE OF BOOPSIE IN ACTION?
YUP! IT HAS TO BE IN LOS ANGELES ASAP!
OKAY IF I WATCH IT FIRST?
I WOULDN'T. THERE'RE ALL SORTS OF ROYALTY ISSUES.

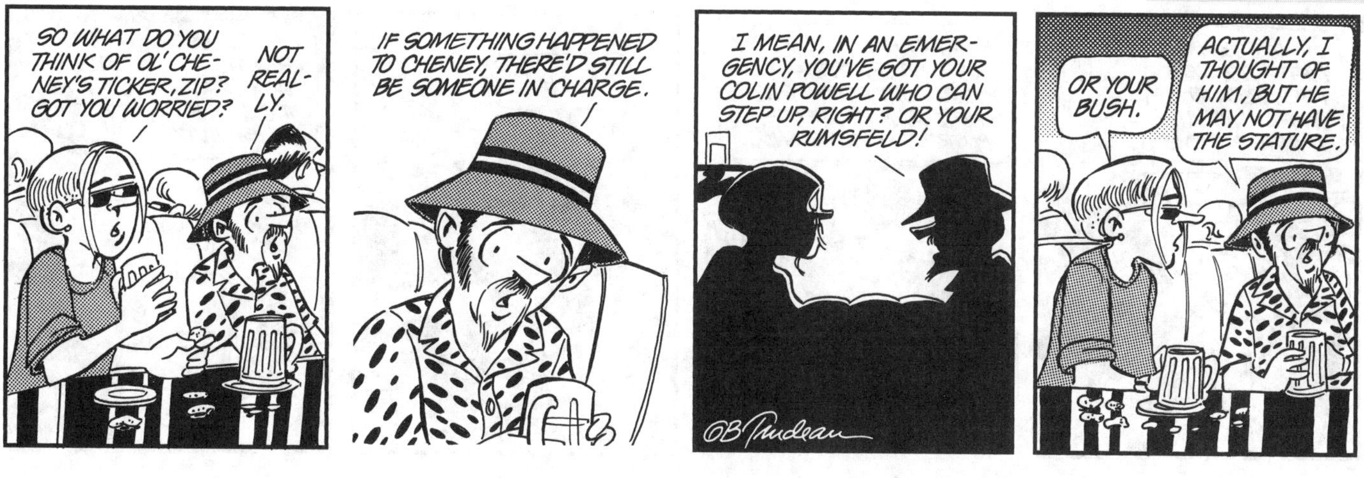
SO WHAT DO YOU THINK OF OL' CHENEY'S TICKER, ZIP? GOT YOU WORRIED?
NOT REALLY.
IF SOMETHING HAPPENED TO CHENEY, THERE'D STILL BE SOMEONE IN CHARGE.
I MEAN, IN AN EMERGENCY, YOU'VE GOT YOUR COLIN POWELL WHO CAN STEP UP, RIGHT? OR YOUR RUMSFELD!
OR YOUR BUSH.
ACTUALLY, I THOUGHT OF HIM, BUT HE MAY NOT HAVE THE STATURE.

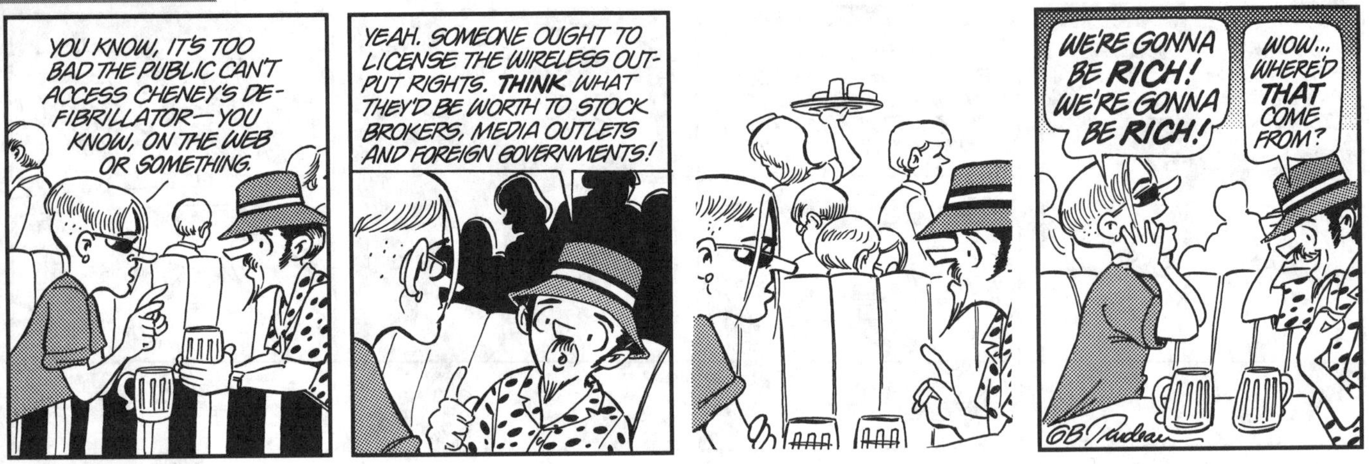
YOU KNOW, IT'S TOO BAD THE PUBLIC CAN'T ACCESS CHENEY'S DEFIBRILLATOR— YOU KNOW, ON THE WEB OR SOMETHING.
YEAH. SOMEONE OUGHT TO LICENSE THE WIRELESS OUTPUT RIGHTS. THINK WHAT THEY'D BE WORTH TO STOCK BROKERS, MEDIA OUTLETS AND FOREIGN GOVERNMENTS!
WE'RE GONNA BE RICH! WE'RE GONNA BE RICH!
WOW... WHERE'D THAT COME FROM?

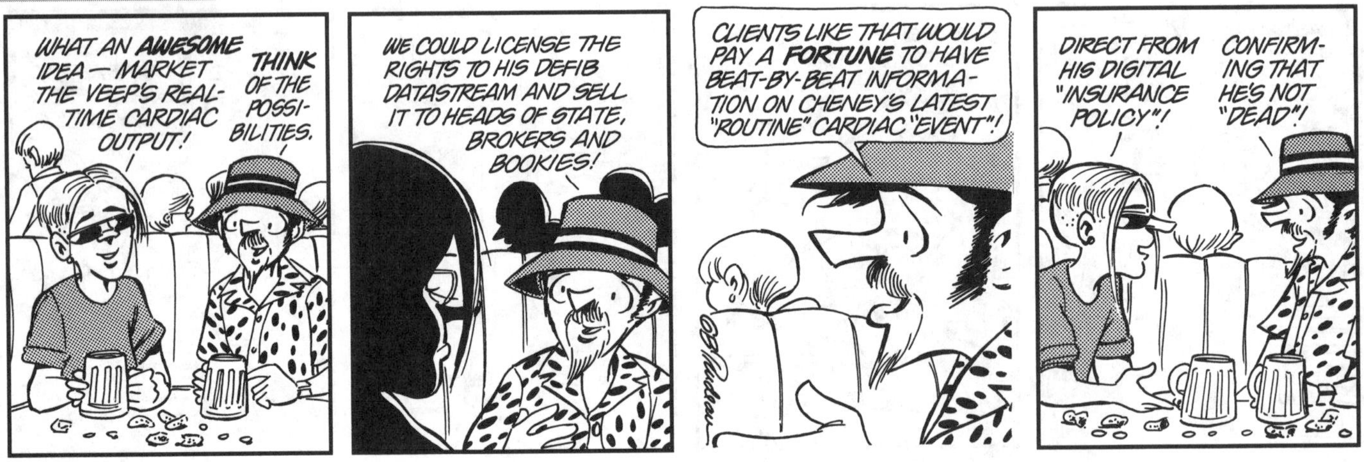
WHAT AN AWESOME IDEA— MARKET THE VEEP'S REAL-TIME CARDIAC OUTPUT!
THINK OF THE POSSIBILITIES.
WE COULD LICENSE THE RIGHTS TO HIS DEFIB DATASTREAM AND SELL IT TO HEADS OF STATE, BROKERS AND BOOKIES!
CLIENTS LIKE THAT WOULD PAY A FORTUNE TO HAVE BEAT-BY-BEAT INFORMATION ON CHENEY'S LATEST "ROUTINE" CARDIAC "EVENT"!
DIRECT FROM HIS DIGITAL "INSURANCE POLICY"!
CONFIRMING THAT HE'S NOT "DEAD"!

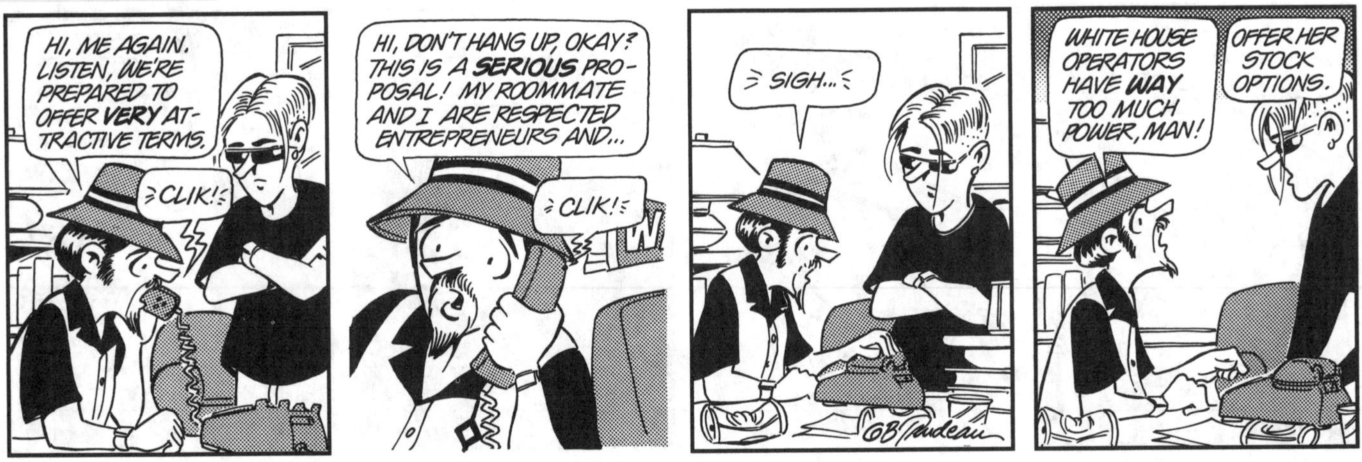
HI, ME AGAIN. LISTEN, WE'RE PREPARED TO OFFER VERY ATTRACTIVE TERMS.
CLIK!
HI, DON'T HANG UP, OKAY? THIS IS A SERIOUS PROPOSAL! MY ROOMMATE AND I ARE RESPECTED ENTREPRENEURS AND...
CLIK!
SIGH...
WHITE HOUSE OPERATORS HAVE WAY TOO MUCH POWER, MAN!
OFFER HER STOCK OPTIONS.

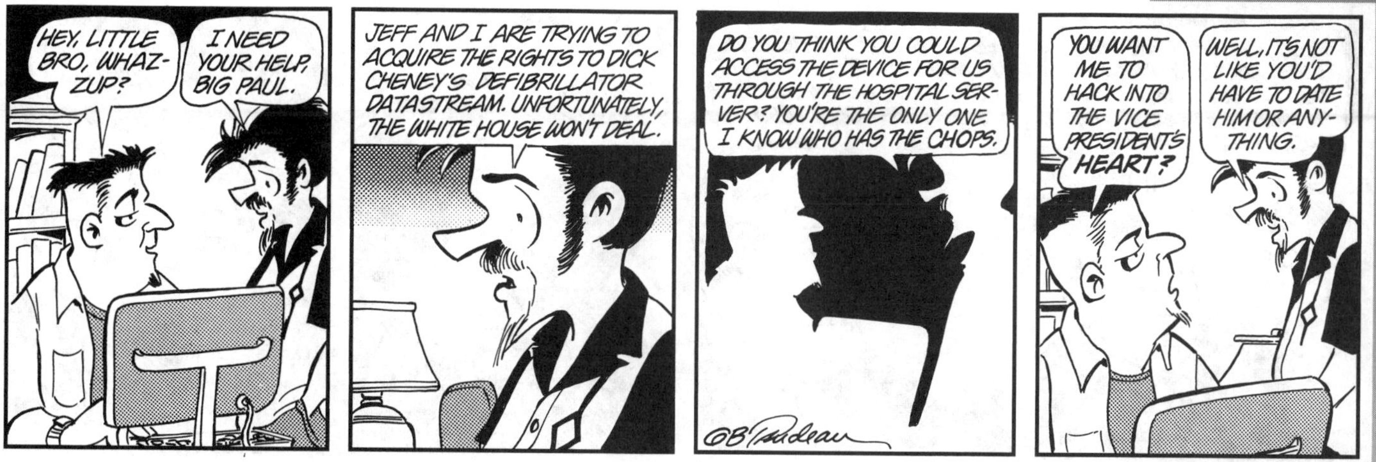
HEY, LITTLE BRO, WHAZZUP?
I NEED YOUR HELP, BIG PAUL.
JEFF AND I ARE TRYING TO ACQUIRE THE RIGHTS TO DICK CHENEY'S DEFIBRILLATOR DATASTREAM. UNFORTUNATELY, THE WHITE HOUSE WON'T DEAL.
DO YOU THINK YOU COULD ACCESS THE DEVICE FOR US THROUGH THE HOSPITAL SERVER? YOU'RE THE ONLY ONE I KNOW WHO HAS THE CHOPS.
YOU WANT ME TO HACK INTO THE VICE PRESIDENT'S **HEART?**
WELL, IT'S NOT LIKE YOU'D HAVE TO DATE HIM OR ANYTHING.

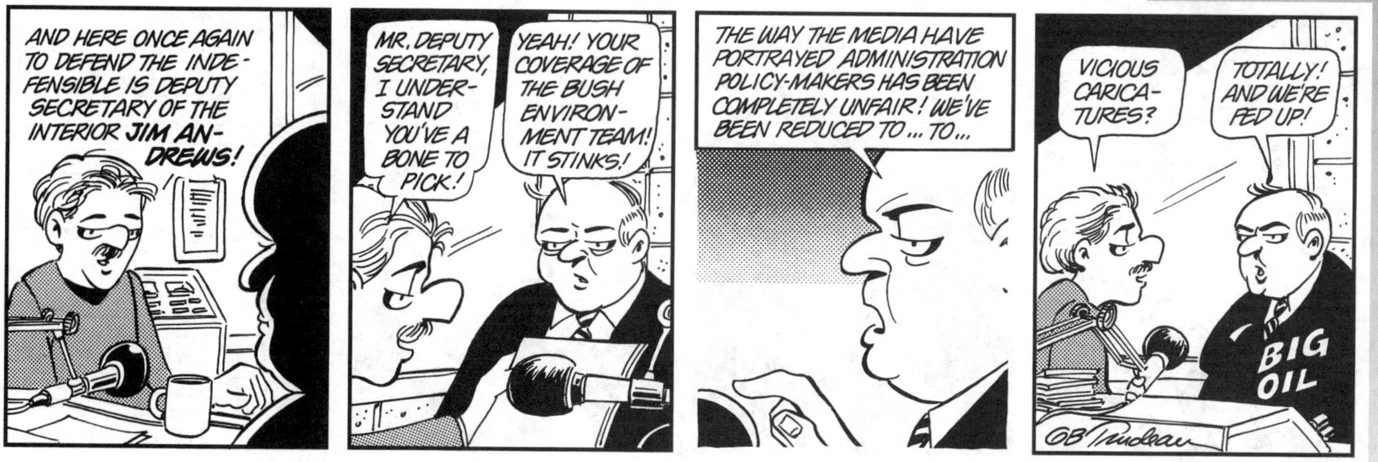
AND HERE ONCE AGAIN TO DEFEND THE INDEFENSIBLE IS DEPUTY SECRETARY OF THE INTERIOR **JIM ANDREWS**!
MR. DEPUTY SECRETARY, I UNDERSTAND YOU'VE A BONE TO PICK!
YEAH! YOUR COVERAGE OF THE BUSH ENVIRONMENT TEAM! IT STINKS!
THE WAY THE MEDIA HAVE PORTRAYED ADMINISTRATION POLICY-MAKERS HAS BEEN COMPLETELY UNFAIR! WE'VE BEEN REDUCED TO ... TO...
VICIOUS CARICATURES?
TOTALLY! AND WE'RE FED UP!
BIG OIL

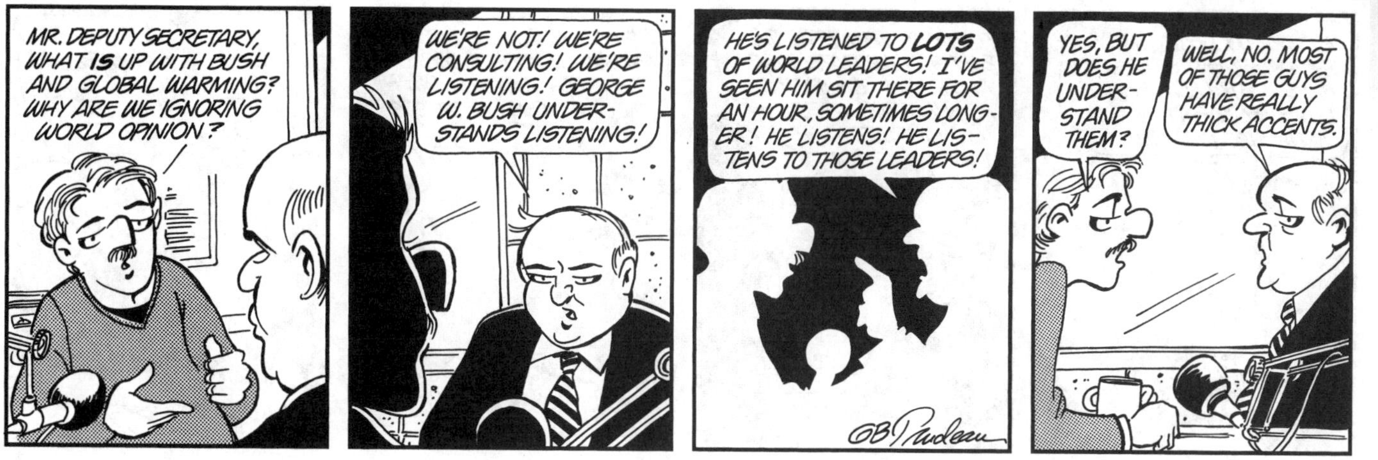
MR. DEPUTY SECRETARY, WHAT **IS** UP WITH BUSH AND GLOBAL WARMING? WHY ARE WE IGNORING WORLD OPINION?
WE'RE NOT! WE'RE CONSULTING! WE'RE LISTENING! GEORGE W. BUSH UNDERSTANDS LISTENING!
HE'S LISTENED TO **LOTS** OF WORLD LEADERS! I'VE SEEN HIM SIT THERE FOR AN HOUR, SOMETIMES LONGER! HE LISTENS! HE LISTENS TO THOSE LEADERS!
YES, BUT DOES HE UNDERSTAND THEM?
WELL, NO. MOST OF THOSE GUYS HAVE REALLY THICK ACCENTS.

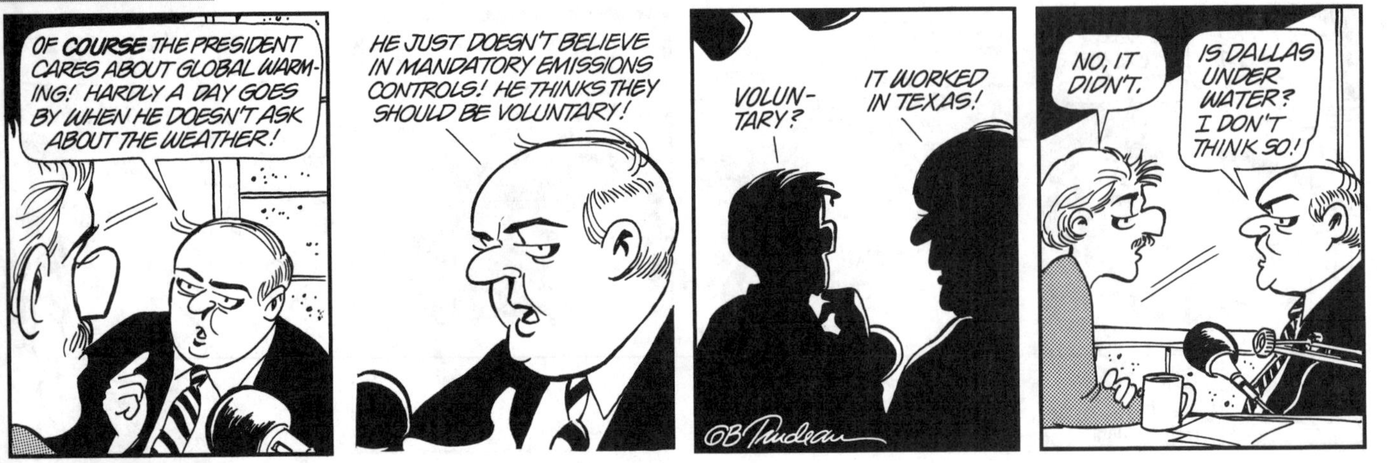
OF **COURSE** THE PRESIDENT CARES ABOUT GLOBAL WARMING! HARDLY A DAY GOES BY WHEN HE DOESN'T ASK ABOUT THE WEATHER!
HE JUST DOESN'T BELIEVE IN MANDATORY EMISSIONS CONTROLS! HE THINKS THEY SHOULD BE VOLUNTARY!
VOLUNTARY?
IT WORKED IN TEXAS!
NO, IT DIDN'T.
IS DALLAS UNDER WATER? I DON'T THINK SO!
©B. Trudeau

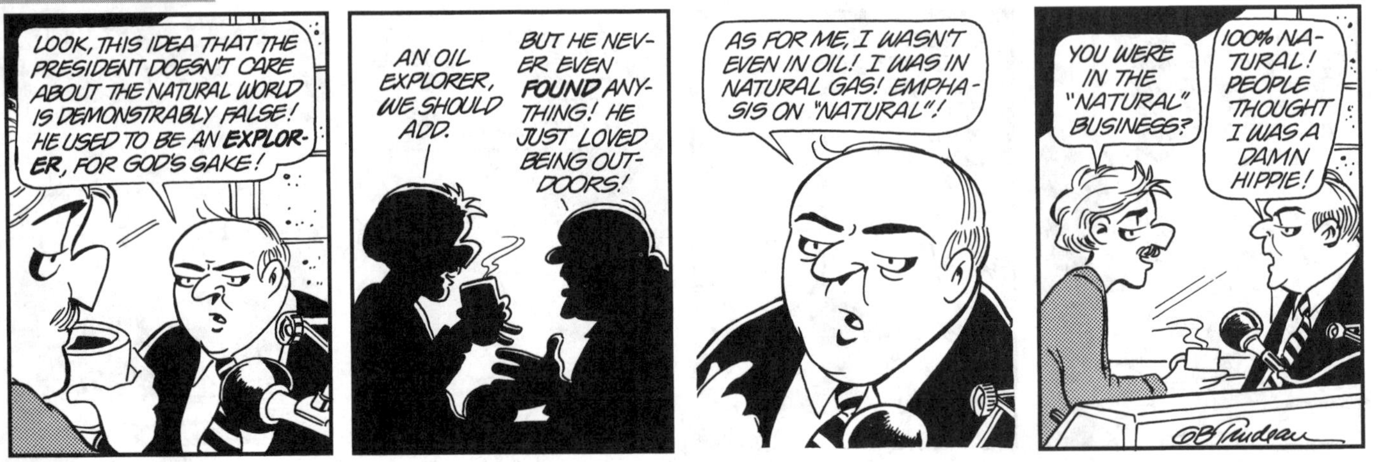
LOOK, THIS IDEA THAT THE PRESIDENT DOESN'T CARE ABOUT THE NATURAL WORLD IS DEMONSTRABLY FALSE! HE USED TO BE AN **EXPLORER**, FOR GOD'S SAKE!
AN OIL EXPLORER, WE SHOULD ADD.
BUT HE NEVER EVEN **FOUND** ANYTHING! HE JUST LOVED BEING OUTDOORS!
AS FOR ME, I WASN'T EVEN IN OIL! I WAS IN NATURAL GAS! EMPHASIS ON "NATURAL"!
YOU WERE IN THE "NATURAL" BUSINESS?
100% NATURAL! PEOPLE THOUGHT I WAS A DAMN HIPPIE!
©B. Trudeau

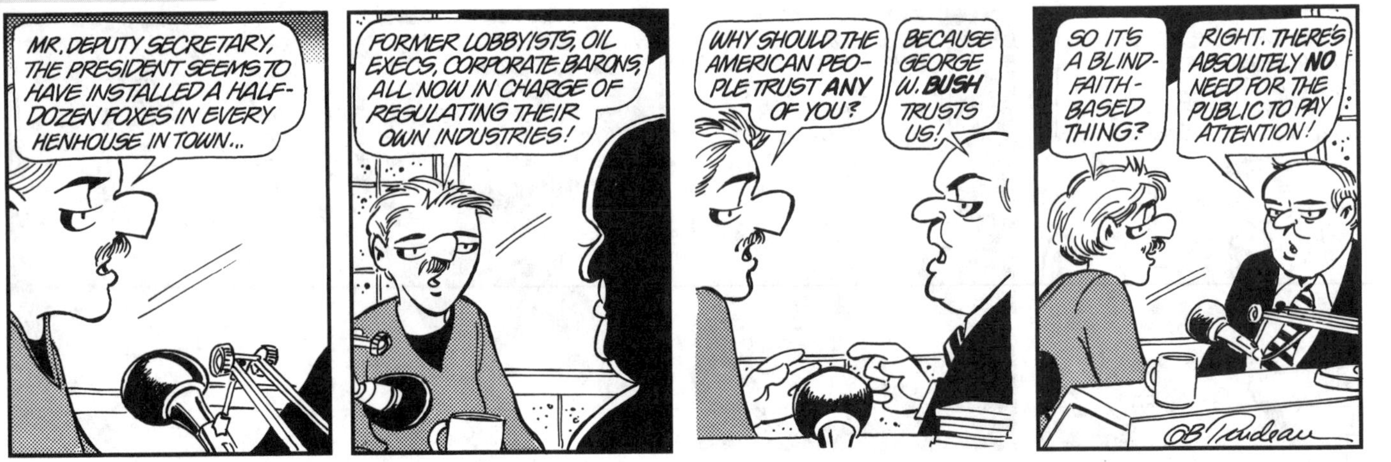
MR. DEPUTY SECRETARY, THE PRESIDENT SEEMS TO HAVE INSTALLED A HALF-DOZEN FOXES IN EVERY HENHOUSE IN TOWN...
FORMER LOBBYISTS, OIL EXECS, CORPORATE BARONS, ALL NOW IN CHARGE OF REGULATING THEIR OWN INDUSTRIES!
WHY SHOULD THE AMERICAN PEOPLE TRUST **ANY** OF YOU?
BECAUSE GEORGE W. **BUSH** TRUSTS US!
SO IT'S A BLIND-FAITH-BASED THING?
RIGHT. THERE'S ABSOLUTELY **NO** NEED FOR THE PUBLIC TO PAY ATTENTION!
©B. Trudeau

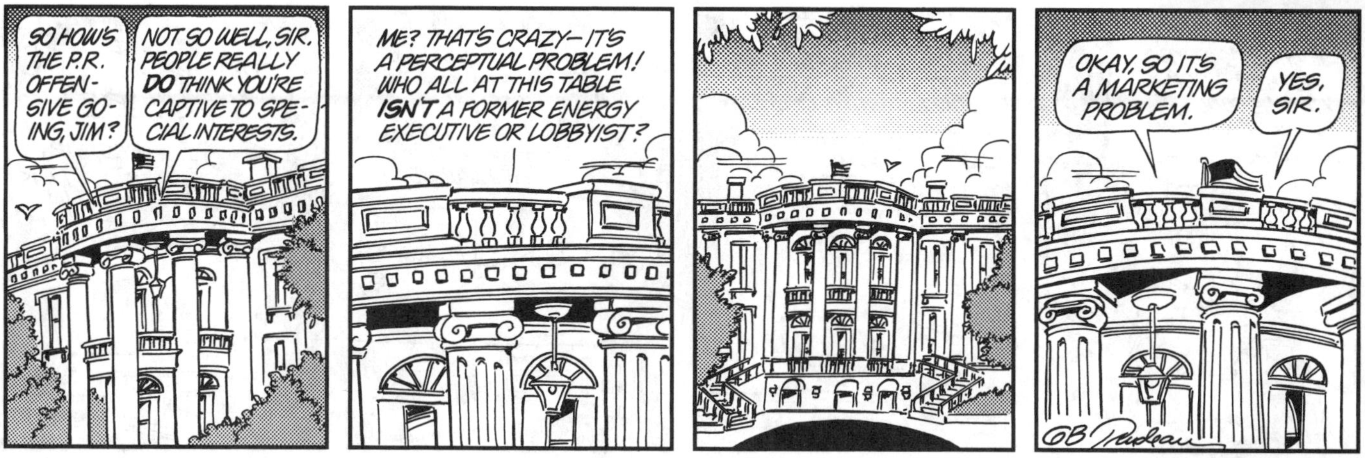
SO HOW'S THE P.R. OFFEN-SIVE GO-ING, JIM?
NOT SO WELL, SIR. PEOPLE REALLY DO THINK YOU'RE CAPTIVE TO SPE-CIAL INTERESTS.
ME? THAT'S CRAZY—IT'S A PERCEPTUAL PROBLEM! WHO ALL AT THIS TABLE ISN'T A FORMER ENERGY EXECUTIVE OR LOBBYIST?
OKAY, SO IT'S A MARKETING PROBLEM.
YES, SIR.
GB Trudeau

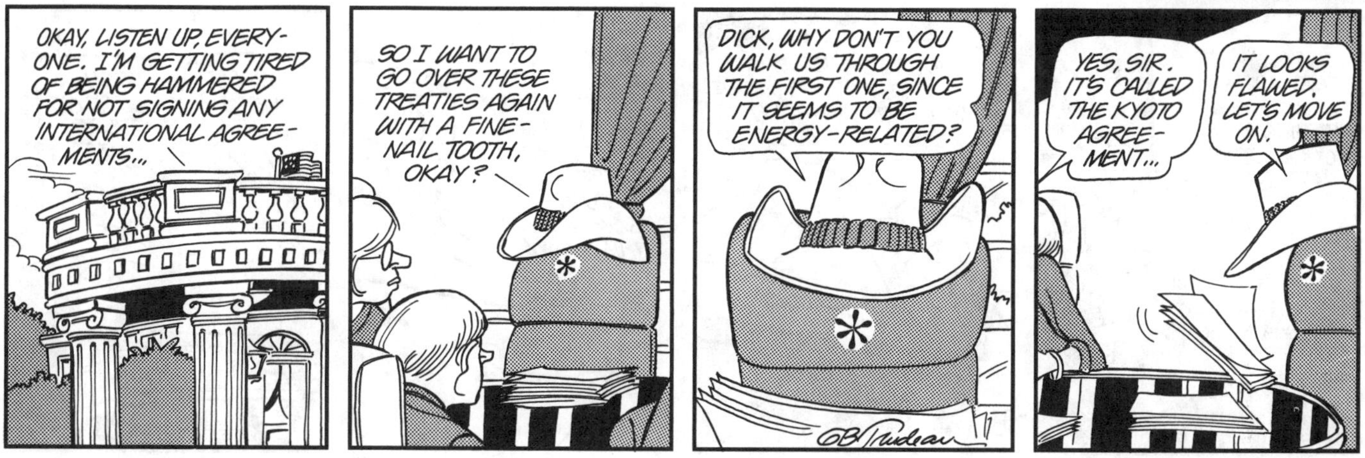
OKAY, LISTEN UP, EVERY-ONE. I'M GETTING TIRED OF BEING HAMMERED FOR NOT SIGNING ANY INTERNATIONAL AGREE-MENTS...
SO I WANT TO GO OVER THESE TREATIES AGAIN WITH A FINE-NAIL TOOTH, OKAY?
DICK, WHY DON'T YOU WALK US THROUGH THE FIRST ONE, SINCE IT SEEMS TO BE ENERGY-RELATED?
YES, SIR. IT'S CALLED THE KYOTO AGREE-MENT...
IT LOOKS FLAWED. LET'S MOVE ON.
GB Trudeau

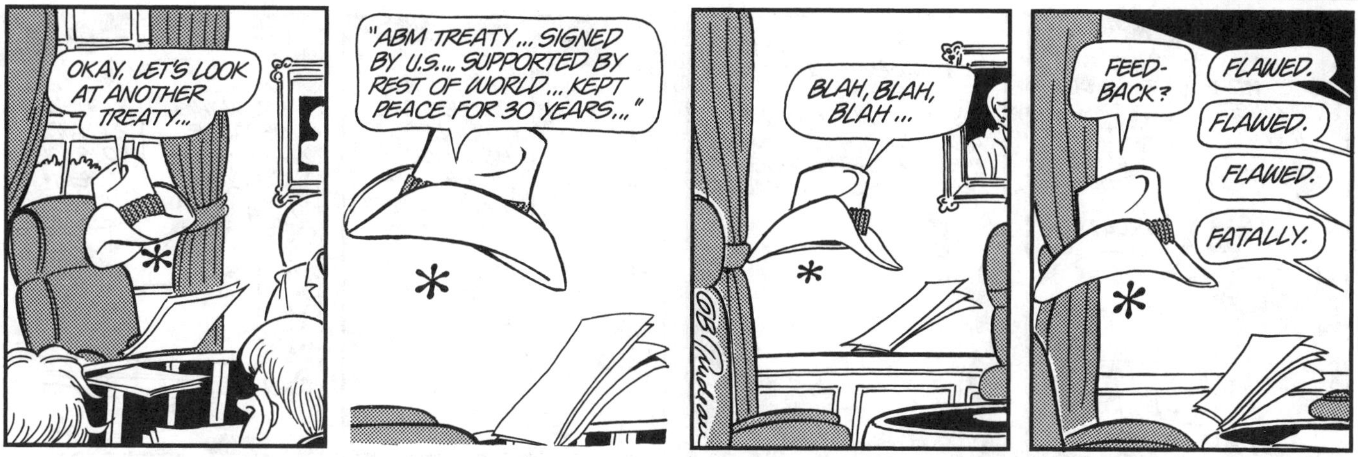
OKAY, LET'S LOOK AT ANOTHER TREATY...
"ABM TREATY... SIGNED BY U.S.... SUPPORTED BY REST OF WORLD... KEPT PEACE FOR 30 YEARS..."
BLAH, BLAH, BLAH...
FEED-BACK?
FLAWED.
FLAWED.
FLAWED.
FATALLY.
GB Trudeau

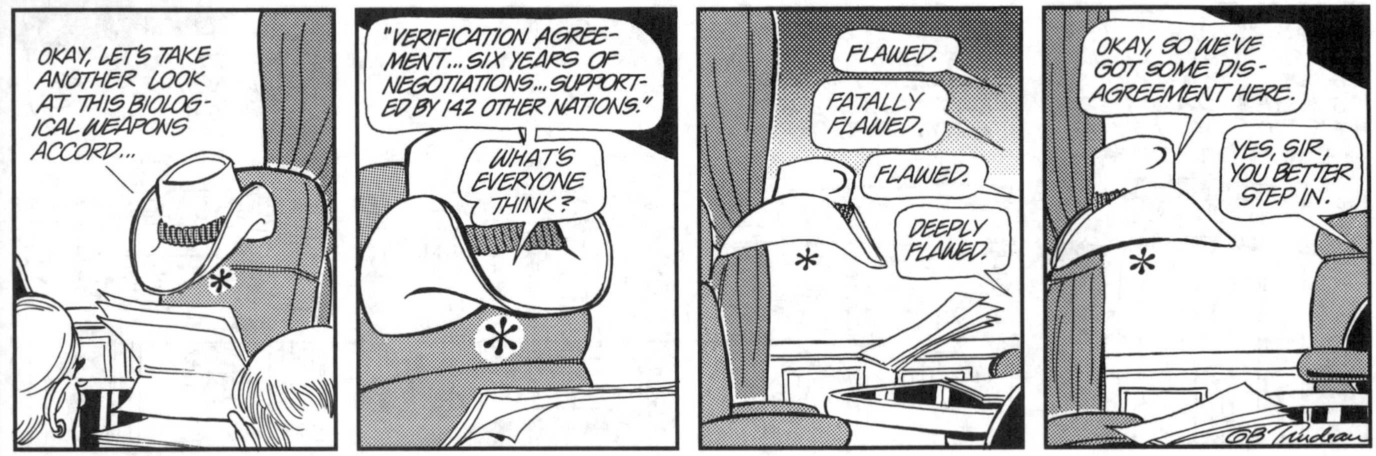
OKAY, LET'S TAKE ANOTHER LOOK AT THIS BIOLOGICAL WEAPONS ACCORD...
"VERIFICATION AGREEMENT... SIX YEARS OF NEGOTIATIONS... SUPPORTED BY 142 OTHER NATIONS."
WHAT'S EVERYONE THINK?
FLAWED.
FATALLY FLAWED.
FLAWED.
DEEPLY FLAWED.
OKAY, SO WE'VE GOT SOME DISAGREEMENT HERE.
YES, SIR, YOU BETTER STEP IN.
GB Trudeau

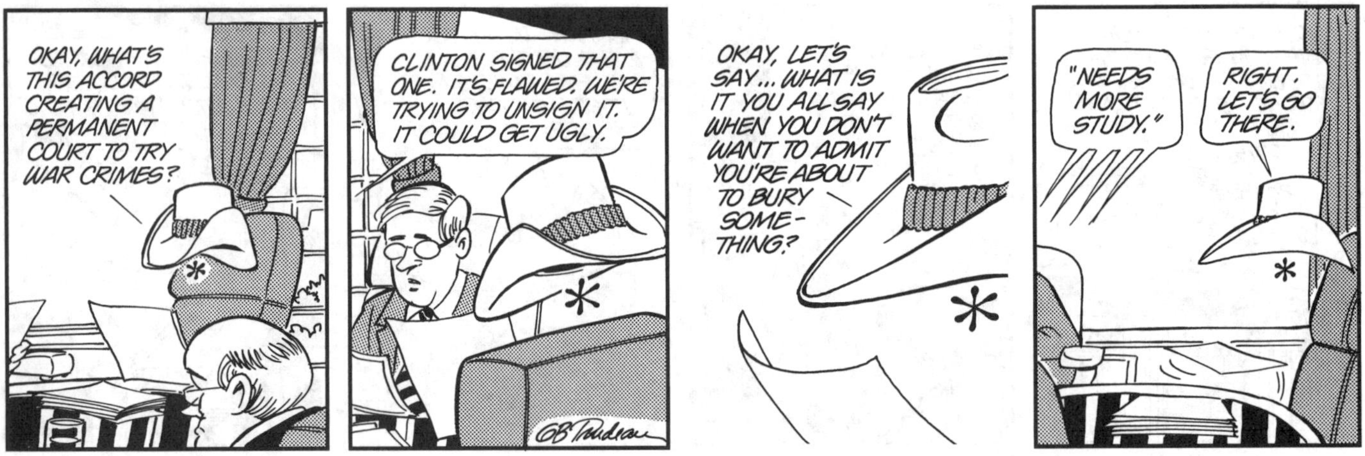
OKAY, WHAT'S THIS ACCORD CREATING A PERMANENT COURT TO TRY WAR CRIMES?
CLINTON SIGNED THAT ONE. IT'S FLAWED. WE'RE TRYING TO UNSIGN IT. IT COULD GET UGLY.
GB Trudeau
OKAY, LET'S SAY... WHAT IS IT YOU ALL SAY WHEN YOU DON'T WANT TO ADMIT YOU'RE ABOUT TO BURY SOMETHING?
"NEEDS MORE STUDY."
RIGHT. LET'S GO THERE.

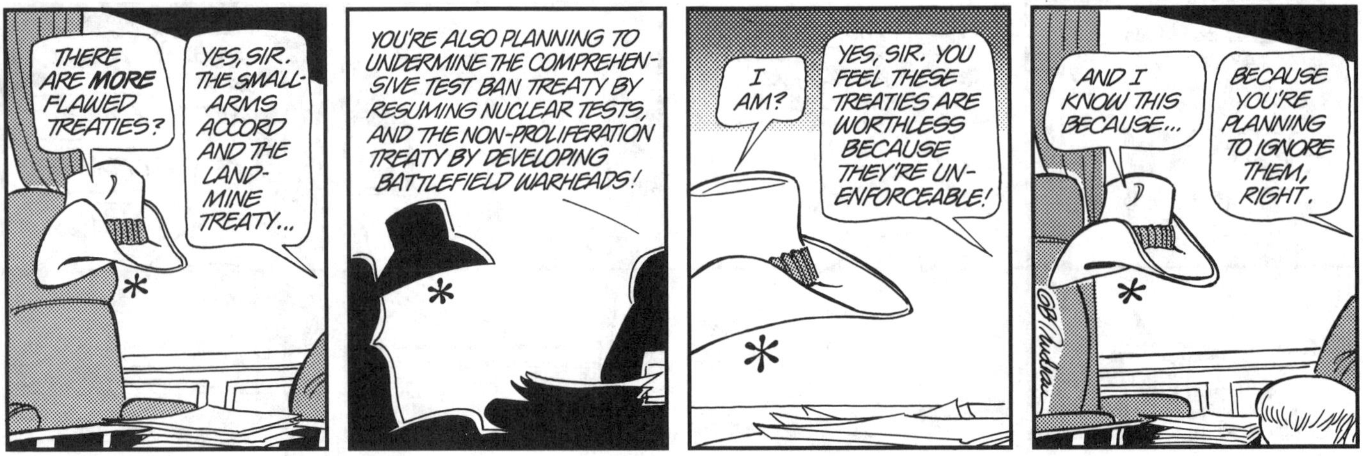
THERE ARE **MORE** FLAWED TREATIES?
YES, SIR. THE SMALL-ARMS ACCORD AND THE LAND-MINE TREATY...
YOU'RE ALSO PLANNING TO UNDERMINE THE COMPREHENSIVE TEST BAN TREATY BY RESUMING NUCLEAR TESTS, AND THE NON-PROLIFERATION TREATY BY DEVELOPING BATTLEFIELD WARHEADS!
I AM?
YES, SIR. YOU FEEL THESE TREATIES ARE WORTHLESS BECAUSE THEY'RE UNENFORCEABLE!
GB Trudeau
AND I KNOW THIS BECAUSE...
BECAUSE YOU'RE PLANNING TO IGNORE THEM, RIGHT.

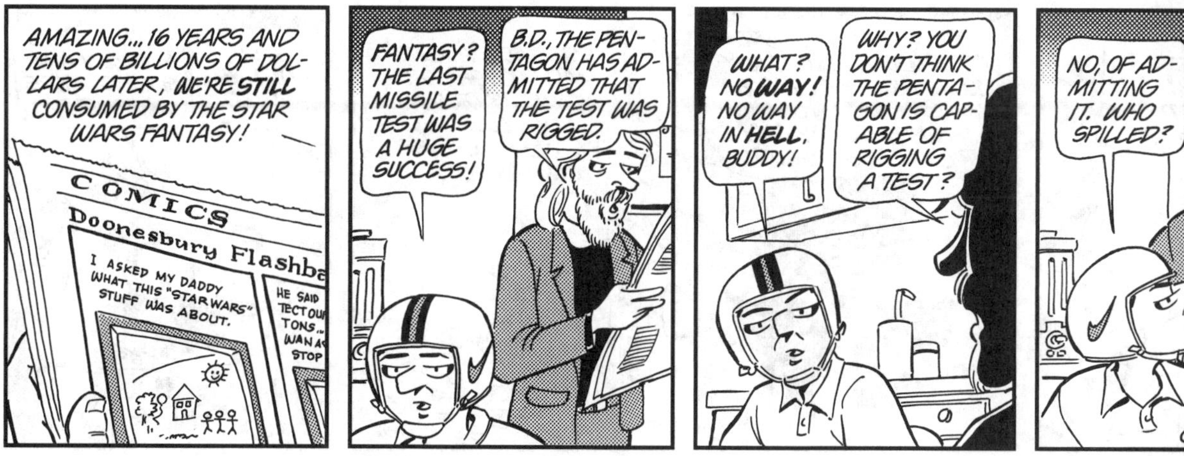
AMAZING... 16 YEARS AND TENS OF BILLIONS OF DOLLARS LATER, WE'RE **STILL** CONSUMED BY THE STAR WARS FANTASY!
COMICS
Doonesbury Flashba
I ASKED MY DADDY WHAT THIS "STAR WARS" STUFF WAS ABOUT.
HE SAID
FANTASY? THE LAST MISSILE TEST WAS A HUGE SUCCESS!
B.D., THE PENTAGON HAS ADMITTED THAT THE TEST WAS RIGGED.
WHAT? NO **WAY**! NO WAY IN **HELL**, BUDDY!
WHY? YOU DON'T THINK THE PENTAGON IS CAPABLE OF RIGGING A TEST?
NO, OF ADMITTING IT. WHO SPILLED?
SOME ARMY OF ONE.
GB Trudeau

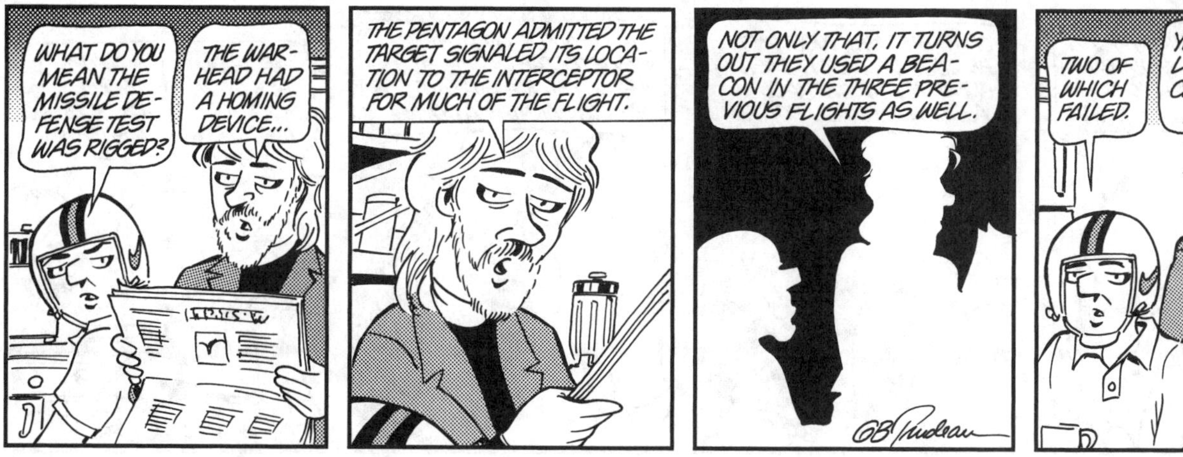
WHAT DO YOU MEAN THE MISSILE DEFENSE TEST WAS RIGGED?
THE WARHEAD HAD A HOMING DEVICE...
THE PENTAGON ADMITTED THE TARGET SIGNALED ITS LOCATION TO THE INTERCEPTOR FOR MUCH OF THE FLIGHT.
NOT ONLY THAT, IT TURNS OUT THEY USED A BEACON IN THE THREE PREVIOUS FLIGHTS AS WELL.
GB Trudeau
TWO OF WHICH FAILED.
YES, APPARENTLY A RELIABLE CHEAT IS SOME YEARS OFF.

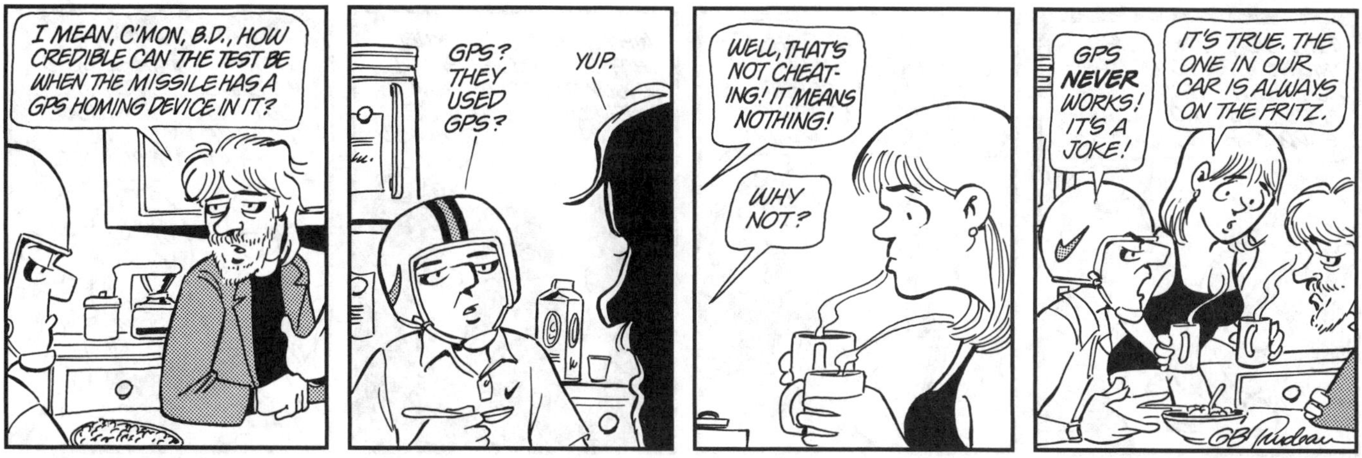
I MEAN, C'MON, B.D., HOW CREDIBLE CAN THE TEST BE WHEN THE MISSILE HAS A GPS HOMING DEVICE IN IT?
GPS? THEY USED GPS?
YUP.
WELL, THAT'S NOT CHEATING! IT MEANS NOTHING!
WHY NOT?
GPS **NEVER** WORKS! IT'S A JOKE!
IT'S TRUE. THE ONE IN OUR CAR IS ALWAYS ON THE FRITZ.
GB Trudeau

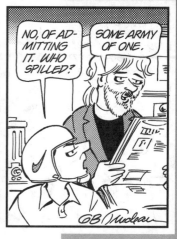

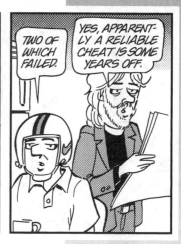

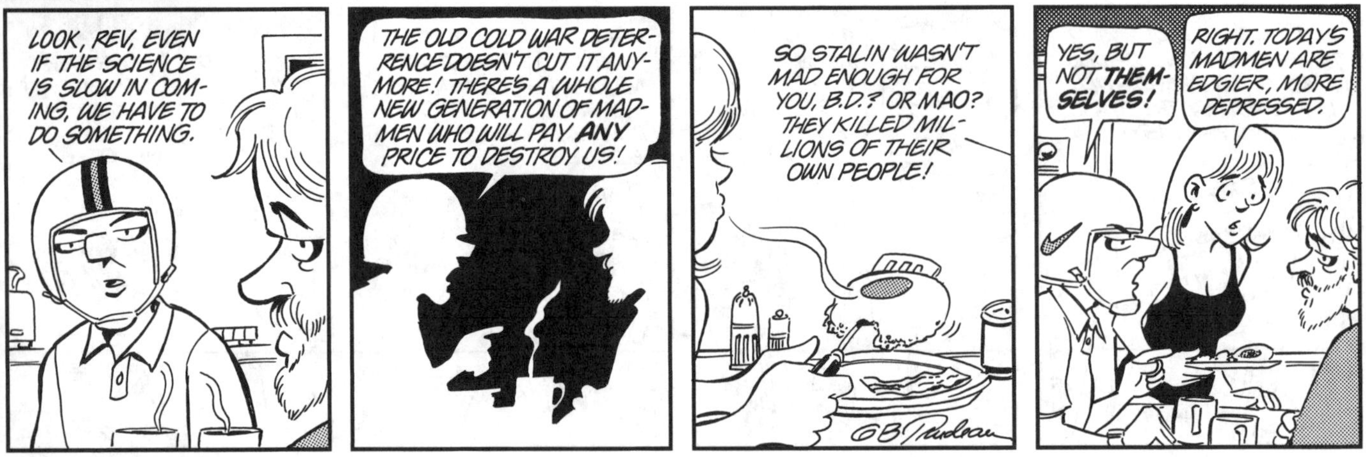
LOOK, REV, EVEN IF THE SCIENCE IS SLOW IN COMING, WE HAVE TO DO SOMETHING.
THE OLD COLD WAR DETERRENCE DOESN'T CUT IT ANYMORE! THERE'S A WHOLE NEW GENERATION OF MADMEN WHO WILL PAY **ANY** PRICE TO DESTROY US!
SO STALIN WASN'T MAD ENOUGH FOR YOU, B.D.? OR MAO? THEY KILLED MILLIONS OF THEIR OWN PEOPLE!
YES, BUT NOT **THEMSELVES!**
RIGHT. TODAY'S MADMEN ARE EDGIER, MORE DEPRESSED.

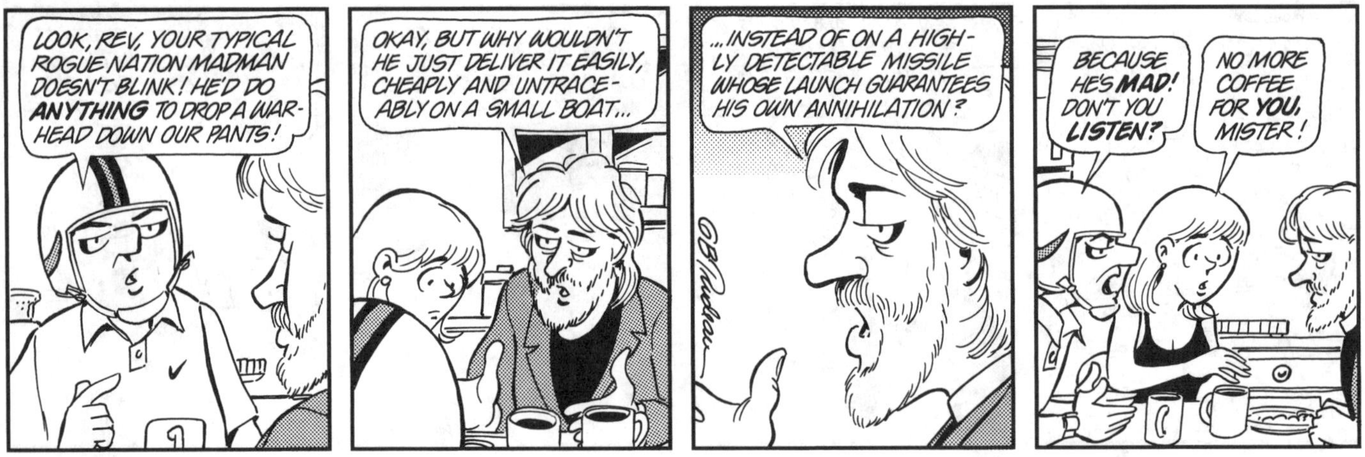
LOOK, REV, YOUR TYPICAL ROGUE NATION MADMAN DOESN'T BLINK! HE'D DO **ANYTHING** TO DROP A WARHEAD DOWN OUR PANTS!
OKAY, BUT WHY WOULDN'T HE JUST DELIVER IT EASILY, CHEAPLY AND UNTRACEABLY ON A SMALL BOAT...
...INSTEAD OF ON A HIGHLY DETECTABLE MISSILE WHOSE LAUNCH GUARANTEES HIS OWN ANNIHILATION?
BECAUSE HE'S **MAD!** DON'T YOU **LISTEN?**
NO MORE COFFEE FOR **YOU,** MISTER!

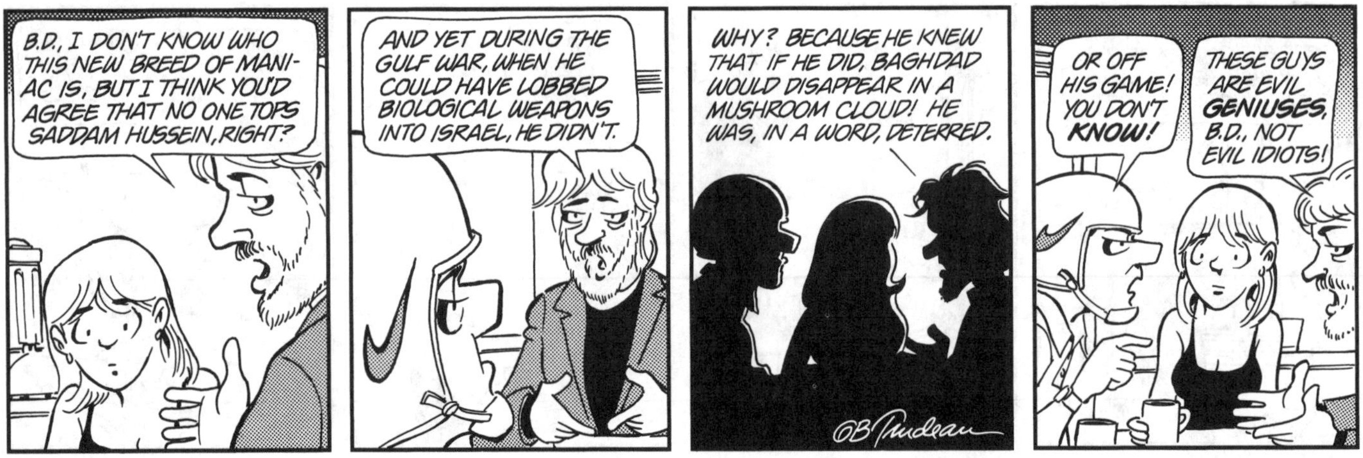
B.D., I DON'T KNOW WHO THIS NEW BREED OF MANIAC IS, BUT I THINK YOU'D AGREE THAT NO ONE TOPS SADDAM HUSSEIN, RIGHT?
AND YET DURING THE GULF WAR, WHEN HE COULD HAVE LOBBED BIOLOGICAL WEAPONS INTO ISRAEL, HE DIDN'T.
WHY? BECAUSE HE KNEW THAT IF HE DID, BAGHDAD WOULD DISAPPEAR IN A MUSHROOM CLOUD! HE WAS, IN A WORD, DETERRED.
OR OFF HIS GAME! YOU DON'T **KNOW!**
THESE GUYS ARE EVIL **GENIUSES,** B.D., NOT EVIL IDIOTS!

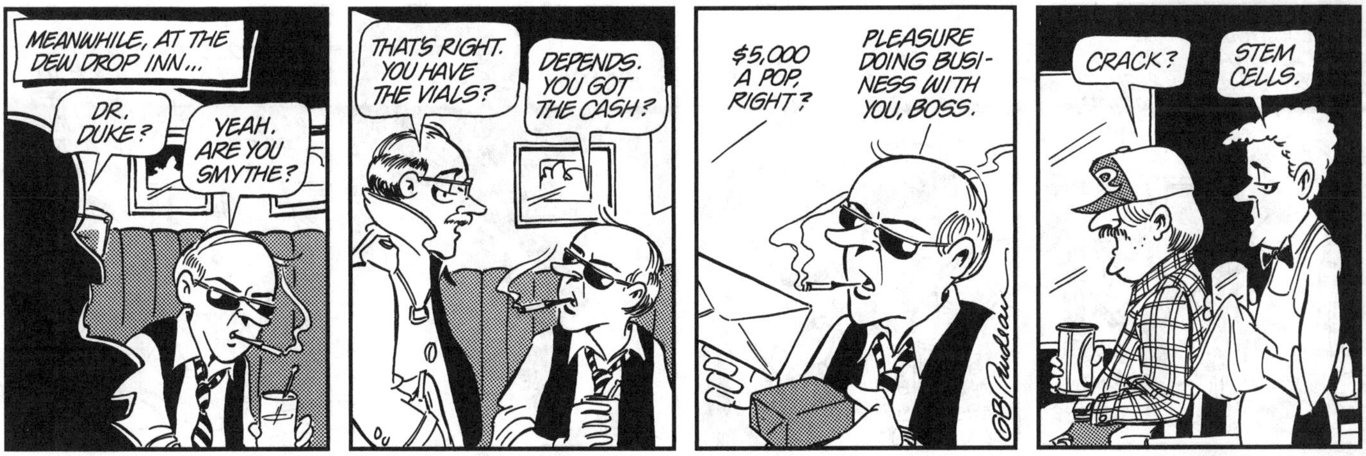
MEANWHILE, AT THE DEW DROP INN...
DR. DUKE?
YEAH. ARE YOU SMYTHE?
THAT'S RIGHT. YOU HAVE THE VIALS?
DEPENDS. YOU GOT THE CASH?
$5,000 A POP, RIGHT?
PLEASURE DOING BUSINESS WITH YOU, BOSS.
CRACK?
STEM CELLS.

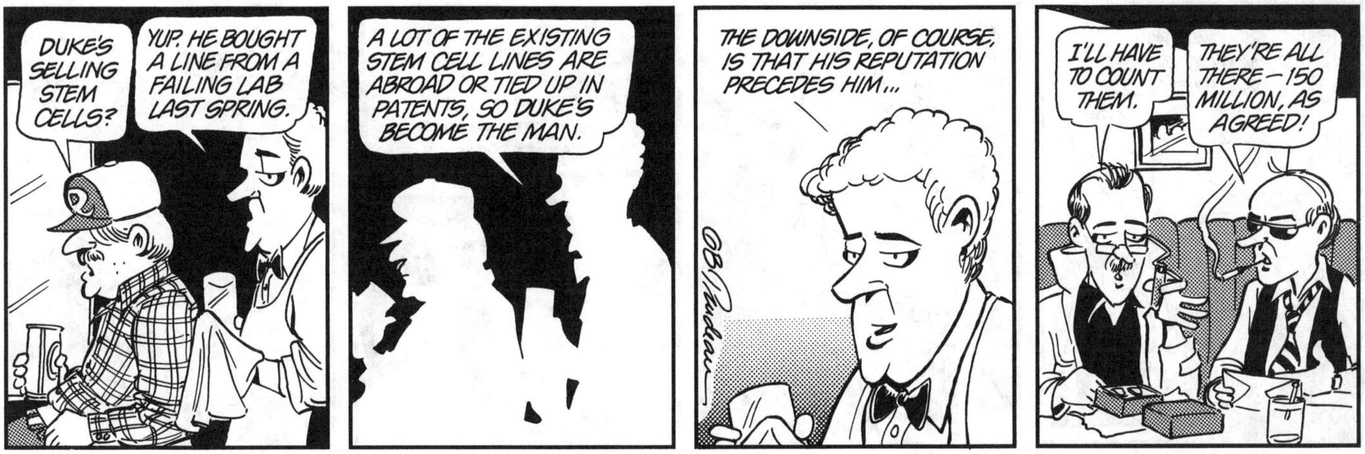
DUKE'S SELLING STEM CELLS?
YUP. HE BOUGHT A LINE FROM A FAILING LAB LAST SPRING.
A LOT OF THE EXISTING STEM CELL LINES ARE ABROAD OR TIED UP IN PATENTS, SO DUKE'S BECOME THE MAN.
THE DOWNSIDE, OF COURSE, IS THAT HIS REPUTATION PRECEDES HIM...
I'LL HAVE TO COUNT THEM.
THEY'RE ALL THERE — 150 MILLION, AS AGREED!

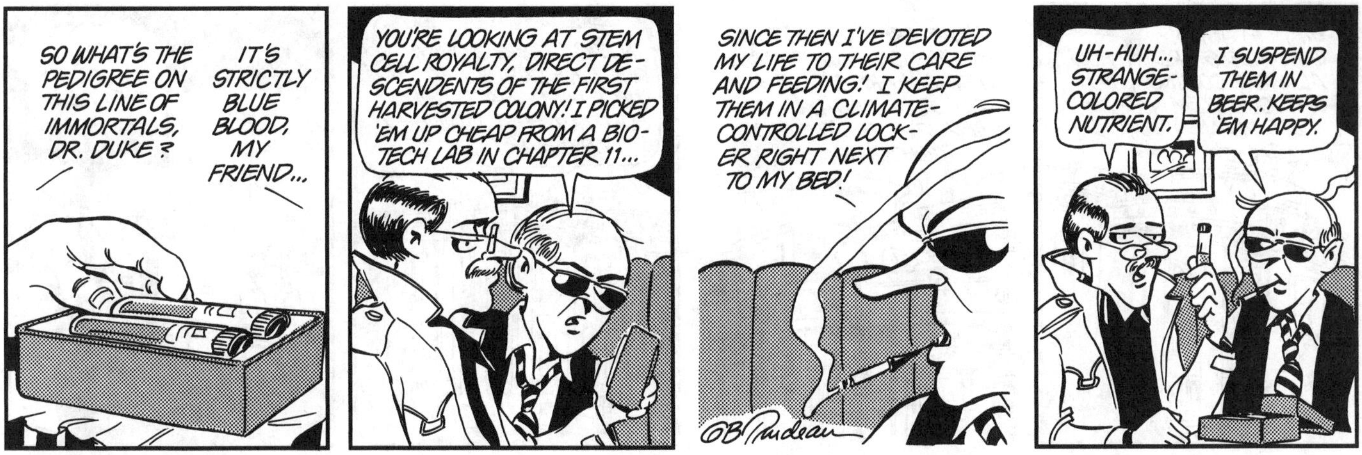
SO WHAT'S THE PEDIGREE ON THIS LINE OF IMMORTALS, DR. DUKE?
IT'S STRICTLY BLUE BLOOD, MY FRIEND...
YOU'RE LOOKING AT STEM CELL ROYALTY, DIRECT DESCENDENTS OF THE FIRST HARVESTED COLONY! I PICKED 'EM UP CHEAP FROM A BIOTECH LAB IN CHAPTER 11...
SINCE THEN I'VE DEVOTED MY LIFE TO THEIR CARE AND FEEDING! I KEEP THEM IN A CLIMATE-CONTROLLED LOCKER RIGHT NEXT TO MY BED!
UH-HUH... STRANGE-COLORED NUTRIENT.
I SUSPEND THEM IN BEER. KEEPS 'EM HAPPY.

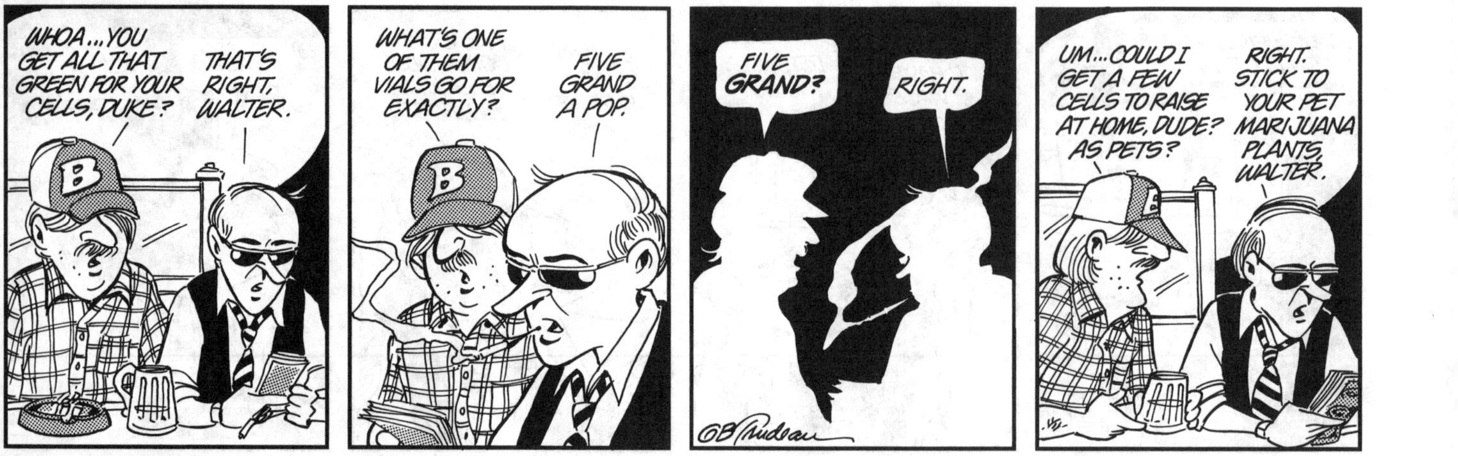
WHOA ... YOU GET ALL THAT GREEN FOR YOUR CELLS, DUKE?
THAT'S RIGHT, WALTER.
WHAT'S ONE OF THEM VIALS GO FOR EXACTLY?
FIVE GRAND A POP.
FIVE GRAND?
RIGHT.
UM... COULD I GET A FEW CELLS TO RAISE AT HOME, DUDE? AS PETS?
RIGHT. STICK TO YOUR PET MARIJUANA PLANTS, WALTER.

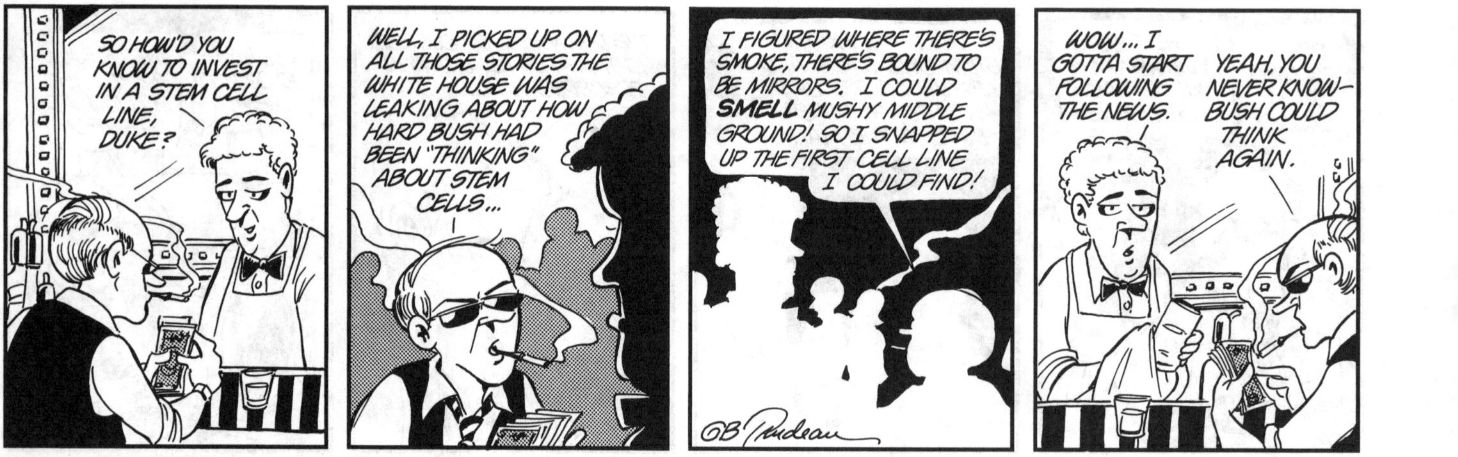
SO HOW'D YOU KNOW TO INVEST IN A STEM CELL LINE, DUKE?
WELL, I PICKED UP ON ALL THOSE STORIES THE WHITE HOUSE WAS LEAKING ABOUT HOW HARD BUSH HAD BEEN "THINKING" ABOUT STEM CELLS...
I FIGURED WHERE THERE'S SMOKE, THERE'S BOUND TO BE MIRRORS. I COULD SMELL MUSHY MIDDLE GROUND! SO I SNAPPED UP THE FIRST CELL LINE I COULD FIND!
WOW... I GOTTA START FOLLOWING THE NEWS.
YEAH, YOU NEVER KNOW–BUSH COULD THINK AGAIN.

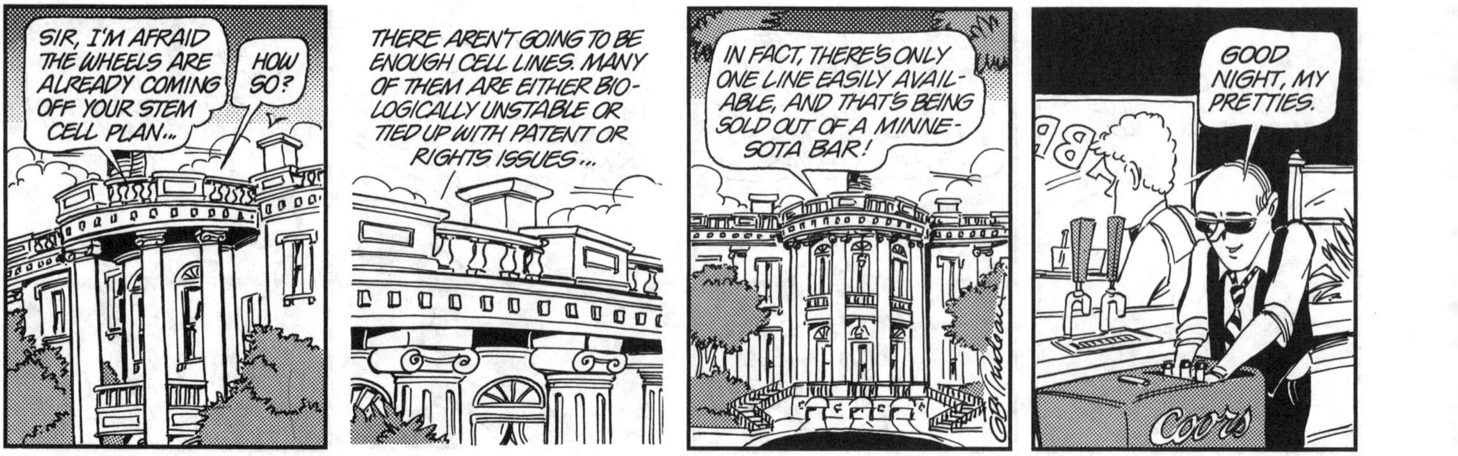
SIR, I'M AFRAID THE WHEELS ARE ALREADY COMING OFF YOUR STEM CELL PLAN...
HOW SO?
THERE AREN'T GOING TO BE ENOUGH CELL LINES. MANY OF THEM ARE EITHER BIOLOGICALLY UNSTABLE OR TIED UP WITH PATENT OR RIGHTS ISSUES...
IN FACT, THERE'S ONLY ONE LINE EASILY AVAILABLE, AND THAT'S BEING SOLD OUT OF A MINNESOTA BAR!
GOOD NIGHT, MY PRETTIES.
Coors

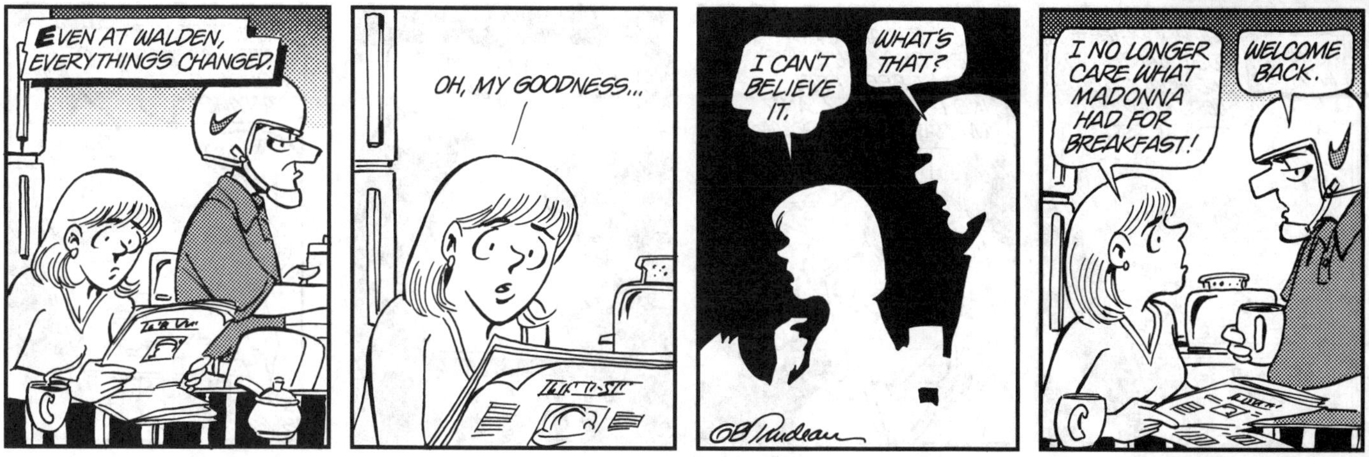
EVEN AT WALDEN, EVERYTHING'S CHANGED.
OH, MY GOODNESS...
I CAN'T BELIEVE IT.
WHAT'S THAT?
I NO LONGER CARE WHAT MADONNA HAD FOR BREAKFAST!
WELCOME BACK.

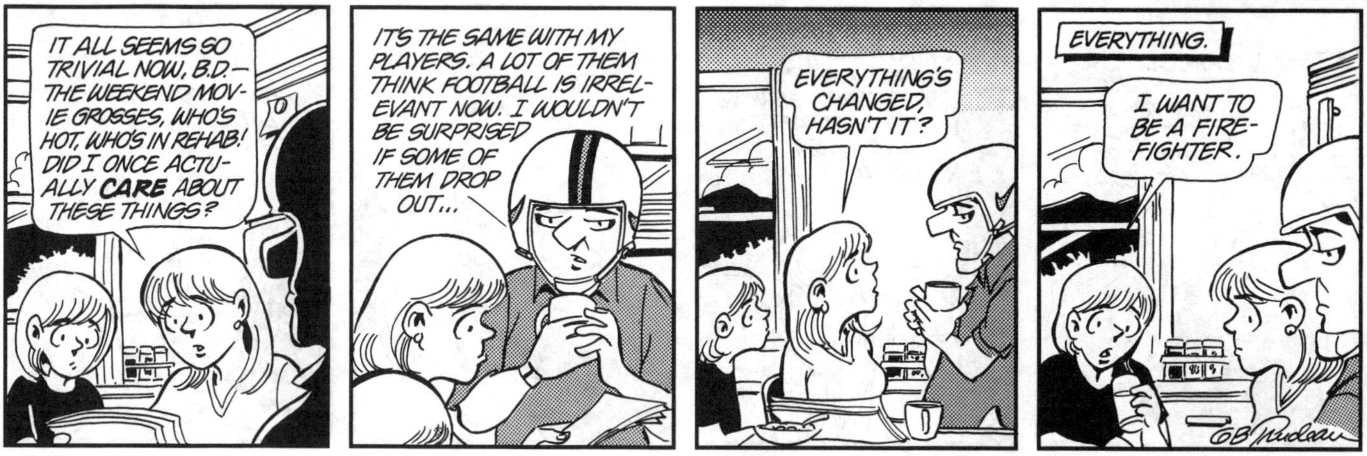
IT ALL SEEMS SO TRIVIAL NOW, B.D.— THE WEEKEND MOVIE GROSSES, WHO'S HOT, WHO'S IN REHAB! DID I ONCE ACTUALLY CARE ABOUT THESE THINGS?
IT'S THE SAME WITH MY PLAYERS. A LOT OF THEM THINK FOOTBALL IS IRRELEVANT NOW. I WOULDN'T BE SURPRISED IF SOME OF THEM DROP OUT...
EVERYTHING'S CHANGED, HASN'T IT?
EVERYTHING.
I WANT TO BE A FIREFIGHTER.

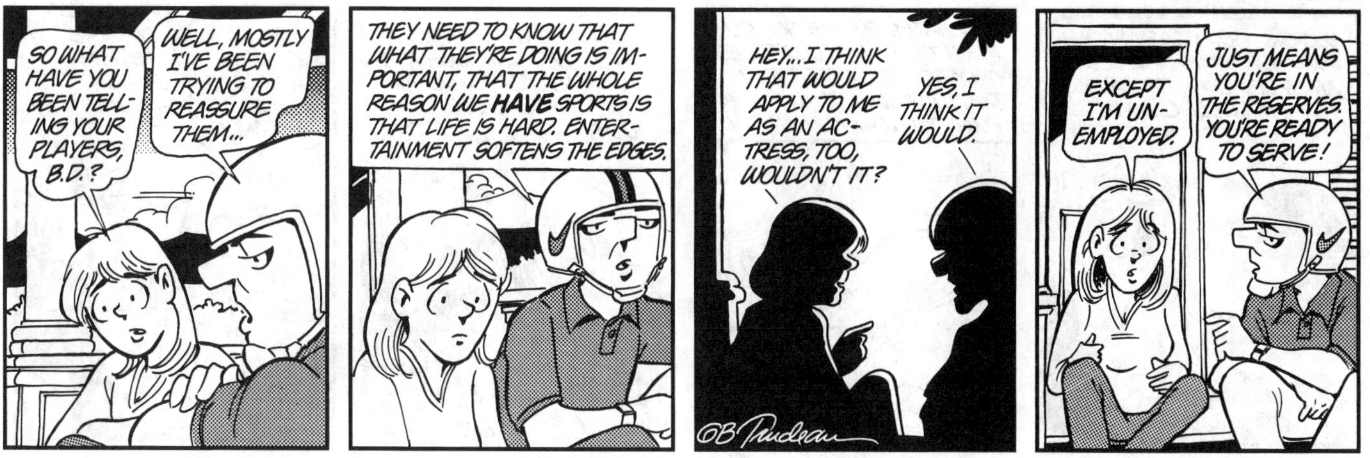
SO WHAT HAVE YOU BEEN TELLING YOUR PLAYERS, B.D.?
WELL, MOSTLY I'VE BEEN TRYING TO REASSURE THEM...
THEY NEED TO KNOW THAT WHAT THEY'RE DOING IS IMPORTANT, THAT THE WHOLE REASON WE HAVE SPORTS IS THAT LIFE IS HARD. ENTERTAINMENT SOFTENS THE EDGES.
HEY... I THINK THAT WOULD APPLY TO ME AS AN ACTRESS, TOO, WOULDN'T IT?
YES, I THINK IT WOULD.
EXCEPT I'M UNEMPLOYED.
JUST MEANS YOU'RE IN THE RESERVES. YOU'RE READY TO SERVE!

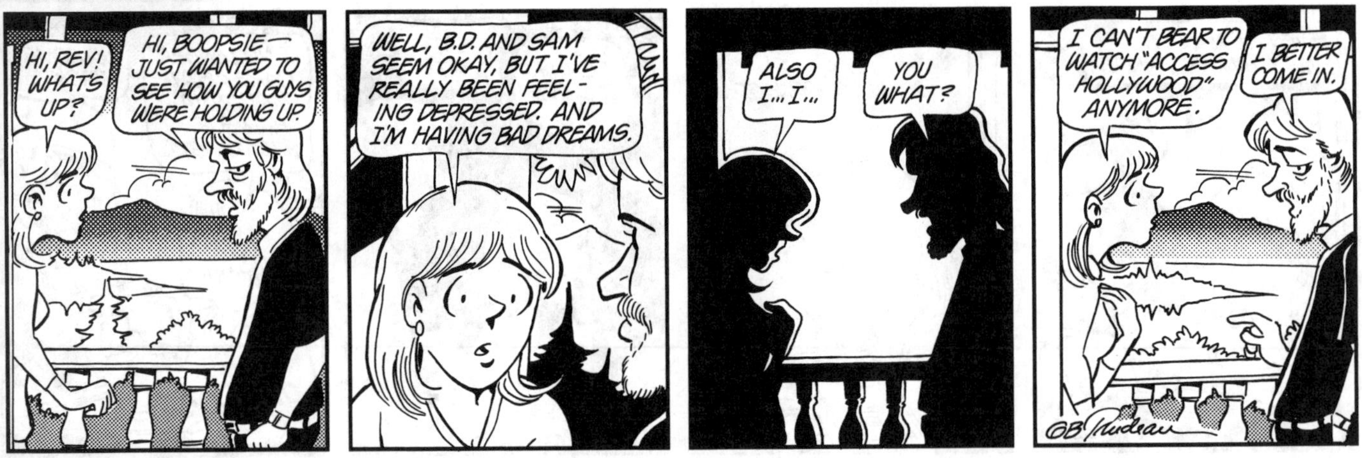
HI, REV! WHAT'S UP?
HI, BOOPSIE— JUST WANTED TO SEE HOW YOU GUYS WERE HOLDING UP.
WELL, B.D. AND SAM SEEM OKAY, BUT I'VE REALLY BEEN FEEL-ING DEPRESSED. AND I'M HAVING BAD DREAMS.
ALSO I... I...
YOU WHAT?
I CAN'T BEAR TO WATCH "ACCESS HOLLYWOOD" ANYMORE.
I BETTER COME IN.
©B Trudeau

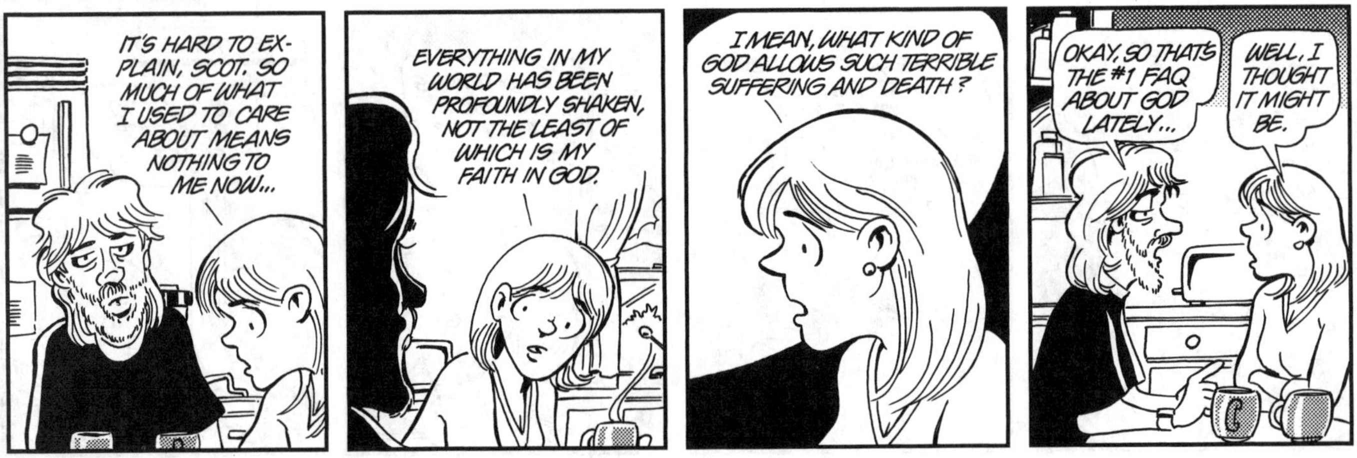
IT'S HARD TO EX-PLAIN, SCOT. SO MUCH OF WHAT I USED TO CARE ABOUT MEANS NOTHING TO ME NOW...
EVERYTHING IN MY WORLD HAS BEEN PROFOUNDLY SHAKEN, NOT THE LEAST OF WHICH IS MY FAITH IN GOD.
I MEAN, WHAT KIND OF GOD ALLOWS SUCH TERRIBLE SUFFERING AND DEATH?
OKAY, SO THAT'S THE #1 FAQ ABOUT GOD LATELY...
WELL, I THOUGHT IT MIGHT BE.

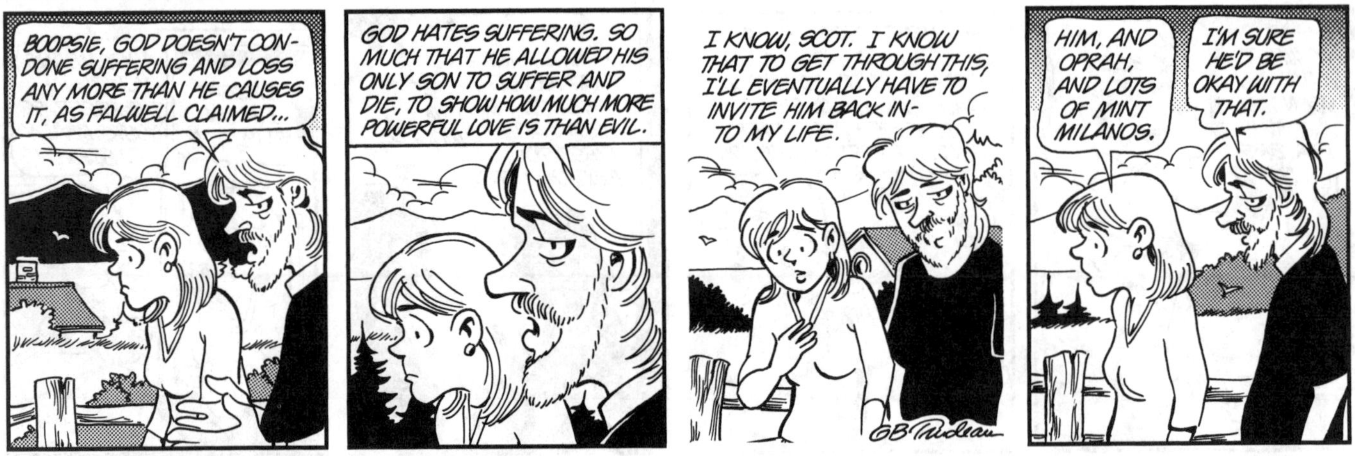
BOOPSIE, GOD DOESN'T CON-DONE SUFFERING AND LOSS ANY MORE THAN HE CAUSES IT, AS FALWELL CLAIMED...
GOD HATES SUFFERING. SO MUCH THAT HE ALLOWED HIS ONLY SON TO SUFFER AND DIE, TO SHOW HOW MUCH MORE POWERFUL LOVE IS THAN EVIL.
I KNOW, SCOT. I KNOW THAT TO GET THROUGH THIS, I'LL EVENTUALLY HAVE TO INVITE HIM BACK IN-TO MY LIFE.
HIM, AND OPRAH, AND LOTS OF MINT MILANOS.
I'M SURE HE'D BE OKAY WITH THAT.
©B Trudeau

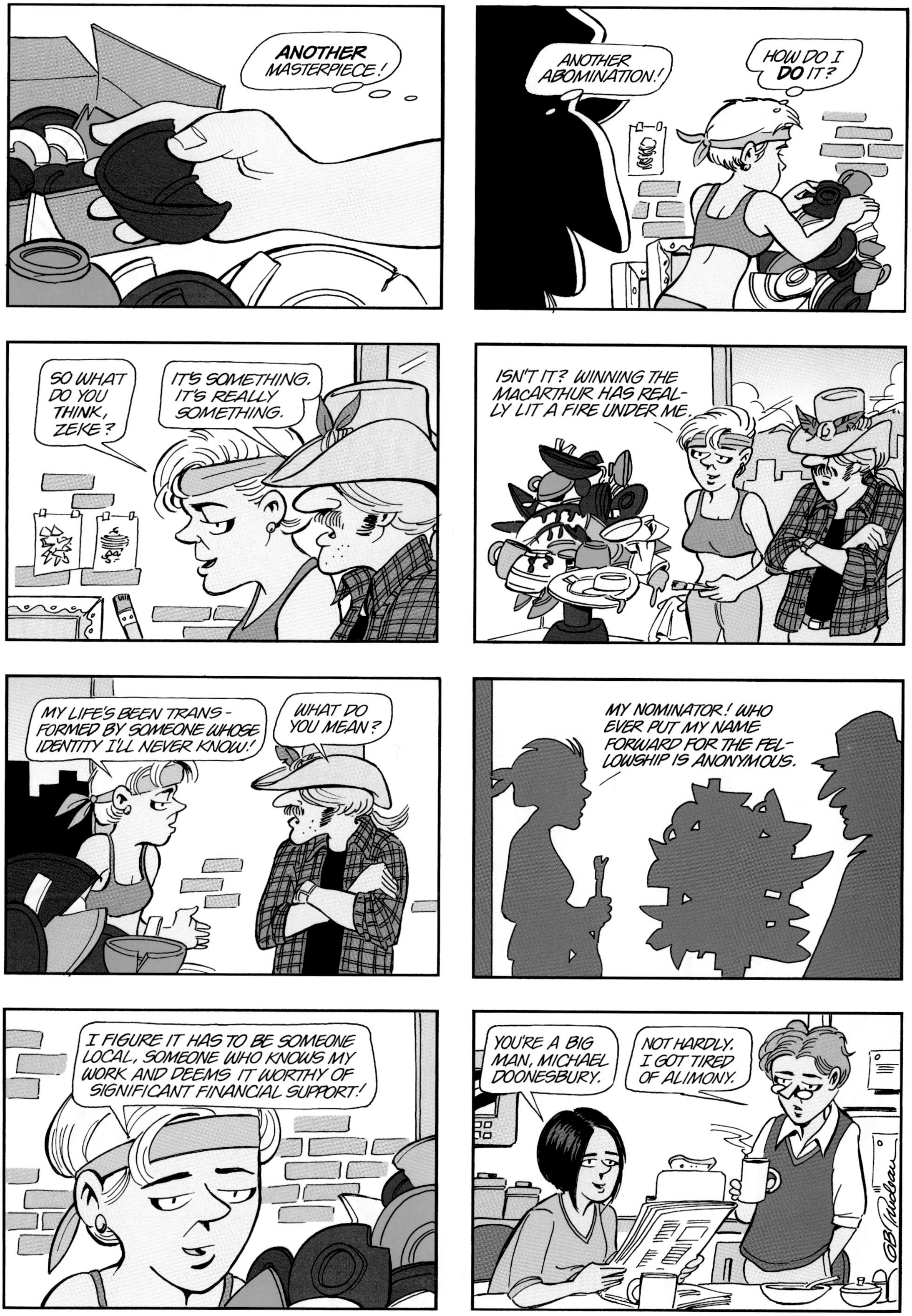
ANOTHER MASTERPIECE!
ANOTHER ABOMINATION!
HOW DO I DO IT?
SO WHAT DO YOU THINK, ZEKE?
IT'S SOMETHING. IT'S REALLY SOMETHING.
ISN'T IT? WINNING THE MACARTHUR HAS REALLY LIT A FIRE UNDER ME.
MY LIFE'S BEEN TRANSFORMED BY SOMEONE WHOSE IDENTITY I'LL NEVER KNOW!
WHAT DO YOU MEAN?
MY NOMINATOR! WHOEVER PUT MY NAME FORWARD FOR THE FELLOWSHIP IS ANONYMOUS.
I FIGURE IT HAS TO BE SOMEONE LOCAL, SOMEONE WHO KNOWS MY WORK AND DEEMS IT WORTHY OF SIGNIFICANT FINANCIAL SUPPORT!
YOU'RE A BIG MAN, MICHAEL DOONESBURY.
NOT HARDLY. I GOT TIRED OF ALIMONY.
GBTrudeau

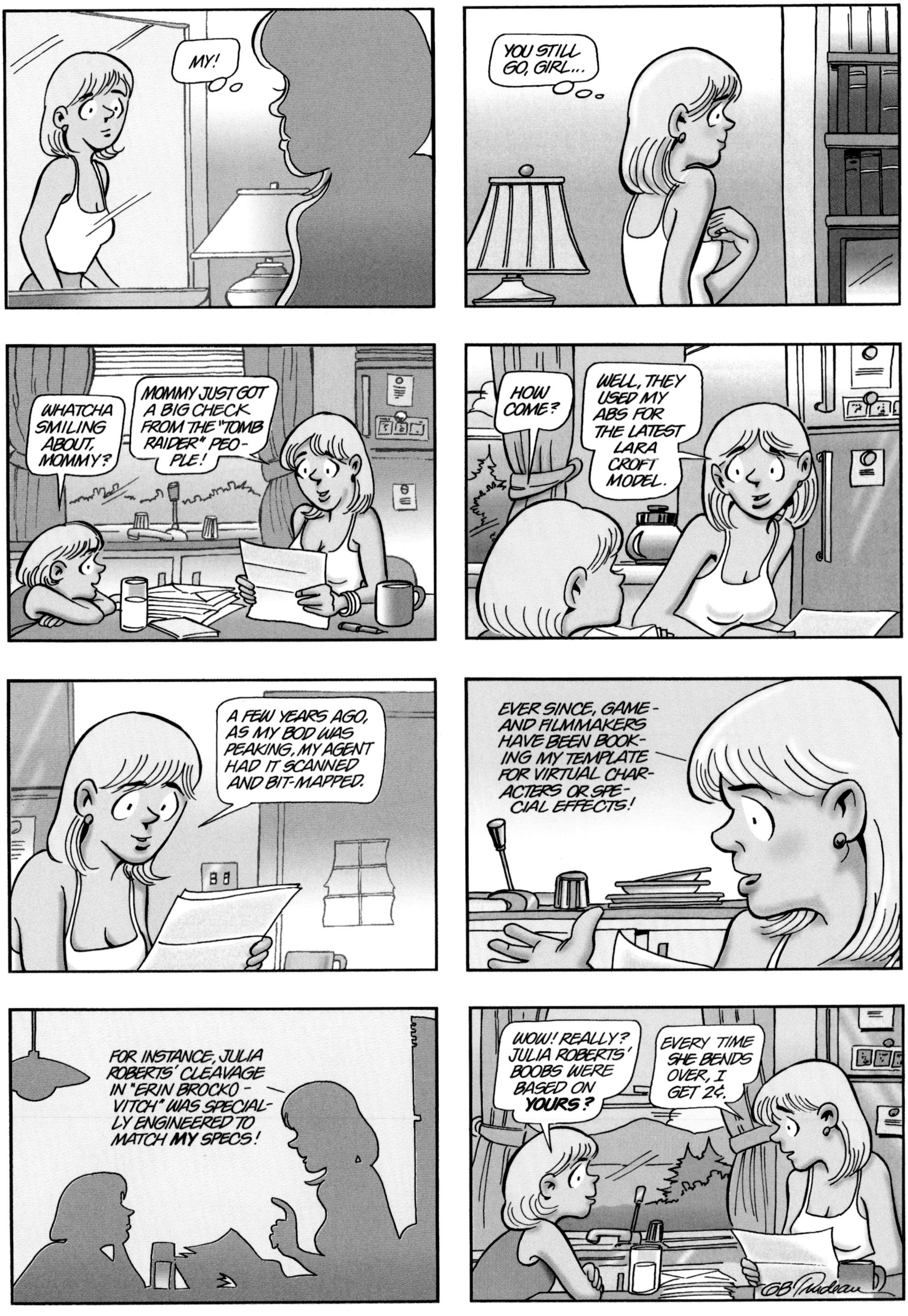
MY!
YOU STILL GO, GIRL...
WHATCHA SMILING ABOUT, MOMMY?
MOMMY JUST GOT A BIG CHECK FROM THE "TOMB RAIDER" PEO-PLE!
HOW COME?
WELL, THEY USED MY ABS FOR THE LATEST LARA CROFT MODEL.
A FEW YEARS AGO, AS MY BOD WAS PEAKING, MY AGENT HAD IT SCANNED AND BIT-MAPPED.
EVER SINCE, GAME- AND FILMMAKERS HAVE BEEN BOOK-ING MY TEMPLATE FOR VIRTUAL CHAR-ACTERS OR SPE-CIAL EFFECTS!
FOR INSTANCE, JULIA ROBERTS' CLEAVAGE IN "ERIN BROCKO-VITCH" WAS SPECIAL-LY ENGINEERED TO MATCH **MY** SPECS!
WOW! REALLY? JULIA ROBERTS' BOOBS WERE BASED ON **YOURS?**
EVERY TIME SHE BENDS OVER, I GET 2¢.

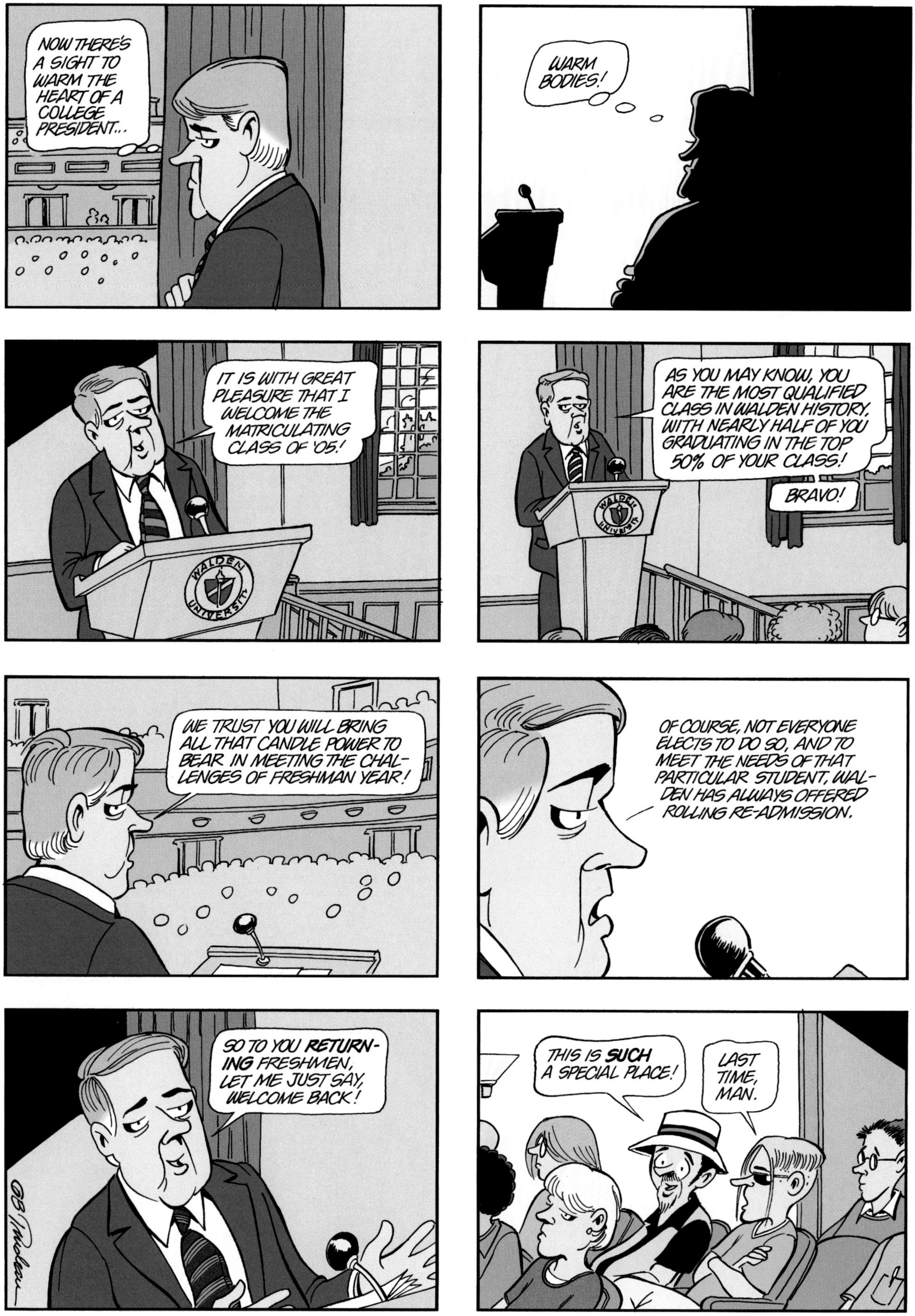
NOW THERE'S A SIGHT TO WARM THE HEART OF A COLLEGE PRESIDENT...
WARM BODIES!
IT IS WITH GREAT PLEASURE THAT I WELCOME THE MATRICULATING CLASS OF '05!
AS YOU MAY KNOW, YOU ARE THE MOST QUALIFIED CLASS IN WALDEN HISTORY, WITH NEARLY HALF OF YOU GRADUATING IN THE TOP 50% OF YOUR CLASS!
BRAVO!
WALDEN UNIVERSITY
WE TRUST YOU WILL BRING ALL THAT CANDLE POWER TO BEAR IN MEETING THE CHALLENGES OF FRESHMAN YEAR!
OF COURSE, NOT EVERYONE ELECTS TO DO SO, AND TO MEET THE NEEDS OF THAT PARTICULAR STUDENT, WALDEN HAS ALWAYS OFFERED ROLLING RE-ADMISSION.
SO TO YOU **RETURNING** FRESHMEN, LET ME JUST SAY, WELCOME BACK!
THIS IS **SUCH** A SPECIAL PLACE!
LAST TIME, MAN.

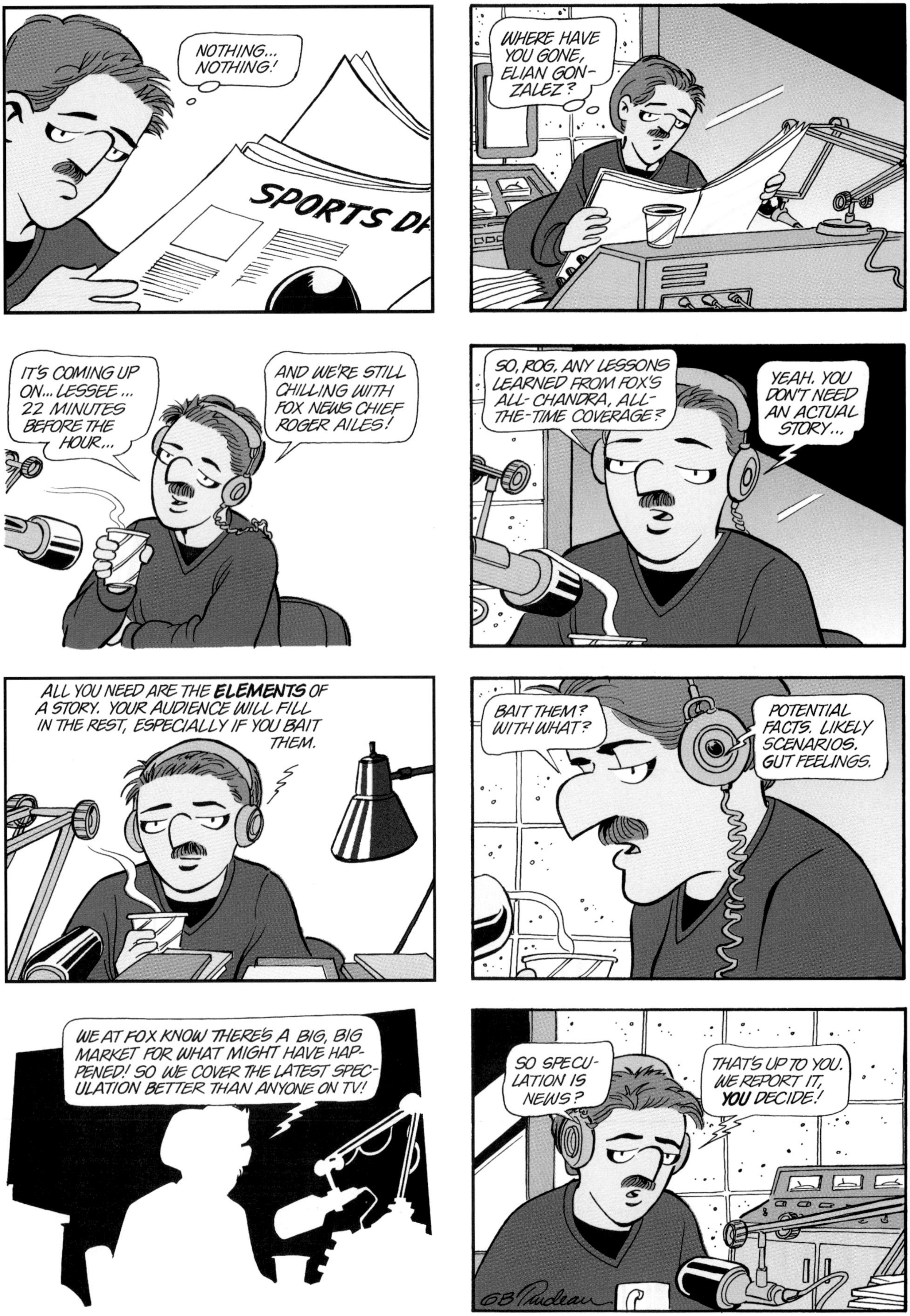
NOTHING... NOTHING!
WHERE HAVE YOU GONE, ELIAN GONZALEZ?
IT'S COMING UP ON... LESSEE... 22 MINUTES BEFORE THE HOUR...
AND WE'RE STILL CHILLING WITH FOX NEWS CHIEF ROGER AILES!
SO, ROG, ANY LESSONS LEARNED FROM FOX'S ALL-CHANDRA, ALL-THE-TIME COVERAGE?
YEAH. YOU DON'T NEED AN ACTUAL STORY...
ALL YOU NEED ARE THE **ELEMENTS** OF A STORY. YOUR AUDIENCE WILL FILL IN THE REST, ESPECIALLY IF YOU BAIT THEM.
BAIT THEM? WITH WHAT?
POTENTIAL FACTS. LIKELY SCENARIOS. GUT FEELINGS.
WE AT FOX KNOW THERE'S A BIG, BIG MARKET FOR WHAT MIGHT HAVE HAPPENED! SO WE COVER THE LATEST SPECULATION BETTER THAN ANYONE ON TV!
SO SPECULATION IS NEWS?
THAT'S UP TO YOU. WE REPORT IT, **YOU** DECIDE!
GB Trudeau

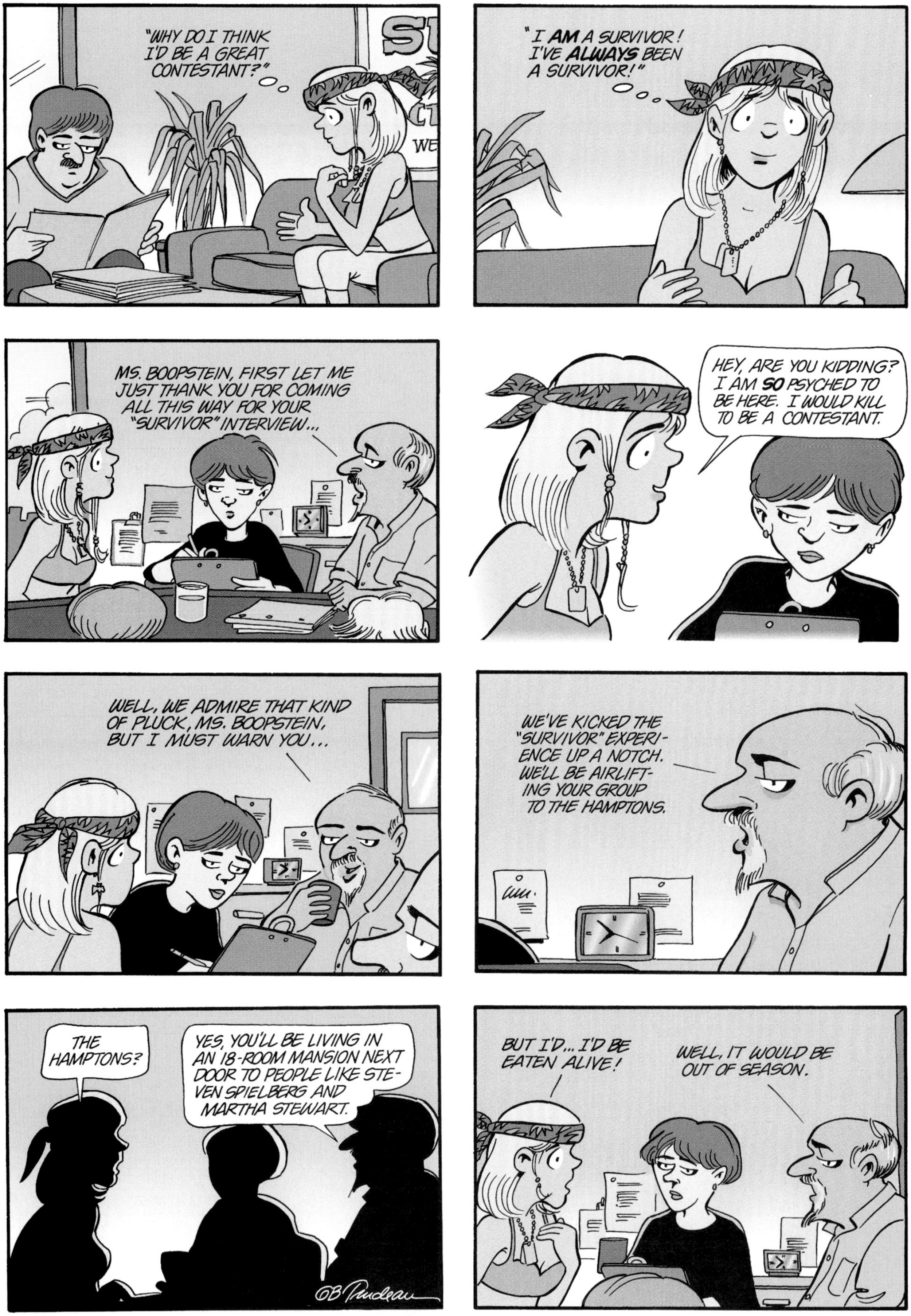
"WHY DO I THINK I'D BE A GREAT CONTESTANT?"
"I AM A SURVIVOR! I'VE ALWAYS BEEN A SURVIVOR!"
MS. BOOPSTEIN, FIRST LET ME JUST THANK YOU FOR COMING ALL THIS WAY FOR YOUR "SURVIVOR" INTERVIEW...
HEY, ARE YOU KIDDING? I AM SO PSYCHED TO BE HERE. I WOULD KILL TO BE A CONTESTANT.
WELL, WE ADMIRE THAT KIND OF PLUCK, MS. BOOPSTEIN, BUT I MUST WARN YOU...
WE'VE KICKED THE "SURVIVOR" EXPERIENCE UP A NOTCH. WE'LL BE AIRLIFTING YOUR GROUP TO THE HAMPTONS.
THE HAMPTONS?
YES, YOU'LL BE LIVING IN AN 18-ROOM MANSION NEXT DOOR TO PEOPLE LIKE STEVEN SPIELBERG AND MARTHA STEWART.
©B Trudeau
BUT I'D... I'D BE EATEN ALIVE!
WELL, IT WOULD BE OUT OF SEASON.

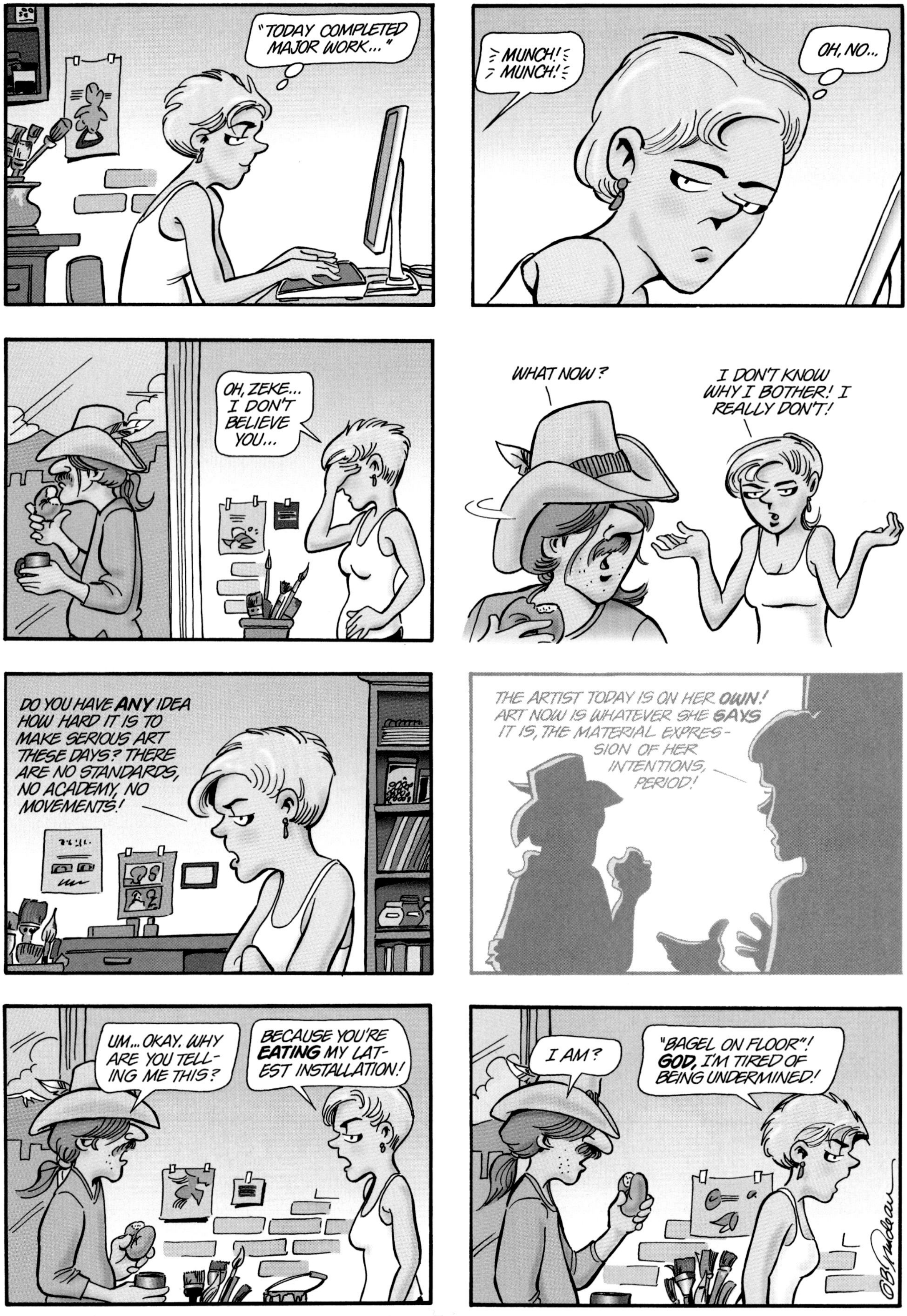
"TODAY COMPLETED MAJOR WORK..."
MUNCH! MUNCH!
OH, NO...
OH, ZEKE... I DON'T BELIEVE YOU...
WHAT NOW?
I DON'T KNOW WHY I BOTHER! I REALLY DON'T!
DO YOU HAVE ANY IDEA HOW HARD IT IS TO MAKE SERIOUS ART THESE DAYS? THERE ARE NO STANDARDS, NO ACADEMY, NO MOVEMENTS!
THE ARTIST TODAY IS ON HER OWN! ART NOW IS WHATEVER SHE SAYS IT IS, THE MATERIAL EXPRESSION OF HER INTENTIONS, PERIOD!
UM... OKAY. WHY ARE YOU TELLING ME THIS?
BECAUSE YOU'RE EATING MY LATEST INSTALLATION!
I AM?
"BAGEL ON FLOOR"! GOD, I'M TIRED OF BEING UNDERMINED!

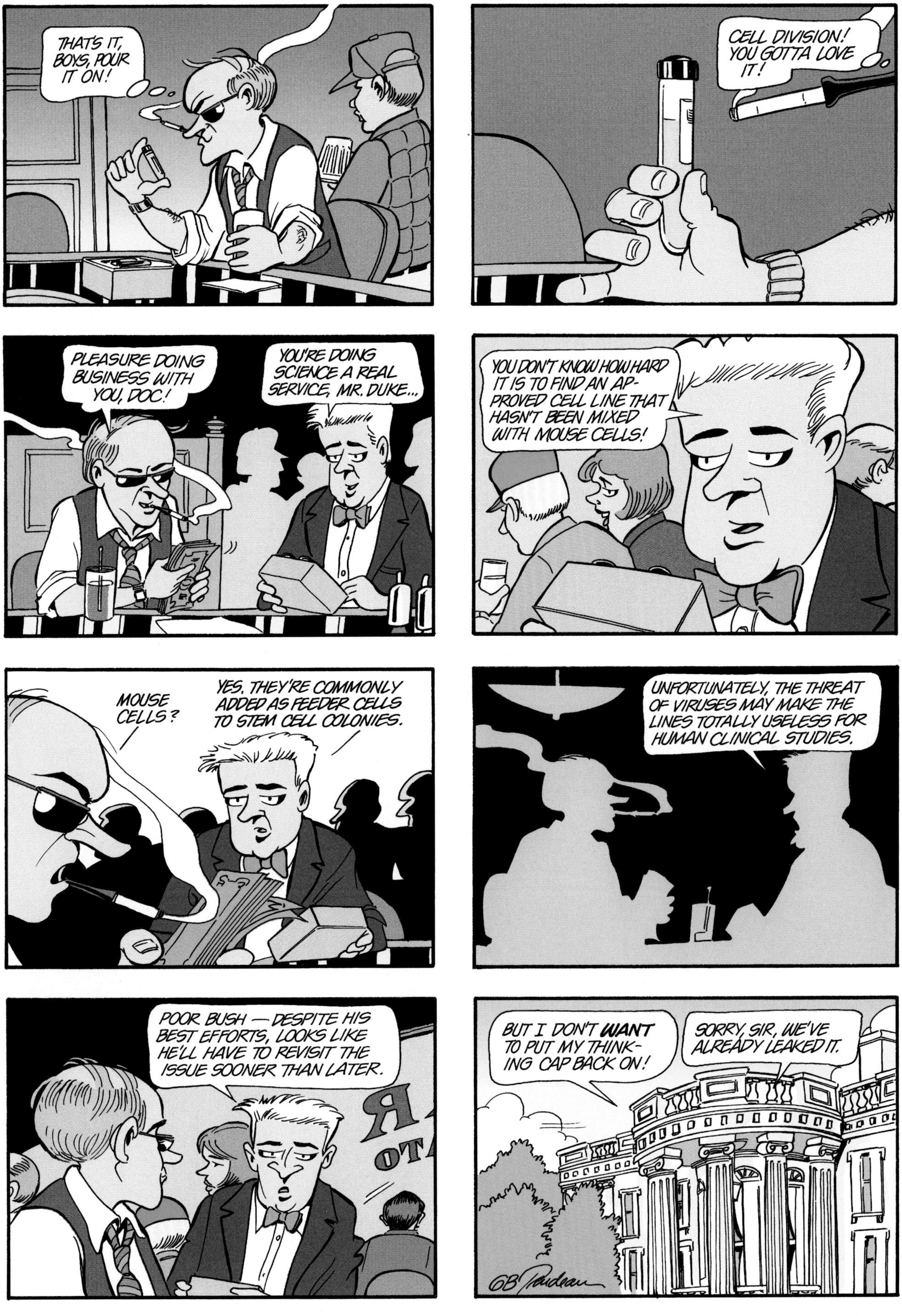
THAT'S IT, BOYS, POUR IT ON!
CELL DIVISION! YOU GOTTA LOVE IT!
PLEASURE DOING BUSINESS WITH YOU, DOC!
YOU'RE DOING SCIENCE A REAL SERVICE, MR. DUKE...
YOU DON'T KNOW HOW HARD IT IS TO FIND AN AP-PROVED CELL LINE THAT HASN'T BEEN MIXED WITH MOUSE CELLS!
MOUSE CELLS?
YES. THEY'RE COMMONLY ADDED AS FEEDER CELLS TO STEM CELL COLONIES.
UNFORTUNATELY, THE THREAT OF VIRUSES MAY MAKE THE LINES TOTALLY USELESS FOR HUMAN CLINICAL STUDIES.
POOR BUSH — DESPITE HIS BEST EFFORTS, LOOKS LIKE HE'LL HAVE TO REVISIT THE ISSUE SOONER THAN LATER.
BUT I DON'T **WANT** TO PUT MY THINK-ING CAP BACK ON!
SORRY, SIR, WE'VE ALREADY LEAKED IT.

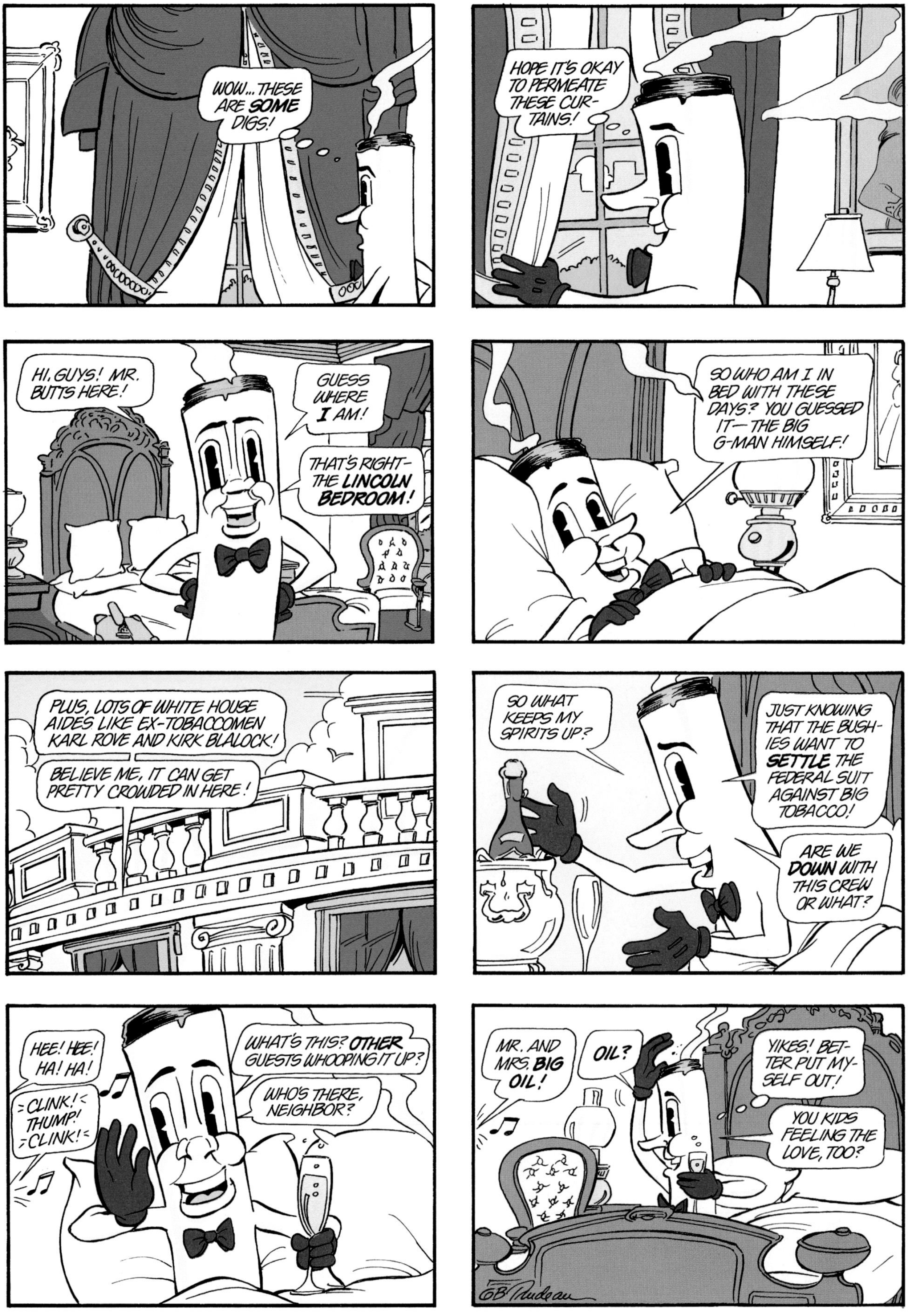
WOW... THESE ARE SOME DIGS!
HOPE IT'S OKAY TO PERMEATE THESE CURTAINS!
HI, GUYS! MR. BUTTS HERE!
GUESS WHERE I AM!
THAT'S RIGHT-THE LINCOLN BEDROOM!
SO WHO AM I IN BED WITH THESE DAYS? YOU GUESSED IT—THE BIG G-MAN HIMSELF!
PLUS, LOTS OF WHITE HOUSE AIDES LIKE EX-TOBACCOMEN KARL ROVE AND KIRK BLALOCK!
BELIEVE ME, IT CAN GET PRETTY CROWDED IN HERE!
SO WHAT KEEPS MY SPIRITS UP?
JUST KNOWING THAT THE BUSHIES WANT TO SETTLE THE FEDERAL SUIT AGAINST BIG TOBACCO!
ARE WE DOWN WITH THIS CREW OR WHAT?
HEE! HEE! HA! HA!
CLINK! THUMP! CLINK!
WHAT'S THIS? OTHER GUESTS WHOOPING IT UP?
WHO'S THERE, NEIGHBOR?
MR. AND MRS. BIG OIL!
OIL?
YIKES! BETTER PUT MYSELF OUT!
YOU KIDS FEELING THE LOVE, TOO?
GB Trudeau

WHAT'S GOING ON OUT THERE?
WE'RE GOING TO GET ANOTHER DELAY OF GAME!
WELL, THERE'S A LOT TO DISCUSS.
HOW ABOUT WE GO WITH... NAH, THAT'S NOT RIGHT... HOW ABOUT ... NO, NO, THAT DOESN'T SEEM APPROPRIATE... UM ...
WHAT'S UP, SKIPPER? YOU SEEM TO HAVE LOST YOUR CONFIDENCE!
THAT'S NOT IT, ZIP. I JUST CAN'T GET MY HEAD INTO THE GAME. IT JUST SEEMS SO... SO IRRELEVANT!
IRRELEVANT TO WHAT?
TO LIFE. I FEEL LIKE THERE ARE MORE IMPORTANT THINGS I COULD BE DOING ON A SATURDAY AFTERNOON, LIKE TUTORING A KID OR SOMETHING...
HEY, ME TOO! I'VE BEEN YEARNING FOR MEANING AS WELL!
NO KIDDING?
DEFINITELY. BEING JUST ANOTHER ENTERTAINER SEEMS SO POINTLESS!
IT'S THE COMPETITIVENESS THAT GETS ME DOWN. AT A TIME LIKE THIS, SHOULDN'T WE ALL BE PULLING TOGETHER?
THERE'S ALSO THE VIOLENCE. IT JUST SEEMS GRATUITOUS NOW...
MAYBE WE COULD CHANGE TO TOUCH FOOTBALL...
AND NOT KEEP SCORE!
TWEET!
DELAY OF GAME!
I MISS SEPTEMBER 10TH.
WHAT, LIKE THIS IS NEW?
©GBTrudeau

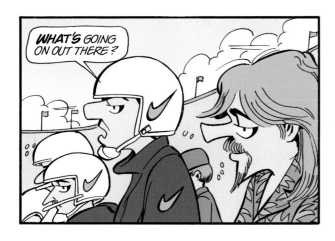

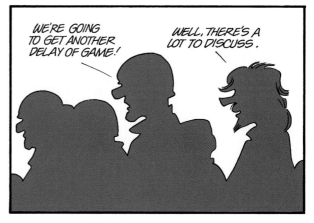

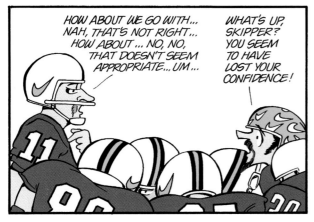

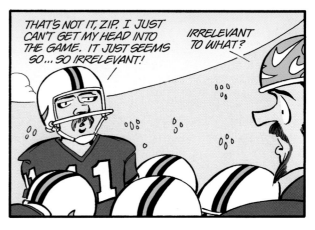

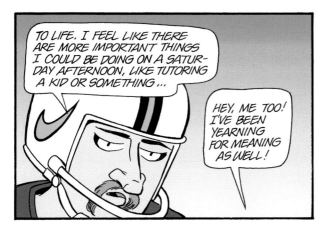

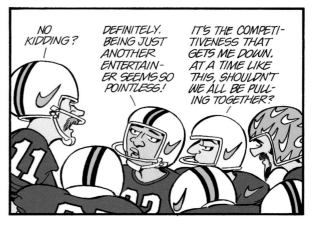

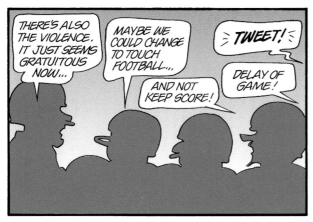

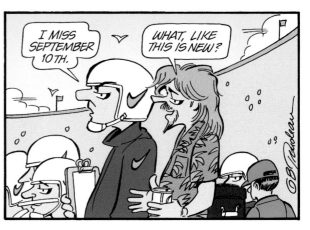

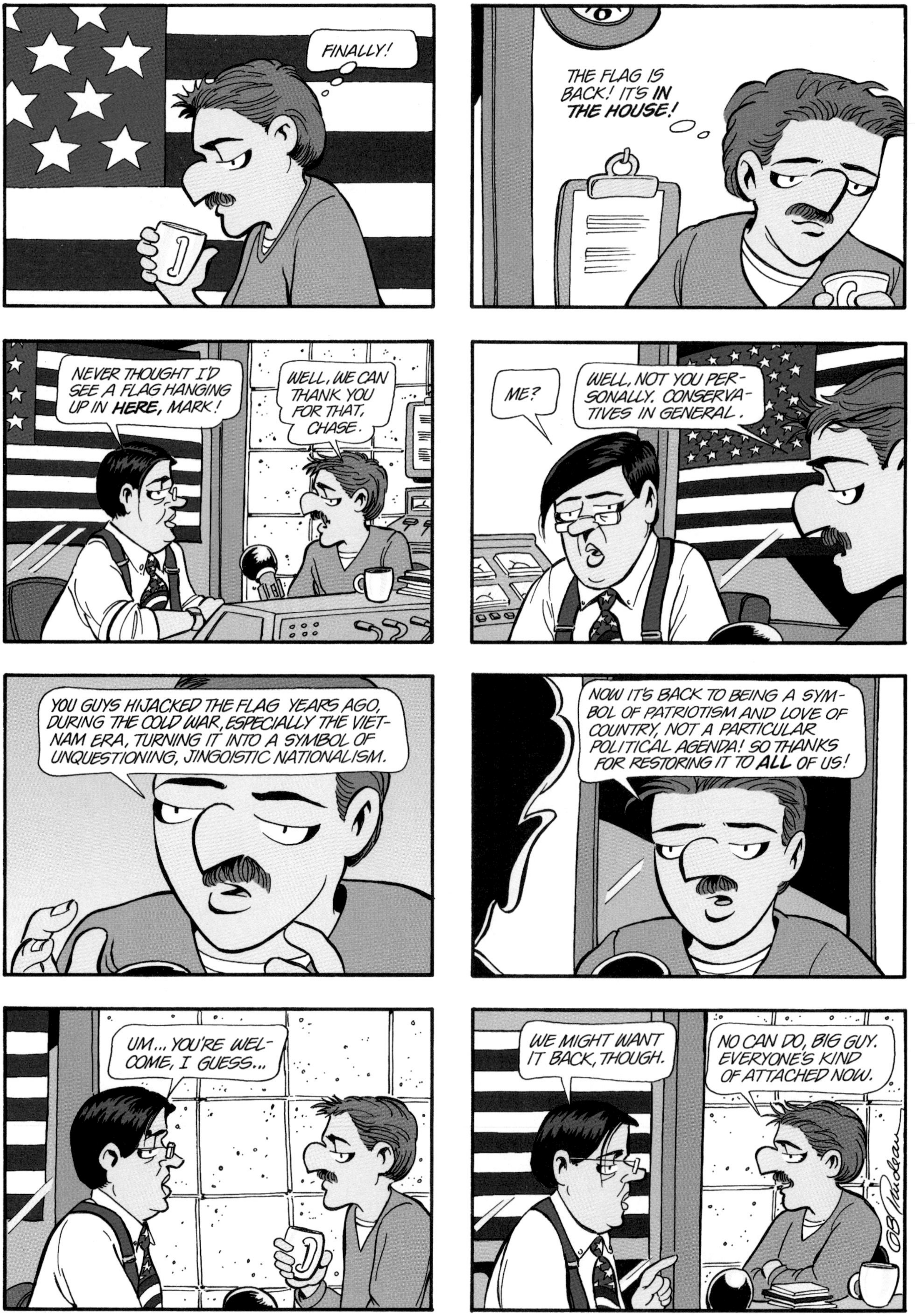
FINALLY!
THE FLAG IS BACK! IT'S IN THE HOUSE!
NEVER THOUGHT I'D SEE A FLAG HANGING UP IN HERE, MARK!
WELL, WE CAN THANK YOU FOR THAT, CHASE.
ME?
WELL, NOT YOU PERSONALLY. CONSERVATIVES IN GENERAL.
YOU GUYS HIJACKED THE FLAG YEARS AGO, DURING THE COLD WAR, ESPECIALLY THE VIETNAM ERA, TURNING IT INTO A SYMBOL OF UNQUESTIONING, JINGOISTIC NATIONALISM.
NOW IT'S BACK TO BEING A SYMBOL OF PATRIOTISM AND LOVE OF COUNTRY, NOT A PARTICULAR POLITICAL AGENDA! SO THANKS FOR RESTORING IT TO ALL OF US!
UM... YOU'RE WELCOME, I GUESS...
WE MIGHT WANT IT BACK, THOUGH.
NO CAN DO, BIG GUY. EVERYONE'S KIND OF ATTACHED NOW.
GBTrudeau

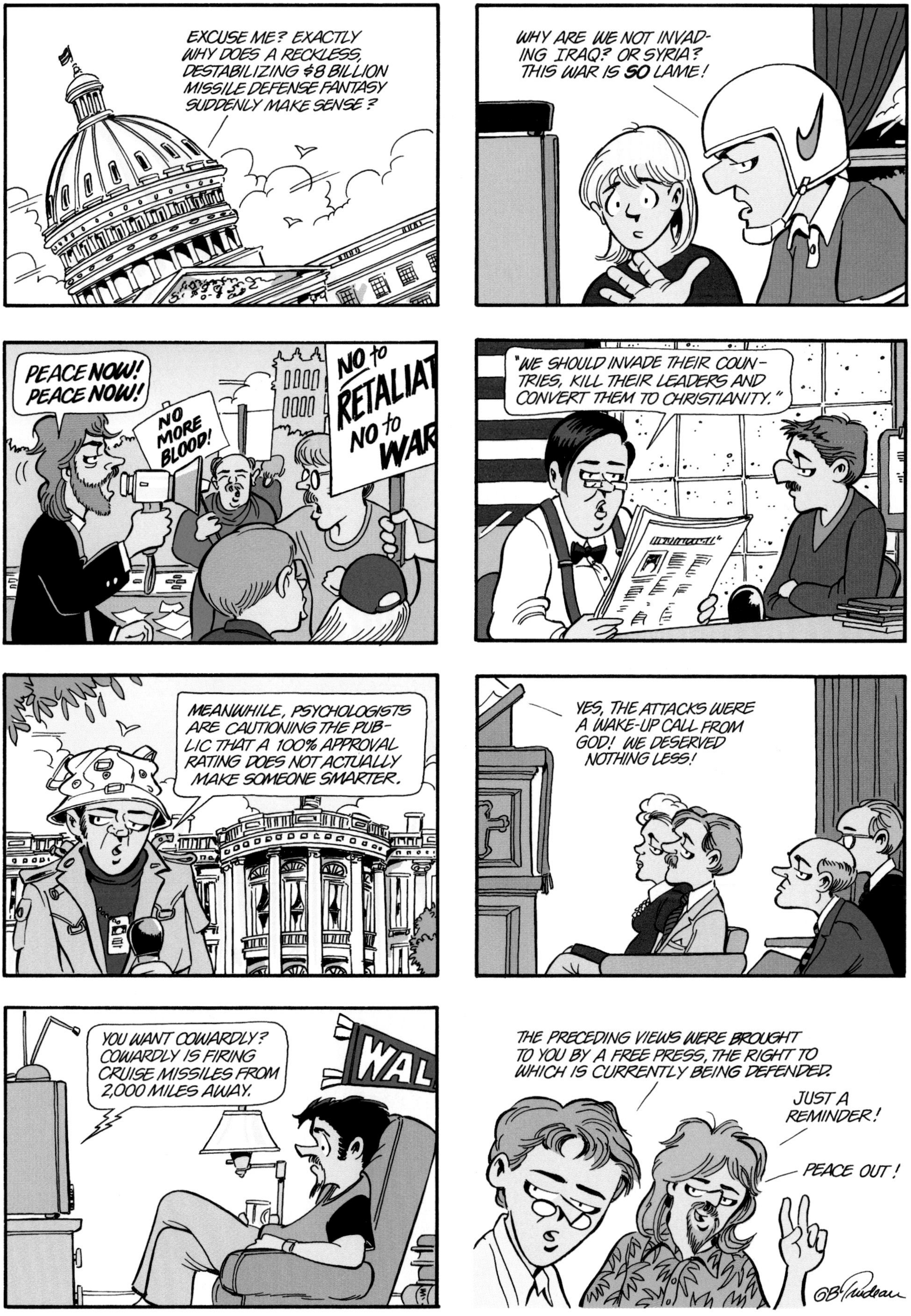
EXCUSE ME? EXACTLY WHY DOES A RECKLESS, DESTABILIZING $8 BILLION MISSILE DEFENSE FANTASY SUDDENLY MAKE SENSE?
WHY ARE WE NOT INVADING IRAQ? OR SYRIA? THIS WAR IS SO LAME!
PEACE NOW! PEACE NOW!
NO MORE BLOOD!
NO to RETALIAT NO to WAR
"WE SHOULD INVADE THEIR COUNTRIES, KILL THEIR LEADERS AND CONVERT THEM TO CHRISTIANITY."
MEANWHILE, PSYCHOLOGISTS ARE CAUTIONING THE PUBLIC THAT A 100% APPROVAL RATING DOES NOT ACTUALLY MAKE SOMEONE SMARTER.
YES, THE ATTACKS WERE A WAKE-UP CALL FROM GOD! WE DESERVED NOTHING LESS!
YOU WANT COWARDLY? COWARDLY IS FIRING CRUISE MISSILES FROM 2,000 MILES AWAY.
WAL
THE PRECEDING VIEWS WERE BROUGHT TO YOU BY A FREE PRESS, THE RIGHT TO WHICH IS CURRENTLY BEING DEFENDED.
JUST A REMINDER!
PEACE OUT!
©B. Trudeau

KARL, IS IT STILL UNPATRIOTIC TO CRITICIZE ME?
YES, SIR.
COOL! THIS IS GREAT...
SIR, YOU'VE BEEN SO BUSY THIS FALL, WE DIDN'T HAVE A CHANCE TO BRIEF YOU ON THIS...
BUT IT TURNED OUT THAT THE MISSILE DEFENSE PROGRAM, AND CORPORATE TAX CUTS, AND SUBSIDIES FOR THE POWER INDUSTRY, AND OIL DRILLING IN ALASKA...
...IN FACT, MOST OF THE ITEMS ON OUR POLITICAL AGENDA...
...ARE **ALL** JUSTIFIED BY THE WAR AGAINST TERRORISM!
WOW... WHAT A COINCIDENCE...
THANKS, EVILDOERS!
THEY'RE SUCH JERKS — IF THEY ONLY KNEW...

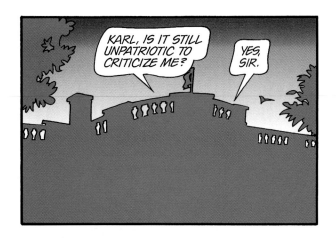

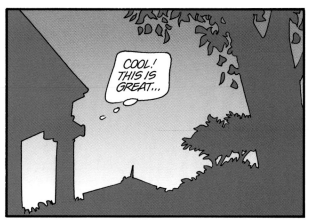

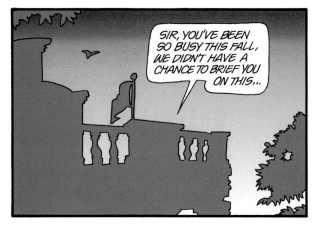

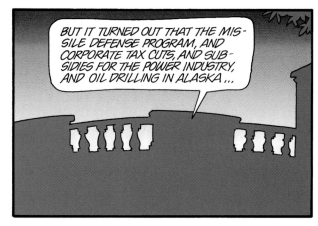

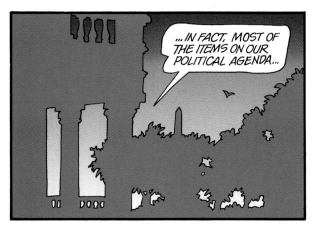

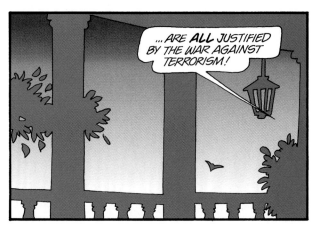

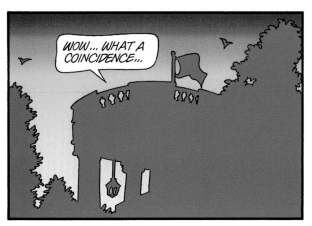

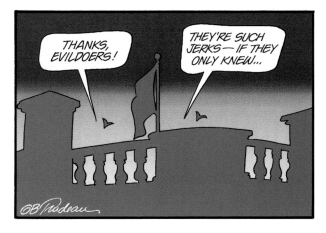

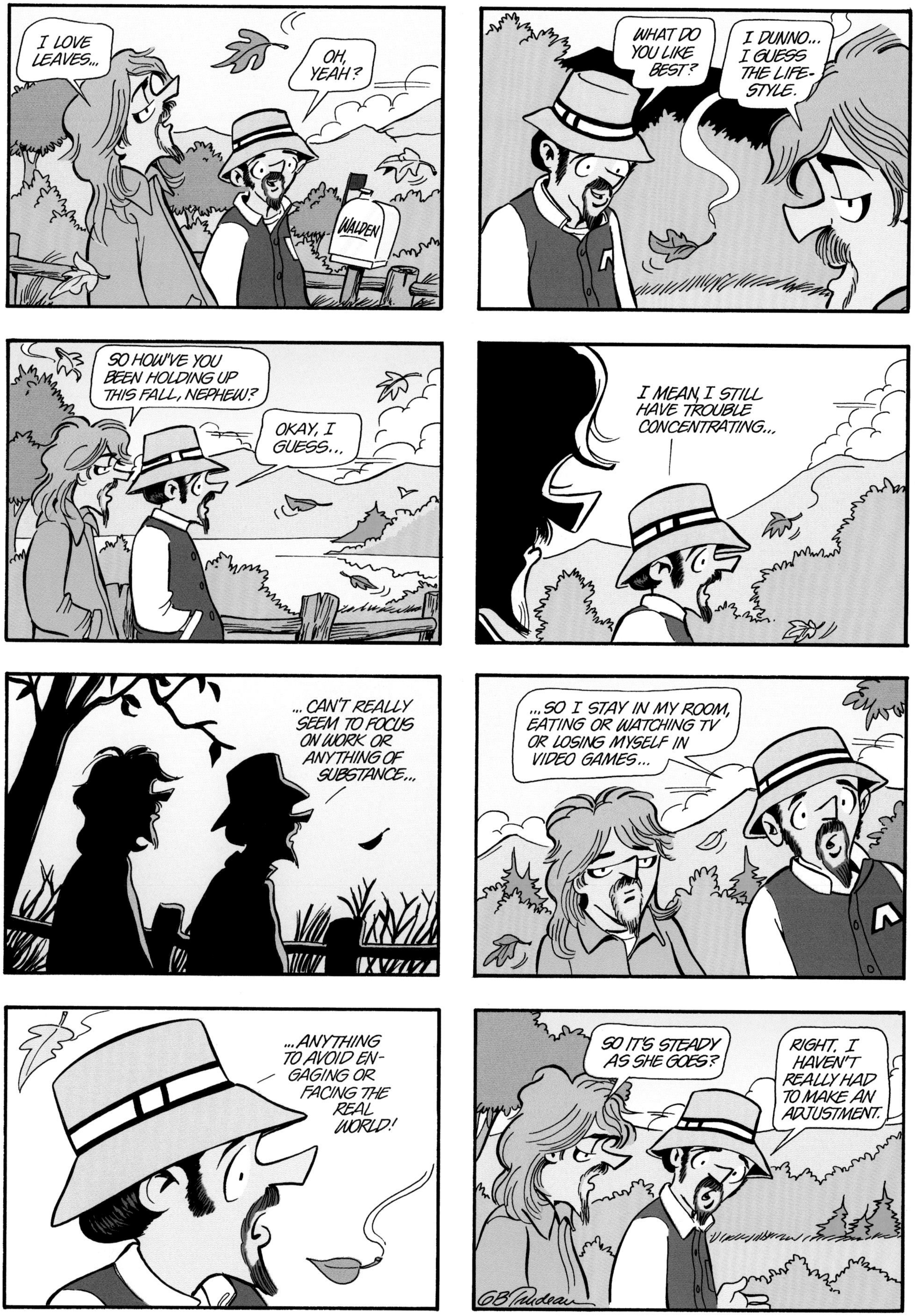
I LOVE LEAVES...
OH, YEAH?
WALDEN
WHAT DO YOU LIKE BEST?
I DUNNO... I GUESS THE LIFE-STYLE.
SO HOW'VE YOU BEEN HOLDING UP THIS FALL, NEPHEW?
OKAY, I GUESS...
I MEAN, I STILL HAVE TROUBLE CONCENTRATING...
...CAN'T REALLY SEEM TO FOCUS ON WORK OR ANYTHING OF SUBSTANCE...
...SO I STAY IN MY ROOM, EATING OR WATCHING TV OR LOSING MYSELF IN VIDEO GAMES...
...ANYTHING TO AVOID EN-GAGING OR FACING THE REAL WORLD!
SO IT'S STEADY AS SHE GOES?
RIGHT. I HAVEN'T REALLY HAD TO MAKE AN ADJUSTMENT.
GB Trudeau

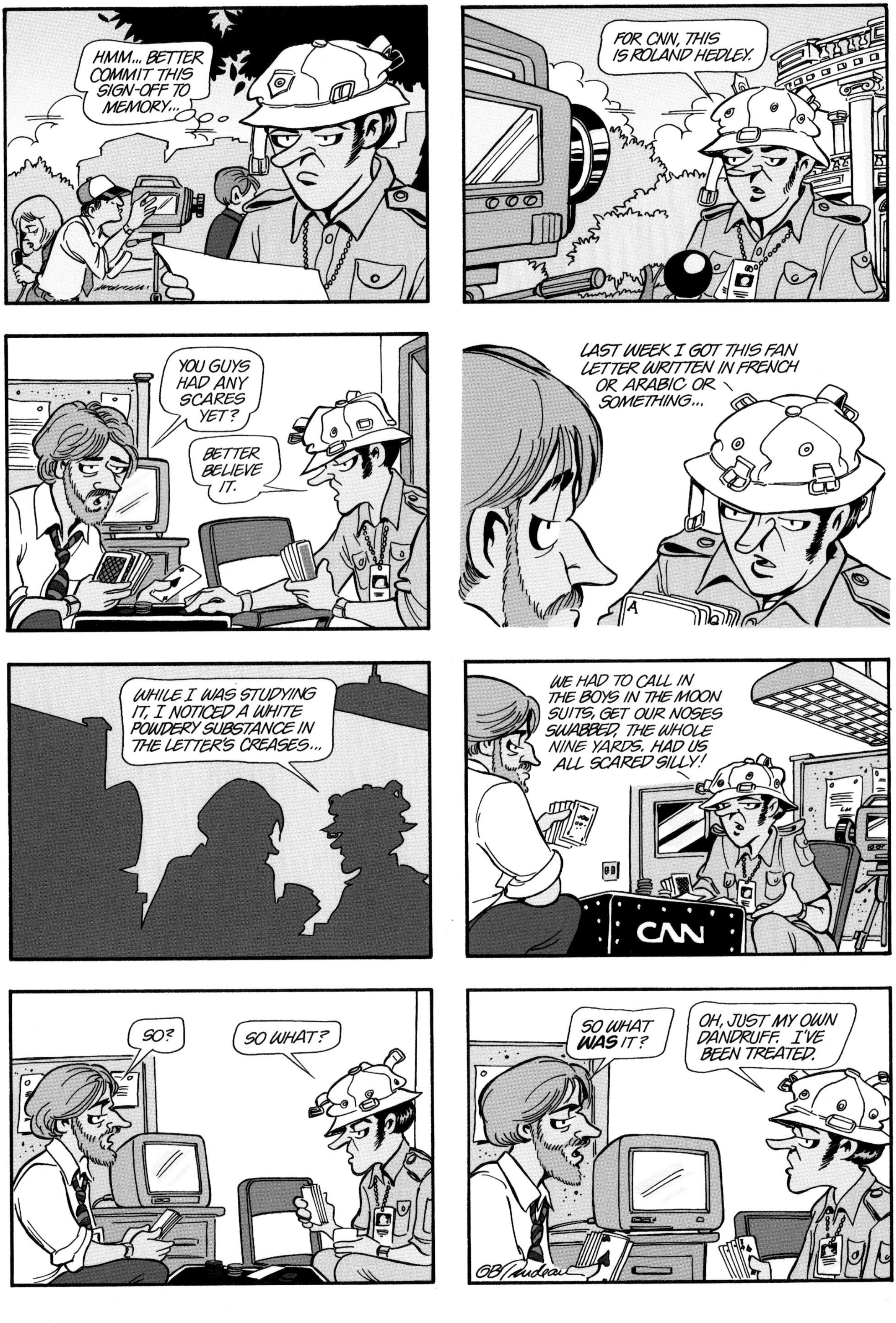
HMM... BETTER COMMIT THIS SIGN-OFF TO MEMORY...
FOR CNN, THIS IS ROLAND HEDLEY.
YOU GUYS HAD ANY SCARES YET?
BETTER BELIEVE IT.
LAST WEEK I GOT THIS FAN LETTER WRITTEN IN FRENCH OR ARABIC OR SOMETHING...
WHILE I WAS STUDYING IT, I NOTICED A WHITE POWDERY SUBSTANCE IN THE LETTER'S CREASES...
WE HAD TO CALL IN THE BOYS IN THE MOON SUITS, GET OUR NOSES SWABBED, THE WHOLE NINE YARDS. HAD US ALL SCARED SILLY!
CNN
SO?
SO WHAT?
SO WHAT **WAS** IT?
OH, JUST MY OWN DANDRUFF. I'VE BEEN TREATED.

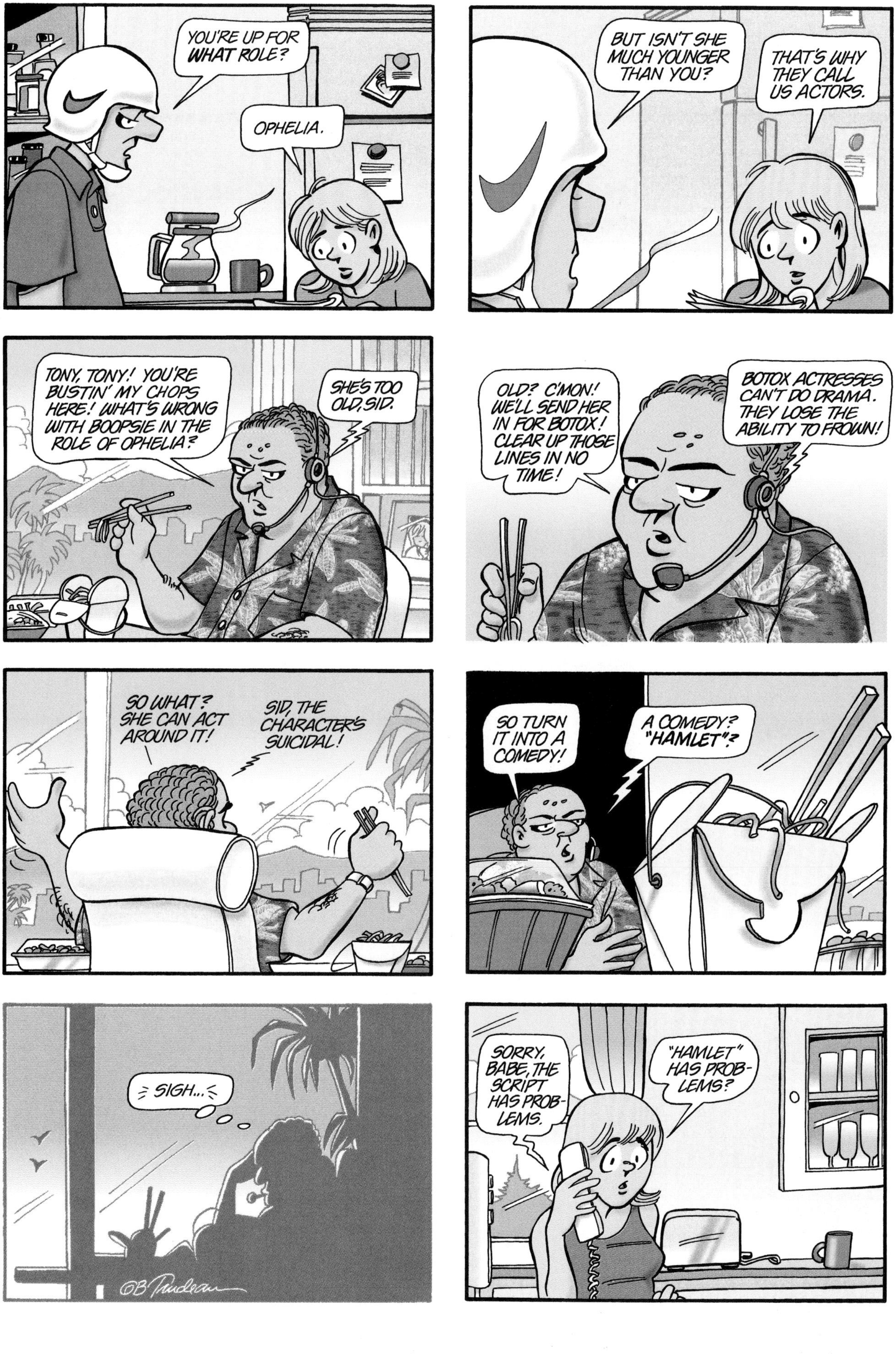
YOU'RE UP FOR WHAT ROLE?
OPHELIA.
BUT ISN'T SHE MUCH YOUNGER THAN YOU?
THAT'S WHY THEY CALL US ACTORS.
TONY, TONY! YOU'RE BUSTIN' MY CHOPS HERE! WHAT'S WRONG WITH BOOPSIE IN THE ROLE OF OPHELIA?
SHE'S TOO OLD, SID.
OLD? C'MON! WE'LL SEND HER IN FOR BOTOX! CLEAR UP THOSE LINES IN NO TIME!
BOTOX ACTRESSES CAN'T DO DRAMA. THEY LOSE THE ABILITY TO FROWN!
SO WHAT? SHE CAN ACT AROUND IT!
SID, THE CHARACTER'S SUICIDAL!
SO TURN IT INTO A COMEDY!
A COMEDY? "HAMLET"?
SIGH...
©B. Trudeau
SORRY, BABE, THE SCRIPT HAS PROBLEMS.
"HAMLET" HAS PROBLEMS?

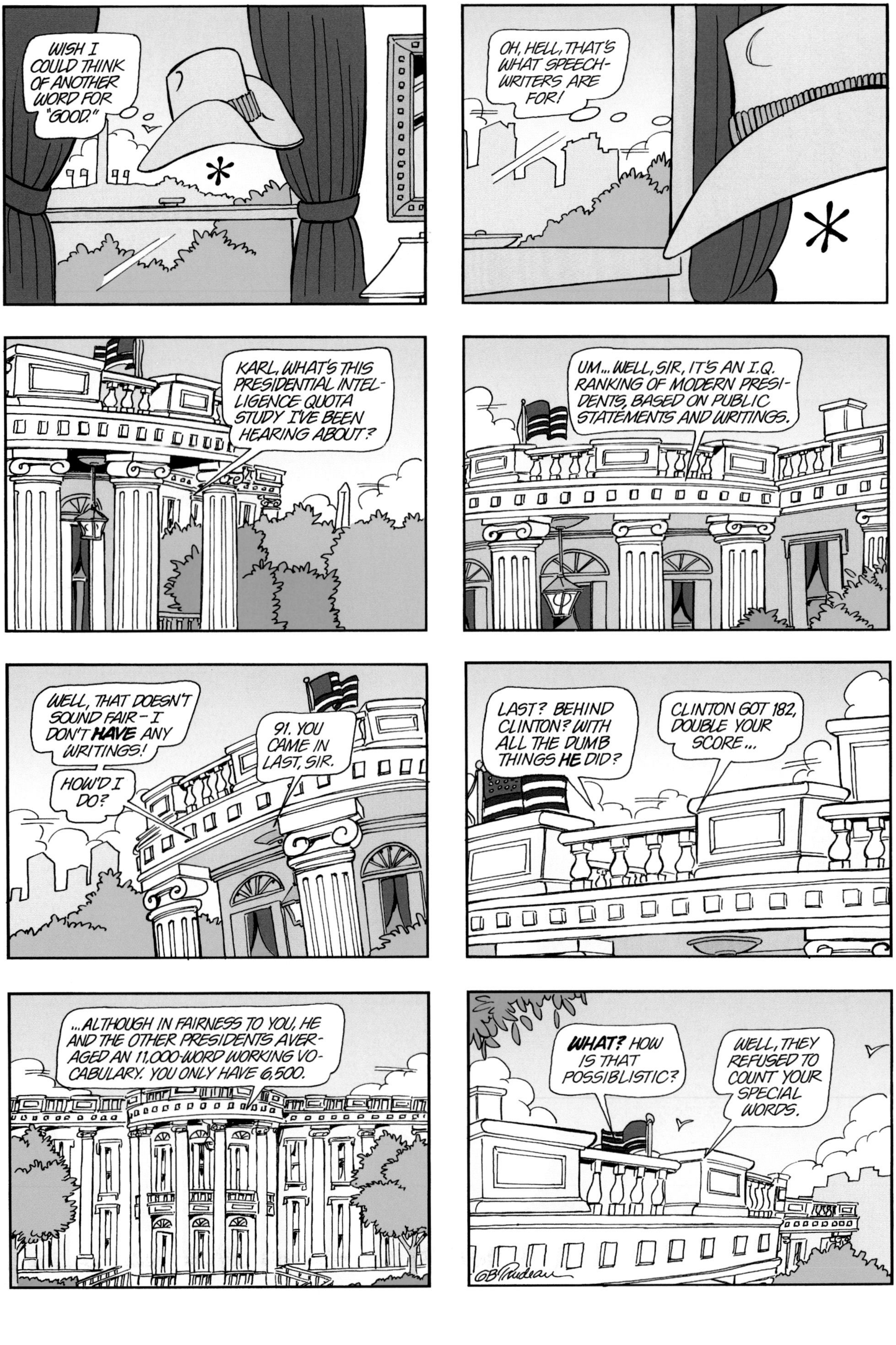

WISH I COULD THINK OF ANOTHER WORD FOR "GOOD."
OH, HELL, THAT'S WHAT SPEECH-WRITERS ARE FOR!
KARL, WHAT'S THIS PRESIDENTIAL INTEL-LIGENCE QUOTA STUDY I'VE BEEN HEARING ABOUT?
UM... WELL, SIR, IT'S AN I.Q. RANKING OF MODERN PRESI-DENTS, BASED ON PUBLIC STATEMENTS AND WRITINGS.
WELL, THAT DOESN'T SOUND FAIR – I DON'T **HAVE** ANY WRITINGS!
HOW'D I DO?
91. YOU CAME IN LAST, SIR.
LAST? BEHIND CLINTON? WITH ALL THE DUMB THINGS **HE** DID?
CLINTON GOT 182, DOUBLE YOUR SCORE...
...ALTHOUGH IN FAIRNESS TO YOU, HE AND THE OTHER PRESIDENTS AVER-AGED AN 11,000-WORD WORKING VO-CABULARY. YOU ONLY HAVE 6,500.
WHAT? HOW IS THAT POSSIBLISTIC?
WELL, THEY REFUSED TO COUNT YOUR SPECIAL WORDS.
GBTrudeau

WHAT IS IT, KARL?
SIR, IT'S ABOUT THAT PRESI-DENTIAL IQ REPORT...
IT TURNS OUT NONE OF IT'S TRUE. IT WAS AN INTERNET HOAX.
A HOAX? YOU MEAN I **DON'T** HAVE AN IQ OF 91?
NO, SIR.
DAMN!
FRANKLY, WE FEEL A LITTLE SILLY BEING TAKEN IN.

I **DON'T** HAVE AN IQ OF 91?
NO, SIR. THE REPORT WAS AN INTER-NET HOAX.
> SIGH < JUST MY LUCK...
UM... YOU SHOULD BE PLEASED, SIR. 91'S NOT SO GREAT.
IT WAS MY FIRST "A," DAMMIT!
LET ME WALK YOU THROUGH THIS, SIR...
GB Trudeau

ARE YOU **SURE** THERE'S NO TRUTH TO THE IQ REPORT?
YES, SIR.
MAN, THAT'S JUST NOT FAIR! I GET ALL THESE POINTS AND IT TURNS OUT TO BE A HOAX!
> SIGH... <
GB Trudeau
COULDN'T WE START OUR **OWN** HOAX?
WELL, THE BUDGET'S ALREADY IN PLAY. COULD BE OVERLOAD.

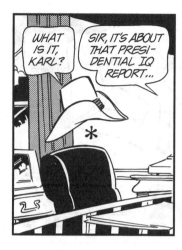

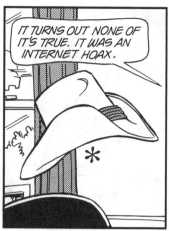

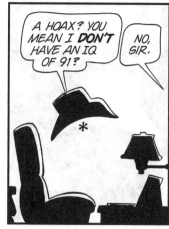

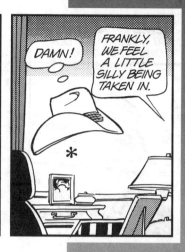

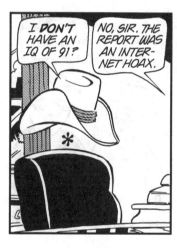

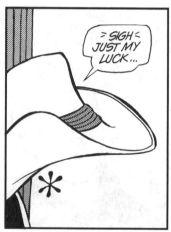

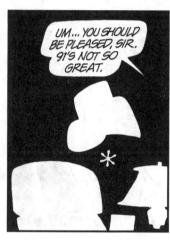

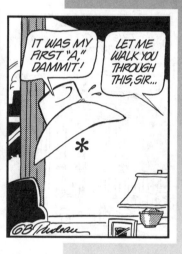

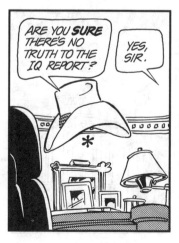

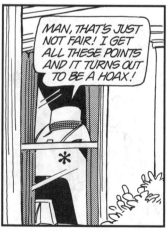

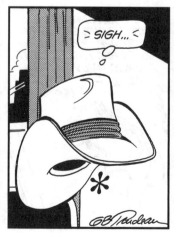

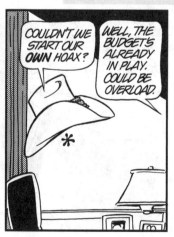

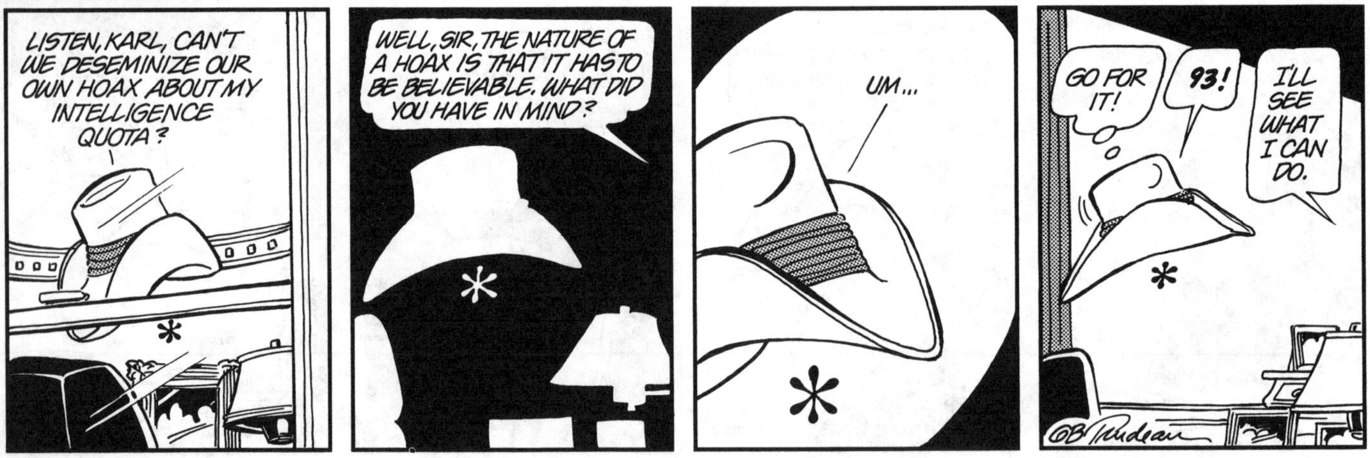
LISTEN, KARL, CAN'T WE DESEMINIZE OUR OWN HOAX ABOUT MY INTELLIGENCE QUOTA?
WELL, SIR, THE NATURE OF A HOAX IS THAT IT HAS TO BE BELIEVABLE. WHAT DID YOU HAVE IN MIND?
UM...
GO FOR IT!
93!
I'LL SEE WHAT I CAN DO.

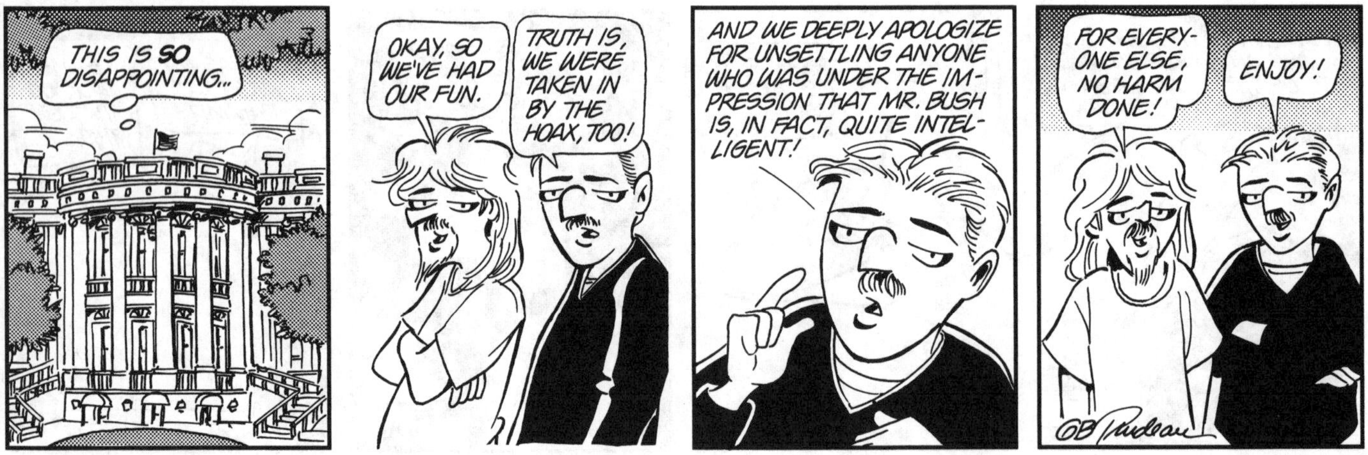
THIS IS SO DISAPPOINTING...
OKAY, SO WE'VE HAD OUR FUN.
TRUTH IS, WE WERE TAKEN IN BY THE HOAX, TOO!
AND WE DEEPLY APOLOGIZE FOR UNSETTLING ANYONE WHO WAS UNDER THE IMPRESSION THAT MR. BUSH IS, IN FACT, QUITE INTELLIGENT!
FOR EVERYONE ELSE, NO HARM DONE!
ENJOY!

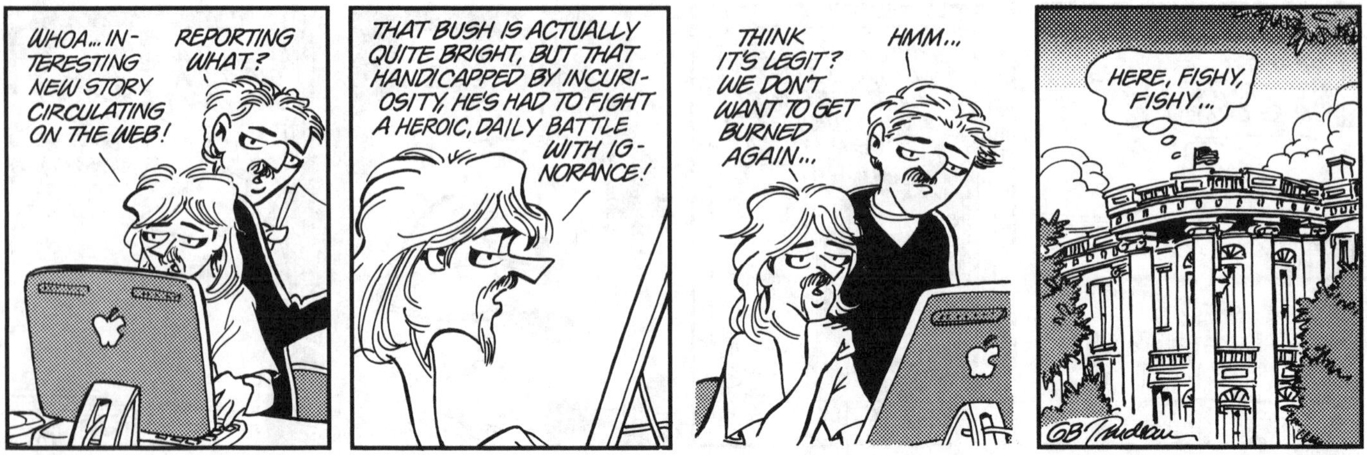
WHOA... INTERESTING NEW STORY CIRCULATING ON THE WEB!
REPORTING WHAT?
THAT BUSH IS ACTUALLY QUITE BRIGHT, BUT THAT HANDICAPPED BY INCURIOSITY, HE'S HAD TO FIGHT A HEROIC, DAILY BATTLE WITH IGNORANCE!
THINK IT'S LEGIT? WE DON'T WANT TO GET BURNED AGAIN...
HMM...
HERE, FISHY, FISHY...

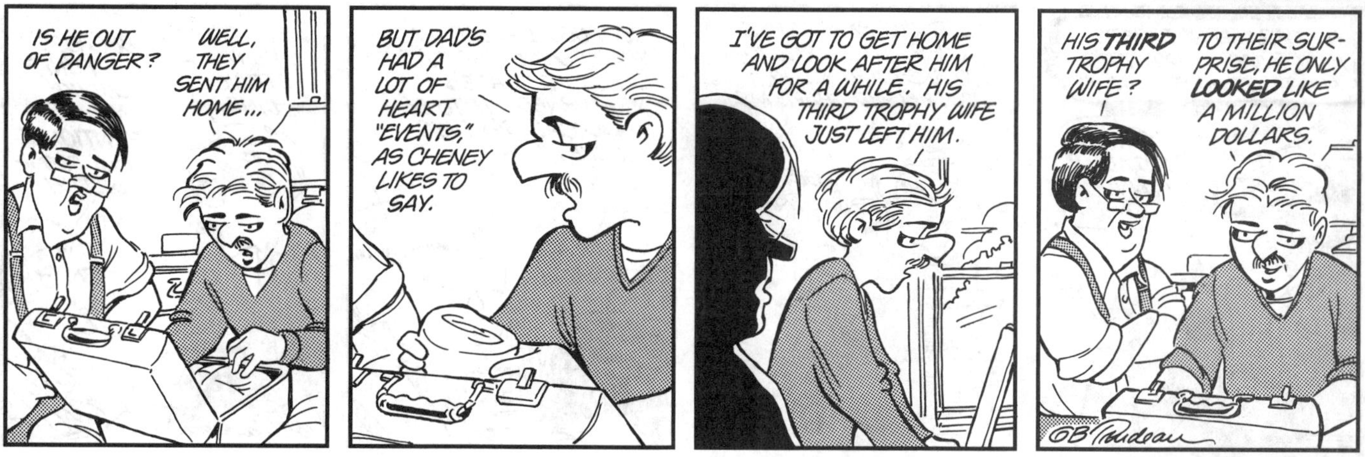
IS HE OUT OF DANGER?
WELL, THEY SENT HIM HOME...
BUT DAD'S HAD A LOT OF HEART "EVENTS," AS CHENEY LIKES TO SAY.
I'VE GOT TO GET HOME AND LOOK AFTER HIM FOR A WHILE. HIS THIRD TROPHY WIFE JUST LEFT HIM.
HIS **THIRD** TROPHY WIFE?
TO THEIR SURPRISE, HE ONLY **LOOKED** LIKE A MILLION DOLLARS.
GB Trudeau

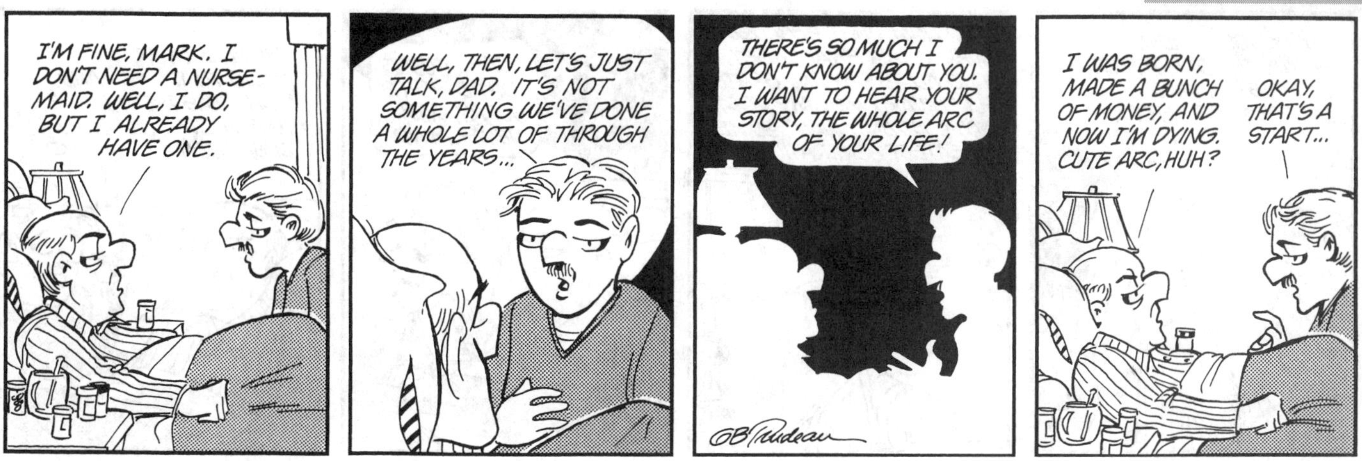
I'M FINE, MARK. I DON'T NEED A NURSE-MAID. WELL, I DO, BUT I ALREADY HAVE ONE.
WELL, THEN, LET'S JUST TALK, DAD. IT'S NOT SOMETHING WE'VE DONE A WHOLE LOT OF THROUGH THE YEARS...
THERE'S SO MUCH I DON'T KNOW ABOUT YOU. I WANT TO HEAR YOUR STORY, THE WHOLE ARC OF YOUR LIFE!
GB Trudeau
I WAS BORN, MADE A BUNCH OF MONEY, AND NOW I'M DYING. CUTE ARC, HUH?
OKAY, THAT'S A START...

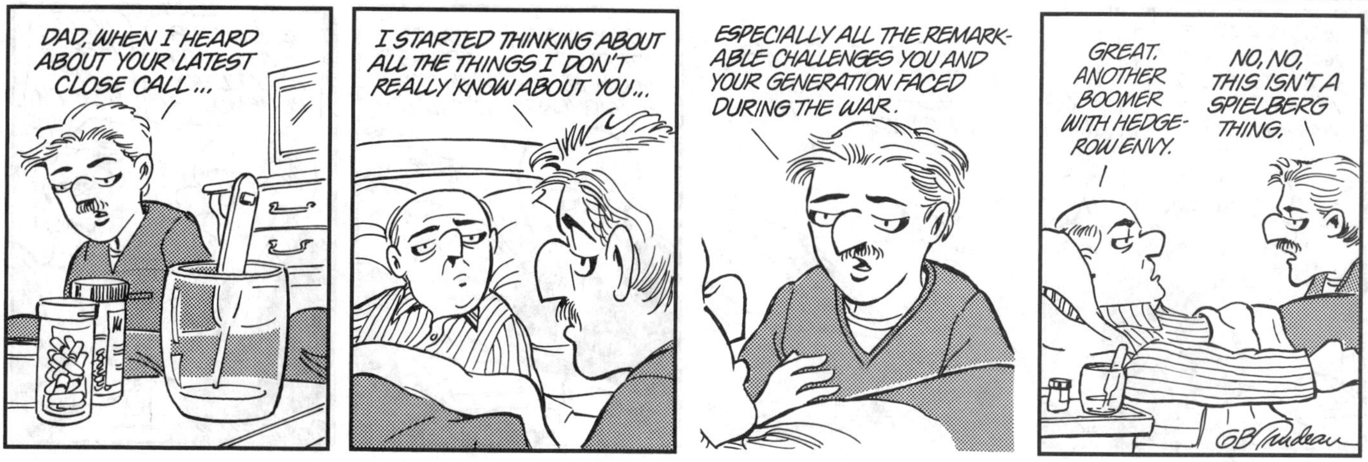
DAD, WHEN I HEARD ABOUT YOUR LATEST CLOSE CALL...
I STARTED THINKING ABOUT ALL THE THINGS I DON'T REALLY KNOW ABOUT YOU...
ESPECIALLY ALL THE REMARKABLE CHALLENGES YOU AND YOUR GENERATION FACED DURING THE WAR.
GREAT, ANOTHER BOOMER WITH HEDGEROW ENVY.
NO, NO, THIS ISN'T A SPIELBERG THING.
GB Trudeau

NO, DAD, IT'S NOT "HEDGE-ROW ENVY"—I DON'T ROMANTICIZE YOUR WAR.
FOR ME, IT'S ABOUT CONNECTIONS...
YOUR WAR EXPERIENCE HELPED MAKE YOU WHO YOU ARE! AND YOU IN TURN HELPED SHAPE ME!
LET ME GET THIS STRAIGHT...
BECAUSE I SPENT TWO YEARS BEING SHOT AT IN EUROPE, THAT'S WHY YOU TURNED OUT TO BE A RADICAL GAY DISC JOCKEY?
WELL, IT'S NOT LIKE IT'S A STRAIGHT LINE...
BECAUSE IT'S FUNNY HOW IKE NEVER MENTIONED THAT POSSIBILITY!

MARK, YOU'VE NEVER SHOWN THE SLIGHTEST INTEREST IN MY WAR EXPERIENCES BEFORE!
AND NOW, JUST BECAUSE EVERYONE'S FINALLY GETTING ALL GUSHY AND GRATEFUL TOWARD MEN MY AGE, YOU SUDDENLY WANT SOME GREATEST GENERATION FAIRY DUST?
YEAH... GUESS YOU'RE RIGHT. SORRY, DAD. NEVER MIND.
THE FLAK OVER ANZIO THAT NIGHT WAS THE WORST I'D EVER SEEN...
AND WE'RE OFF!

WELL, MARK, IF YOU REALLY WANT TO KNOW ABOUT MY WAR EXPERIENCES...
YOU MIGHT BE INTERESTED IN THIS—ALL 724 PAGES OF IT!
WHAT IS IT?
MY MEMOIR—TURNED DOWN BY 23 PUBLISHERS!
YOU'RE KIDDING! WHAT'S IT CALLED?
"HELL IN TRIPLICATE: A COMPANY CLERK REMEMBERS!"
WELL, THERE'S YOUR PROBLEM.

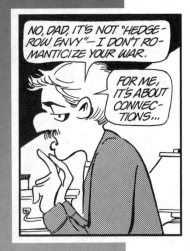

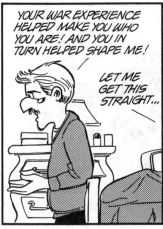

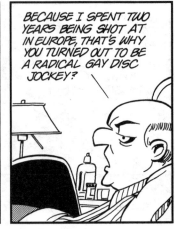

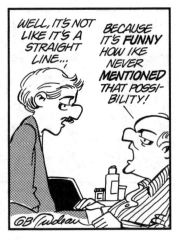

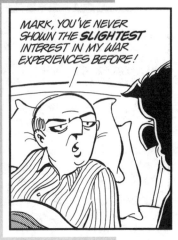

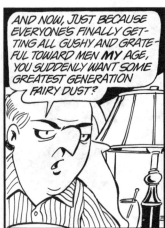

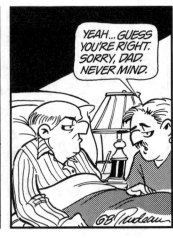

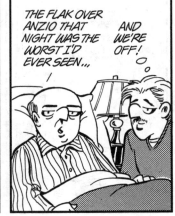

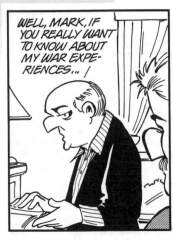

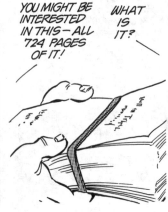

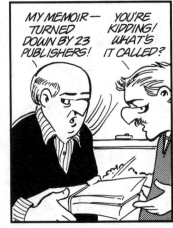

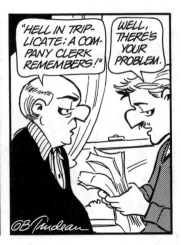

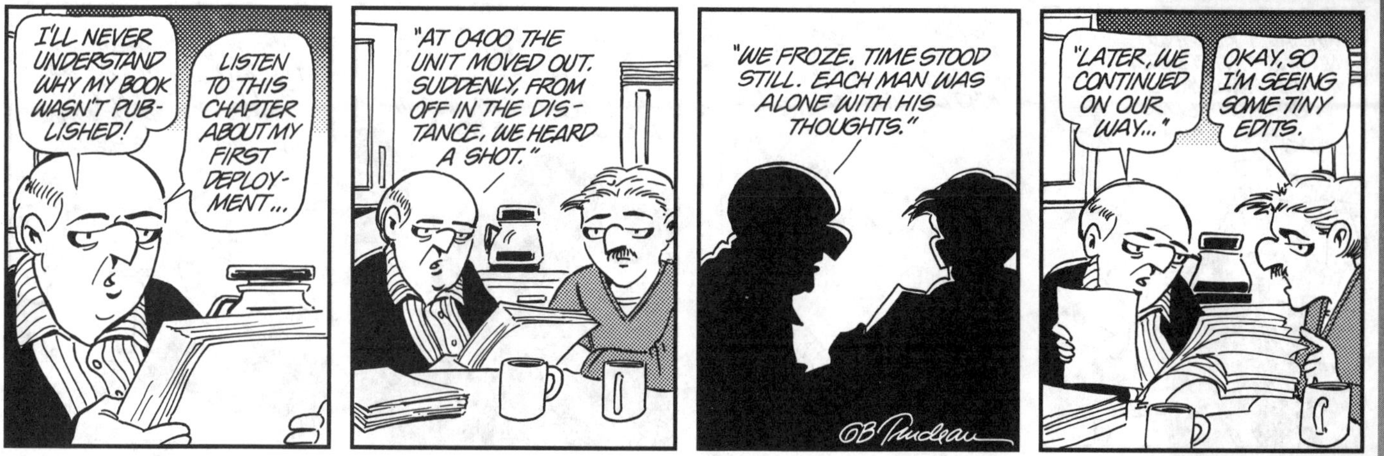
I'LL NEVER UNDERSTAND WHY MY BOOK WASN'T PUB-LISHED!
LISTEN TO THIS CHAPTER ABOUT MY FIRST DEPLOY-MENT...
"AT 0400 THE UNIT MOVED OUT. SUDDENLY, FROM OFF IN THE DIS-TANCE, WE HEARD A SHOT."
"WE FROZE. TIME STOOD STILL. EACH MAN WAS ALONE WITH HIS THOUGHTS."
GB Trudeau
"LATER, WE CONTINUED ON OUR WAY..."
OKAY, SO I'M SEEING SOME TINY EDITS.

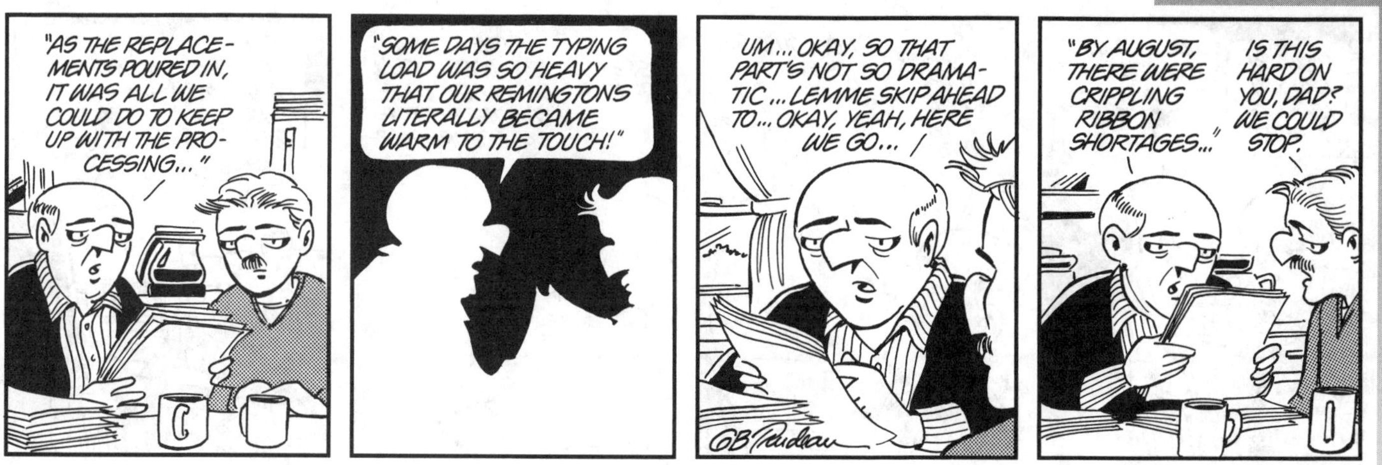
"AS THE REPLACE-MENTS POURED IN, IT WAS ALL WE COULD DO TO KEEP UP WITH THE PRO-CESSING..."
"SOME DAYS THE TYPING LOAD WAS SO HEAVY THAT OUR REMINGTONS LITERALLY BECAME WARM TO THE TOUCH!"
UM... OKAY, SO THAT PART'S NOT SO DRAMA-TIC... LEMME SKIP AHEAD TO... OKAY, YEAH, HERE WE GO...
GB Trudeau
"BY AUGUST, THERE WERE CRIPPLING RIBBON SHORTAGES..."
IS THIS HARD ON YOU, DAD? WE COULD STOP.

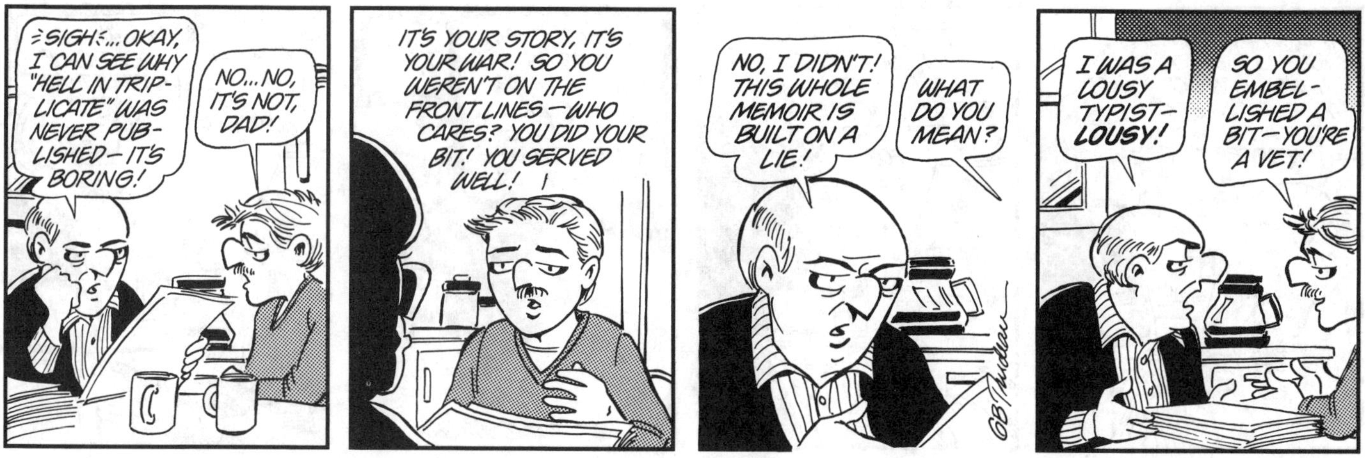
SIGH... OKAY, I CAN SEE WHY "HELL IN TRIP-LICATE" WAS NEVER PUB-LISHED — IT'S BORING!
NO... NO, IT'S NOT, DAD!
IT'S YOUR STORY, IT'S YOUR WAR! SO YOU WEREN'T ON THE FRONT LINES — WHO CARES? YOU DID YOUR BIT! YOU SERVED WELL!
NO, I DIDN'T! THIS WHOLE MEMOIR IS BUILT ON A LIE!
WHAT DO YOU MEAN?
GB Trudeau
I WAS A LOUSY TYPIST — LOUSY!
SO YOU EMBEL-LISHED A BIT — YOU'RE A VET!

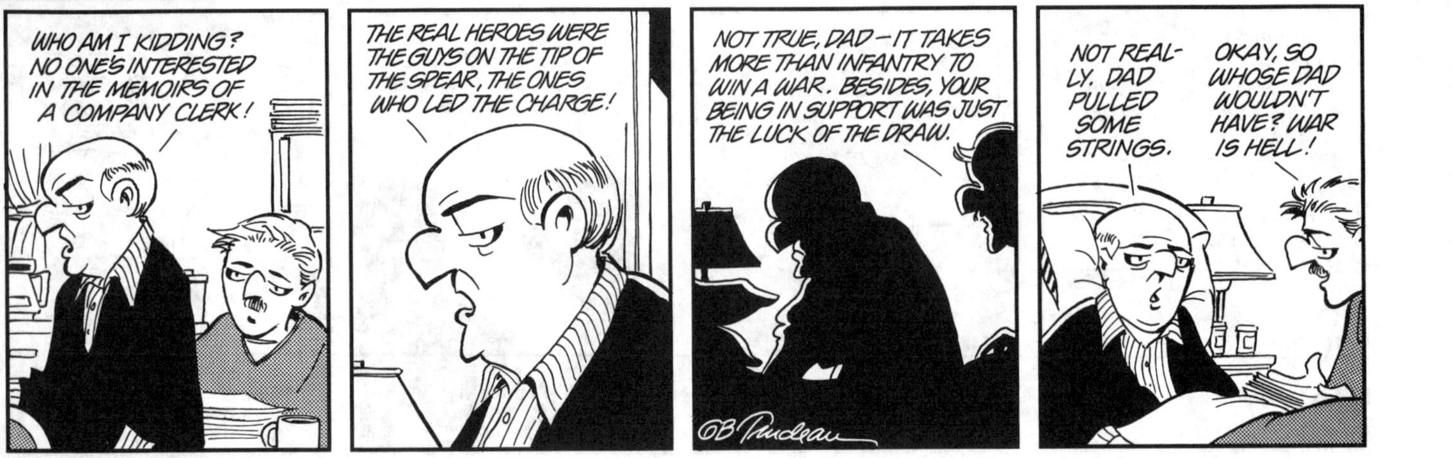
WHO AM I KIDDING? NO ONE'S INTERESTED IN THE MEMOIRS OF A COMPANY CLERK!
THE REAL HEROES WERE THE GUYS ON THE TIP OF THE SPEAR, THE ONES WHO LED THE CHARGE!
NOT TRUE, DAD—IT TAKES MORE THAN INFANTRY TO WIN A WAR. BESIDES, YOUR BEING IN SUPPORT WAS JUST THE LUCK OF THE DRAW.
NOT REALLY. DAD PULLED SOME STRINGS.
OKAY, SO WHOSE DAD WOULDN'T HAVE? WAR IS HELL!
©B Trudeau

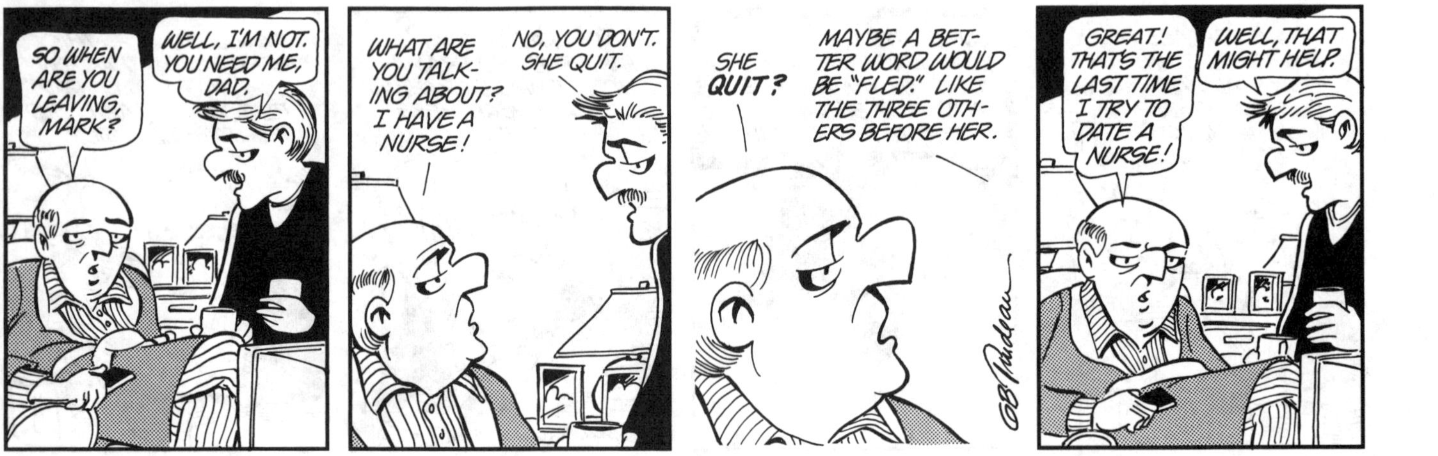
SO WHEN ARE YOU LEAVING, MARK?
WELL, I'M NOT. YOU NEED ME, DAD.
WHAT ARE YOU TALKING ABOUT? I HAVE A NURSE!
NO, YOU DON'T. SHE QUIT.
SHE QUIT?
MAYBE A BETTER WORD WOULD BE "FLED." LIKE THE THREE OTHERS BEFORE HER.
©B Trudeau
GREAT! THAT'S THE LAST TIME I TRY TO DATE A NURSE!
WELL, THAT MIGHT HELP.

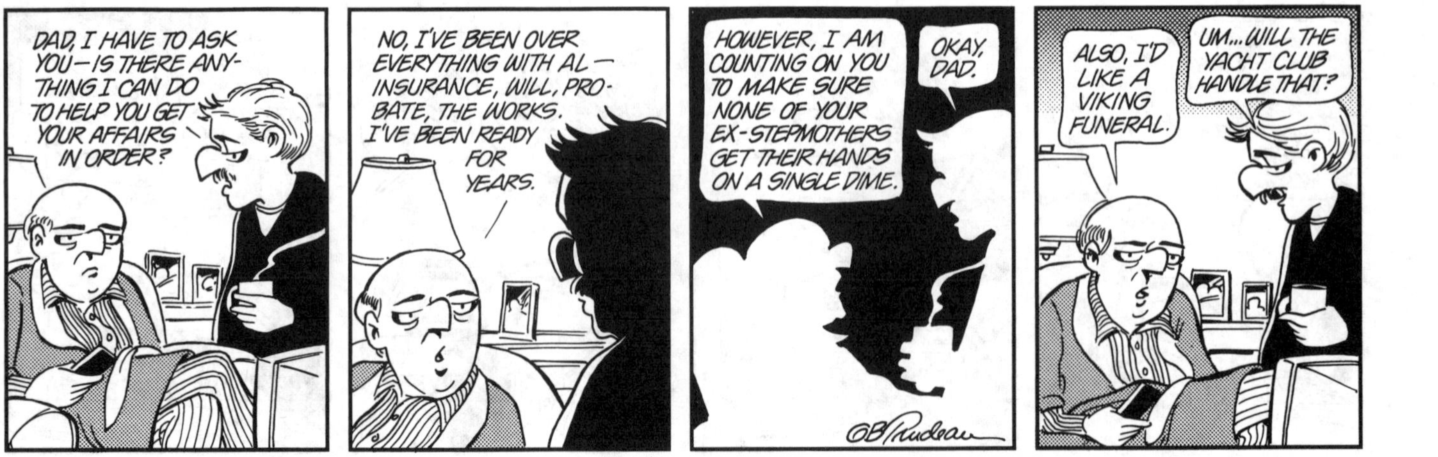
DAD, I HAVE TO ASK YOU—IS THERE ANYTHING I CAN DO TO HELP YOU GET YOUR AFFAIRS IN ORDER?
NO, I'VE BEEN OVER EVERYTHING WITH AL—INSURANCE, WILL, PROBATE, THE WORKS. I'VE BEEN READY FOR YEARS.
HOWEVER, I AM COUNTING ON YOU TO MAKE SURE NONE OF YOUR EX-STEPMOTHERS GET THEIR HANDS ON A SINGLE DIME.
OKAY, DAD.
©B Trudeau
ALSO, I'D LIKE A VIKING FUNERAL.
UM... WILL THE YACHT CLUB HANDLE THAT?

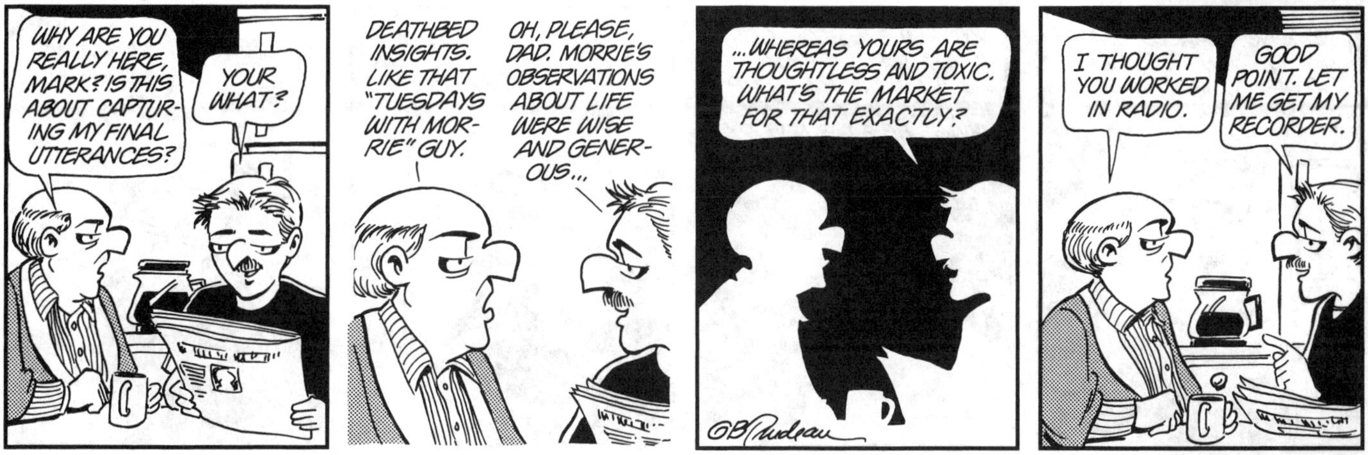
WHY ARE YOU REALLY HERE, MARK? IS THIS ABOUT CAPTURING MY FINAL UTTERANCES?
YOUR WHAT?
DEATHBED INSIGHTS. LIKE THAT "TUESDAYS WITH MORRIE" GUY.
OH, PLEASE, DAD. MORRIE'S OBSERVATIONS ABOUT LIFE WERE WISE AND GENEROUS...
...WHEREAS YOURS ARE THOUGHTLESS AND TOXIC. WHAT'S THE MARKET FOR THAT EXACTLY?
I THOUGHT YOU WORKED IN RADIO.
GOOD POINT. LET ME GET MY RECORDER.

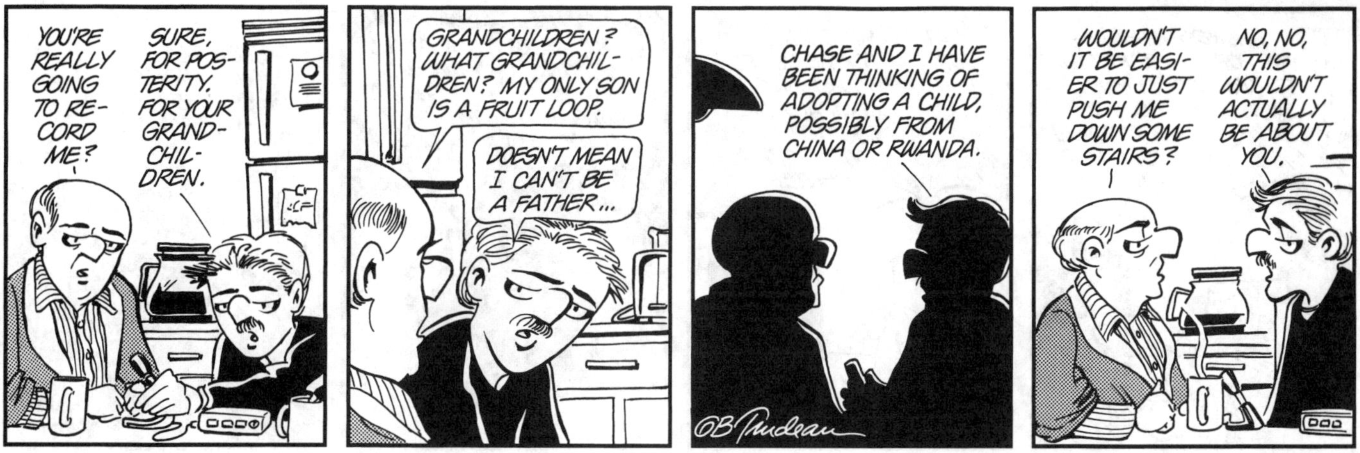
YOU'RE REALLY GOING TO RECORD ME?
SURE, FOR POSTERITY. FOR YOUR GRANDCHILDREN.
GRANDCHILDREN? WHAT GRANDCHILDREN? MY ONLY SON IS A FRUIT LOOP.
DOESN'T MEAN I CAN'T BE A FATHER...
CHASE AND I HAVE BEEN THINKING OF ADOPTING A CHILD, POSSIBLY FROM CHINA OR RWANDA.
WOULDN'T IT BE EASIER TO JUST PUSH ME DOWN SOME STAIRS?
NO, NO, THIS WOULDN'T ACTUALLY BE ABOUT YOU.

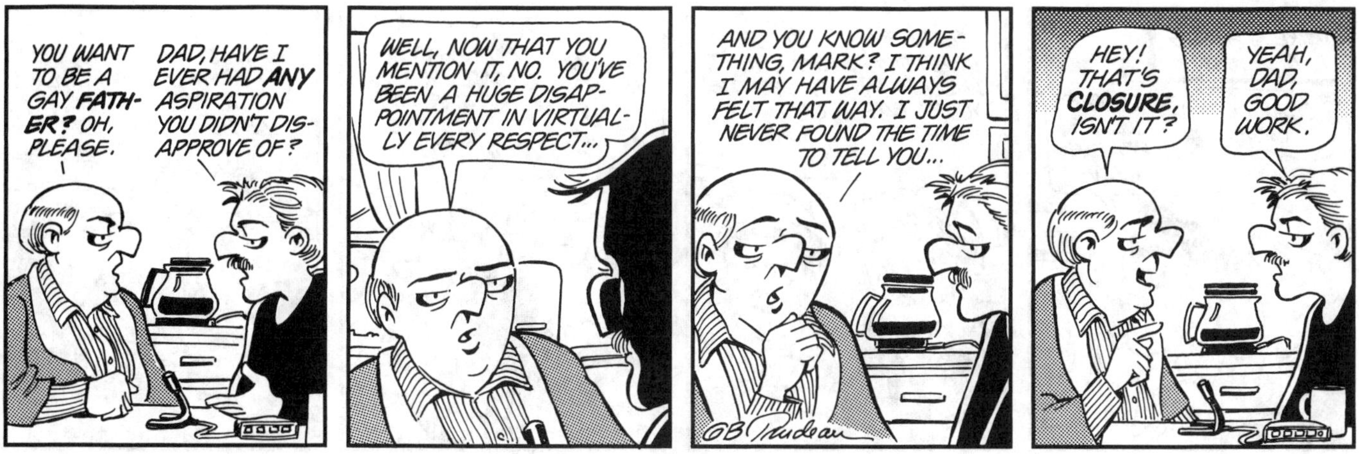
YOU WANT TO BE A GAY **FATHER?** OH, PLEASE.
DAD, HAVE I EVER HAD **ANY** ASPIRATION YOU DIDN'T DISAPPROVE OF?
WELL, NOW THAT YOU MENTION IT, NO. YOU'VE BEEN A HUGE DISAPPOINTMENT IN VIRTUALLY EVERY RESPECT...
AND YOU KNOW SOMETHING, MARK? I THINK I MAY HAVE ALWAYS FELT THAT WAY. I JUST NEVER FOUND THE TIME TO TELL YOU...
HEY! THAT'S **CLOSURE,** ISN'T IT?
YEAH, DAD, GOOD WORK.

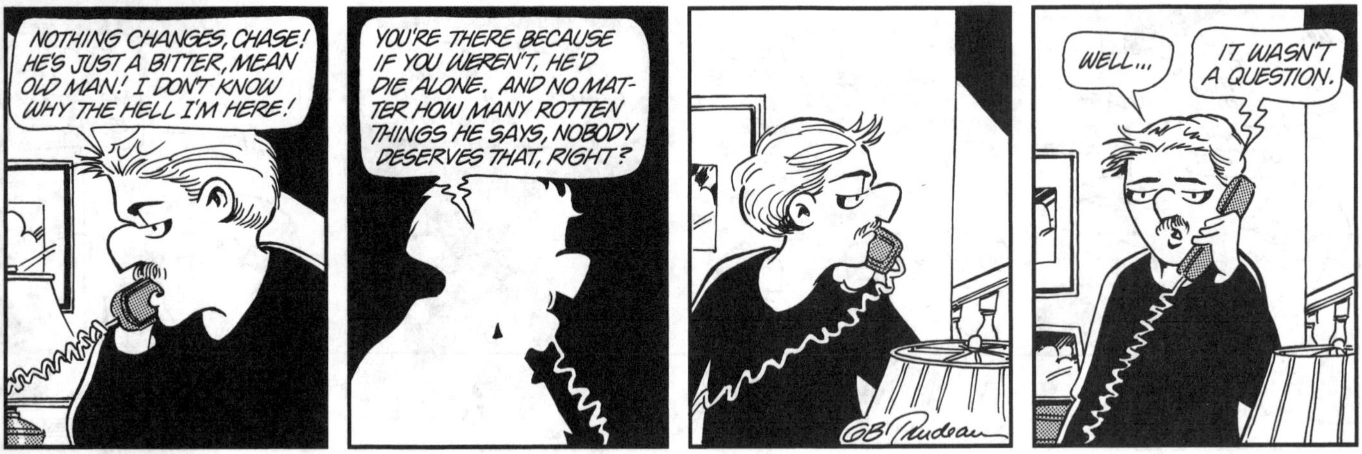
NOTHING CHANGES, CHASE! HE'S JUST A BITTER, MEAN OLD MAN! I DON'T KNOW WHY THE HELL I'M HERE!
YOU'RE THERE BECAUSE IF YOU WEREN'T, HE'D DIE ALONE. AND NO MATTER HOW MANY ROTTEN THINGS HE SAYS, NOBODY DESERVES THAT, RIGHT?
WELL...
IT WASN'T A QUESTION.
GBTrudeau

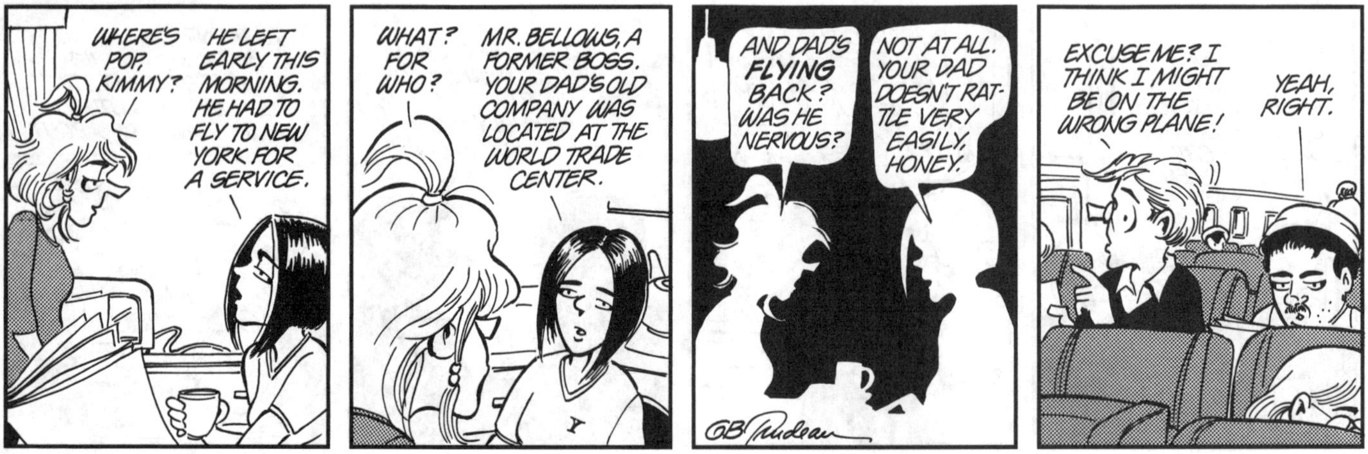
WHERE'S POP, KIMMY?
HE LEFT EARLY THIS MORNING. HE HAD TO FLY TO NEW YORK FOR A SERVICE.
WHAT? FOR WHO?
MR. BELLOWS, A FORMER BOSS. YOUR DAD'S OLD COMPANY WAS LOCATED AT THE WORLD TRADE CENTER.
AND DAD'S FLYING BACK? WAS HE NERVOUS?
NOT AT ALL. YOUR DAD DOESN'T RATTLE VERY EASILY, HONEY.
GBTrudeau
EXCUSE ME? I THINK I MIGHT BE ON THE WRONG PLANE!
YEAH, RIGHT.

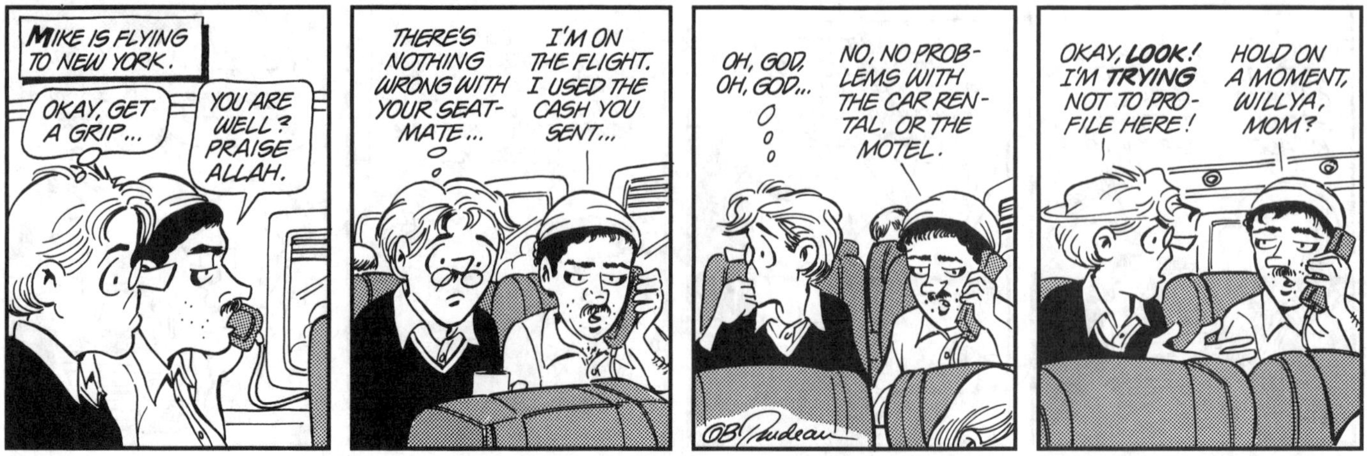
MIKE IS FLYING TO NEW YORK.
OKAY, GET A GRIP...
YOU ARE WELL? PRAISE ALLAH.
THERE'S NOTHING WRONG WITH YOUR SEATMATE...
I'M ON THE FLIGHT. I USED THE CASH YOU SENT...
OH, GOD, OH, GOD...
NO, NO PROBLEMS WITH THE CAR RENTAL. OR THE MOTEL.
GBTrudeau
OKAY, LOOK! I'M TRYING NOT TO PROFILE HERE!
HOLD ON A MOMENT, WILLYA, MOM?

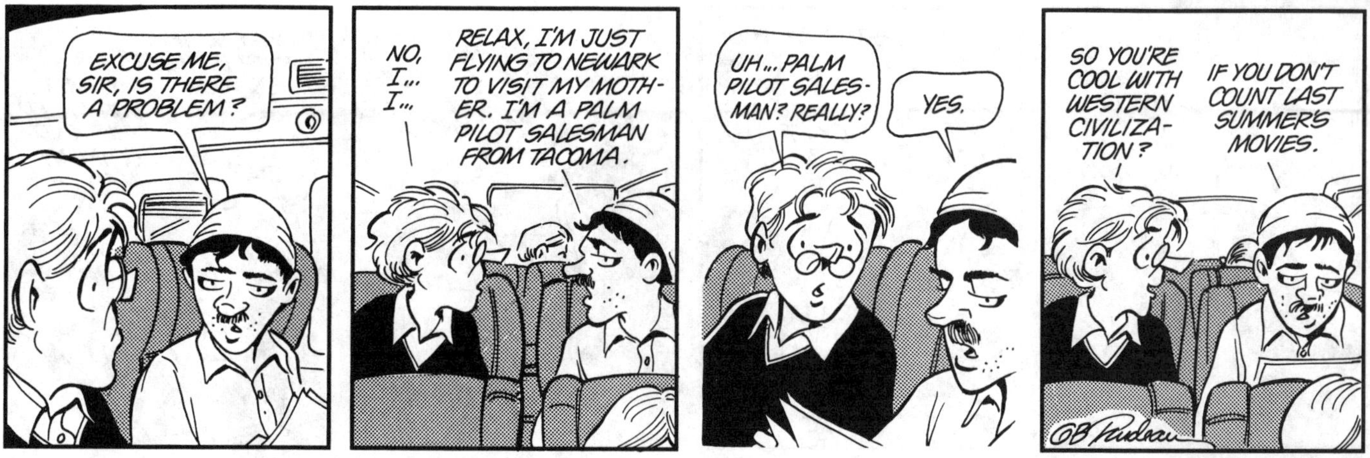
EXCUSE ME, SIR, IS THERE A PROBLEM?
NO, I... I...
RELAX, I'M JUST FLYING TO NEWARK TO VISIT MY MOTHER. I'M A PALM PILOT SALESMAN FROM TACOMA.
UH... PALM PILOT SALESMAN? REALLY?
YES.
SO YOU'RE COOL WITH WESTERN CIVILIZATION?
IF YOU DON'T COUNT LAST SUMMER'S MOVIES.
©B Trudeau

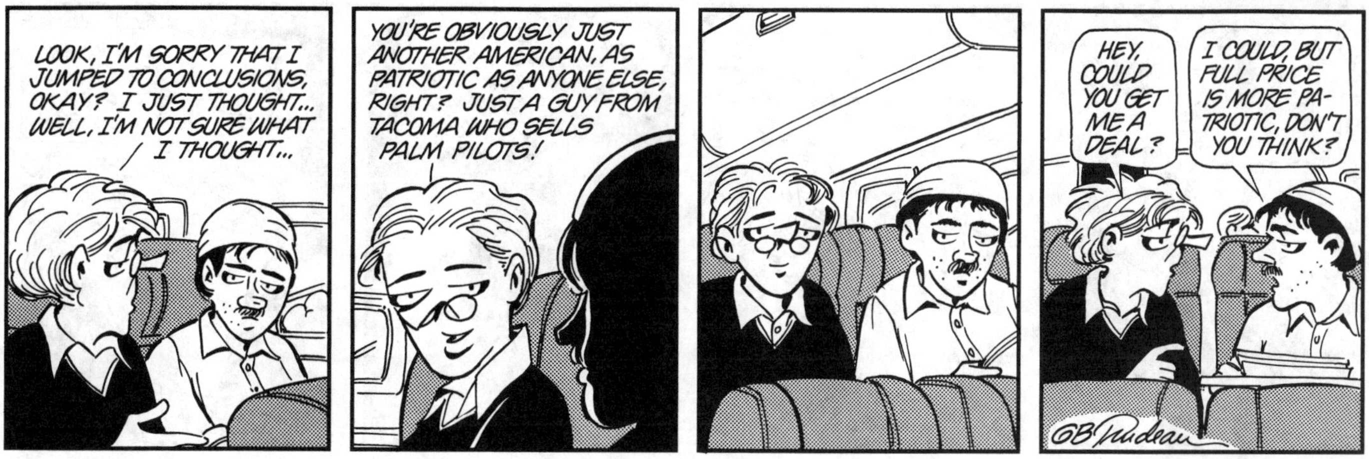
LOOK, I'M SORRY THAT I JUMPED TO CONCLUSIONS, OKAY? I JUST THOUGHT... WELL, I'M NOT SURE WHAT I THOUGHT...
YOU'RE OBVIOUSLY JUST ANOTHER AMERICAN, AS PATRIOTIC AS ANYONE ELSE, RIGHT? JUST A GUY FROM TACOMA WHO SELLS PALM PILOTS!
HEY, COULD YOU GET ME A DEAL?
I COULD, BUT FULL PRICE IS MORE PATRIOTIC, DON'T YOU THINK?
©B Trudeau

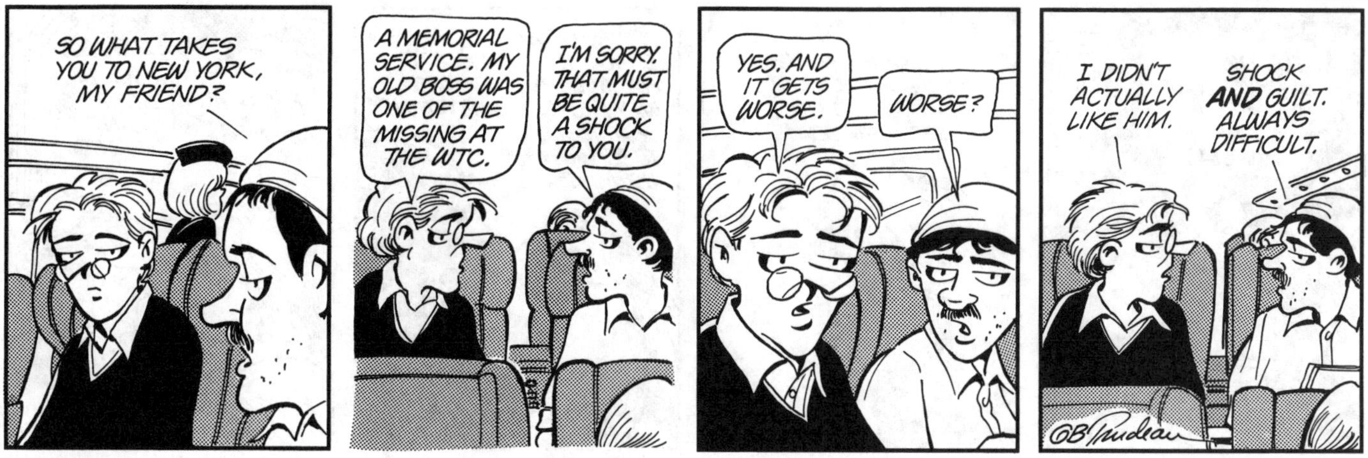
SO WHAT TAKES YOU TO NEW YORK, MY FRIEND?
A MEMORIAL SERVICE. MY OLD BOSS WAS ONE OF THE MISSING AT THE WTC.
I'M SORRY. THAT MUST BE QUITE A SHOCK TO YOU.
YES. AND IT GETS WORSE.
WORSE?
I DIDN'T ACTUALLY LIKE HIM.
SHOCK AND GUILT. ALWAYS DIFFICULT.
©B Trudeau

HEY, BUDDY. WHAT'S THE STORY ON THE GUY YOU'RE SITTING WITH?
HE'S A SALESMAN FROM TACOMA. HE'S FLYING HOME TO SEE HIS MOTHER.
OH... THAT'S A RELIEF!
WELL, NOT A RELIEF, EXACTLY, JUST... WELL, YOU KNOW.
OKAY, SO THIS MUST BE WEIRD FOR YOU.
YEAH. I DON'T NEED THIS KIND OF IRONY IN MY LIFE.

MARCIA?
MIKE! YOU MADE IT!
WELL, I THOUGHT I SHOULD BE HERE...
MR. BELLOWS WOULD HAVE BEEN TOUCHED.
AND YOU'RE OKAY?
I'M FINE, MIKE, BUT I KNOW WHAT YOU'RE WONDERING...
YOU DO?
THE ANSWER'S YES. I'M STILL SINGLE. WHY DO YOU ASK?

SO HOW IS EVERYONE AT THE AGENCY COPING, MARCIA?
IT VARIES. SOME PEOPLE ARE OKAY. OTHERS ARE STILL DEVASTATED.
IT WAS GOOD OF YOU TO FLY ALL THE WAY FROM SEATTLE TO BE WITH US, MIKE.
WELL, IT SEEMED IMPORTANT.
PACKAGE?
UM... YEAH. "LION KING" AND "PHANTOM."

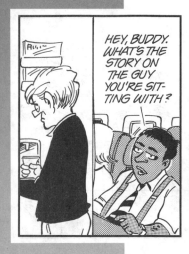

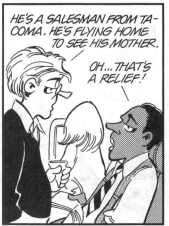

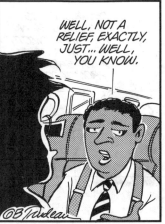

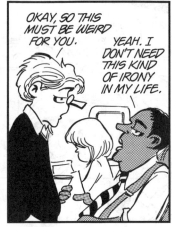

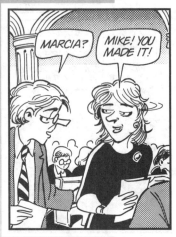

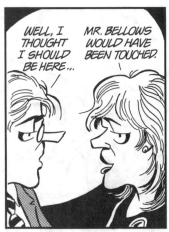

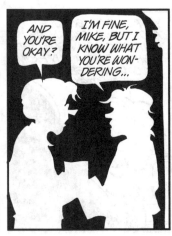

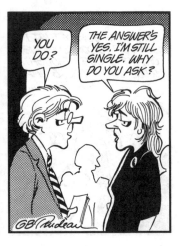

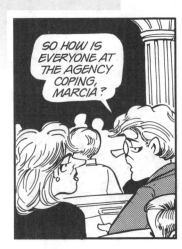

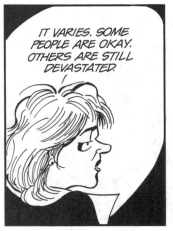

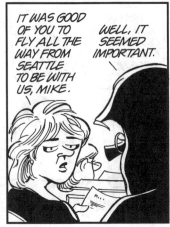

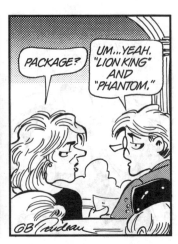

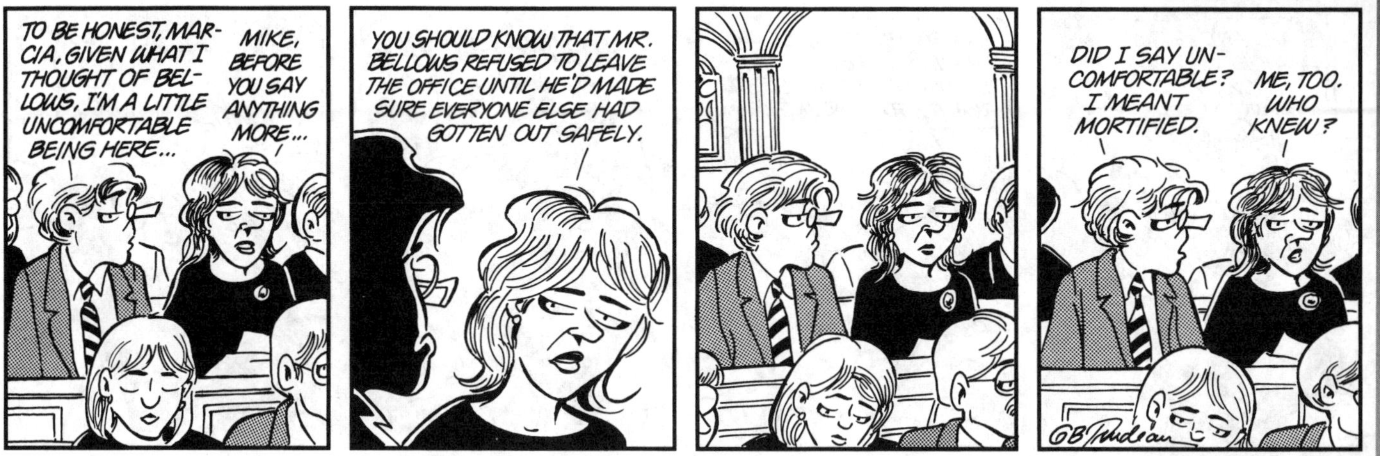
TO BE HONEST, MARCIA, GIVEN WHAT I THOUGHT OF BELLOWS, I'M A LITTLE UNCOMFORTABLE BEING HERE...
MIKE, BEFORE YOU SAY ANYTHING MORE...
YOU SHOULD KNOW THAT MR. BELLOWS REFUSED TO LEAVE THE OFFICE UNTIL HE'D MADE SURE EVERYONE ELSE HAD GOTTEN OUT SAFELY.
DID I SAY UNCOMFORTABLE? I MEANT MORTIFIED.
ME, TOO. WHO KNEW?

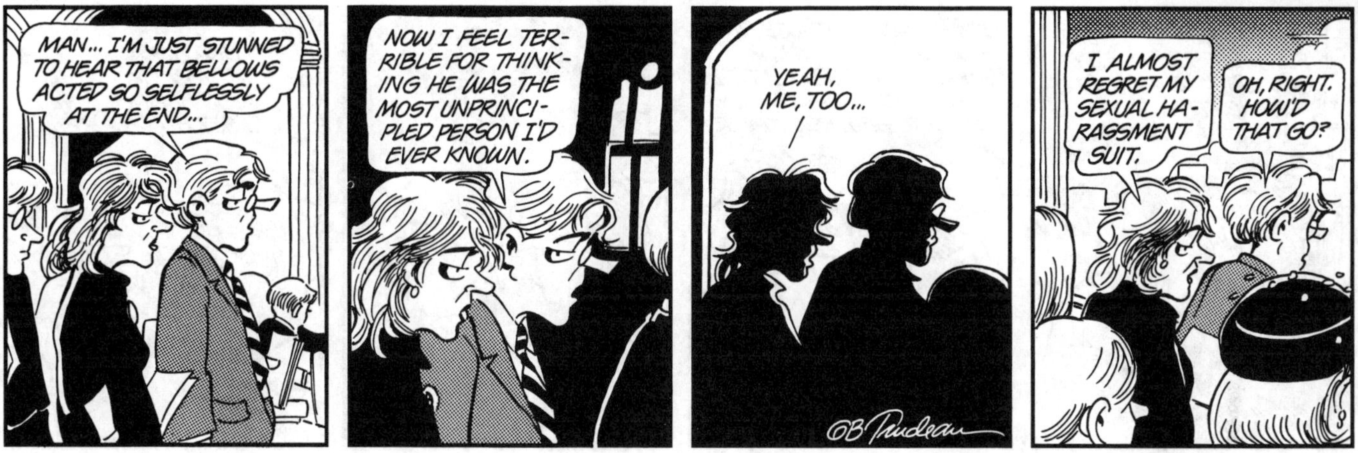
MAN... I'M JUST STUNNED TO HEAR THAT BELLOWS ACTED SO SELFLESSLY AT THE END...
NOW I FEEL TERRIBLE FOR THINKING HE WAS THE MOST UNPRINCIPLED PERSON I'D EVER KNOWN.
YEAH, ME, TOO...
I ALMOST REGRET MY SEXUAL HARASSMENT SUIT.
OH, RIGHT. HOW'D THAT GO?

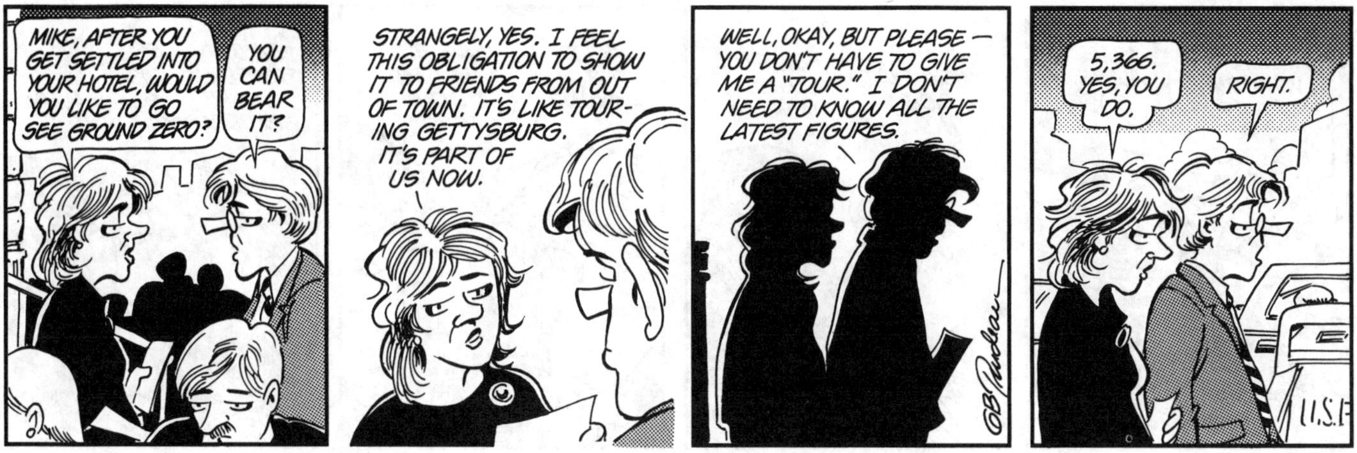
MIKE, AFTER YOU GET SETTLED INTO YOUR HOTEL, WOULD YOU LIKE TO GO SEE GROUND ZERO?
YOU CAN BEAR IT?
STRANGELY, YES. I FEEL THIS OBLIGATION TO SHOW IT TO FRIENDS FROM OUT OF TOWN. IT'S LIKE TOURING GETTYSBURG. IT'S PART OF US NOW.
WELL, OKAY, BUT PLEASE — YOU DON'T HAVE TO GIVE ME A "TOUR." I DON'T NEED TO KNOW ALL THE LATEST FIGURES.
5,366. YES, YOU DO.
RIGHT.

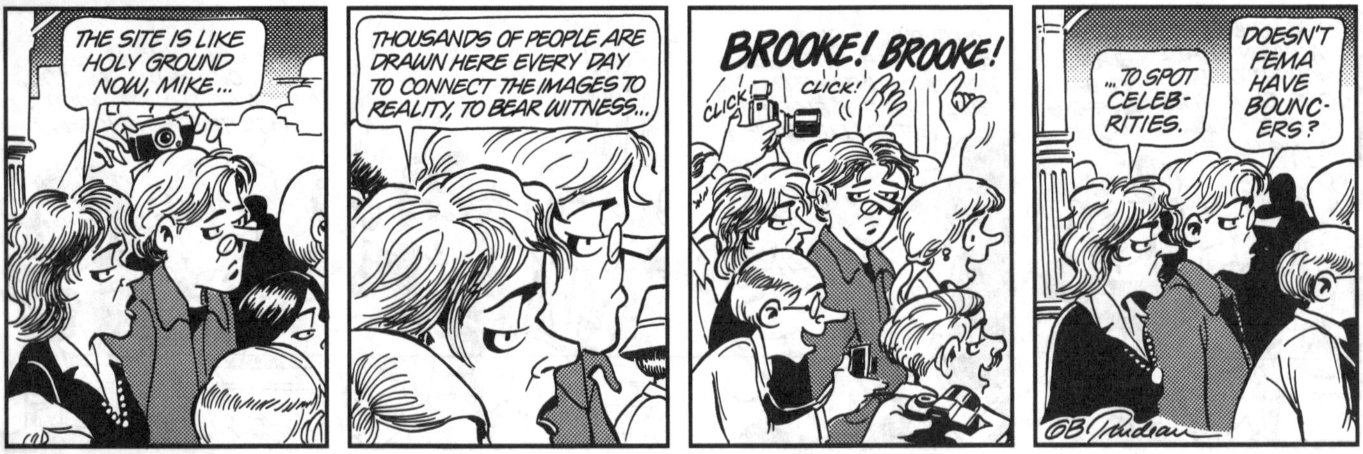
THE SITE IS LIKE HOLY GROUND NOW, MIKE...
THOUSANDS OF PEOPLE ARE DRAWN HERE EVERY DAY TO CONNECT THE IMAGES TO REALITY, TO BEAR WITNESS...
BROOKE! BROOKE!
CLICK
CLICK!
...TO SPOT CELEB-RITIES.
DOESN'T FEMA HAVE BOUNC-ERS?
©B Trudeau

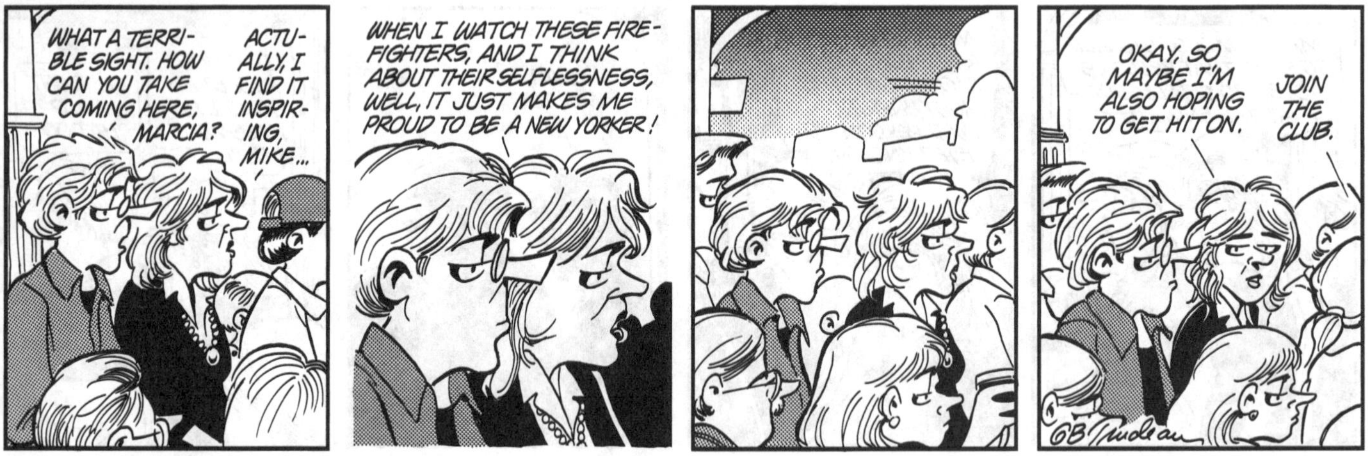
WHAT A TERRI-BLE SIGHT. HOW CAN YOU TAKE COMING HERE, MARCIA?
ACTU-ALLY, I FIND IT INSPIR-ING, MIKE...
WHEN I WATCH THESE FIRE-FIGHTERS, AND I THINK ABOUT THEIR SELFLESSNESS, WELL, IT JUST MAKES ME PROUD TO BE A NEW YORKER!
OKAY, SO MAYBE I'M ALSO HOPING TO GET HIT ON.
JOIN THE CLUB.
©B Trudeau

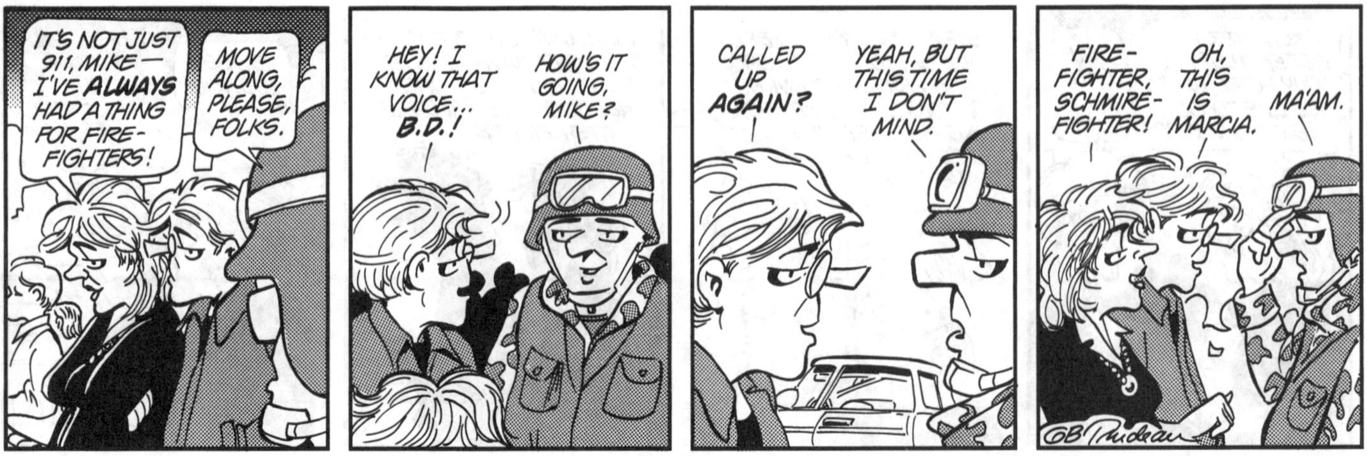
IT'S NOT JUST 9/11, MIKE— I'VE **ALWAYS** HAD A THING FOR FIRE-FIGHTERS!
MOVE ALONG, PLEASE, FOLKS.
HEY! I KNOW THAT VOICE... **B.D.!**
HOW'S IT GOING, MIKE?
CALLED UP **AGAIN?**
YEAH, BUT THIS TIME I DON'T MIND.
FIRE-FIGHTER, SCHMIRE-FIGHTER!
OH, THIS IS MARCIA.
MA'AM.
©B Trudeau

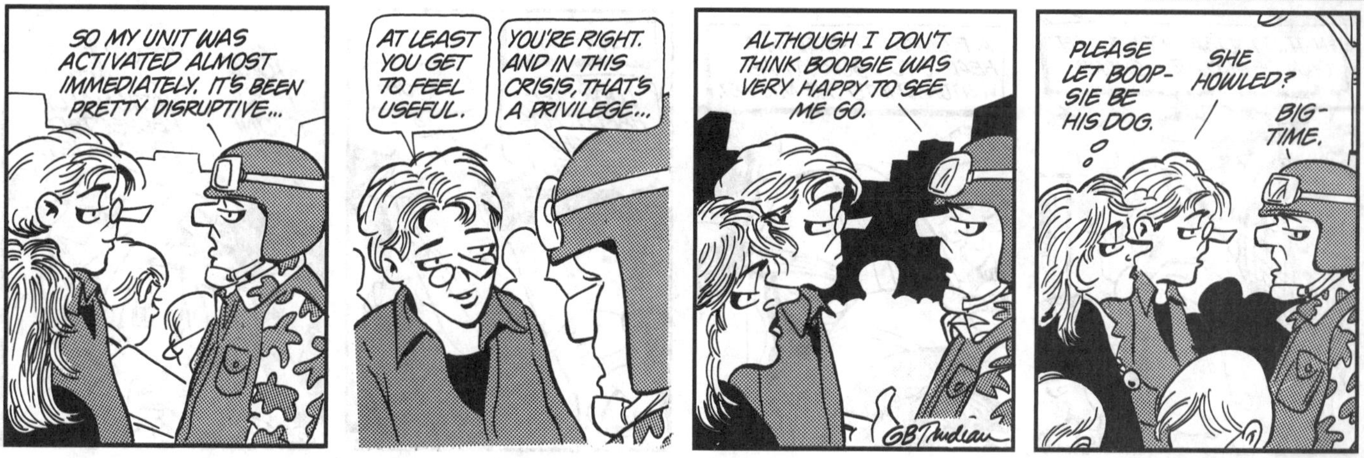
SO MY UNIT WAS ACTIVATED ALMOST IMMEDIATELY. IT'S BEEN PRETTY DISRUPTIVE...
AT LEAST YOU GET TO FEEL USEFUL.
YOU'RE RIGHT. AND IN THIS CRISIS, THAT'S A PRIVILEGE...
ALTHOUGH I DON'T THINK BOOPSIE WAS VERY HAPPY TO SEE ME GO.
PLEASE LET BOOPSIE BE HIS DOG.
SHE HOWLED?
BIG-TIME.

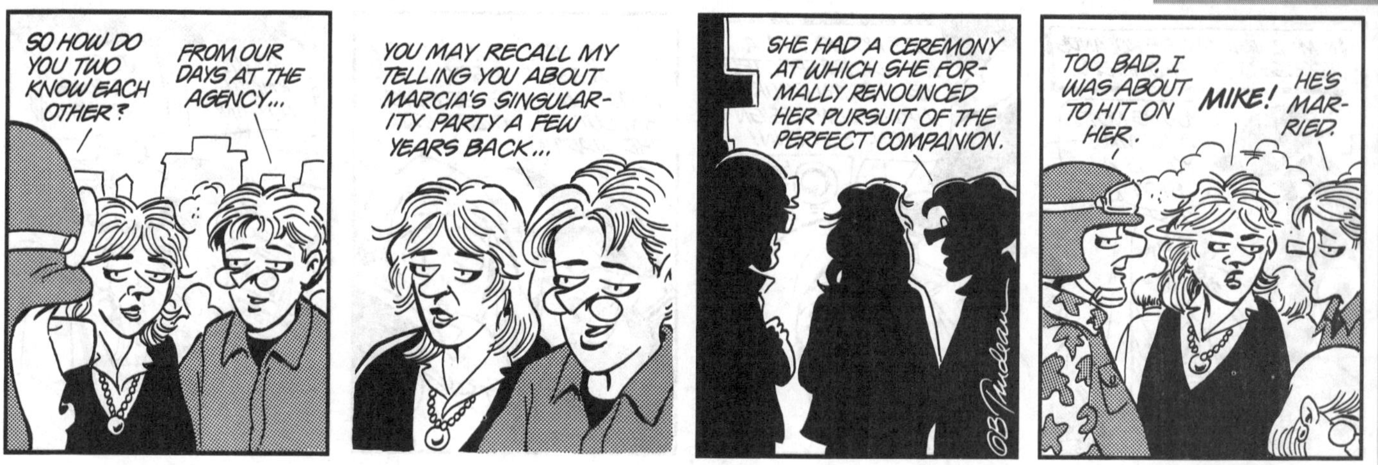
SO HOW DO YOU TWO KNOW EACH OTHER?
FROM OUR DAYS AT THE AGENCY...
YOU MAY RECALL MY TELLING YOU ABOUT MARCIA'S SINGULARITY PARTY A FEW YEARS BACK...
SHE HAD A CEREMONY AT WHICH SHE FORMALLY RENOUNCED HER PURSUIT OF THE PERFECT COMPANION.
TOO BAD. I WAS ABOUT TO HIT ON HER.
MIKE!
HE'S MARRIED.

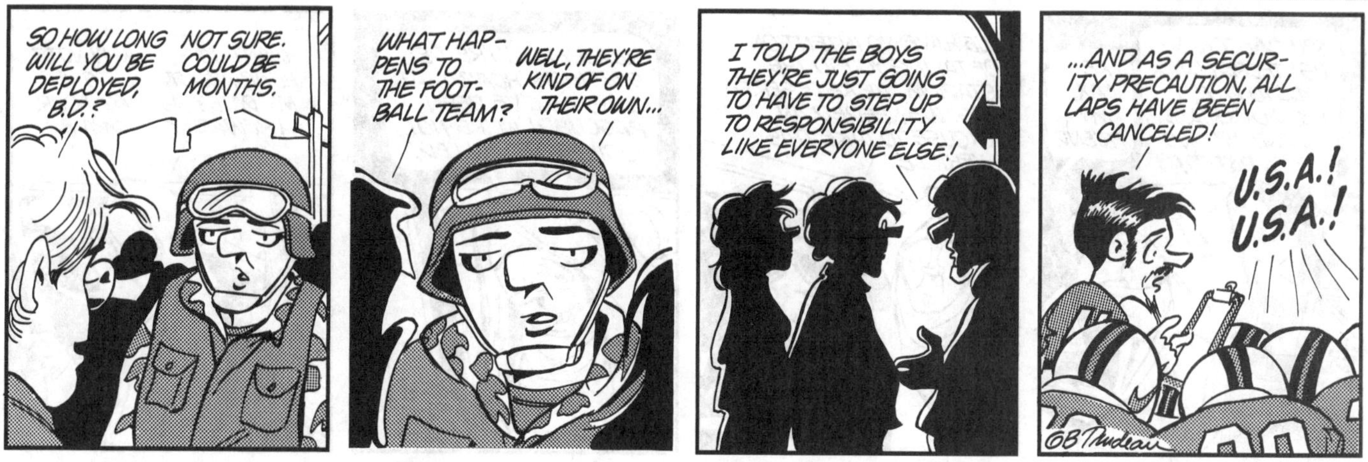
SO HOW LONG WILL YOU BE DEPLOYED, B.D.?
NOT SURE. COULD BE MONTHS.
WHAT HAPPENS TO THE FOOTBALL TEAM?
WELL, THEY'RE KIND OF ON THEIR OWN...
I TOLD THE BOYS THEY'RE JUST GOING TO HAVE TO STEP UP TO RESPONSIBILITY LIKE EVERYONE ELSE!
...AND AS A SECURITY PRECAUTION, ALL LAPS HAVE BEEN CANCELED!
U.S.A.! U.S.A.!

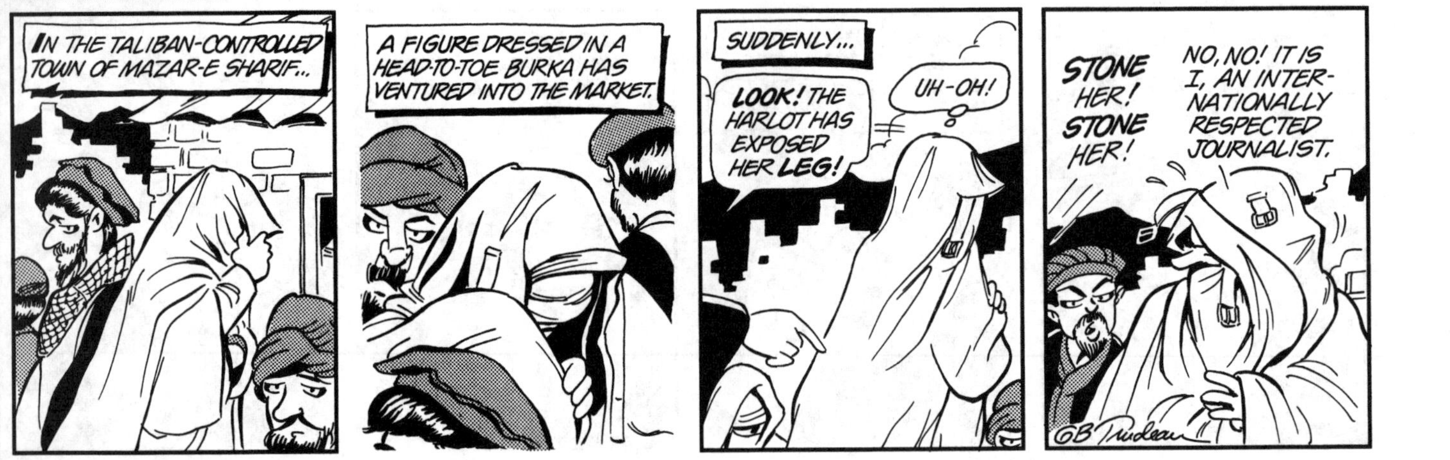
IN THE TALIBAN-CONTROLLED TOWN OF MAZAR-E SHARIF...
A FIGURE DRESSED IN A HEAD-TO-TOE BURKA HAS VENTURED INTO THE MARKET.
SUDDENLY...
LOOK! THE HARLOT HAS EXPOSED HER LEG!
UH-OH!
STONE HER! STONE HER!
NO, NO! IT IS I, AN INTERNATIONALLY RESPECTED JOURNALIST.
©B Trudeau

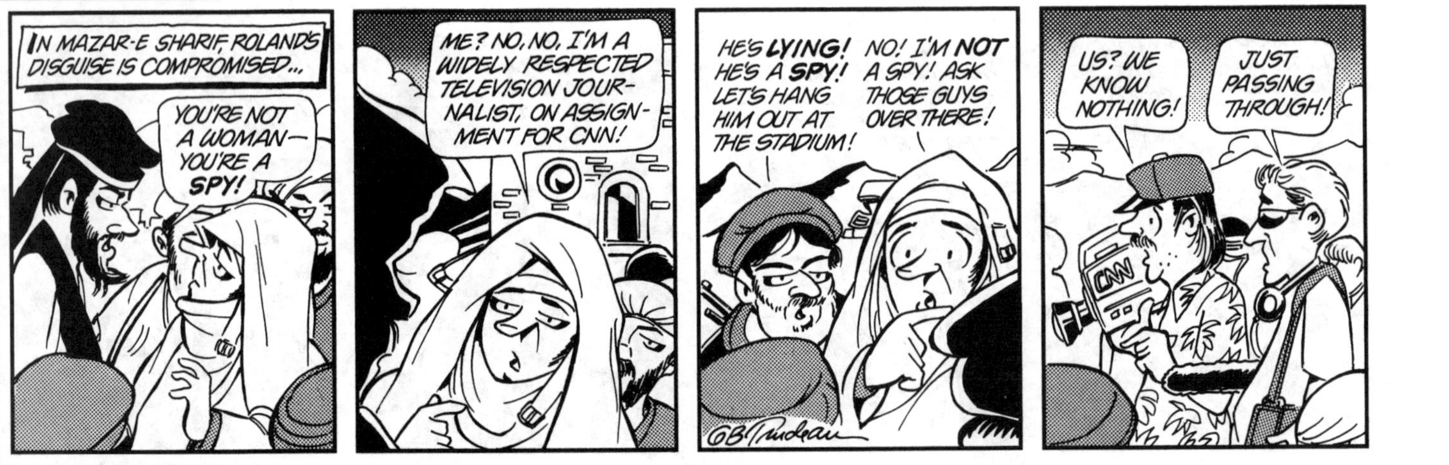
IN MAZAR-E SHARIF, ROLAND'S DISGUISE IS COMPROMISED...
YOU'RE NOT A WOMAN—YOU'RE A SPY!
ME? NO, NO, I'M A WIDELY RESPECTED TELEVISION JOURNALIST, ON ASSIGNMENT FOR CNN!
HE'S LYING! HE'S A SPY! LET'S HANG HIM OUT AT THE STADIUM!
NO! I'M NOT A SPY! ASK THOSE GUYS OVER THERE!
©B Trudeau
US? WE KNOW NOTHING!
JUST PASSING THROUGH!
CNN

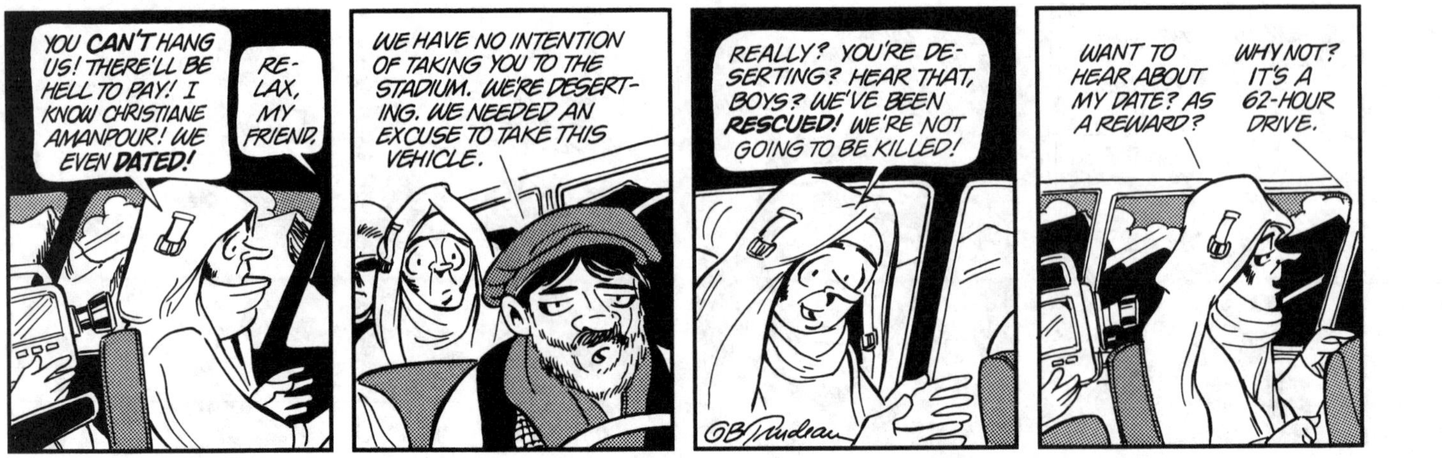
YOU CAN'T HANG US! THERE'LL BE HELL TO PAY! I KNOW CHRISTIANE AMANPOUR! WE EVEN DATED!
RELAX, MY FRIEND.
WE HAVE NO INTENTION OF TAKING YOU TO THE STADIUM. WE'RE DESERTING. WE NEEDED AN EXCUSE TO TAKE THIS VEHICLE.
REALLY? YOU'RE DESERTING? HEAR THAT, BOYS? WE'VE BEEN RESCUED! WE'RE NOT GOING TO BE KILLED!
©B Trudeau
WANT TO HEAR ABOUT MY DATE? AS A REWARD?
WHY NOT? IT'S A 62-HOUR DRIVE.

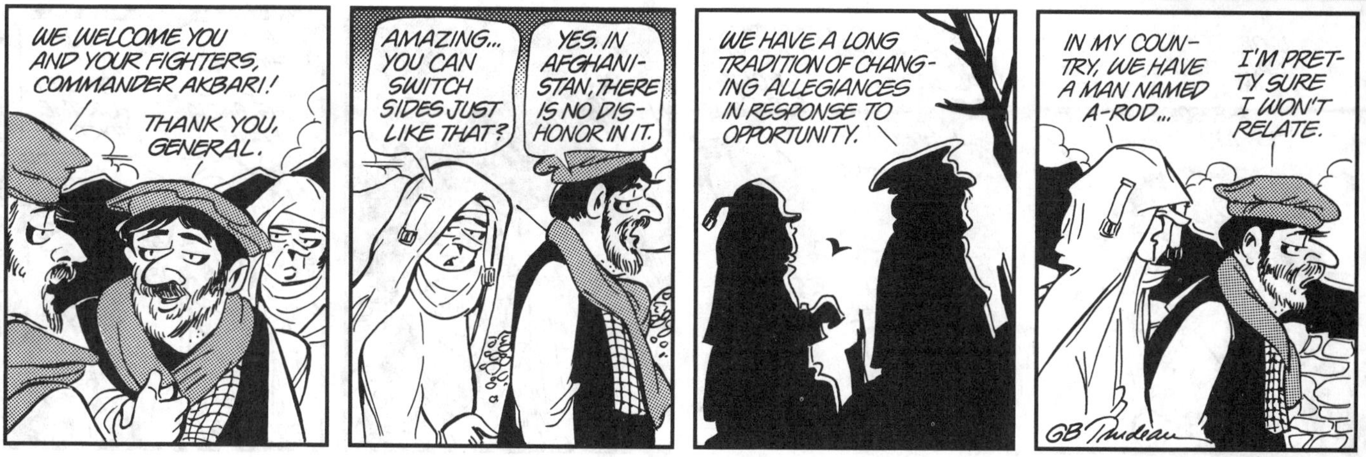
WE WELCOME YOU AND YOUR FIGHTERS, COMMANDER AKBARI!
THANK YOU, GENERAL.
AMAZING... YOU CAN SWITCH SIDES JUST LIKE THAT?
YES, IN AFGHANI-STAN, THERE IS NO DIS-HONOR IN IT.
WE HAVE A LONG TRADITION OF CHANG-ING ALLEGIANCES IN RESPONSE TO OPPORTUNITY.
IN MY COUN-TRY, WE HAVE A MAN NAMED A-ROD...
I'M PRET-TY SURE I WON'T RELATE.
GB Trudeau

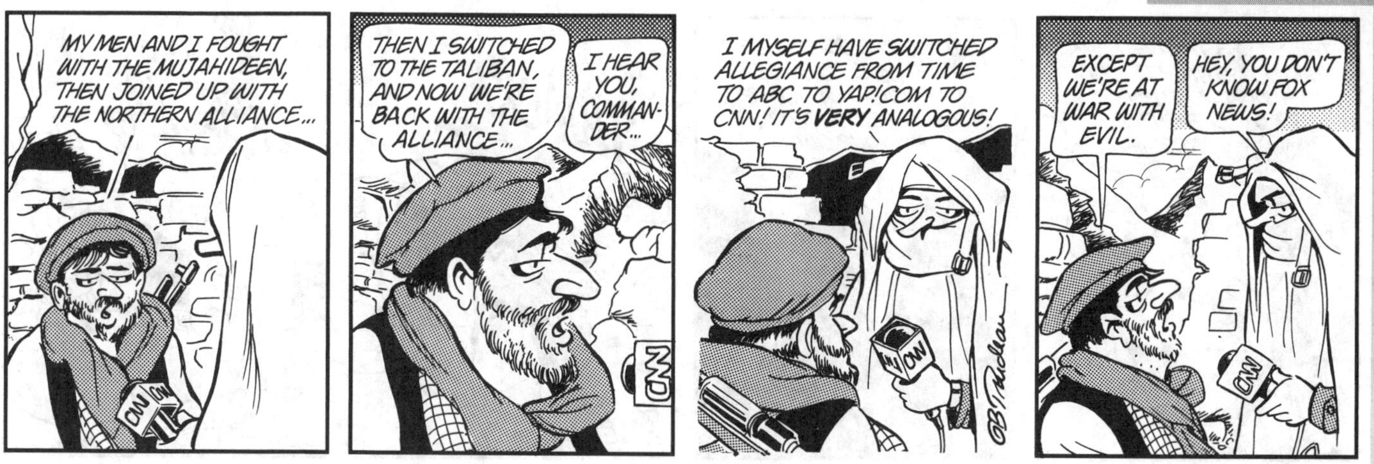
MY MEN AND I FOUGHT WITH THE MUJAHIDEEN, THEN JOINED UP WITH THE NORTHERN ALLIANCE...
CNN
THEN I SWITCHED TO THE TALIBAN, AND NOW WE'RE BACK WITH THE ALLIANCE...
I HEAR YOU, COMMAN-DER...
CNN
I MYSELF HAVE SWITCHED ALLEGIANCE FROM TIME TO ABC TO YAP!COM TO CNN! IT'S **VERY** ANALOGOUS!
CNN
GB Trudeau
EXCEPT WE'RE AT WAR WITH EVIL.
HEY, YOU DON'T KNOW FOX NEWS!
CNN

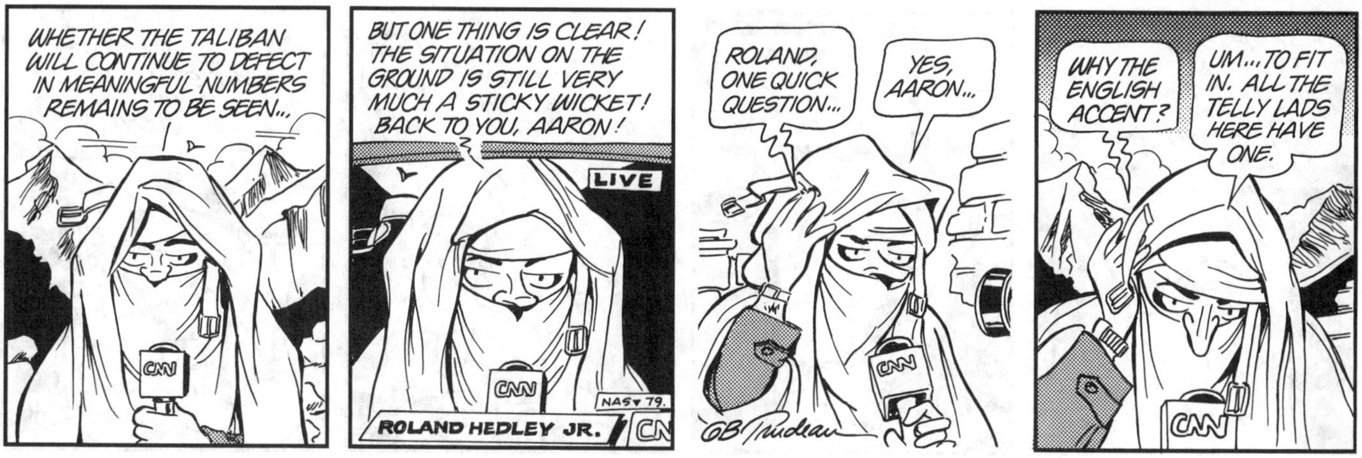
WHETHER THE TALIBAN WILL CONTINUE TO DEFECT IN MEANINGFUL NUMBERS REMAINS TO BE SEEN...
CNN
BUT ONE THING IS CLEAR! THE SITUATION ON THE GROUND IS STILL VERY MUCH A STICKY WICKET! BACK TO YOU, AARON!
LIVE
CNN
ROLAND HEDLEY JR.
ROLAND, ONE QUICK QUESTION...
YES, AARON...
CNN
GB Trudeau
WHY THE ENGLISH ACCENT?
UM... TO FIT IN. ALL THE TELLY LADS HERE HAVE ONE.
CNN

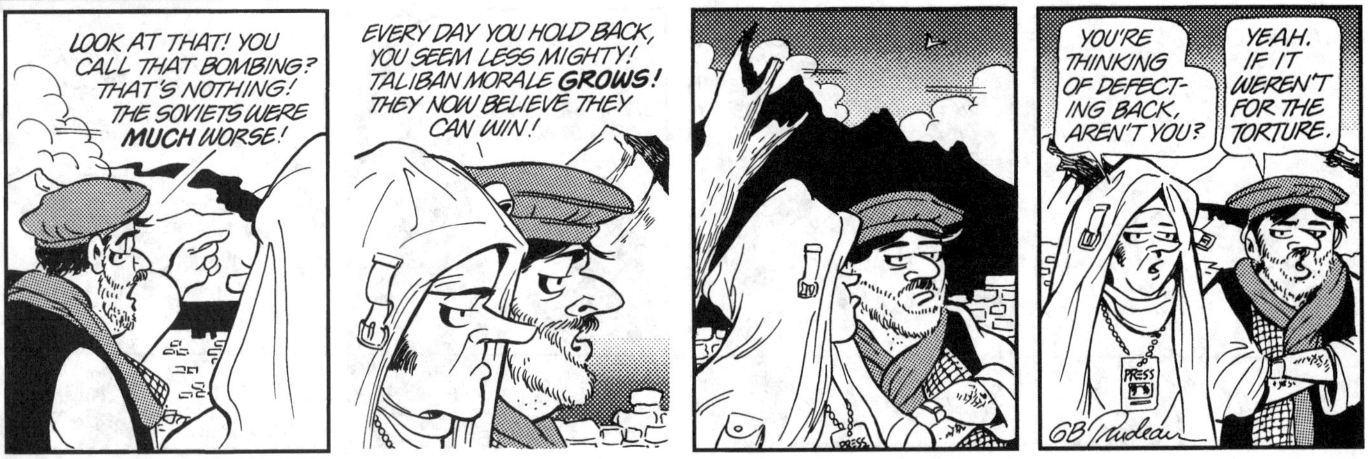
LOOK AT THAT! YOU CALL THAT BOMBING? THAT'S NOTHING! THE SOVIETS WERE **MUCH** WORSE!
EVERY DAY YOU HOLD BACK, YOU SEEM LESS MIGHTY! TALIBAN MORALE **GROWS**! THEY NOW BELIEVE THEY CAN WIN!
YOU'RE THINKING OF DEFECTING BACK, AREN'T YOU?
YEAH. IF IT WEREN'T FOR THE TORTURE.
PRESS
GB Trudeau

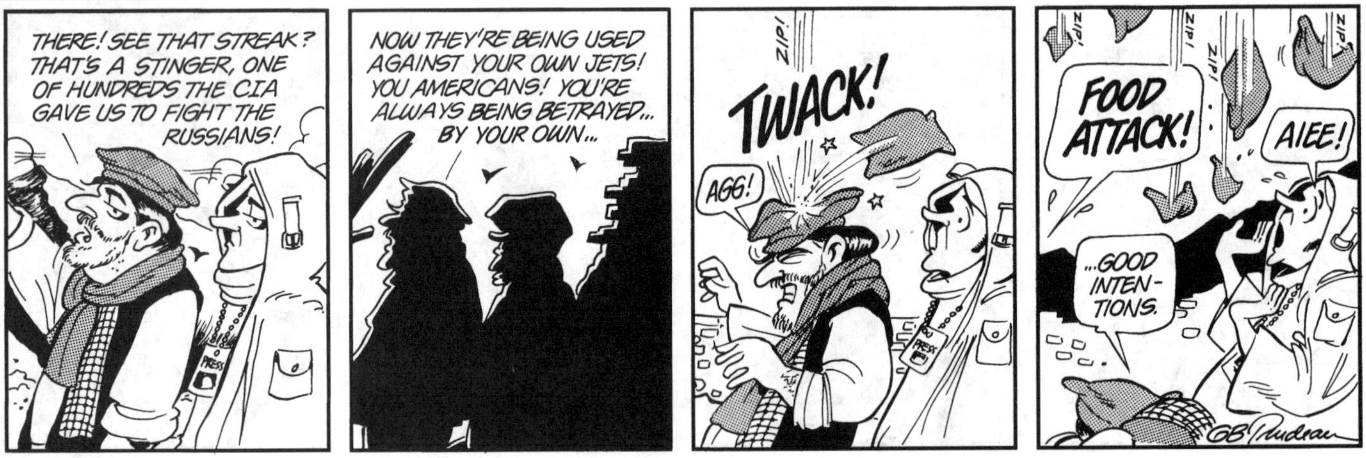
THERE! SEE THAT STREAK? THAT'S A STINGER, ONE OF HUNDREDS THE C.I.A. GAVE US TO FIGHT THE RUSSIANS!
PRESS
NOW THEY'RE BEING USED AGAINST YOUR OWN JETS! YOU AMERICANS! YOU'RE ALWAYS BEING BETRAYED... BY YOUR OWN...
ZIP!
TWACK!
AGG!
PRESS
ZIP!
ZIP!
ZIP!
ZIP!
FOOD ATTACK!
AIEE!
...GOOD INTENTIONS.
GB Trudeau

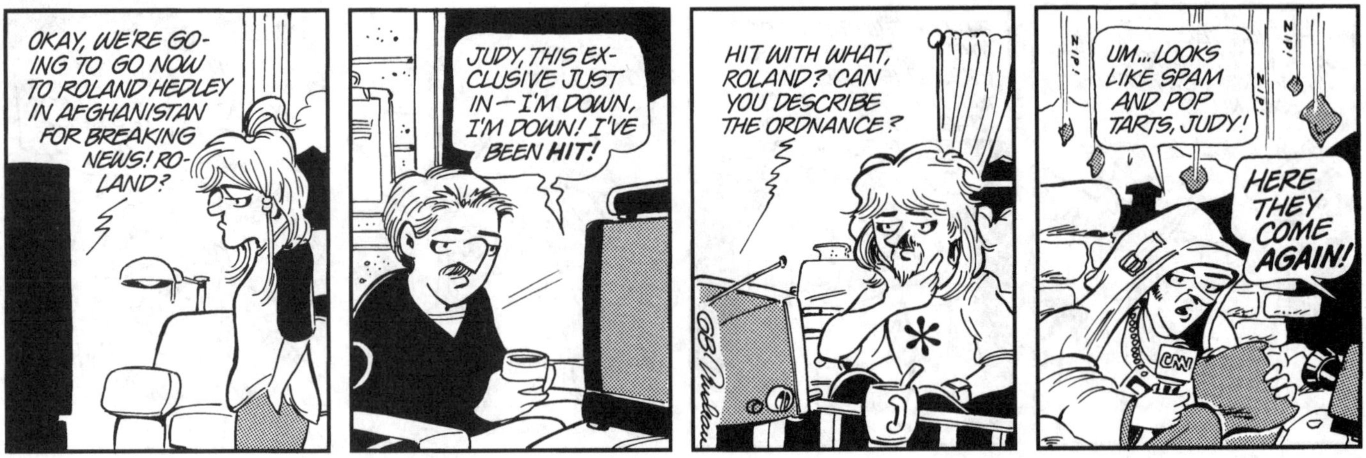
OKAY, WE'RE GOING TO GO NOW TO ROLAND HEDLEY IN AFGHANISTAN FOR BREAKING NEWS! ROLAND?
JUDY, THIS EXCLUSIVE JUST IN—I'M DOWN, I'M DOWN! I'VE BEEN **HIT**!
HIT WITH WHAT, ROLAND? CAN YOU DESCRIBE THE ORDNANCE?
GB Trudeau
ZIP!
ZIP!
ZIP!
UM...LOOKS LIKE SPAM AND POP TARTS, JUDY!
HERE THEY COME AGAIN!
CNN

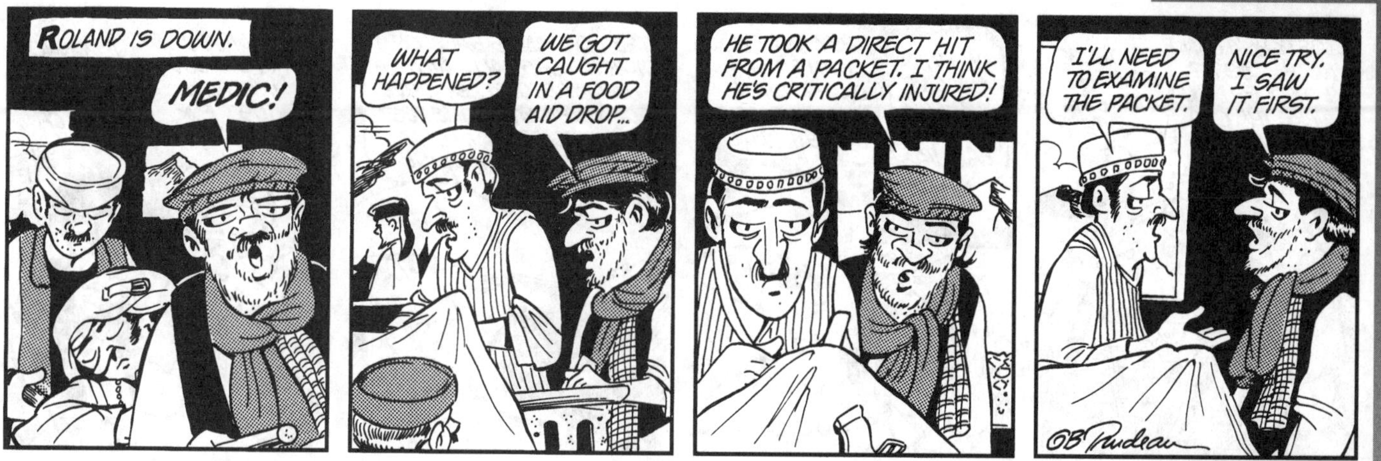
ROLAND IS DOWN.
MEDIC!
WHAT HAPPENED?
WE GOT CAUGHT IN A FOOD AID DROP...
HE TOOK A DIRECT HIT FROM A PACKET. I THINK HE'S CRITICALLY INJURED!
I'LL NEED TO EXAMINE THE PACKET.
NICE TRY. I SAW IT FIRST.
©B Trudeau

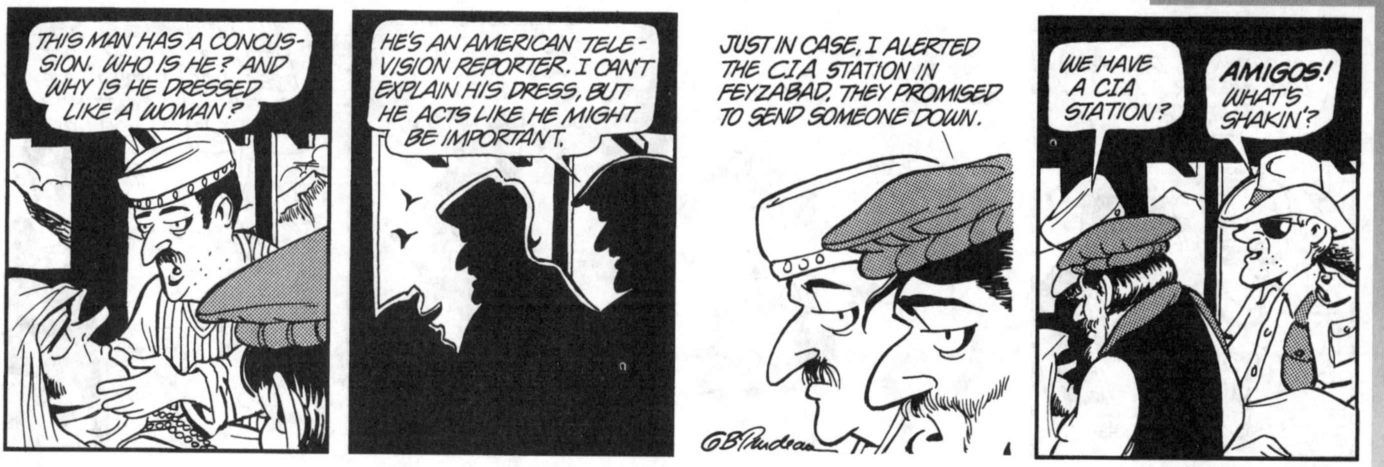
THIS MAN HAS A CONCUSSION. WHO IS HE? AND WHY IS HE DRESSED LIKE A WOMAN?
HE'S AN AMERICAN TELEVISION REPORTER. I CAN'T EXPLAIN HIS DRESS, BUT HE ACTS LIKE HE MIGHT BE IMPORTANT.
JUST IN CASE, I ALERTED THE CIA STATION IN FEYZABAD. THEY PROMISED TO SEND SOMEONE DOWN.
©B Trudeau
WE HAVE A CIA STATION?
AMIGOS! WHAT'S SHAKIN'?

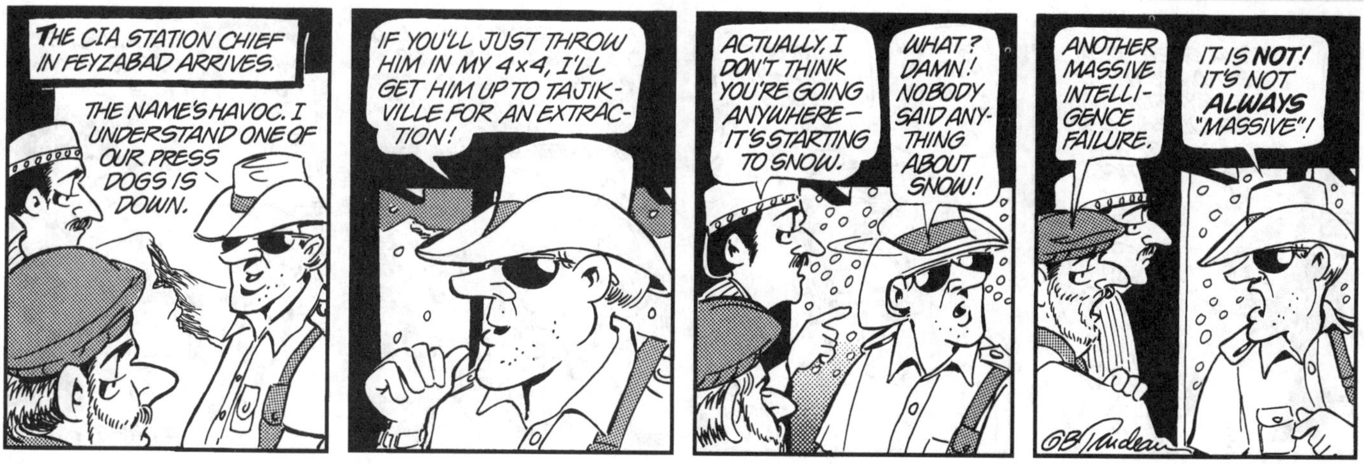
THE CIA STATION CHIEF IN FEYZABAD ARRIVES.
THE NAME'S HAVOC. I UNDERSTAND ONE OF OUR PRESS DOGS IS DOWN.
IF YOU'LL JUST THROW HIM IN MY 4×4, I'LL GET HIM UP TO TAJIKVILLE FOR AN EXTRACTION!
ACTUALLY, I DON'T THINK YOU'RE GOING ANYWHERE – IT'S STARTING TO SNOW.
WHAT? DAMN! NOBODY SAID ANYTHING ABOUT SNOW!
ANOTHER MASSIVE INTELLIGENCE FAILURE.
IT IS NOT! IT'S NOT ALWAYS "MASSIVE"!
©B Trudeau

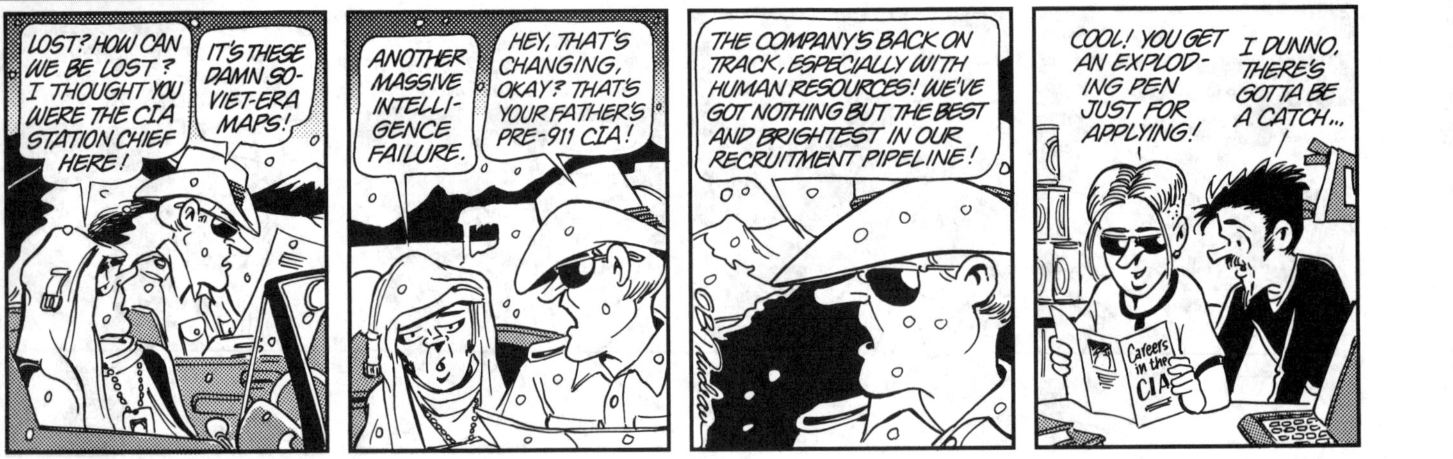
LOST? HOW CAN WE BE LOST? I THOUGHT YOU WERE THE CIA STATION CHIEF HERE!
IT'S THESE DAMN SO-VIET-ERA MAPS!
ANOTHER MASSIVE INTELLI-GENCE FAILURE.
HEY, THAT'S CHANGING, OKAY? THAT'S YOUR FATHER'S PRE-911 CIA!
THE COMPANY'S BACK ON TRACK, ESPECIALLY WITH HUMAN RESOURCES! WE'VE GOT NOTHING BUT THE BEST AND BRIGHTEST IN OUR RECRUITMENT PIPELINE!
COOL! YOU GET AN EXPLOD-ING PEN JUST FOR APPLYING!
I DUNNO. THERE'S GOTTA BE A CATCH...
Careers in the CIA

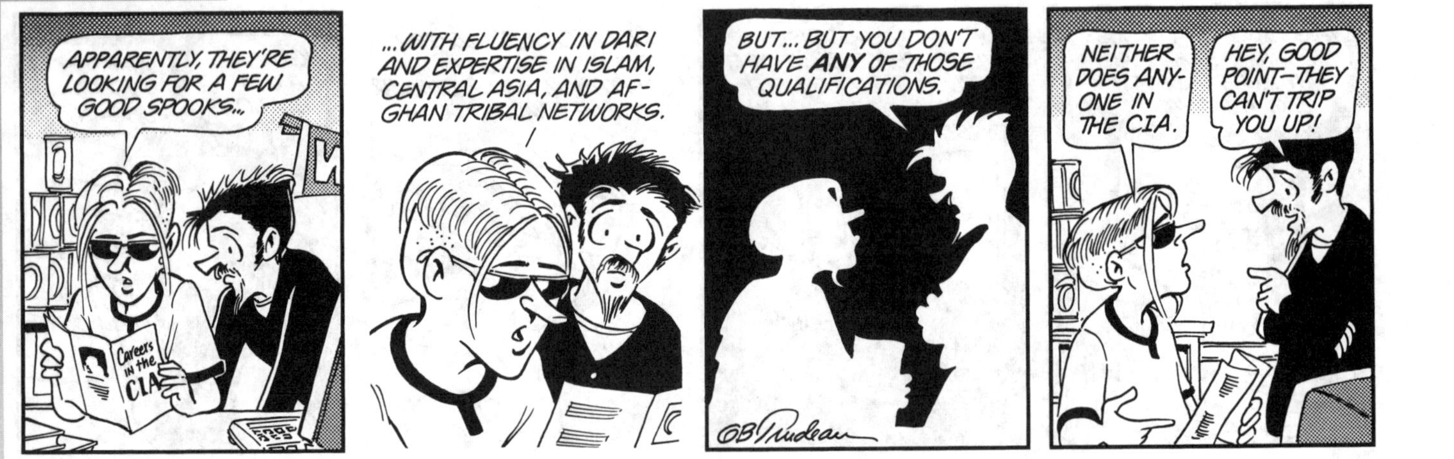
APPARENTLY, THEY'RE LOOKING FOR A FEW GOOD SPOOKS...
Careers in the CIA
...WITH FLUENCY IN DARI AND EXPERTISE IN ISLAM, CENTRAL ASIA, AND AF-GHAN TRIBAL NETWORKS.
BUT... BUT YOU DON'T HAVE ANY OF THOSE QUALIFICATIONS.
NEITHER DOES ANY-ONE IN THE CIA.
HEY, GOOD POINT—THEY CAN'T TRIP YOU UP!

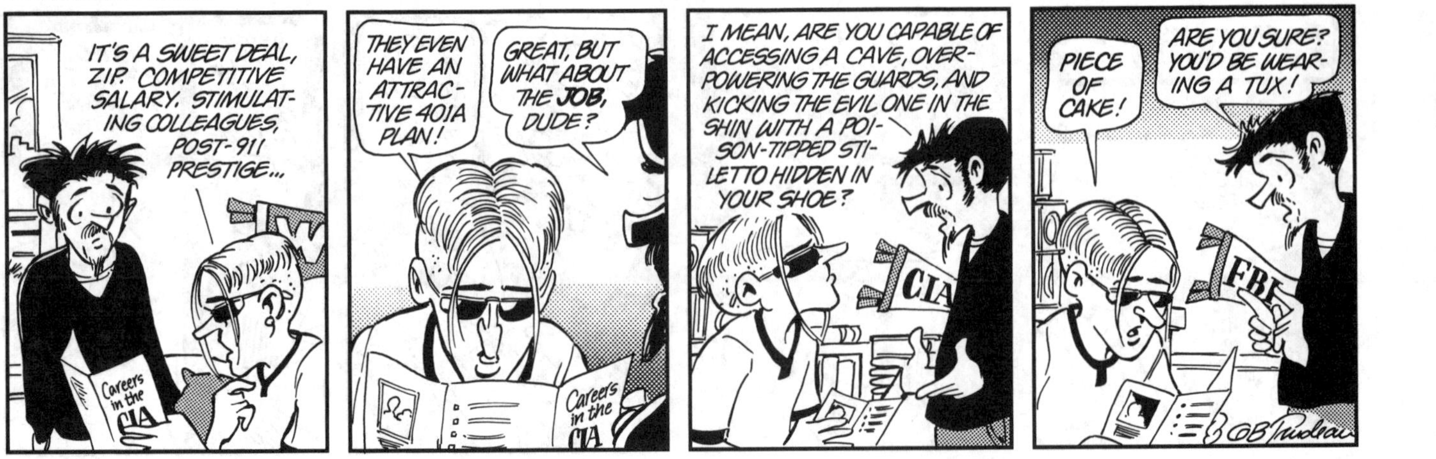
IT'S A SWEET DEAL, ZIP. COMPETITIVE SALARY. STIMULAT-ING COLLEAGUES, POST-911 PRESTIGE...
Careers in the CIA
THEY EVEN HAVE AN ATTRAC-TIVE 401A PLAN!
GREAT, BUT WHAT ABOUT THE JOB, DUDE?
Careers in the CIA
I MEAN, ARE YOU CAPABLE OF ACCESSING A CAVE, OVER-POWERING THE GUARDS, AND KICKING THE EVIL ONE IN THE SHIN WITH A POI-SON-TIPPED STI-LETTO HIDDEN IN YOUR SHOE?
CIA
PIECE OF CAKE!
ARE YOU SURE? YOU'D BE WEAR-ING A TUX!
FBI

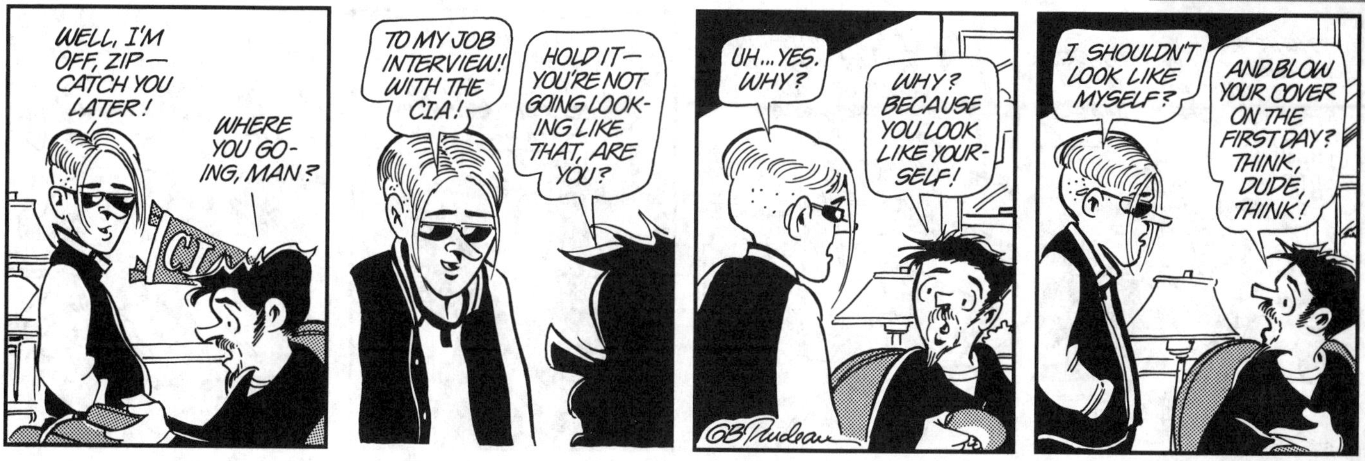
WELL, I'M OFF, ZIP— CATCH YOU LATER!
WHERE YOU GO-ING, MAN?
TO MY JOB INTERVIEW! WITH THE CIA!
HOLD IT— YOU'RE NOT GOING LOOK-ING LIKE THAT, ARE YOU?
UH... YES. WHY?
WHY? BECAUSE YOU LOOK LIKE YOUR-SELF!
I SHOULDN'T LOOK LIKE MYSELF?
AND BLOW YOUR COVER ON THE FIRST DAY? THINK, DUDE, THINK!
©B Trudeau

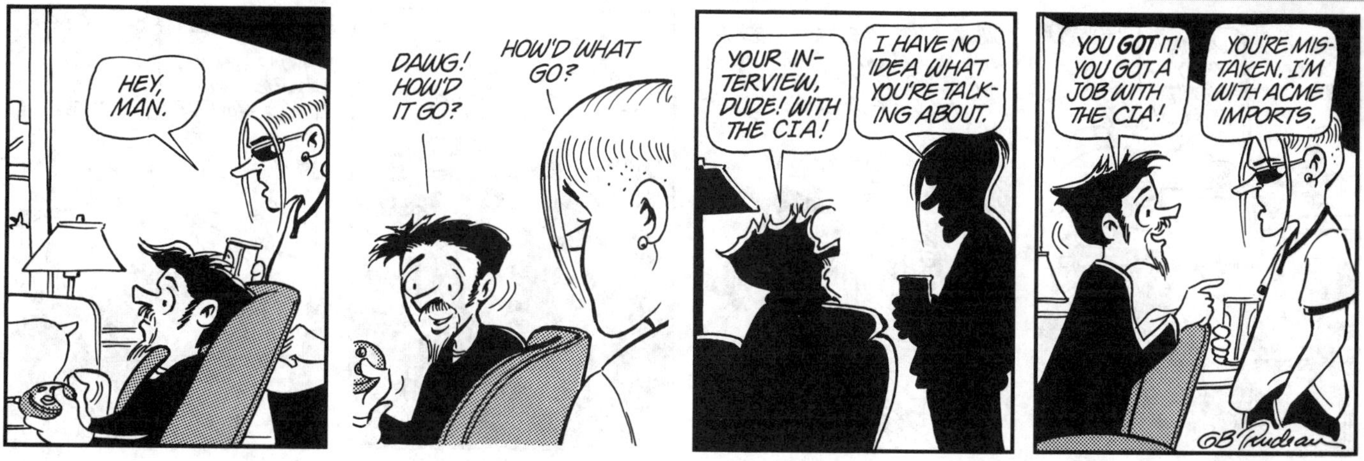
HEY, MAN.
DAWG! HOW'D IT GO?
HOW'D WHAT GO?
YOUR IN-TERVIEW, DUDE! WITH THE CIA!
I HAVE NO IDEA WHAT YOU'RE TALK-ING ABOUT.
YOU GOT IT! YOU GOT A JOB WITH THE CIA!
YOU'RE MIS-TAKEN. I'M WITH ACME IMPORTS.
©B Trudeau

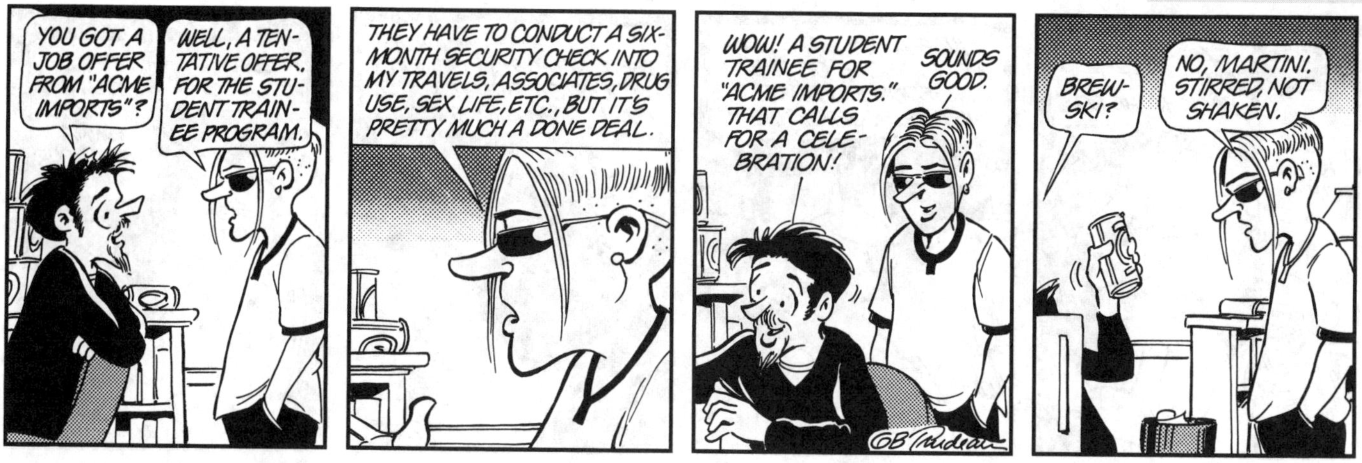
YOU GOT A JOB OFFER FROM "ACME IMPORTS"?
WELL, A TEN-TATIVE OFFER. FOR THE STU-DENT TRAIN-EE PROGRAM.
THEY HAVE TO CONDUCT A SIX-MONTH SECURITY CHECK INTO MY TRAVELS, ASSOCIATES, DRUG USE, SEX LIFE, ETC., BUT IT'S PRETTY MUCH A DONE DEAL.
WOW! A STUDENT TRAINEE FOR "ACME IMPORTS." THAT CALLS FOR A CELE-BRATION!
SOUNDS GOOD.
BREW-SKI?
NO, MARTINI. STIRRED, NOT SHAKEN.
©B Trudeau

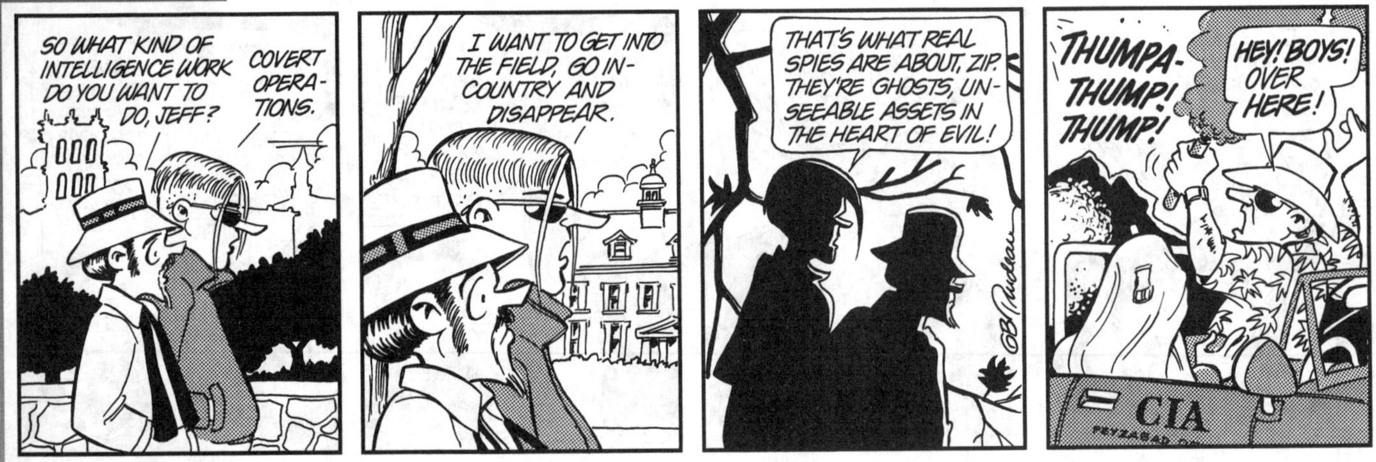
SO WHAT KIND OF INTELLIGENCE WORK DO YOU WANT TO DO, JEFF?
COVERT OPERATIONS.
I WANT TO GET INTO THE FIELD, GO IN-COUNTRY AND DISAPPEAR.
THAT'S WHAT REAL SPIES ARE ABOUT, ZIP. THEY'RE GHOSTS, UN-SEEABLE ASSETS IN THE HEART OF EVIL!
THUMPA-THUMP! THUMP!
HEY! BOYS! OVER HERE!
CIA

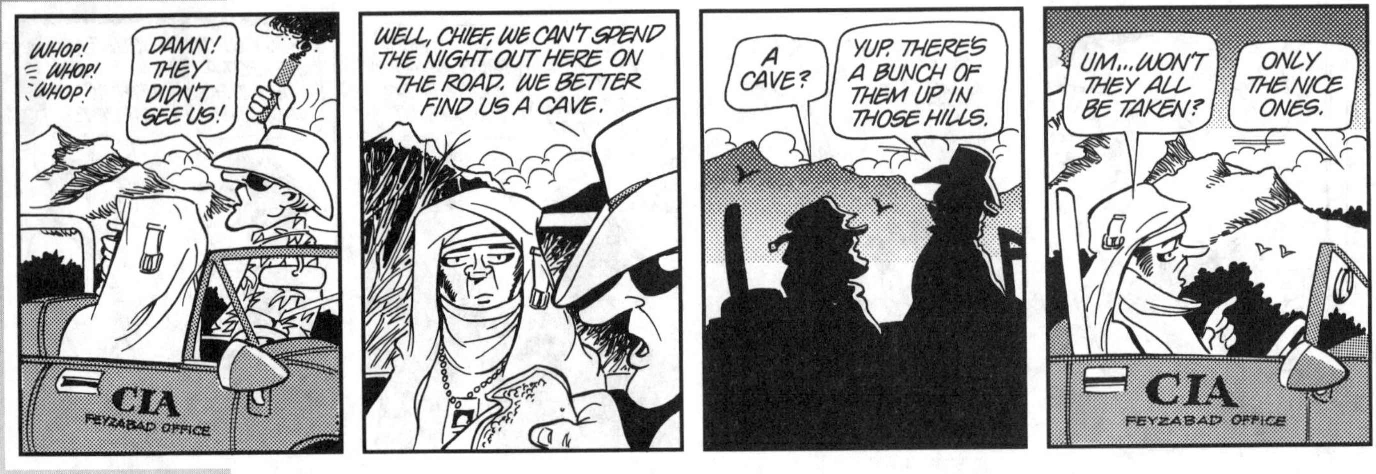
WHOP! WHOP! WHOP!
DAMN! THEY DIDN'T SEE US!
CIA
FEYZABAD OFFICE
WELL, CHIEF, WE CAN'T SPEND THE NIGHT OUT HERE ON THE ROAD. WE BETTER FIND US A CAVE.
A CAVE?
YUP. THERE'S A BUNCH OF THEM UP IN THOSE HILLS.
UM... WON'T THEY ALL BE TAKEN?
ONLY THE NICE ONES.
CIA
FEYZABAD OFFICE

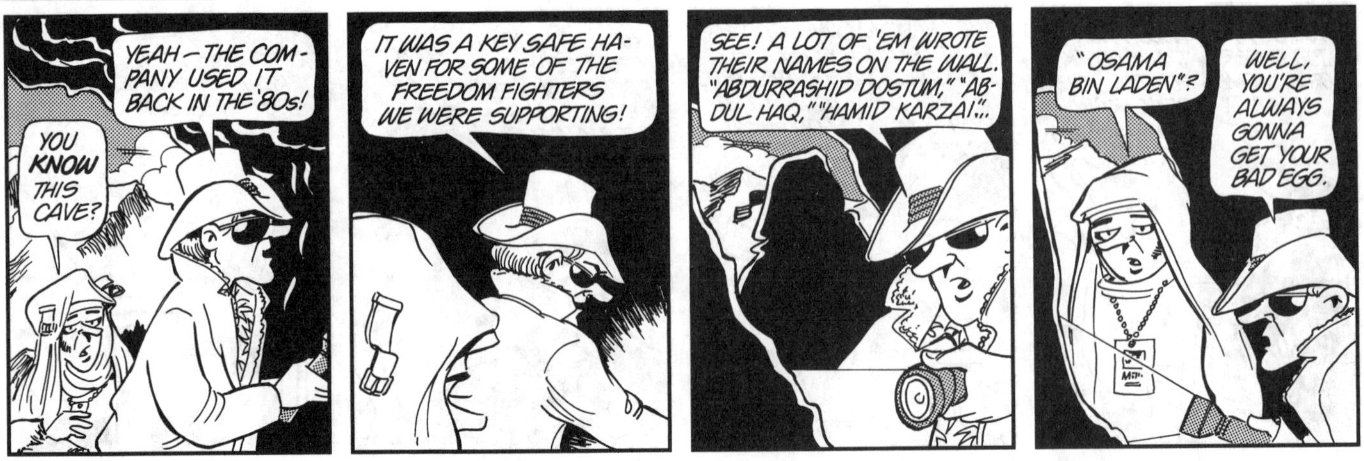
YOU KNOW THIS CAVE?
YEAH – THE COMPANY USED IT BACK IN THE '80s!
IT WAS A KEY SAFE HAVEN FOR SOME OF THE FREEDOM FIGHTERS WE WERE SUPPORTING!
SEE! A LOT OF 'EM WROTE THEIR NAMES ON THE WALL. "ABDURRASHID DOSTUM," "ABDUL HAQ," "HAMID KARZAI"...
"OSAMA BIN LADEN"?
WELL, YOU'RE ALWAYS GONNA GET YOUR BAD EGG.

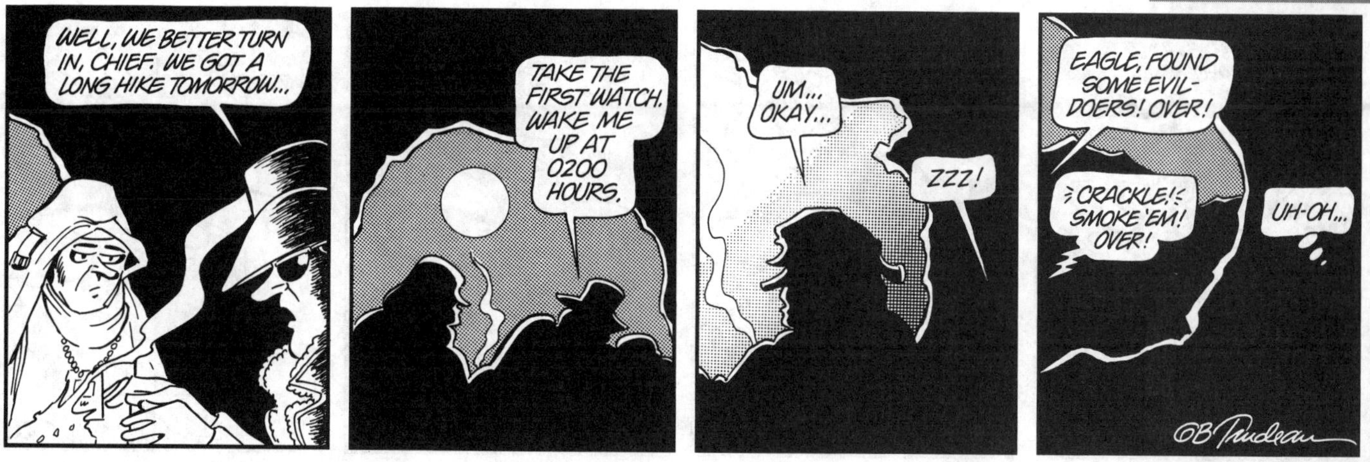
WELL, WE BETTER TURN IN, CHIEF. WE GOT A LONG HIKE TOMORROW...
TAKE THE FIRST WATCH. WAKE ME UP AT 0200 HOURS.
UM... OKAY...
ZZZ!
EAGLE, FOUND SOME EVIL-DOERS! OVER!
CRACKLE! SMOKE 'EM! OVER!
UH-OH...
©B Trudeau

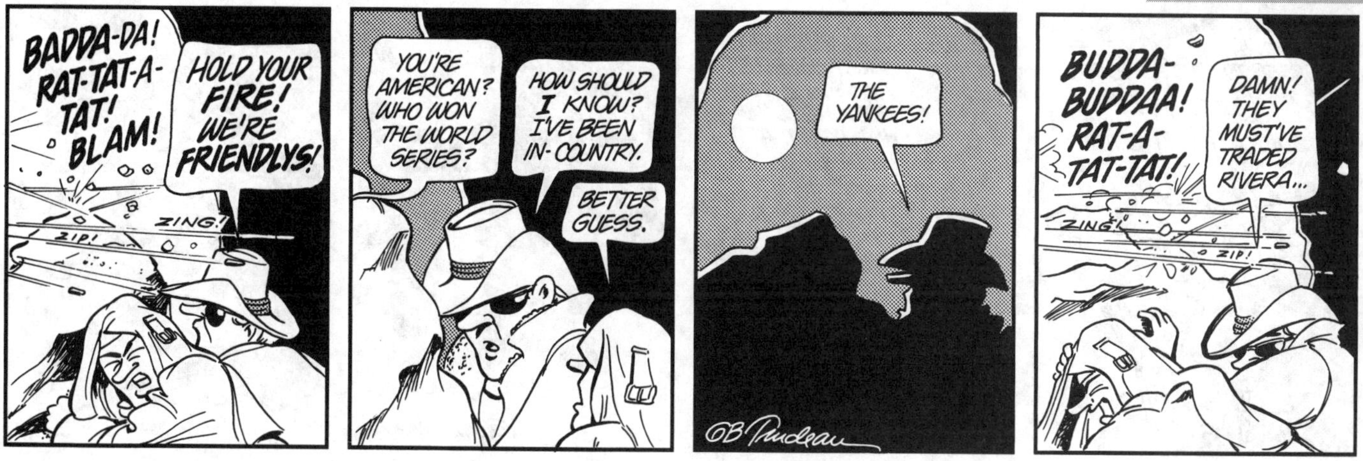
BADDA-DA! RAT-TAT-A-TAT! BLAM!
HOLD YOUR FIRE! WE'RE FRIENDLYS!
ZIP!
ZING!
YOU'RE AMERICAN? WHO WON THE WORLD SERIES?
HOW SHOULD I KNOW? I'VE BEEN IN-COUNTRY.
BETTER GUESS.
THE YANKEES!
©B Trudeau
BUDDA-BUDDAA! RAT-A-TAT-TAT!
DAMN! THEY MUST'VE TRADED RIVERA...
ZING!
ZIP!

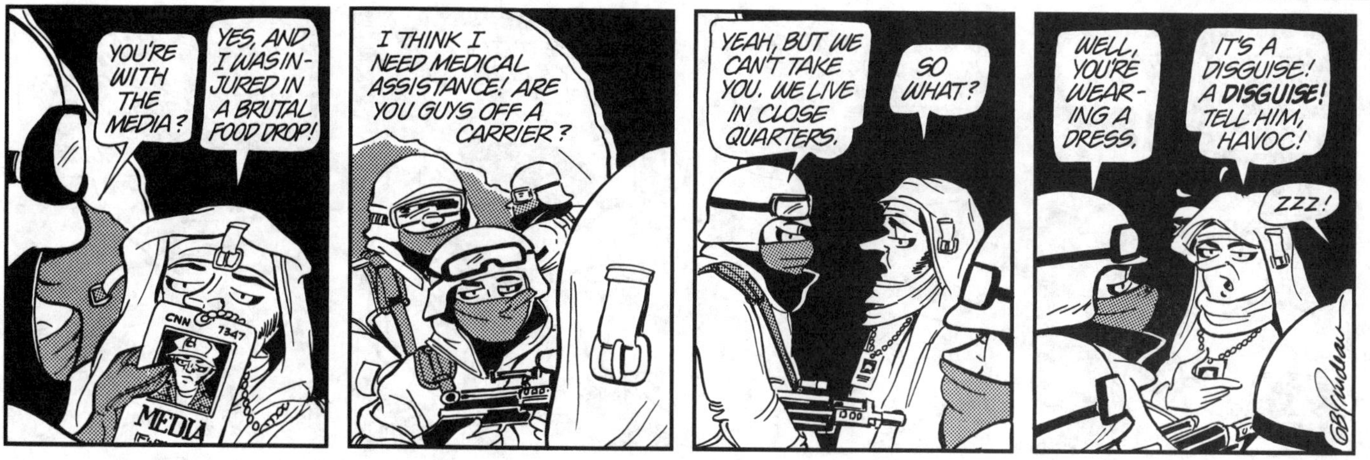
YOU'RE WITH THE MEDIA?
YES, AND I WAS INJURED IN A BRUTAL FOOD DROP!
CNN
7347
MEDIA
I THINK I NEED MEDICAL ASSISTANCE! ARE YOU GUYS OFF A CARRIER?
YEAH, BUT WE CAN'T TAKE YOU. WE LIVE IN CLOSE QUARTERS.
SO WHAT?
WELL, YOU'RE WEARING A DRESS.
IT'S A DISGUISE! A DISGUISE! TELL HIM, HAVOC!
ZZZ!
©B Trudeau

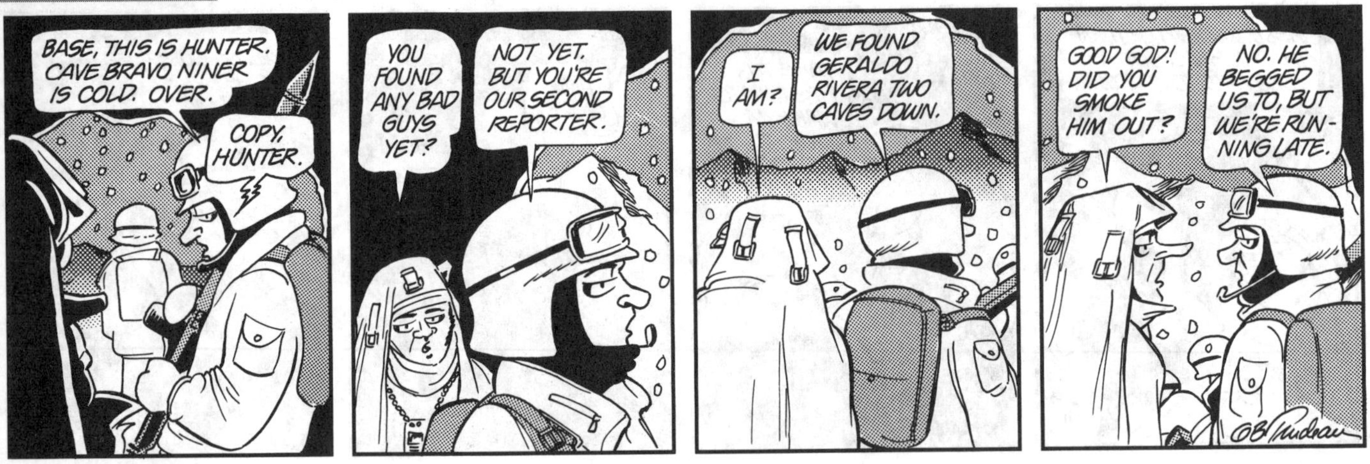
BASE, THIS IS HUNTER. CAVE BRAVO NINER IS COLD. OVER.
COPY, HUNTER.
YOU FOUND ANY BAD GUYS YET?
NOT YET. BUT YOU'RE OUR SECOND REPORTER.
I AM?
WE FOUND GERALDO RIVERA TWO CAVES DOWN.
GOOD GOD! DID YOU SMOKE HIM OUT?
NO. HE BEGGED US TO, BUT WE'RE RUNNING LATE.
©B Trudeau

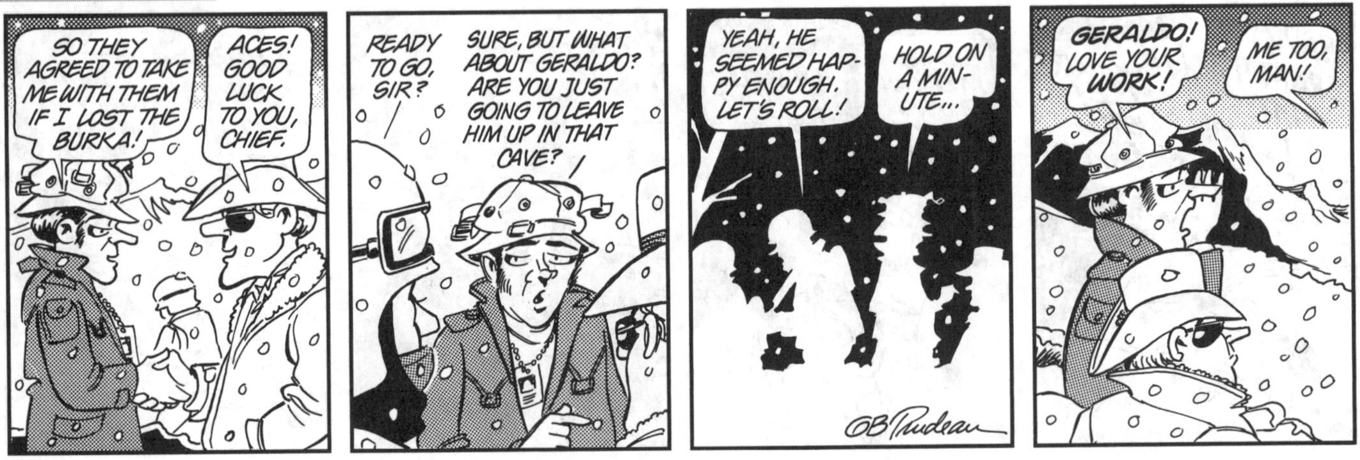
SO THEY AGREED TO TAKE ME WITH THEM IF I LOST THE BURKA!
ACES! GOOD LUCK TO YOU, CHIEF.
READY TO GO, SIR?
SURE, BUT WHAT ABOUT GERALDO? ARE YOU JUST GOING TO LEAVE HIM UP IN THAT CAVE?
YEAH, HE SEEMED HAPPY ENOUGH. LET'S ROLL!
HOLD ON A MINUTE...
©B Trudeau
GERALDO! LOVE YOUR WORK!
ME TOO, MAN!

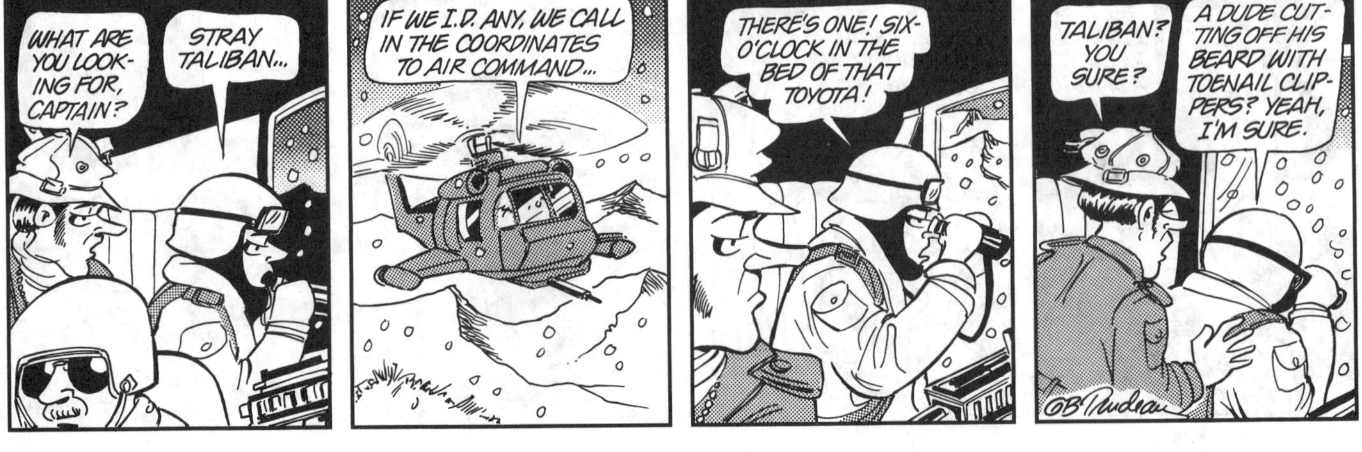
WHAT ARE YOU LOOKING FOR, CAPTAIN?
STRAY TALIBAN...
IF WE I.D. ANY, WE CALL IN THE COORDINATES TO AIR COMMAND...
THERE'S ONE! SIX-O'CLOCK IN THE BED OF THAT TOYOTA!
TALIBAN? YOU SURE?
A DUDE CUTTING OFF HIS BEARD WITH TOENAIL CLIPPERS? YEAH, I'M SURE.
©B Trudeau

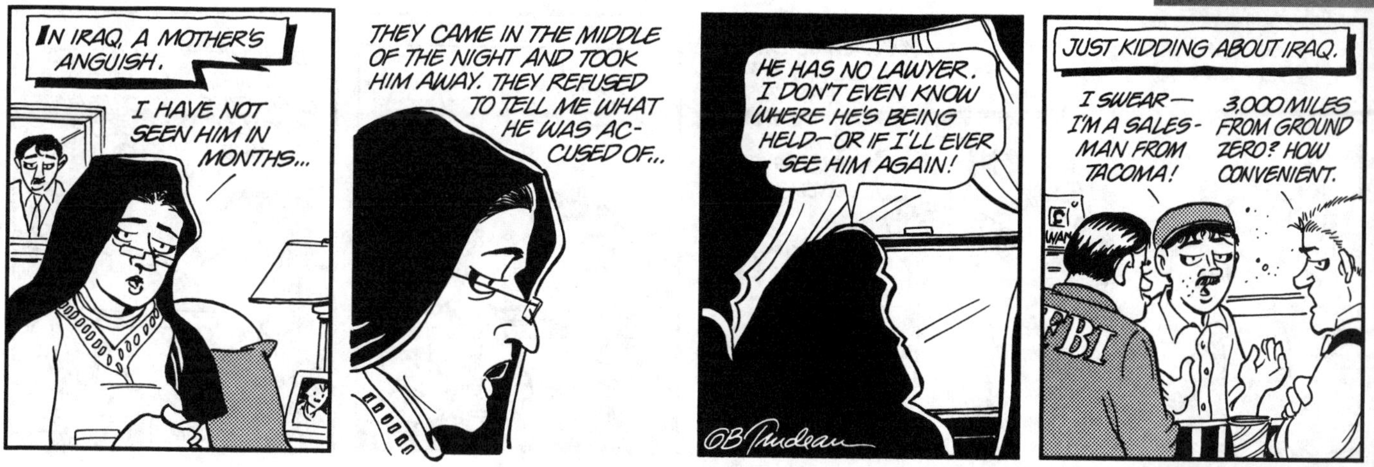
IN IRAQ, A MOTHER'S ANGUISH.
I HAVE NOT SEEN HIM IN MONTHS...
THEY CAME IN THE MIDDLE OF THE NIGHT AND TOOK HIM AWAY. THEY REFUSED TO TELL ME WHAT HE WAS ACCUSED OF...
HE HAS NO LAWYER. I DON'T EVEN KNOW WHERE HE'S BEING HELD—OR IF I'LL EVER SEE HIM AGAIN!
GB Trudeau
JUST KIDDING ABOUT IRAQ.
I SWEAR— I'M A SALESMAN FROM TACOMA!
3,000 MILES FROM GROUND ZERO? HOW CONVENIENT.
FBI

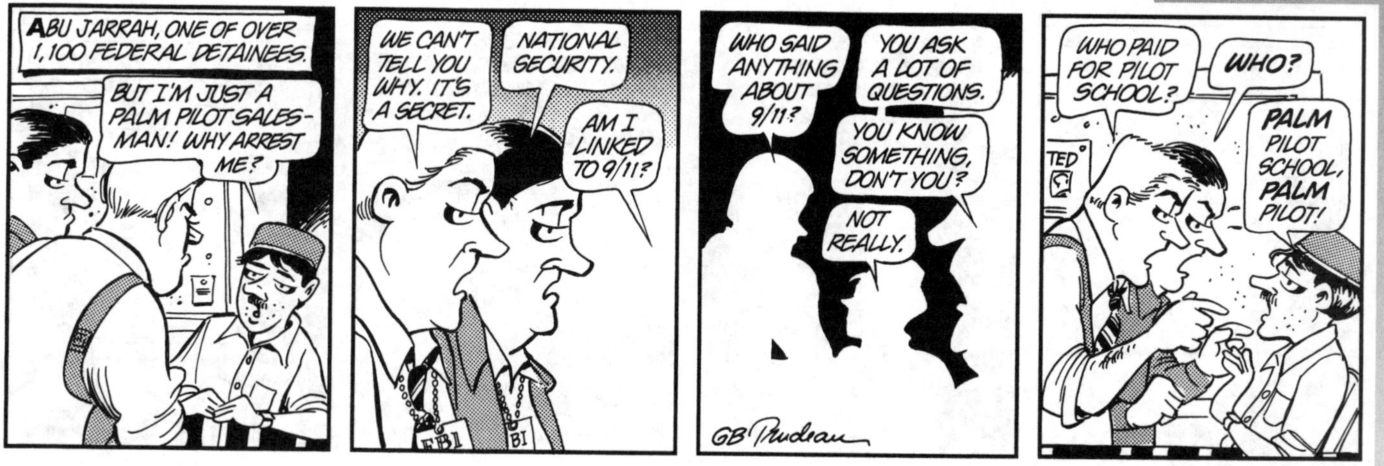
ABU JARRAH, ONE OF OVER 1,100 FEDERAL DETAINEES.
BUT I'M JUST A PALM PILOT SALESMAN! WHY ARREST ME?
WE CAN'T TELL YOU WHY. IT'S A SECRET.
NATIONAL SECURITY.
AM I LINKED TO 9/11?
FBI
WHO SAID ANYTHING ABOUT 9/11?
YOU ASK A LOT OF QUESTIONS.
YOU KNOW SOMETHING, DON'T YOU?
NOT REALLY.
GB Trudeau
WHO PAID FOR PILOT SCHOOL?
WHO?
PALM PILOT SCHOOL, PALM PILOT!

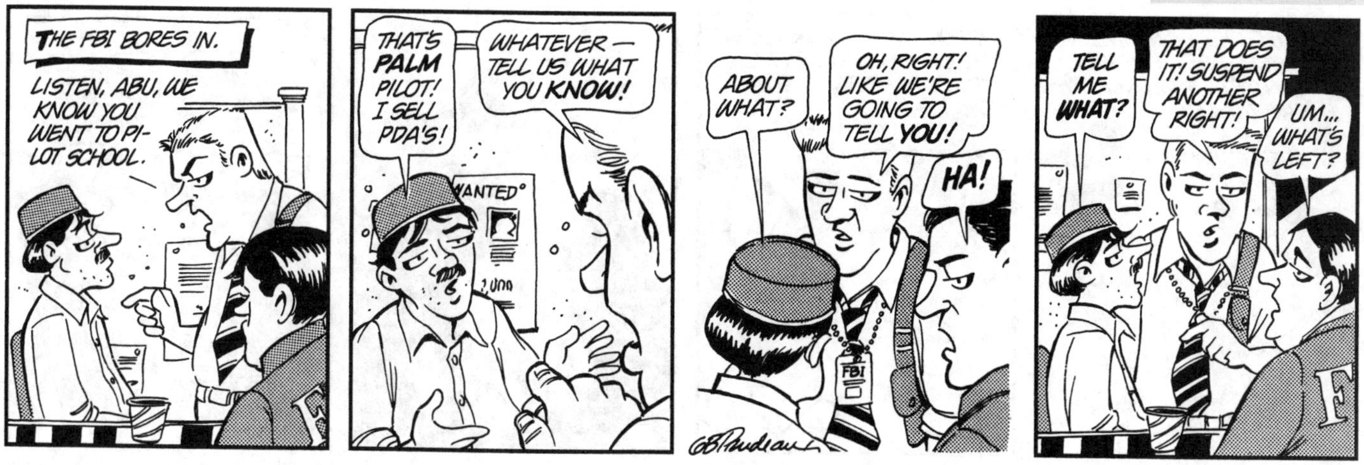
THE FBI BORES IN.
LISTEN, ABU, WE KNOW YOU WENT TO PILOT SCHOOL.
THAT'S PALM PILOT! I SELL PDA'S!
WHATEVER— TELL US WHAT YOU KNOW!
WANTED
ABOUT WHAT?
OH, RIGHT! LIKE WE'RE GOING TO TELL YOU!
HA!
FBI
GB Trudeau
TELL ME WHAT?
THAT DOES IT! SUSPEND ANOTHER RIGHT!
UM... WHAT'S LEFT?

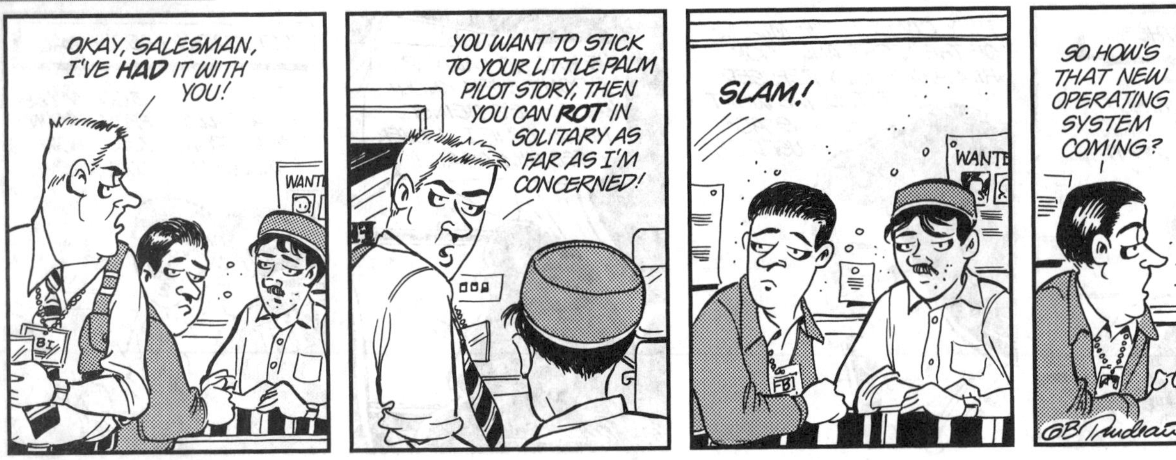

OKAY, SALESMAN, I'VE **HAD** IT WITH YOU!
YOU WANT TO STICK TO YOUR LITTLE PALM PILOT STORY, THEN YOU CAN **ROT** IN SOLITARY AS FAR AS I'M CONCERNED!
SLAM!
SO HOW'S THAT NEW OPERATING SYSTEM COMING?
OH, PLEASE. LIKE I DON'T KNOW WHAT A "GOOD COP" IS?

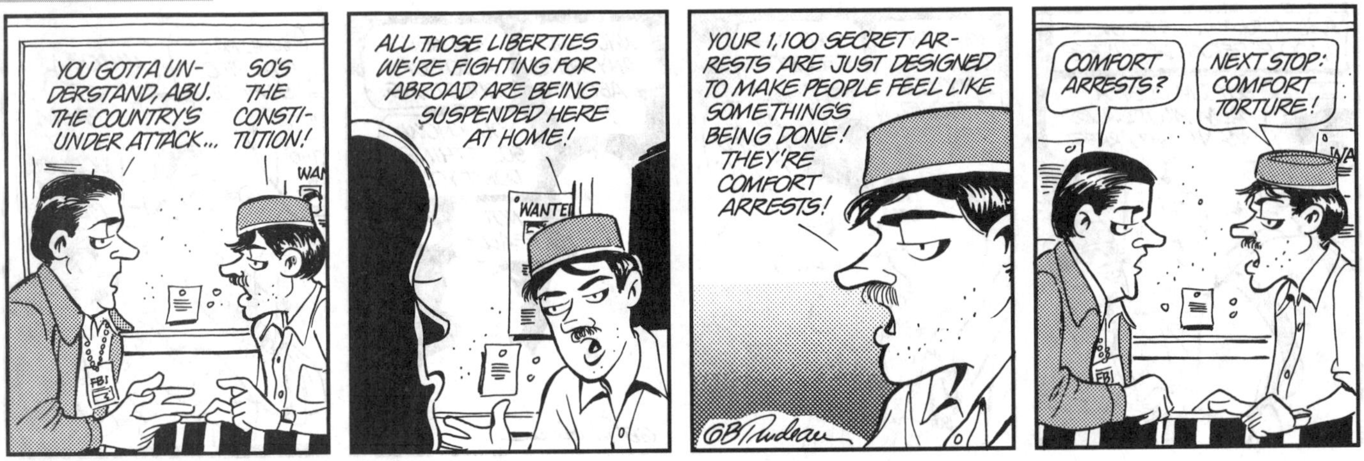

YOU GOTTA UNDERSTAND, ABU. THE COUNTRY'S UNDER ATTACK...
SO'S THE CONSTITUTION!
ALL THOSE LIBERTIES WE'RE FIGHTING FOR ABROAD ARE BEING SUSPENDED HERE AT HOME!
YOUR 1,100 SECRET ARRESTS ARE JUST DESIGNED TO MAKE PEOPLE FEEL LIKE SOMETHING'S BEING DONE! THEY'RE COMFORT ARRESTS!
COMFORT ARRESTS?
NEXT STOP: COMFORT TORTURE!

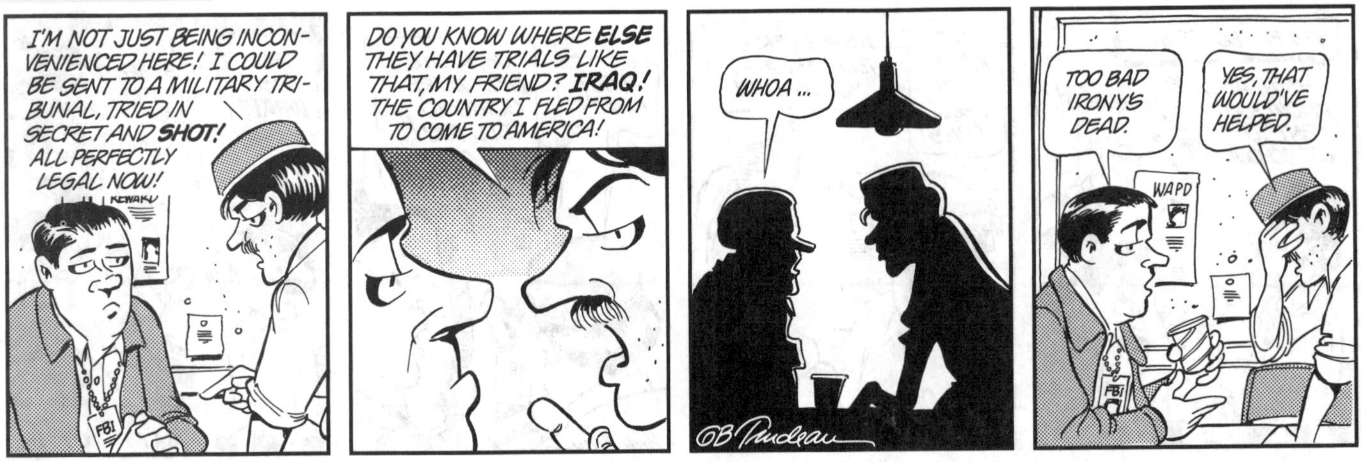

I'M NOT JUST BEING INCONVENIENCED HERE! I COULD BE SENT TO A MILITARY TRIBUNAL, TRIED IN SECRET AND **SHOT!** ALL PERFECTLY LEGAL NOW!
REWARD
DO YOU KNOW WHERE **ELSE** THEY HAVE TRIALS LIKE THAT, MY FRIEND? **IRAQ!** THE COUNTRY I FLED FROM TO COME TO AMERICA!
WHOA ...
TOO BAD IRONY'S DEAD.
YES, THAT WOULD'VE HELPED.
WAPD

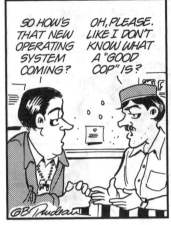

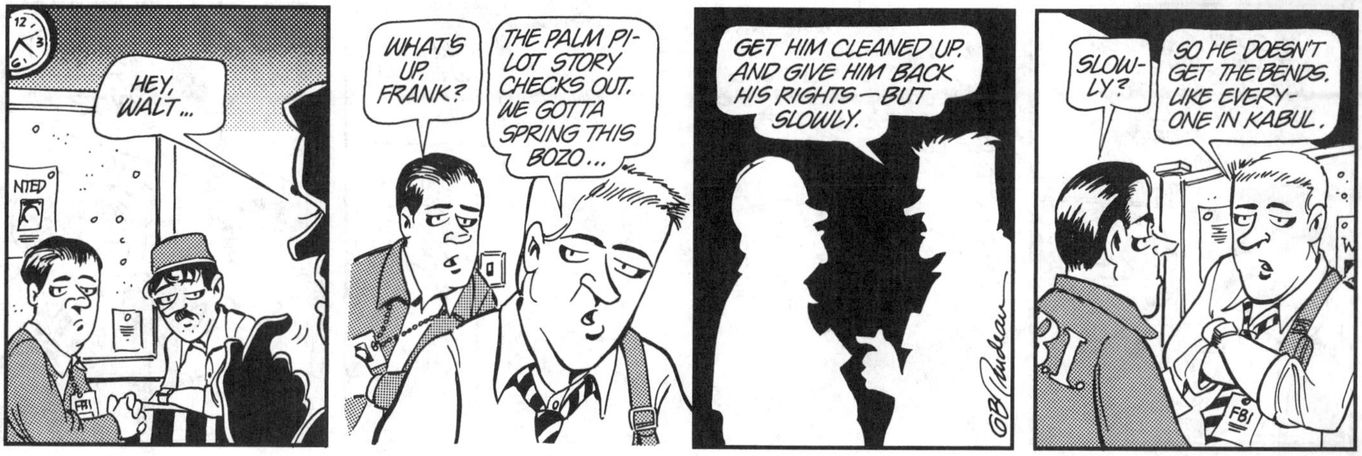
HEY, WALT...
WHAT'S UP, FRANK?
THE PALM PILOT STORY CHECKS OUT. WE GOTTA SPRING THIS BOZO...
GET HIM CLEANED UP, AND GIVE HIM BACK HIS RIGHTS—BUT SLOWLY.
SLOWLY?
SO HE DOESN'T GET THE BENDS, LIKE EVERYONE IN KABUL.

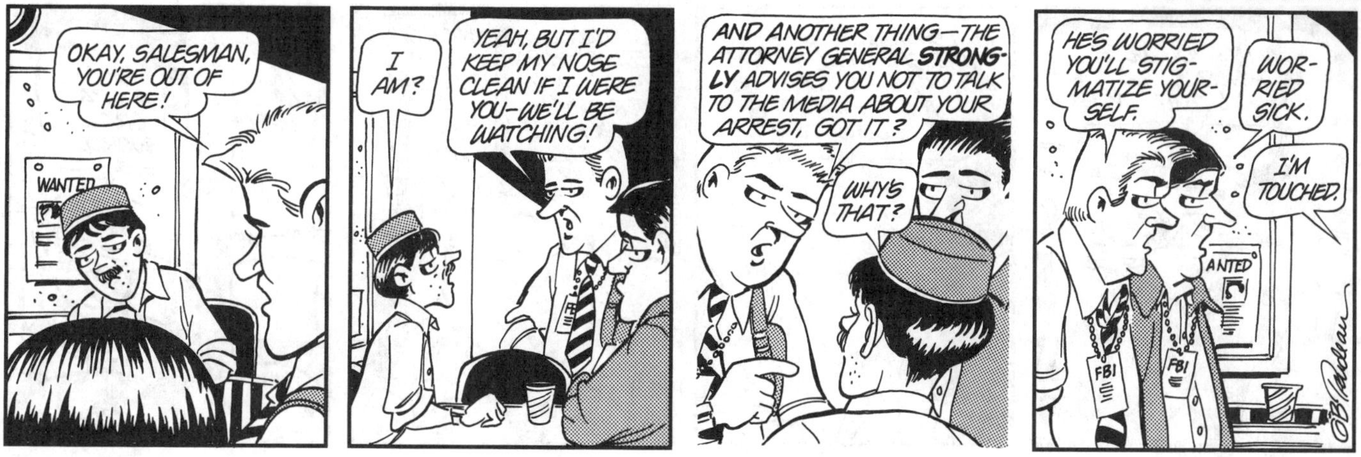
OKAY, SALESMAN, YOU'RE OUT OF HERE!
I AM?
YEAH, BUT I'D KEEP MY NOSE CLEAN IF I WERE YOU—WE'LL BE WATCHING!
AND ANOTHER THING—THE ATTORNEY GENERAL **STRONGLY** ADVISES YOU NOT TO TALK TO THE MEDIA ABOUT YOUR ARREST, GOT IT?
WHY'S THAT?
HE'S WORRIED YOU'LL STIGMATIZE YOURSELF.
WORRIED SICK.
I'M TOUCHED.

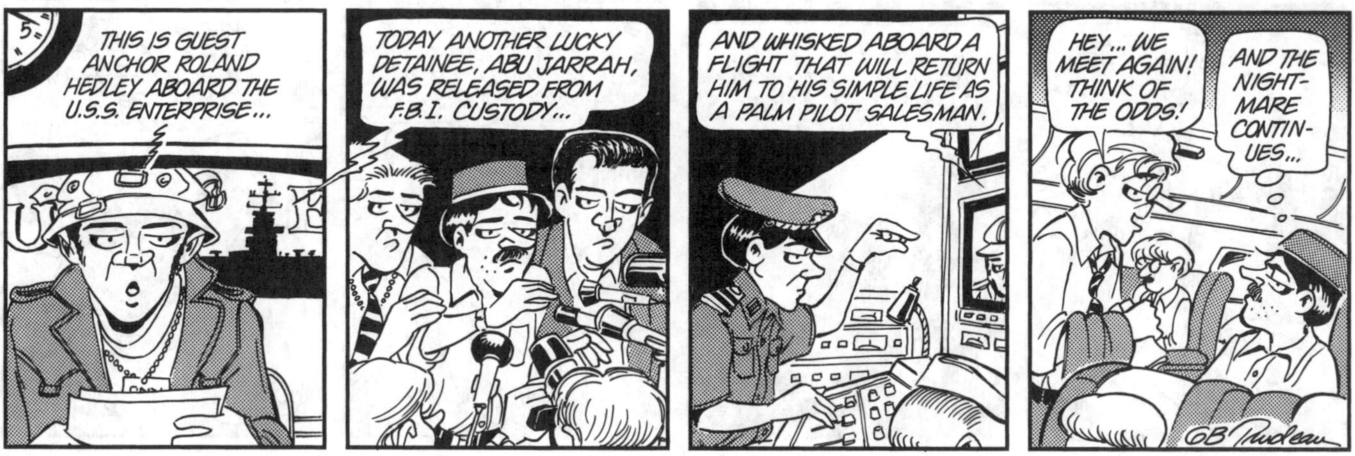
THIS IS GUEST ANCHOR ROLAND HEDLEY ABOARD THE U.S.S. ENTERPRISE...
TODAY ANOTHER LUCKY DETAINEE, ABU JARRAH, WAS RELEASED FROM F.B.I. CUSTODY...
AND WHISKED ABOARD A FLIGHT THAT WILL RETURN HIM TO HIS SIMPLE LIFE AS A PALM PILOT SALESMAN.
HEY... WE MEET AGAIN! THINK OF THE ODDS!
AND THE NIGHTMARE CONTINUES...

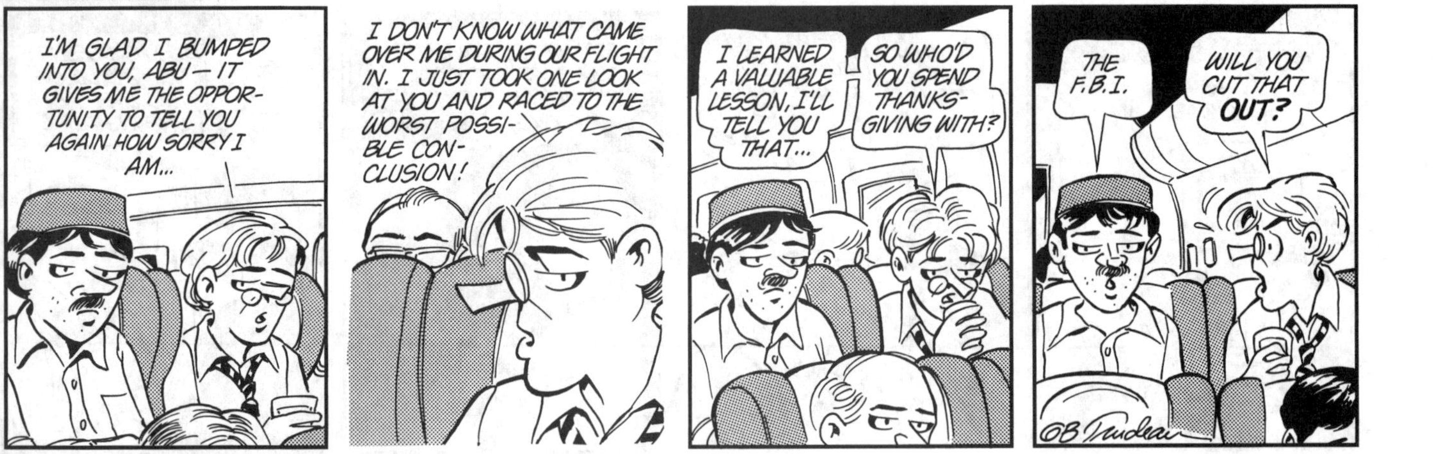
I'M GLAD I BUMPED INTO YOU, ABU— IT GIVES ME THE OPPORTUNITY TO TELL YOU AGAIN HOW SORRY I AM...
I DON'T KNOW WHAT CAME OVER ME DURING OUR FLIGHT IN. I JUST TOOK ONE LOOK AT YOU AND RACED TO THE WORST POSSIBLE CONCLUSION!
I LEARNED A VALUABLE LESSON, I'LL TELL YOU THAT...
SO WHO'D YOU SPEND THANKSGIVING WITH?
THE F.B.I.
WILL YOU CUT THAT **OUT?**

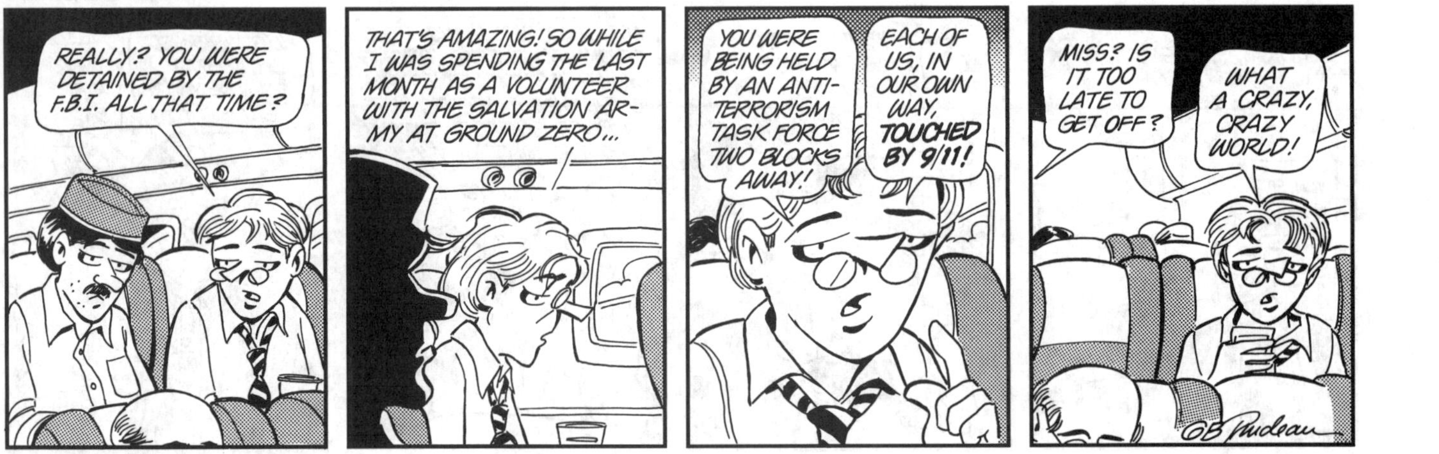
REALLY? YOU WERE DETAINED BY THE F.B.I. ALL THAT TIME?
THAT'S AMAZING! SO WHILE I WAS SPENDING THE LAST MONTH AS A VOLUNTEER WITH THE SALVATION ARMY AT GROUND ZERO...
YOU WERE BEING HELD BY AN ANTI-TERRORISM TASK FORCE TWO BLOCKS AWAY!
EACH OF US, IN OUR OWN WAY, **TOUCHED BY 9/11!**
MISS? IS IT TOO LATE TO GET OFF?
WHAT A CRAZY, CRAZY WORLD!

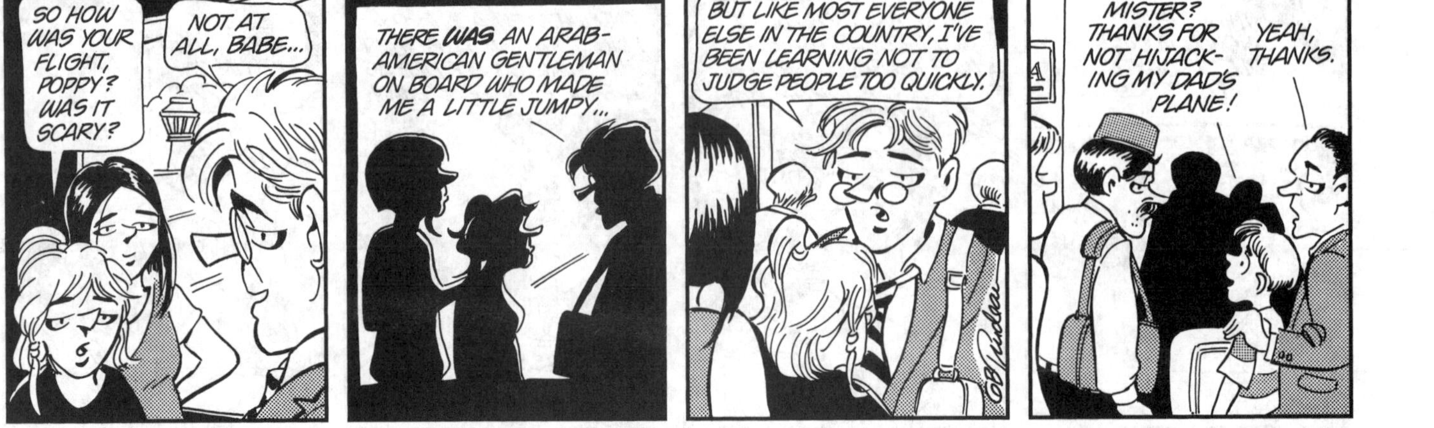
SO HOW WAS YOUR FLIGHT, POPPY? WAS IT SCARY?
NOT AT ALL, BABE...
THERE **WAS** AN ARAB-AMERICAN GENTLEMAN ON BOARD WHO MADE ME A LITTLE JUMPY...
BUT LIKE MOST EVERYONE ELSE IN THE COUNTRY, I'VE BEEN LEARNING NOT TO JUDGE PEOPLE TOO QUICKLY.
MISTER? THANKS FOR NOT HIJACKING MY DAD'S PLANE!
YEAH, THANKS.

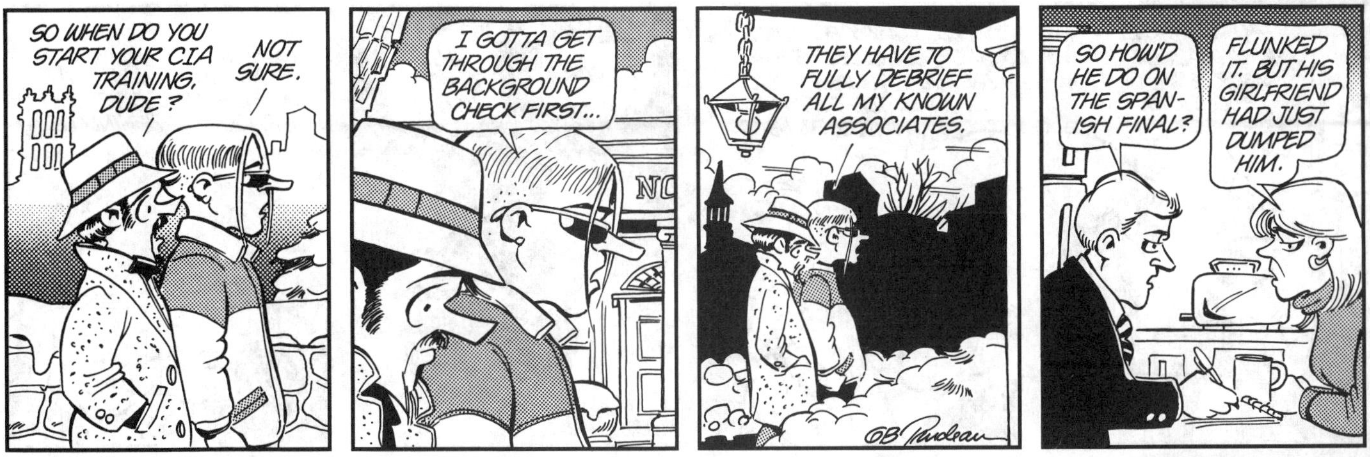
SO WHEN DO YOU START YOUR CIA TRAINING, DUDE?
NOT SURE.
I GOTTA GET THROUGH THE BACKGROUND CHECK FIRST...
THEY HAVE TO FULLY DEBRIEF ALL MY KNOWN ASSOCIATES.
SO HOW'D HE DO ON THE SPAN-ISH FINAL?
FLUNKED IT. BUT HIS GIRLFRIEND HAD JUST DUMPED HIM.

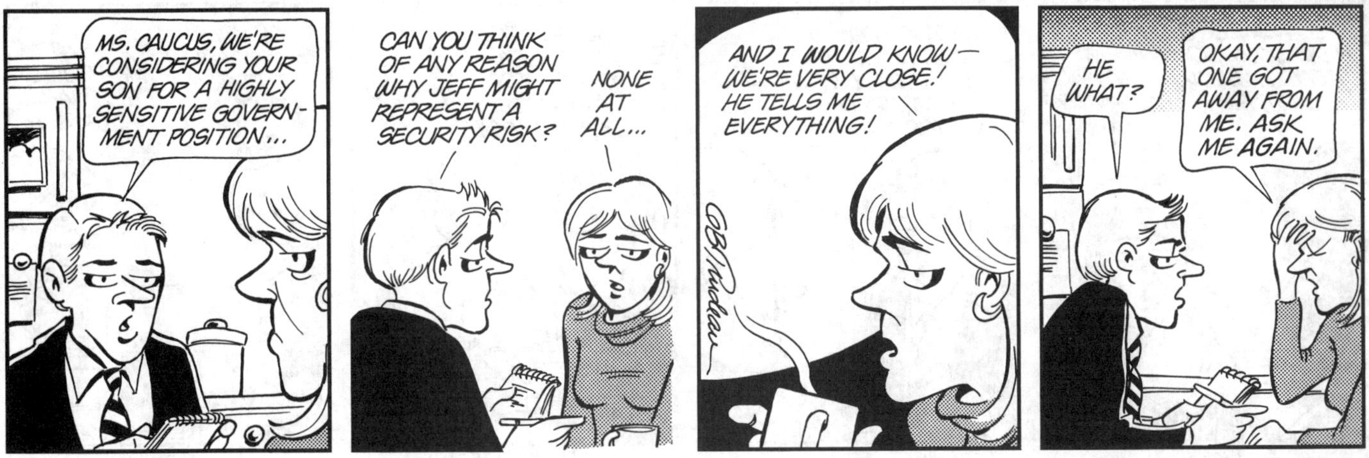
MS. CAUCUS, WE'RE CONSIDERING YOUR SON FOR A HIGHLY SENSITIVE GOVERN-MENT POSITION...
CAN YOU THINK OF ANY REASON WHY JEFF MIGHT REPRESENT A SECURITY RISK?
NONE AT ALL...
AND I WOULD KNOW— WE'RE VERY CLOSE! HE TELLS ME EVERYTHING!
HE WHAT?
OKAY, THAT ONE GOT AWAY FROM ME. ASK ME AGAIN.

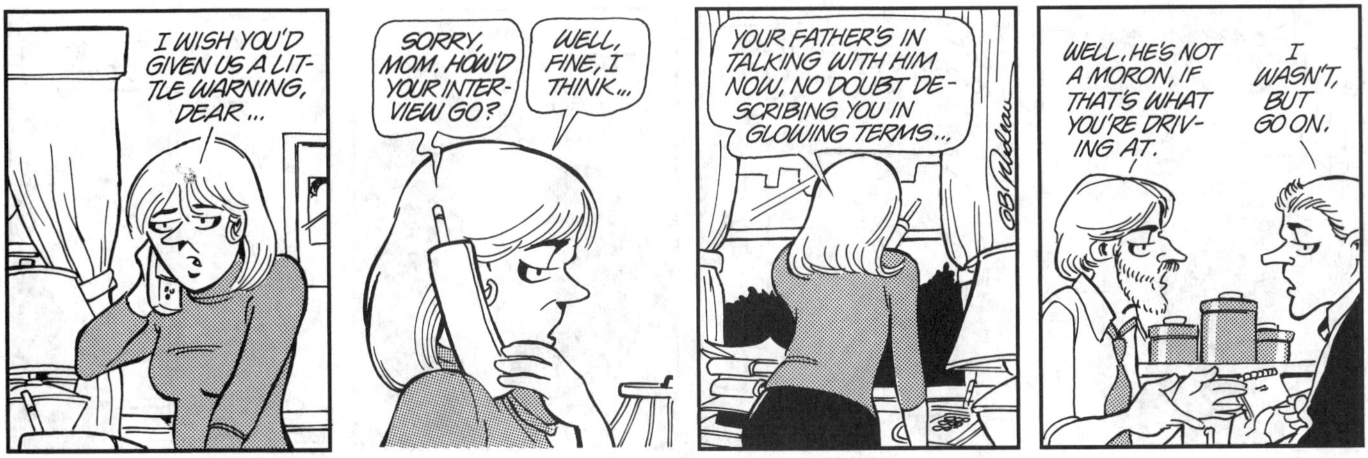
I WISH YOU'D GIVEN US A LIT-TLE WARNING, DEAR...
SORRY, MOM. HOW'D YOUR INTER-VIEW GO?
WELL, FINE, I THINK...
YOUR FATHER'S IN TALKING WITH HIM NOW, NO DOUBT DE-SCRIBING YOU IN GLOWING TERMS...
WELL, HE'S NOT A MORON, IF THAT'S WHAT YOU'RE DRIV-ING AT.
I WASN'T, BUT GO ON.

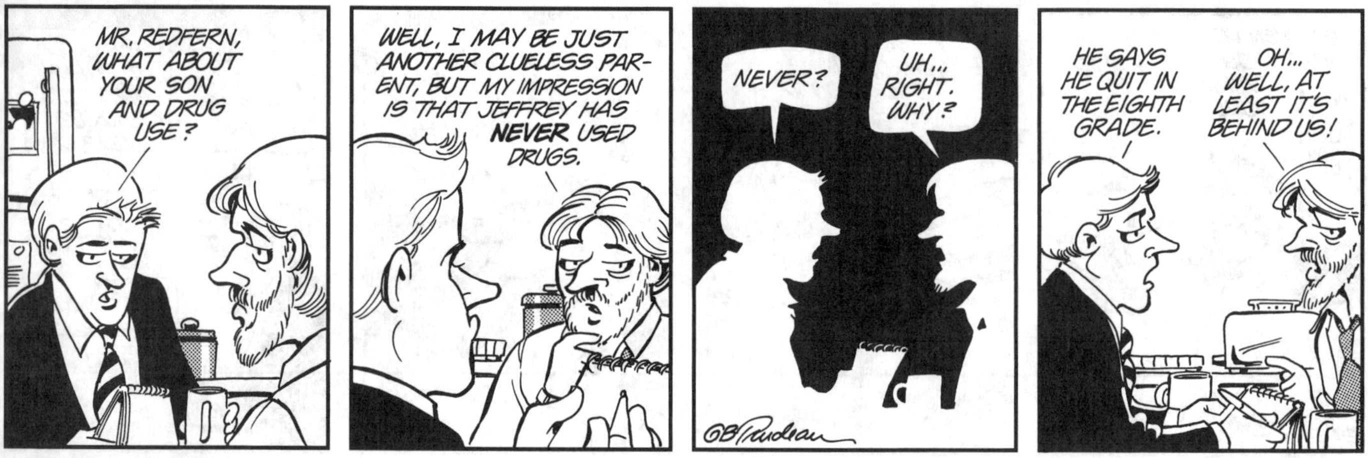
MR. REDFERN, WHAT ABOUT YOUR SON AND DRUG USE?
WELL, I MAY BE JUST ANOTHER CLUELESS PARENT, BUT MY IMPRESSION IS THAT JEFFREY HAS **NEVER** USED DRUGS.
NEVER?
UH... RIGHT. WHY?
HE SAYS HE QUIT IN THE EIGHTH GRADE.
OH... WELL, AT LEAST IT'S BEHIND US!
©B. Trudeau

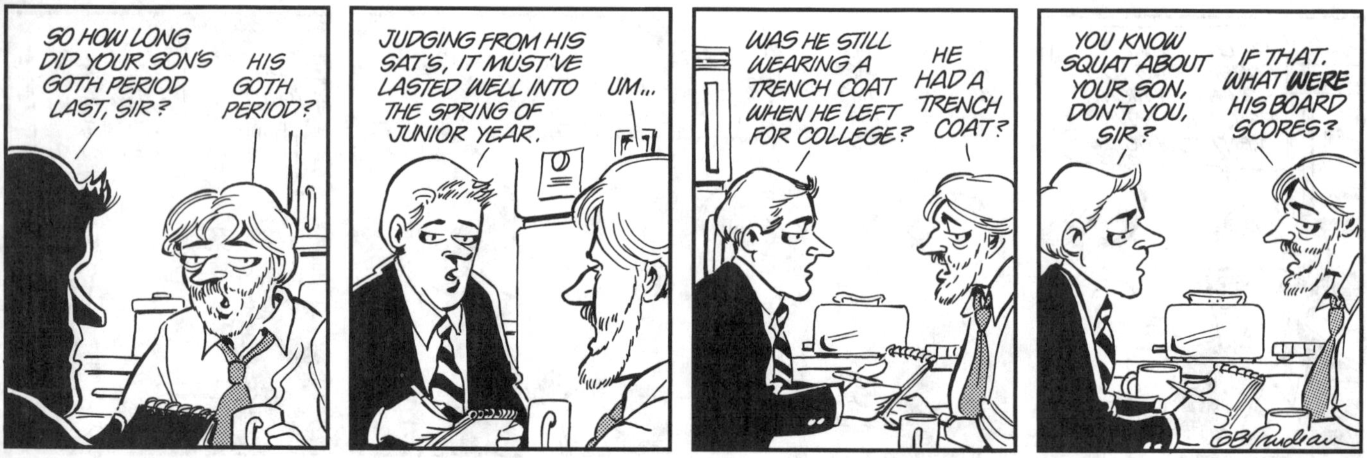
SO HOW LONG DID YOUR SON'S GOTH PERIOD LAST, SIR?
HIS GOTH PERIOD?
JUDGING FROM HIS SAT'S, IT MUST'VE LASTED WELL INTO THE SPRING OF JUNIOR YEAR.
UM...
WAS HE STILL WEARING A TRENCH COAT WHEN HE LEFT FOR COLLEGE?
HE HAD A TRENCH COAT?
YOU KNOW SQUAT ABOUT YOUR SON, DON'T YOU, SIR?
IF THAT. WHAT **WERE** HIS BOARD SCORES?
©B. Trudeau

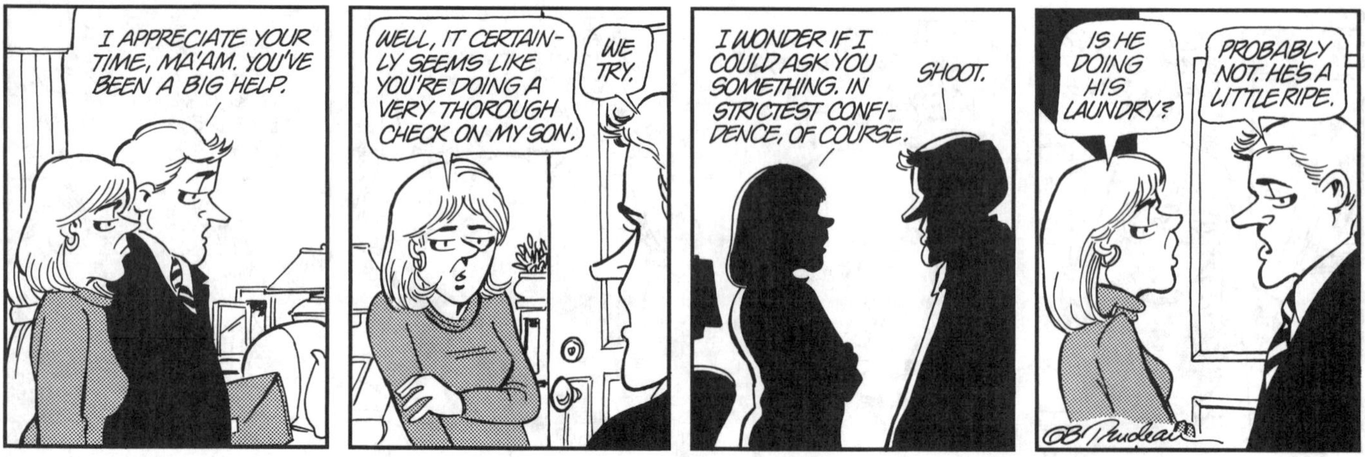
I APPRECIATE YOUR TIME, MA'AM. YOU'VE BEEN A BIG HELP.
WELL, IT CERTAINLY SEEMS LIKE YOU'RE DOING A VERY THOROUGH CHECK ON MY SON.
WE TRY.
I WONDER IF I COULD ASK YOU SOMETHING. IN STRICTEST CONFIDENCE, OF COURSE.
SHOOT.
IS HE DOING HIS LAUNDRY?
PROBABLY NOT. HE'S A LITTLE RIPE.
©B. Trudeau

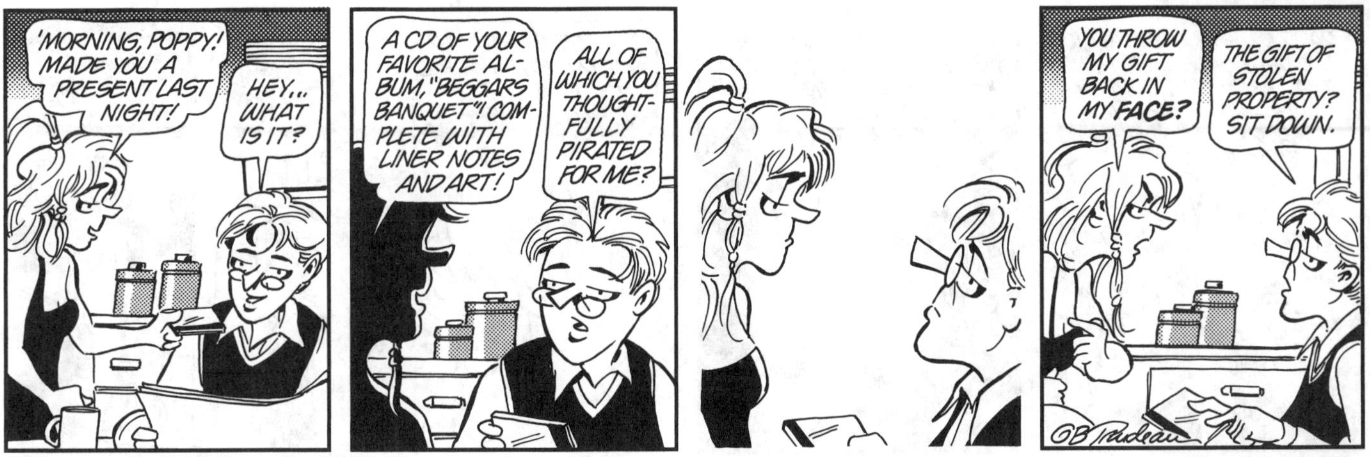
'MORNING, POPPY! MADE YOU A PRESENT LAST NIGHT!
HEY... WHAT IS IT?
A CD OF YOUR FAVORITE ALBUM, "BEGGARS BANQUET"! COMPLETE WITH LINER NOTES AND ART!
ALL OF WHICH YOU THOUGHTFULLY PIRATED FOR ME?
YOU THROW MY GIFT BACK IN MY FACE?
THE GIFT OF STOLEN PROPERTY? SIT DOWN.

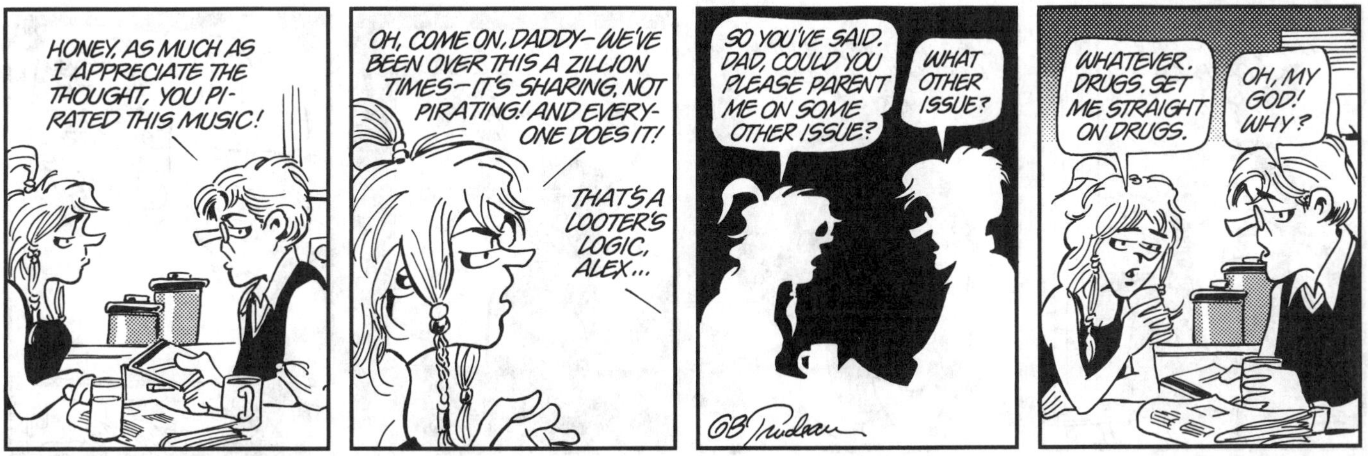
HONEY, AS MUCH AS I APPRECIATE THE THOUGHT, YOU PIRATED THIS MUSIC!
OH, COME ON, DADDY—WE'VE BEEN OVER THIS A ZILLION TIMES—IT'S SHARING, NOT PIRATING! AND EVERYONE DOES IT!
THAT'S A LOOTER'S LOGIC, ALEX...
SO YOU'VE SAID. DAD, COULD YOU PLEASE PARENT ME ON SOME OTHER ISSUE?
WHAT OTHER ISSUE?
WHATEVER. DRUGS. SET ME STRAIGHT ON DRUGS.
OH, MY GOD! WHY?

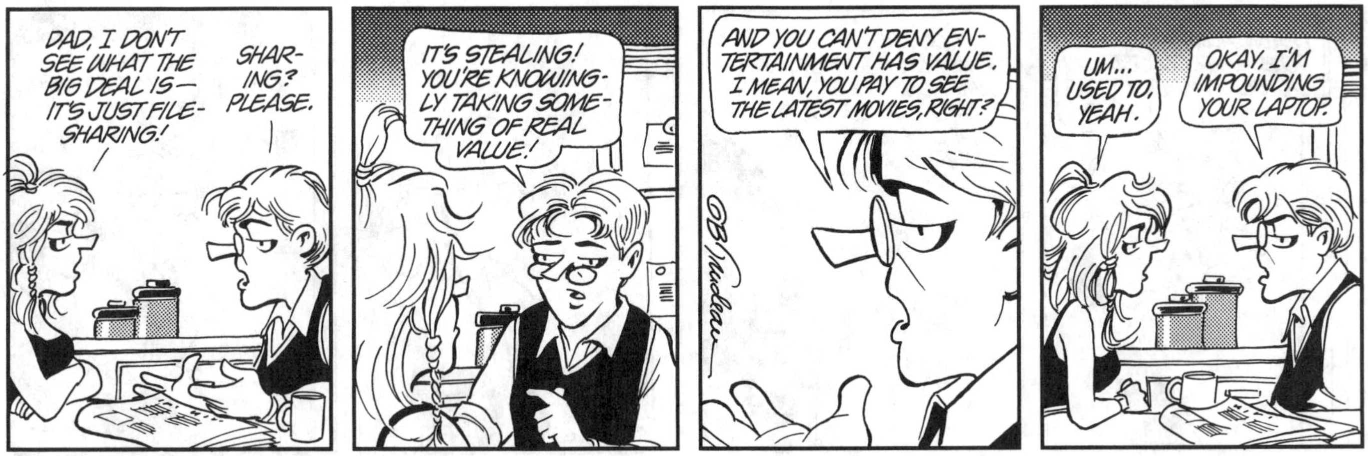
DAD, I DON'T SEE WHAT THE BIG DEAL IS—IT'S JUST FILE-SHARING!
SHARING? PLEASE.
IT'S STEALING! YOU'RE KNOWINGLY TAKING SOMETHING OF REAL VALUE!
AND YOU CAN'T DENY ENTERTAINMENT HAS VALUE. I MEAN, YOU PAY TO SEE THE LATEST MOVIES, RIGHT?
UM... USED TO, YEAH.
OKAY, I'M IMPOUNDING YOUR LAPTOP.

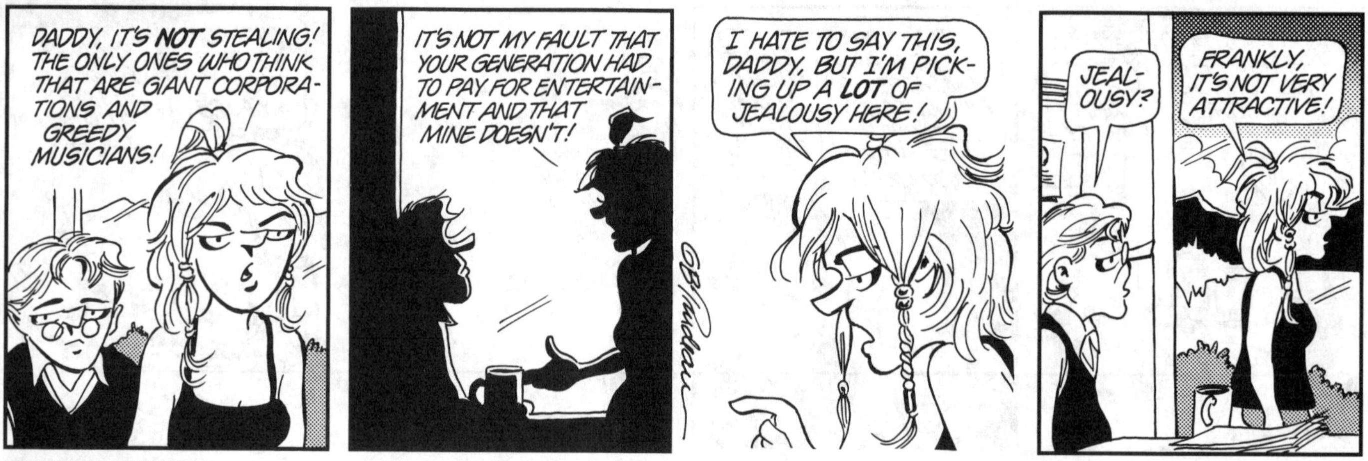
DADDY, IT'S **NOT** STEALING! THE ONLY ONES WHO THINK THAT ARE GIANT CORPORATIONS AND GREEDY MUSICIANS!
IT'S NOT MY FAULT THAT YOUR GENERATION HAD TO PAY FOR ENTERTAINMENT AND THAT MINE DOESN'T!
I HATE TO SAY THIS, DADDY, BUT I'M PICKING UP A **LOT** OF JEALOUSY HERE!
JEALOUSY?
FRANKLY, IT'S NOT VERY ATTRACTIVE!

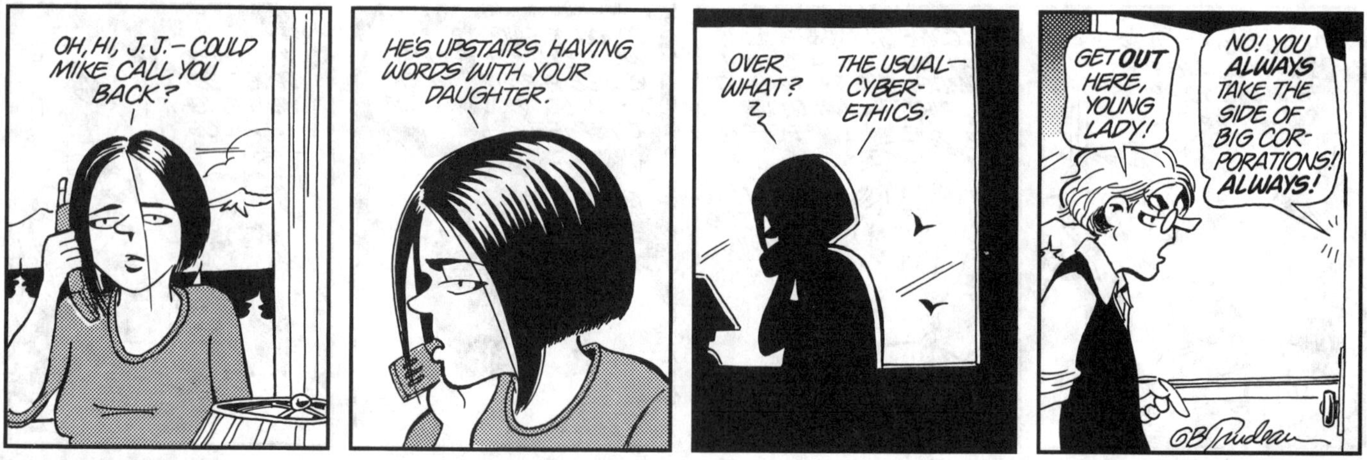
OH, HI, J.J.– COULD MIKE CALL YOU BACK?
HE'S UPSTAIRS HAVING WORDS WITH YOUR DAUGHTER.
OVER WHAT?
THE USUAL– CYBER-ETHICS.
GET **OUT** HERE, YOUNG LADY!
NO! YOU **ALWAYS** TAKE THE SIDE OF BIG CORPORATIONS! **ALWAYS!**

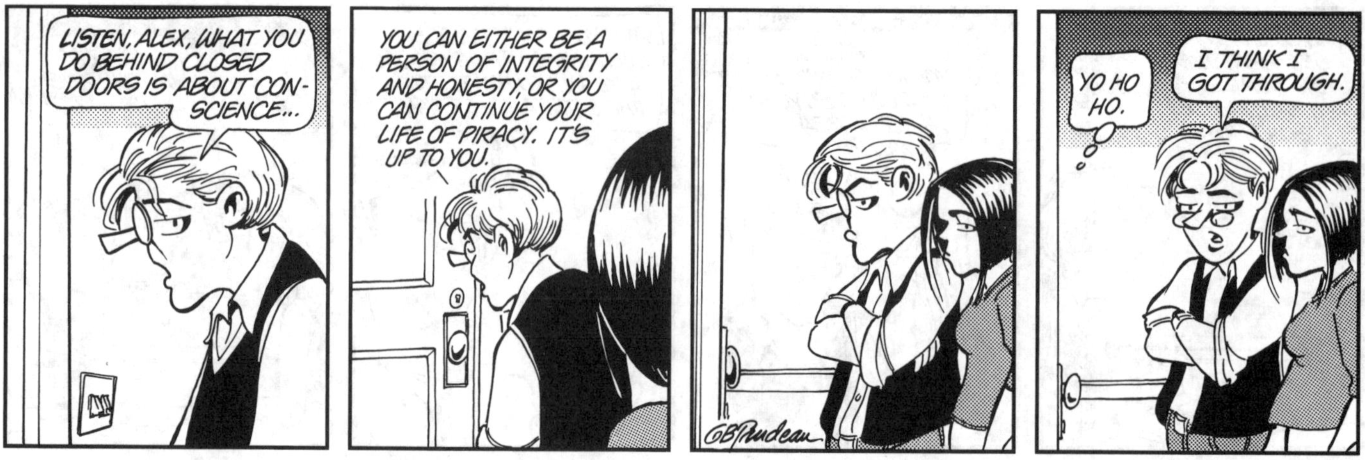
LISTEN, ALEX, WHAT YOU DO BEHIND CLOSED DOORS IS ABOUT CONSCIENCE...
YOU CAN EITHER BE A PERSON OF INTEGRITY AND HONESTY, OR YOU CAN CONTINUE YOUR LIFE OF PIRACY. IT'S UP TO YOU.
YO HO HO.
I THINK I GOT THROUGH.

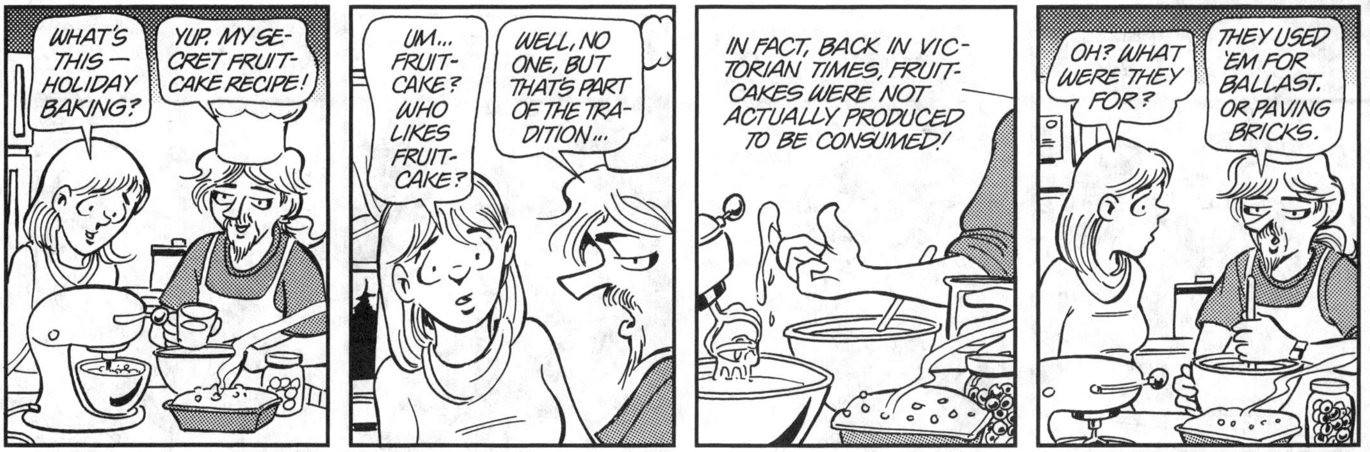
WHAT'S THIS — HOLIDAY BAKING?
YUP. MY SECRET FRUITCAKE RECIPE!
UM... FRUITCAKE? WHO LIKES FRUITCAKE?
WELL, NO ONE, BUT THAT'S PART OF THE TRADITION...
IN FACT, BACK IN VICTORIAN TIMES, FRUITCAKES WERE NOT ACTUALLY PRODUCED TO BE CONSUMED!
OH? WHAT WERE THEY FOR?
THEY USED 'EM FOR BALLAST. OR PAVING BRICKS.

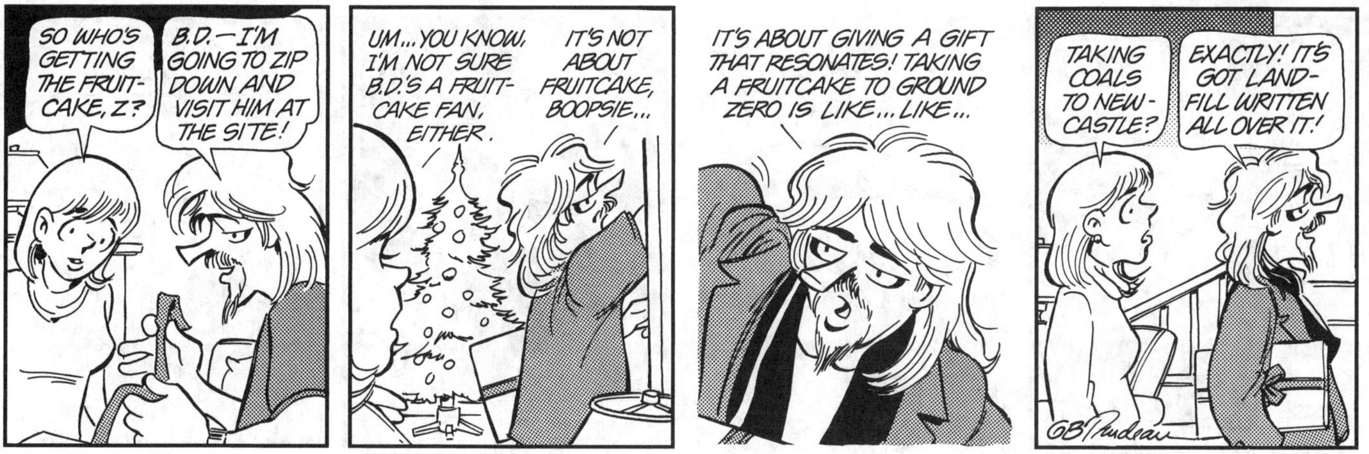
SO WHO'S GETTING THE FRUITCAKE, Z?
B.D.—I'M GOING TO ZIP DOWN AND VISIT HIM AT THE SITE!
UM... YOU KNOW, I'M NOT SURE B.D.'S A FRUITCAKE FAN, EITHER.
IT'S NOT ABOUT FRUITCAKE, BOOPSIE...
IT'S ABOUT GIVING A GIFT THAT RESONATES! TAKING A FRUITCAKE TO GROUND ZERO IS LIKE... LIKE...
TAKING COALS TO NEWCASTLE?
EXACTLY! IT'S GOT LANDFILL WRITTEN ALL OVER IT!

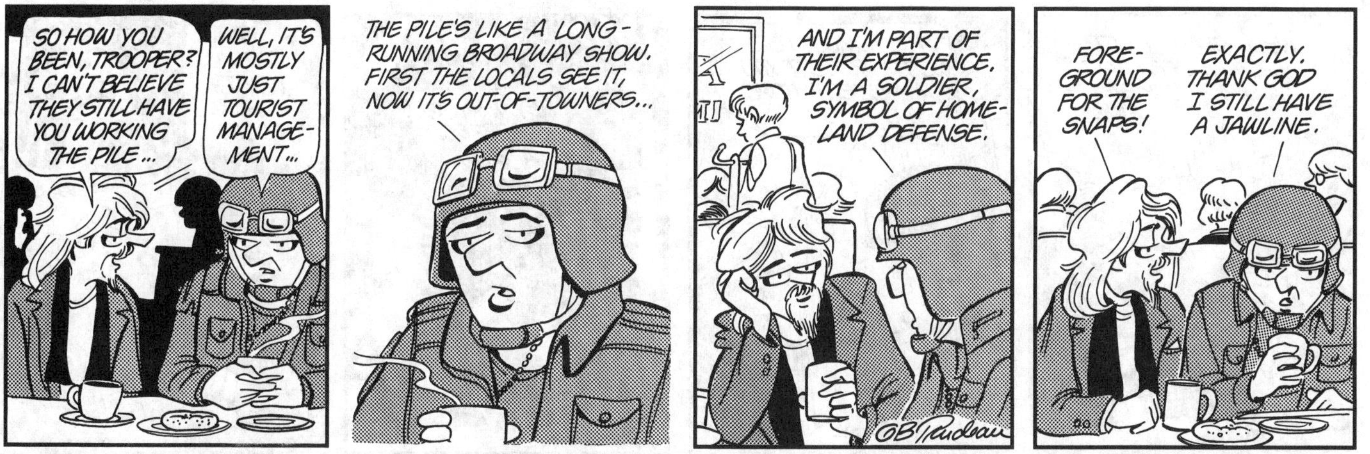
SO HOW YOU BEEN, TROOPER? I CAN'T BELIEVE THEY STILL HAVE YOU WORKING THE PILE...
WELL, IT'S MOSTLY JUST TOURIST MANAGEMENT...
THE PILE'S LIKE A LONG-RUNNING BROADWAY SHOW. FIRST THE LOCALS SEE IT, NOW IT'S OUT-OF-TOWNERS...
AND I'M PART OF THEIR EXPERIENCE. I'M A SOLDIER, SYMBOL OF HOMELAND DEFENSE.
FOREGROUND FOR THE SNAPS!
EXACTLY. THANK GOD I STILL HAVE A JAWLINE.

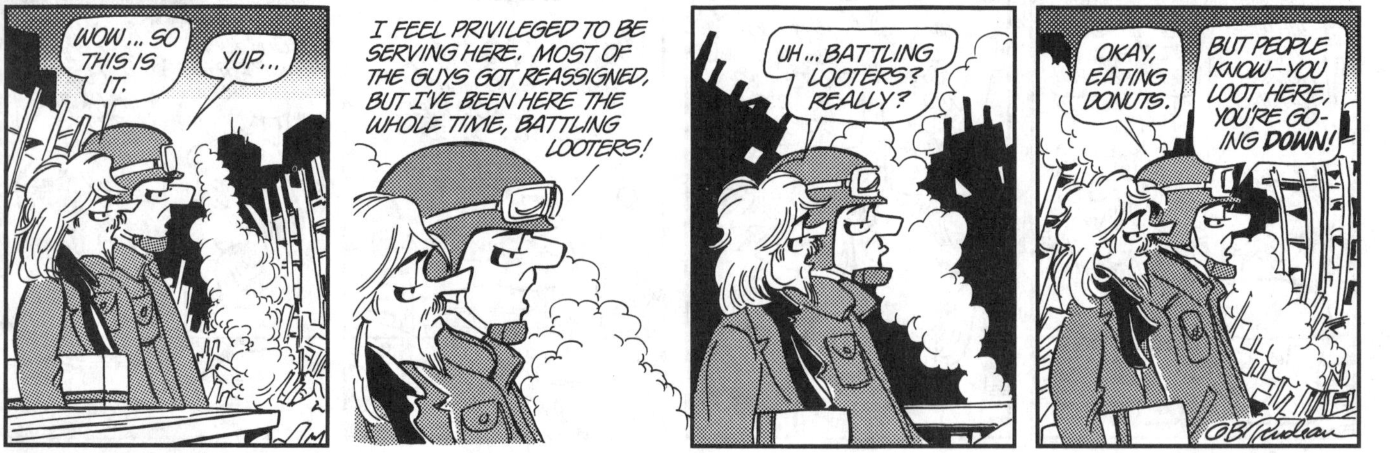
WOW ... SO THIS IS IT.
YUP ...
I FEEL PRIVILEGED TO BE SERVING HERE. MOST OF THE GUYS GOT REASSIGNED, BUT I'VE BEEN HERE THE WHOLE TIME, BATTLING LOOTERS!
UH ... BATTLING LOOTERS? REALLY?
OKAY, EATING DONUTS.
BUT PEOPLE KNOW—YOU LOOT HERE, YOU'RE GOING **DOWN**!
©B. Trudeau

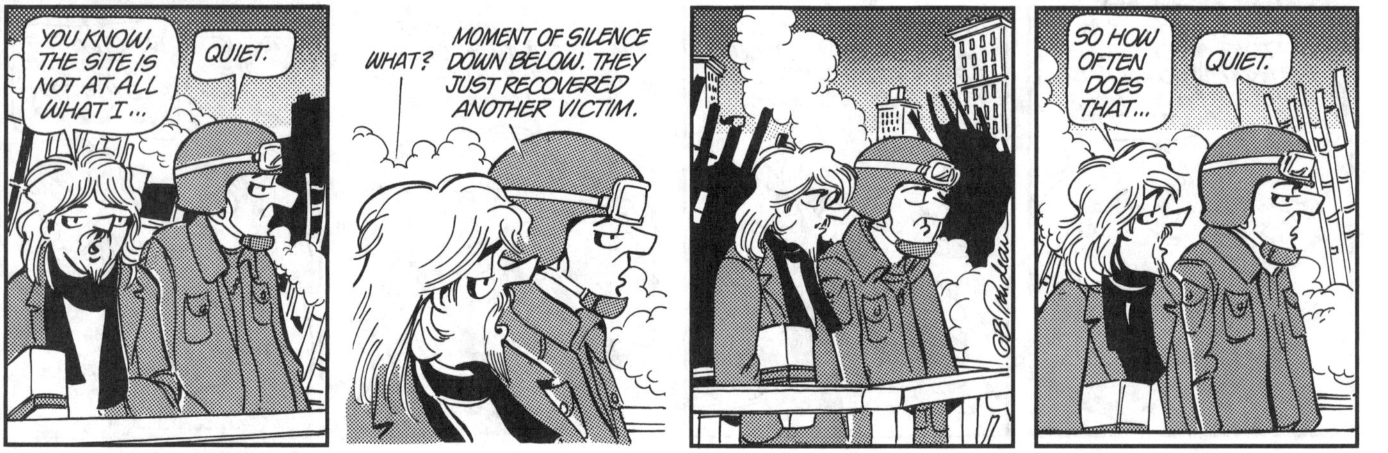
YOU KNOW, THE SITE IS NOT AT ALL WHAT I ...
QUIET.
WHAT?
MOMENT OF SILENCE DOWN BELOW. THEY JUST RECOVERED ANOTHER VICTIM.
©B. Trudeau
SO HOW OFTEN DOES THAT...
QUIET.

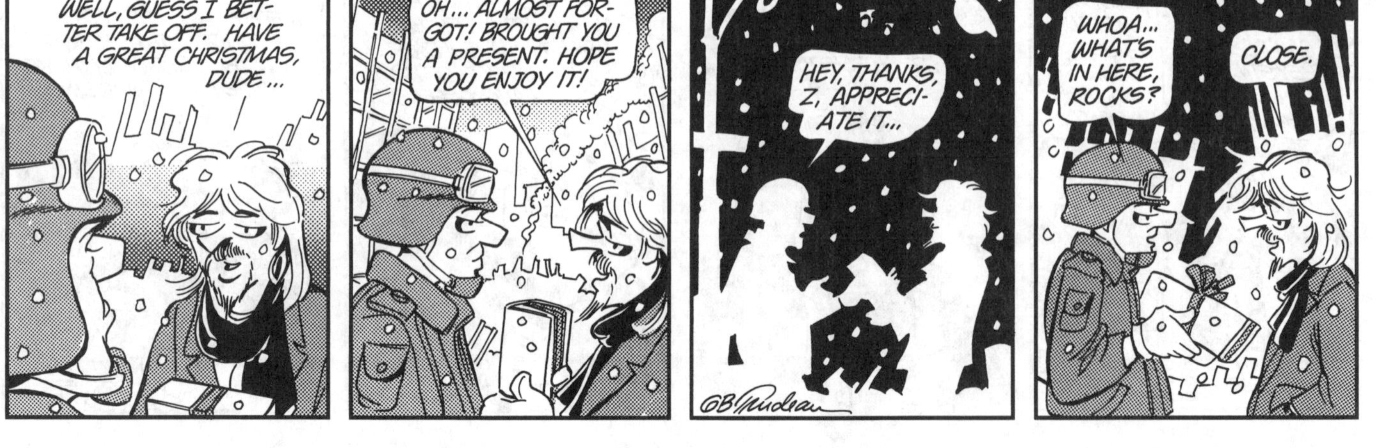
WELL, GUESS I BETTER TAKE OFF. HAVE A GREAT CHRISTMAS, DUDE ...
OH ... ALMOST FORGOT! BROUGHT YOU A PRESENT. HOPE YOU ENJOY IT!
HEY, THANKS, Z, APPRECIATE IT...
©B. Trudeau
WHOA... WHAT'S IN HERE, ROCKS?
CLOSE.

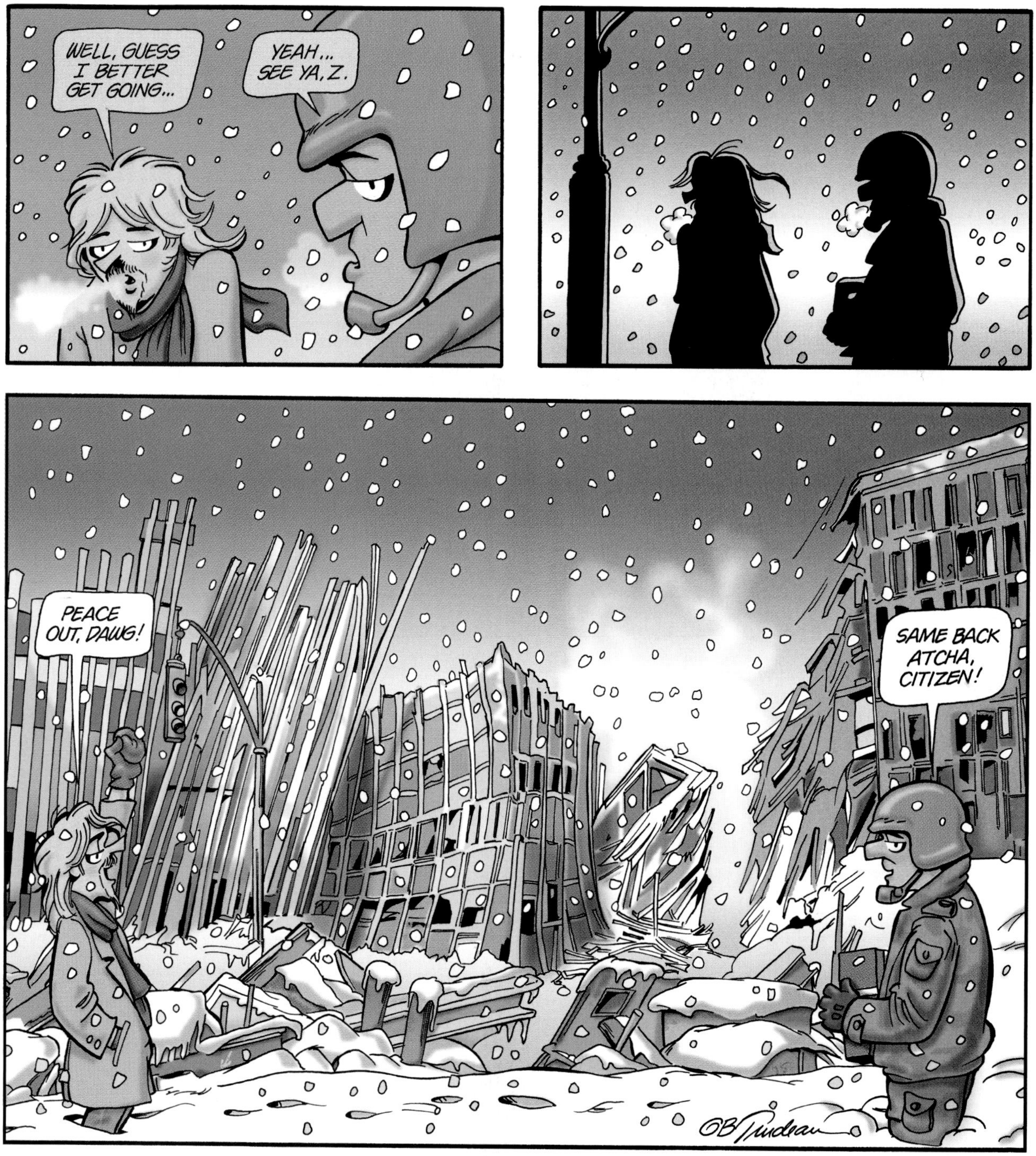
WELL, GUESS I BETTER GET GOING...
YEAH... SEE YA, Z.
PEACE OUT, DAWG!
SAME BACK ATCHA, CITIZEN!
GB Trudeau

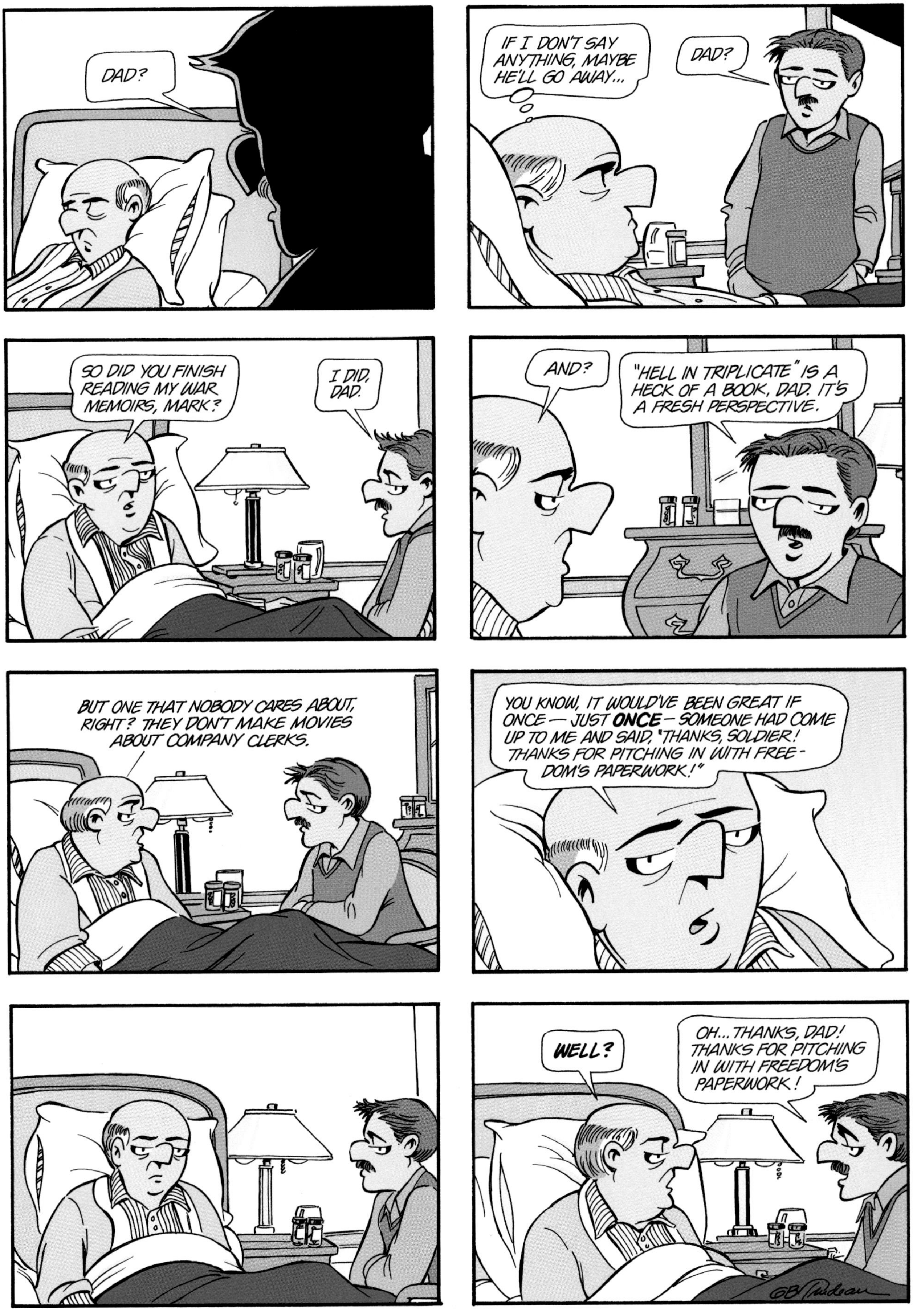
DAD?
IF I DON'T SAY ANYTHING, MAYBE HE'LL GO AWAY...
DAD?
SO DID YOU FINISH READING MY WAR MEMOIRS, MARK?
I DID, DAD.
AND?
"HELL IN TRIPLICATE" IS A HECK OF A BOOK, DAD. IT'S A FRESH PERSPECTIVE.
BUT ONE THAT NOBODY CARES ABOUT, RIGHT? THEY DON'T MAKE MOVIES ABOUT COMPANY CLERKS.
YOU KNOW, IT WOULD'VE BEEN GREAT IF ONCE — JUST ONCE — SOMEONE HAD COME UP TO ME AND SAID, "THANKS, SOLDIER! THANKS FOR PITCHING IN WITH FREE-DOM'S PAPERWORK!"
WELL?
OH... THANKS, DAD! THANKS FOR PITCHING IN WITH FREEDOM'S PAPERWORK!
©B Trudeau

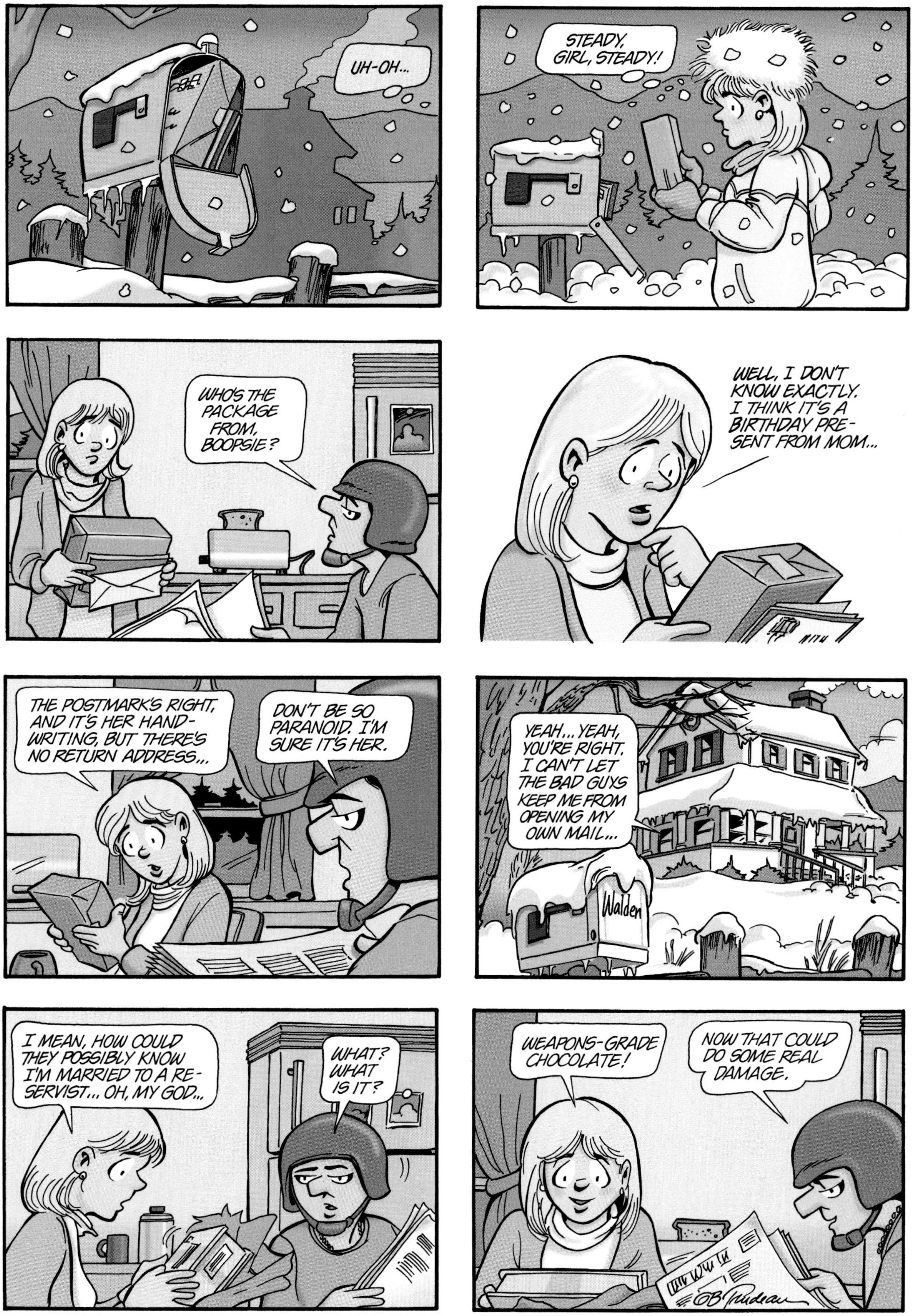
UH-OH...
STEADY, GIRL, STEADY!
WHO'S THE PACKAGE FROM, BOOPSIE?
WELL, I DON'T KNOW EXACTLY. I THINK IT'S A BIRTHDAY PRE-SENT FROM MOM...
THE POSTMARK'S RIGHT, AND IT'S HER HAND-WRITING, BUT THERE'S NO RETURN ADDRESS...
DON'T BE SO PARANOID. I'M SURE IT'S HER.
YEAH... YEAH, YOU'RE RIGHT. I CAN'T LET THE BAD GUYS KEEP ME FROM OPENING MY OWN MAIL...
Walden
I MEAN, HOW COULD THEY POSSIBLY KNOW I'M MARRIED TO A RE-SERVIST... OH, MY GOD...
WHAT? WHAT IS IT?
WEAPONS-GRADE CHOCOLATE!
NOW THAT COULD DO SOME REAL DAMAGE.
GBTrudeau

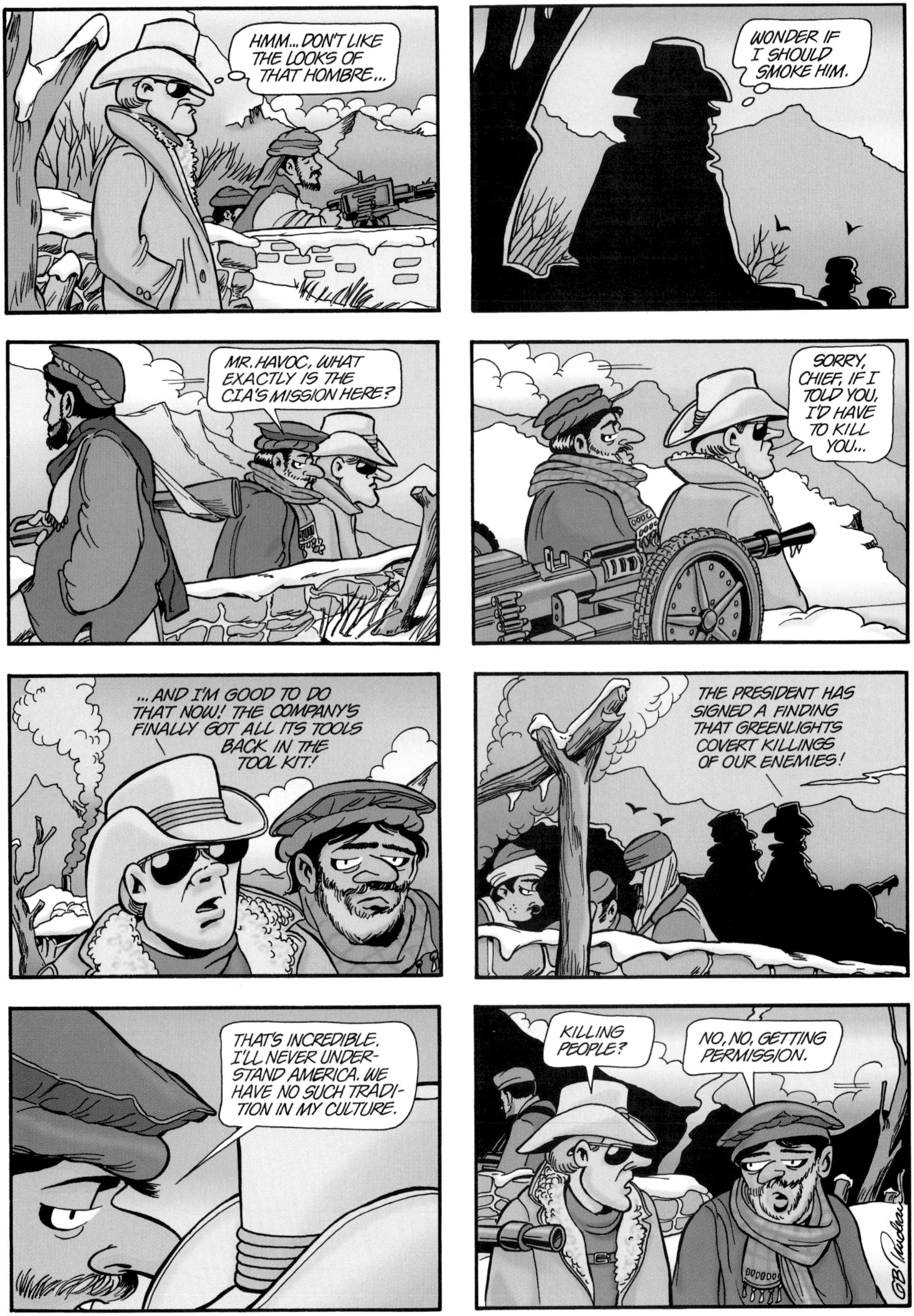
HMM... DON'T LIKE THE LOOKS OF THAT HOMBRE...
WONDER IF I SHOULD SMOKE HIM.
MR. HAVOC, WHAT EXACTLY IS THE CIA'S MISSION HERE?
SORRY, CHIEF, IF I TOLD YOU, I'D HAVE TO KILL YOU...
...AND I'M GOOD TO DO THAT NOW! THE COMPANY'S FINALLY GOT ALL ITS TOOLS BACK IN THE TOOL KIT!
THE PRESIDENT HAS SIGNED A FINDING THAT GREENLIGHTS COVERT KILLINGS OF OUR ENEMIES!
THAT'S INCREDIBLE. I'LL NEVER UNDERSTAND AMERICA. WE HAVE NO SUCH TRADITION IN MY CULTURE.
KILLING PEOPLE?
NO, NO, GETTING PERMISSION.

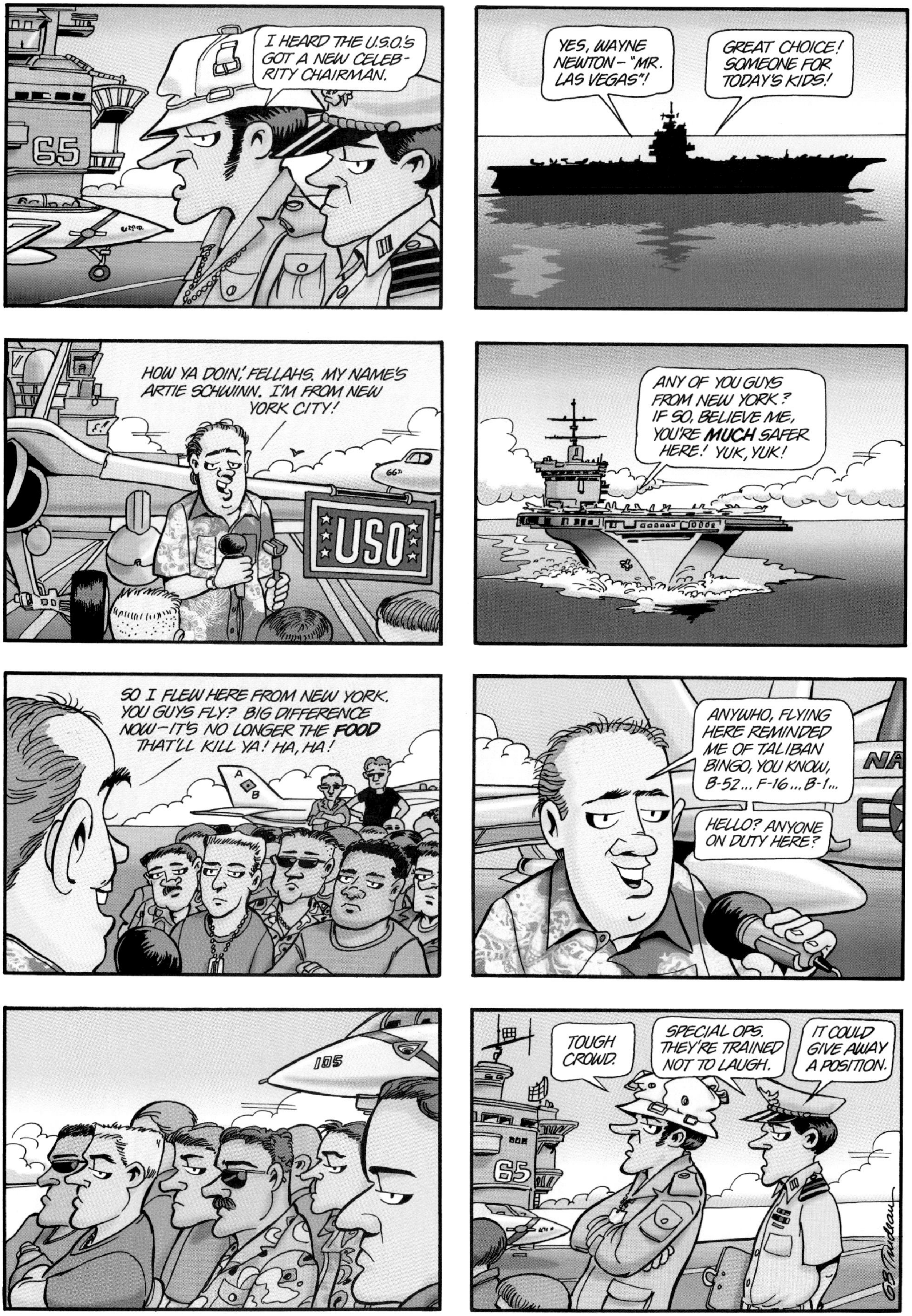
I HEARD THE U.S.O.'S GOT A NEW CELEB-RITY CHAIRMAN.
YES, WAYNE NEWTON – "MR. LAS VEGAS"!
GREAT CHOICE! SOMEONE FOR TODAY'S KIDS!
HOW YA DOIN,' FELLAHS. MY NAME'S ARTIE SCHWINN. I'M FROM NEW YORK CITY!
USO
ANY OF YOU GUYS FROM NEW YORK? IF SO, BELIEVE ME, YOU'RE **MUCH** SAFER HERE! YUK, YUK!
SO I FLEW HERE FROM NEW YORK. YOU GUYS FLY? BIG DIFFERENCE NOW–IT'S NO LONGER THE **FOOD** THAT'LL KILL YA! HA, HA!
ANYWHO, FLYING HERE REMINDED ME OF TALIBAN BINGO, YOU KNOW, B-52... F-16... B-1...
HELLO? ANYONE ON DUTY HERE?
TOUGH CROWD.
SPECIAL OPS. THEY'RE TRAINED NOT TO LAUGH.
IT COULD GIVE AWAY A POSITION.
GB Trudeau

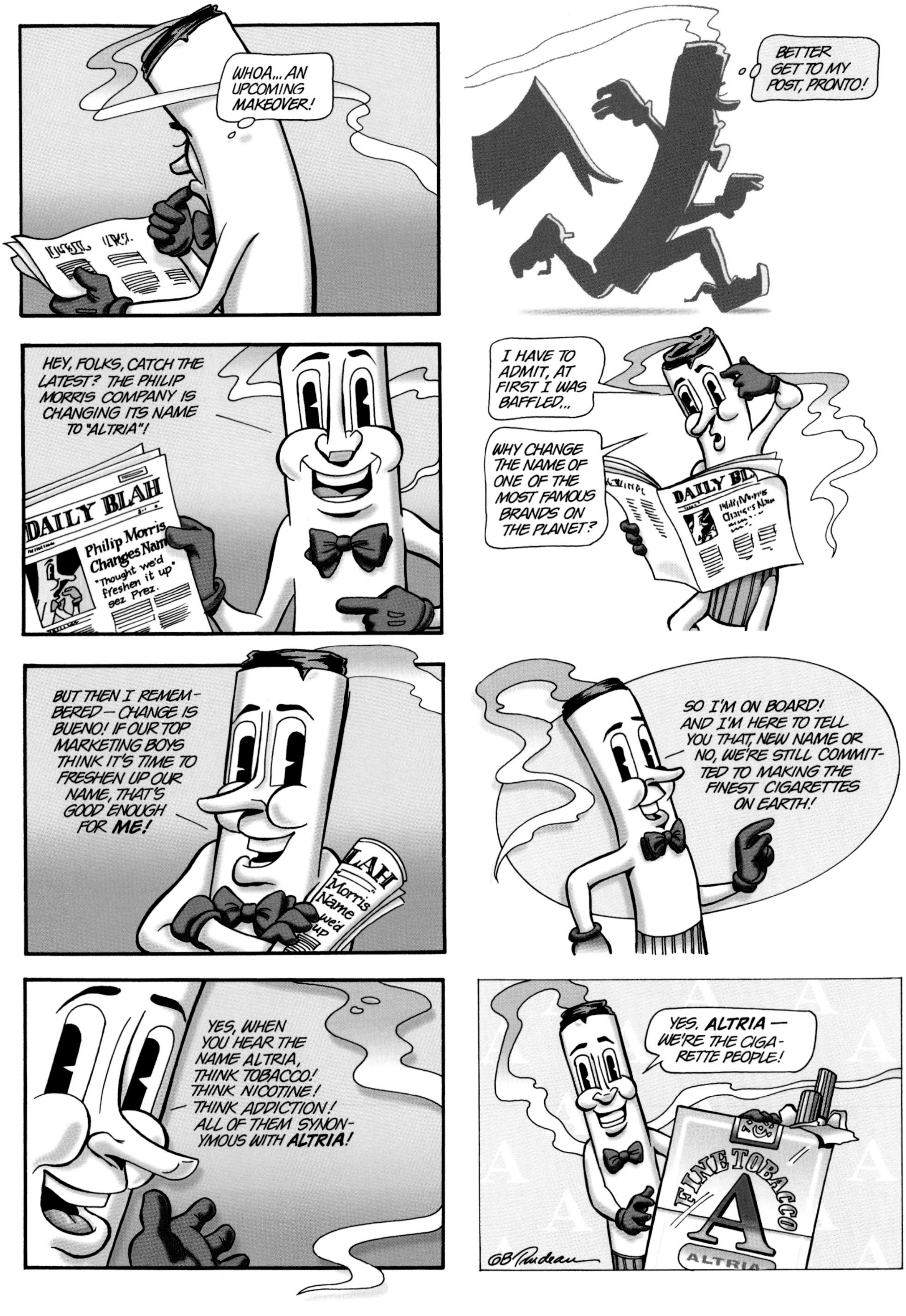
WHOA... AN UPCOMING MAKEOVER!
BETTER GET TO MY POST, PRONTO!
HEY, FOLKS, CATCH THE LATEST? THE PHILIP MORRIS COMPANY IS CHANGING ITS NAME TO "ALTRIA"!
DAILY BLAH
Philip Morris Changes Name
"Thought we'd freshen it up" sez Prez.
I HAVE TO ADMIT, AT FIRST I WAS BAFFLED...
WHY CHANGE THE NAME OF ONE OF THE MOST FAMOUS BRANDS ON THE PLANET?
DAILY BLAH
BUT THEN I REMEMBERED — CHANGE IS BUENO! IF OUR TOP MARKETING BOYS THINK IT'S TIME TO FRESHEN UP OUR NAME, THAT'S GOOD ENOUGH FOR ME!
SO I'M ON BOARD! AND I'M HERE TO TELL YOU THAT, NEW NAME OR NO, WE'RE STILL COMMITTED TO MAKING THE FINEST CIGARETTES ON EARTH!
YES, WHEN YOU HEAR THE NAME ALTRIA, THINK TOBACCO! THINK NICOTINE! THINK ADDICTION! ALL OF THEM SYNONYMOUS WITH ALTRIA!
YES. ALTRIA — WE'RE THE CIGARETTE PEOPLE!
FINE TOBACCO
A
ALTRIA
GB Trudeau

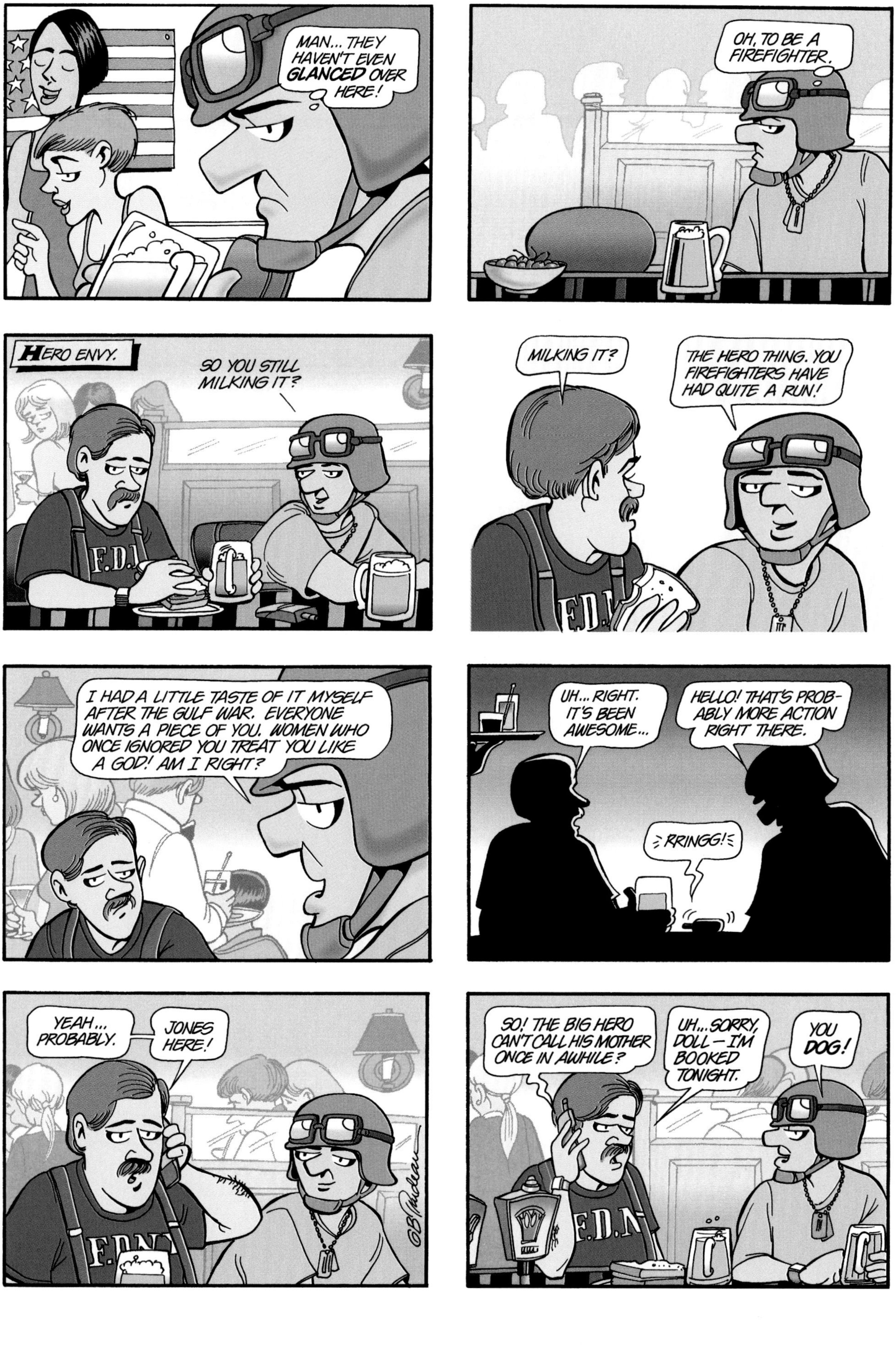

MAN... THEY HAVEN'T EVEN **GLANCED** OVER HERE!
OH, TO BE A FIREFIGHTER.
HERO ENVY.
SO YOU STILL MILKING IT?
F.D.N
MILKING IT?
THE HERO THING. YOU FIREFIGHTERS HAVE HAD QUITE A RUN!
I HAD A LITTLE TASTE OF IT MYSELF AFTER THE GULF WAR. EVERYONE WANTS A PIECE OF YOU. WOMEN WHO ONCE IGNORED YOU TREAT YOU LIKE A GOD! AM I RIGHT?
UH... RIGHT. IT'S BEEN AWESOME...
HELLO! THAT'S PROBABLY MORE ACTION RIGHT THERE.
RRINGG!
YEAH... PROBABLY.
JONES HERE!
SO! THE BIG HERO CAN'T CALL HIS MOTHER ONCE IN AWHILE?
UH... SORRY, DOLL — I'M BOOKED TONIGHT.
YOU **DOG**!

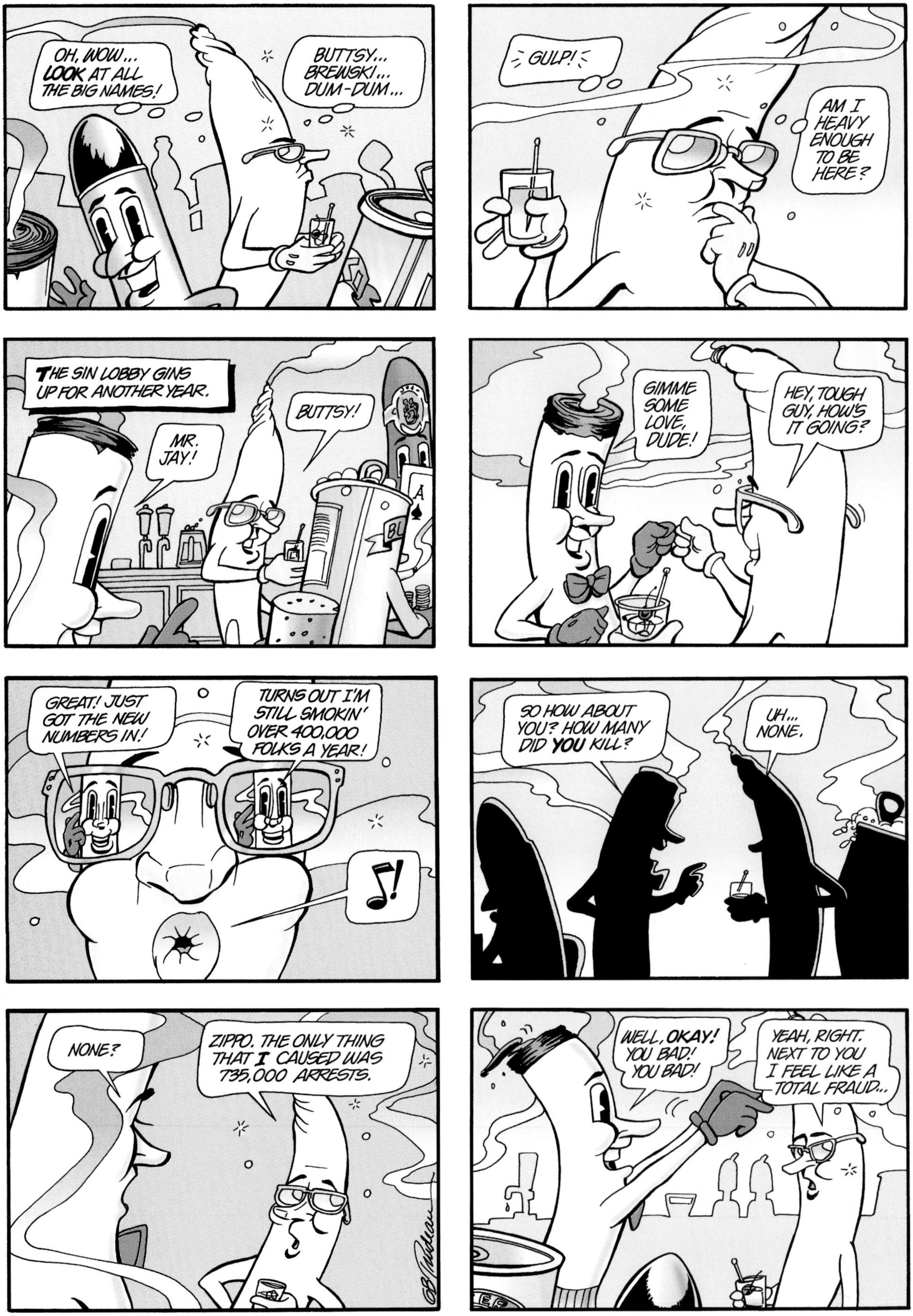
OH, WOW... LOOK AT ALL THE BIG NAMES!
BUTTSY... BREWSKI... DUM-DUM...
GULP!
AM I HEAVY ENOUGH TO BE HERE?
THE SIN LOBBY GINS UP FOR ANOTHER YEAR.
MR. JAY!
BUTTSY!
GIMME SOME LOVE, DUDE!
HEY, TOUGH GUY, HOW'S IT GOING?
GREAT! JUST GOT THE NEW NUMBERS IN!
TURNS OUT I'M STILL SMOKIN' OVER 400,000 FOLKS A YEAR!
SO HOW ABOUT YOU? HOW MANY DID YOU KILL?
UH... NONE.
NONE?
ZIPPO. THE ONLY THING THAT I CAUSED WAS 735,000 ARRESTS.
WELL, OKAY! YOU BAD! YOU BAD!
YEAH, RIGHT. NEXT TO YOU I FEEL LIKE A TOTAL FRAUD...

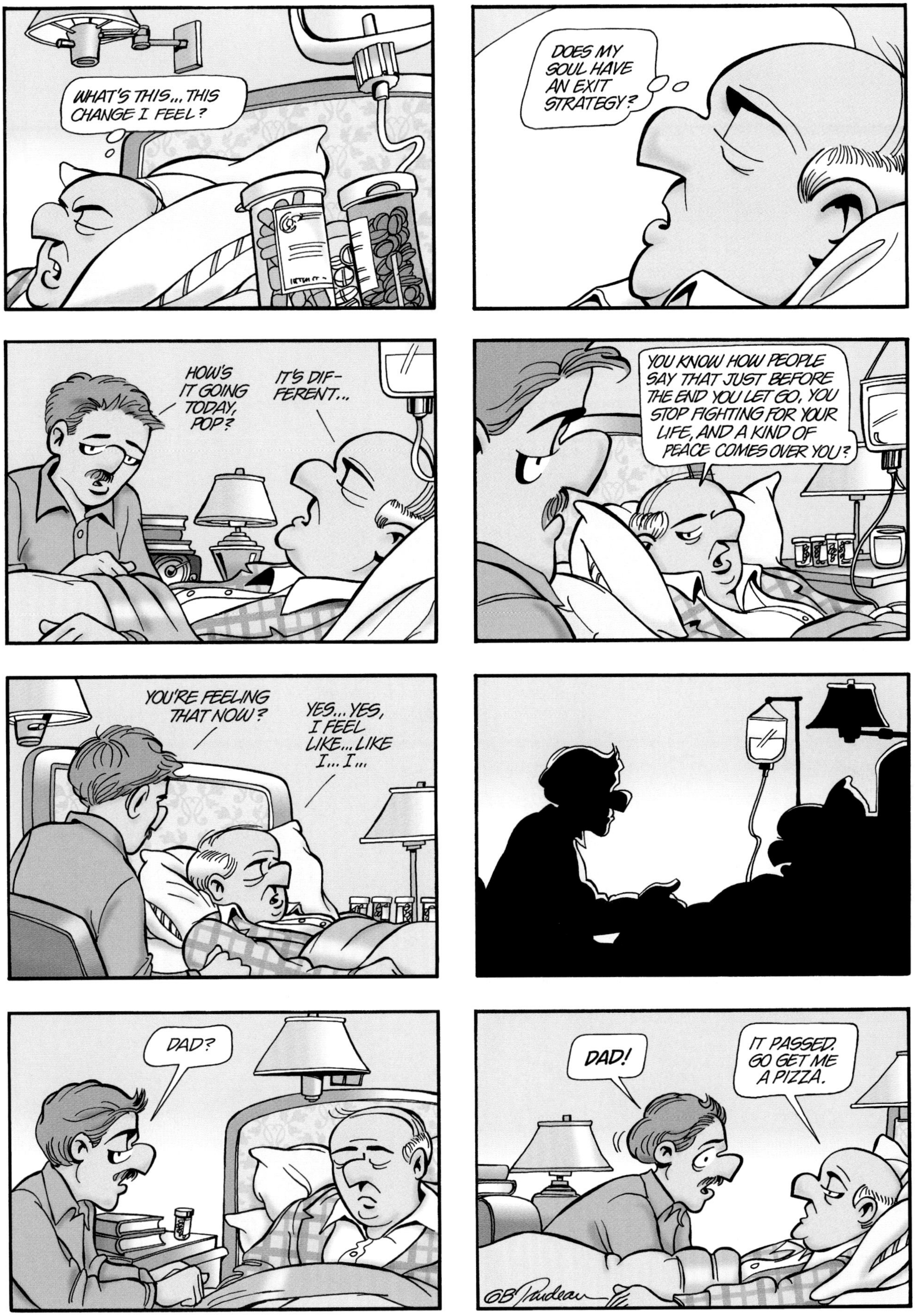
WHAT'S THIS... THIS CHANGE I FEEL?
DOES MY SOUL HAVE AN EXIT STRATEGY?
HOW'S IT GOING TODAY, POP?
IT'S DIF-FERENT...
YOU KNOW HOW PEOPLE SAY THAT JUST BEFORE THE END YOU LET GO, YOU STOP FIGHTING FOR YOUR LIFE, AND A KIND OF PEACE COMES OVER YOU?
YOU'RE FEELING THAT NOW?
YES... YES, I FEEL LIKE... LIKE I... I...
DAD?
DAD!
IT PASSED. GO GET ME A PIZZA.
GB Trudeau

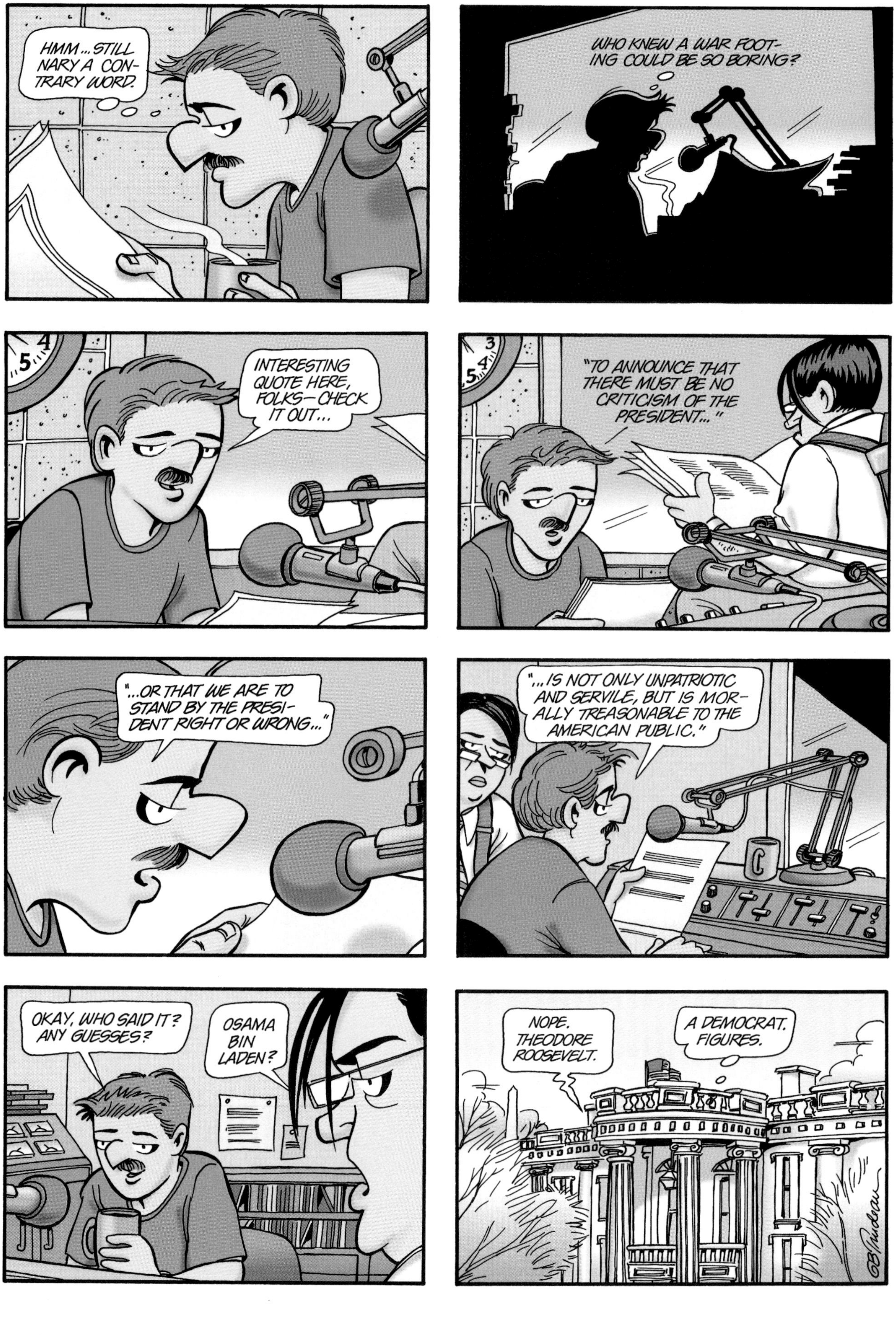

HMM... STILL NARY A CONTRARY WORD.
WHO KNEW A WAR FOOTING COULD BE SO BORING?
INTERESTING QUOTE HERE, FOLKS—CHECK IT OUT...
"TO ANNOUNCE THAT THERE MUST BE NO CRITICISM OF THE PRESIDENT..."
"...OR THAT WE ARE TO STAND BY THE PRESIDENT RIGHT OR WRONG..."
"...IS NOT ONLY UNPATRIOTIC AND SERVILE, BUT IS MORALLY TREASONABLE TO THE AMERICAN PUBLIC."
OKAY, WHO SAID IT? ANY GUESSES?
OSAMA BIN LADEN?
NOPE. THEODORE ROOSEVELT.
A DEMOCRAT. FIGURES.
GBTrudeau

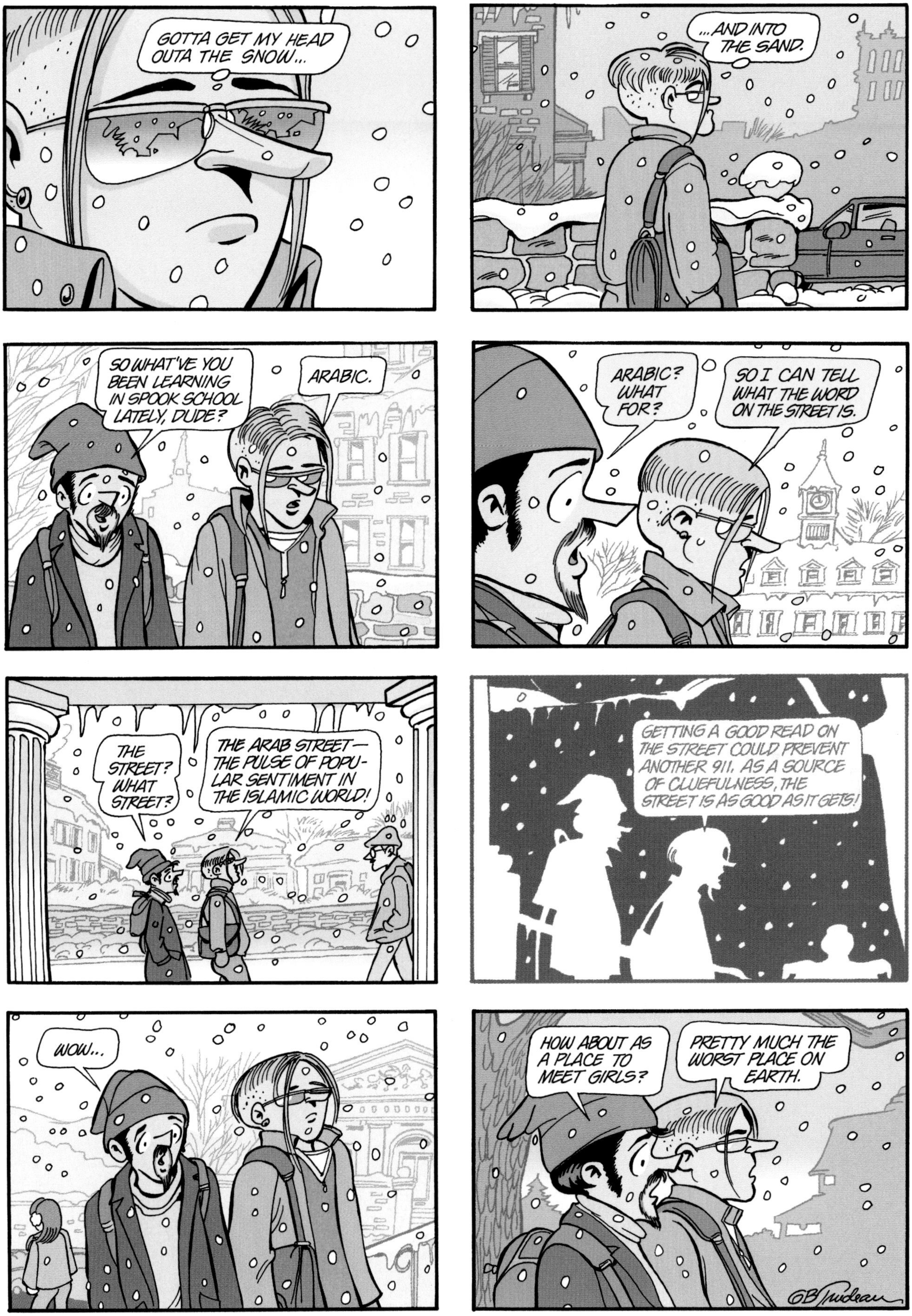
GOTTA GET MY HEAD OUTA THE SNOW...
...AND INTO THE SAND.
SO WHAT'VE YOU BEEN LEARNING IN SPOOK SCHOOL LATELY, DUDE?
ARABIC.
ARABIC? WHAT FOR?
SO I CAN TELL WHAT THE WORD ON THE STREET IS.
THE STREET? WHAT STREET?
THE ARAB STREET— THE PULSE OF POPULAR SENTIMENT IN THE ISLAMIC WORLD!
GETTING A GOOD READ ON THE STREET COULD PREVENT ANOTHER 911. AS A SOURCE OF CLUEFULNESS, THE STREET IS AS GOOD AS IT GETS!
WOW...
HOW ABOUT AS A PLACE TO MEET GIRLS?
PRETTY MUCH THE WORST PLACE ON EARTH.
GBTrudeau

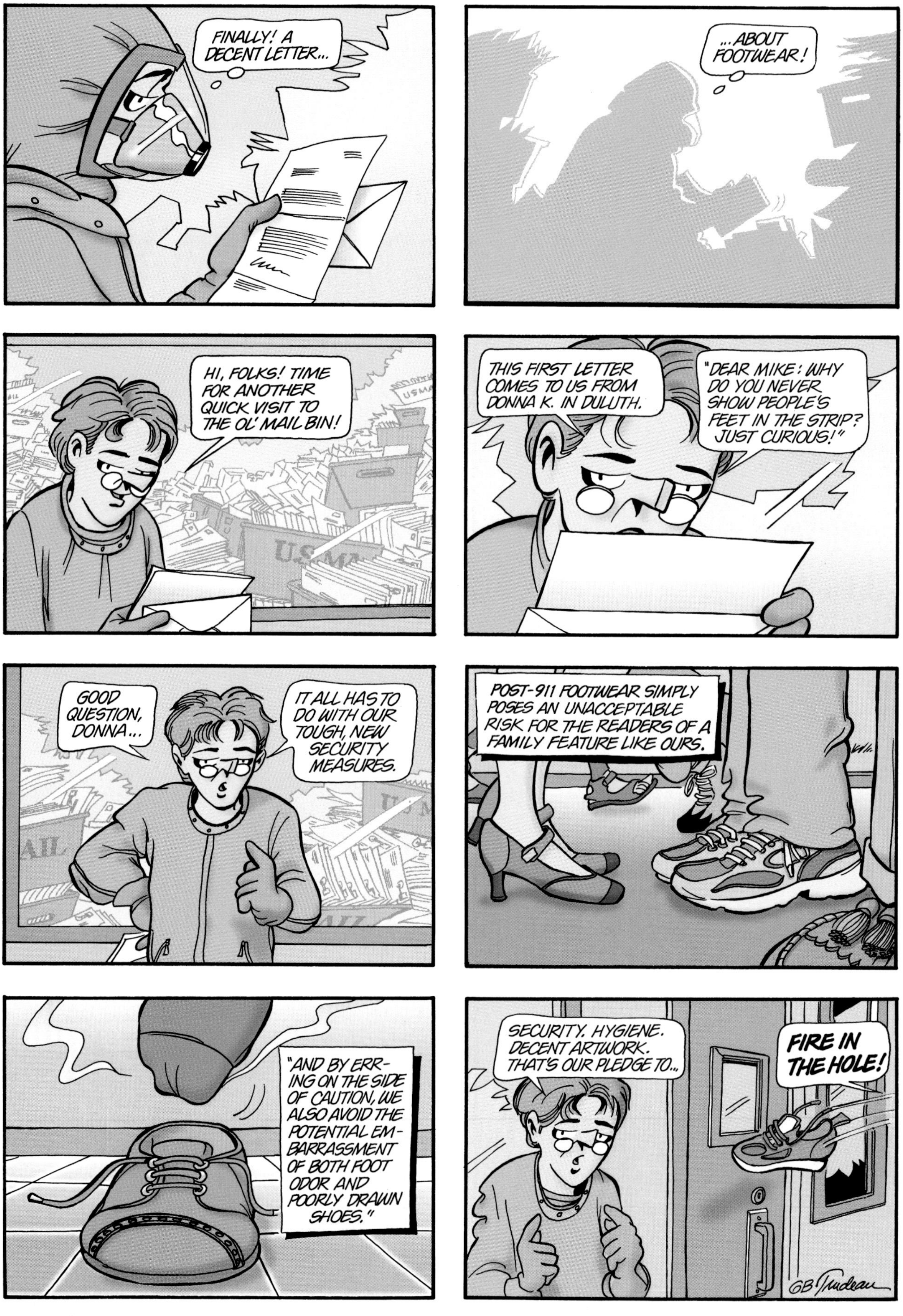
FINALLY! A DECENT LETTER...
...ABOUT FOOTWEAR!
HI, FOLKS! TIME FOR ANOTHER QUICK VISIT TO THE OL' MAIL BIN!
THIS FIRST LETTER COMES TO US FROM DONNA K. IN DULUTH.
"DEAR MIKE: WHY DO YOU NEVER SHOW PEOPLE'S FEET IN THE STRIP? JUST CURIOUS!"
GOOD QUESTION, DONNA...
IT ALL HAS TO DO WITH OUR TOUGH, NEW SECURITY MEASURES.
POST-911 FOOTWEAR SIMPLY POSES AN UNACCEPTABLE RISK FOR THE READERS OF A FAMILY FEATURE LIKE OURS.
"AND BY ERRING ON THE SIDE OF CAUTION, WE ALSO AVOID THE POTENTIAL EMBARRASSMENT OF BOTH FOOT ODOR AND POORLY DRAWN SHOES."
SECURITY. HYGIENE. DECENT ARTWORK. THAT'S OUR PLEDGE TO...
FIRE IN THE HOLE!
GB Trudeau

HMM... COULD BE TIME TO SPEND SOME MORE POLITICAL CAPITAL...
USE IT OR LOSE IT!
YES, THIS IS THE PRESIDENT. I WANT TO WITHDRAW SOME MORE POLITICAL CAPITAL.
UM... I'M SORRY, SIR. WE'RE SHOWING YOUR CAPITAL IS TOTALLY ALLOCATED.
WHAT? HOW IS THAT POSSIBLE?
YOU'VE BEEN SPENDING A LOT ON ENRON, SIR...
THAT PLUS YOUR "STIMULUS PACKAGE" FOR THE RICH HAS PEOPLE WONDERING WHOSE SIDE YOU'RE ON...
THEN THERE'S THE RECESSION AND THE RETURN TO DEFICIT SPENDING AND THE RETREAT ON ENVIRONMENTAL PROTECTIONS - ALL OF IT HAS COST YOU!
SIGH...
OKAY, I WANT TO OPEN A NEW ACCOUNT.
GOT WAR?

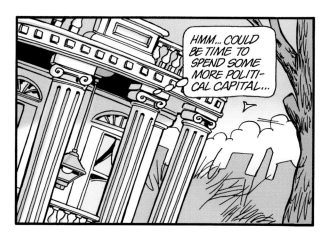

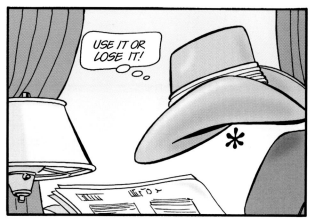

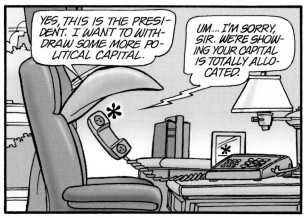

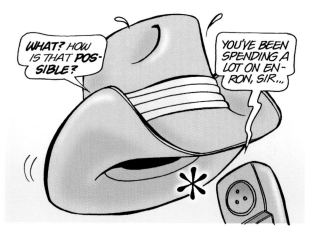

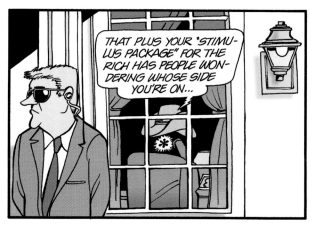

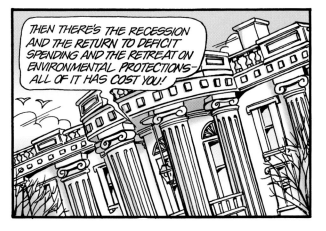

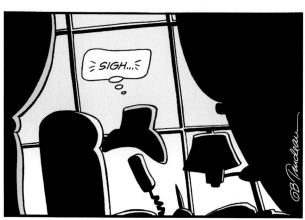

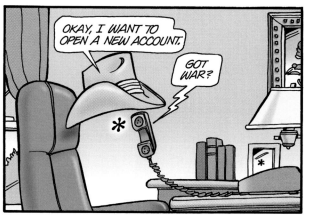

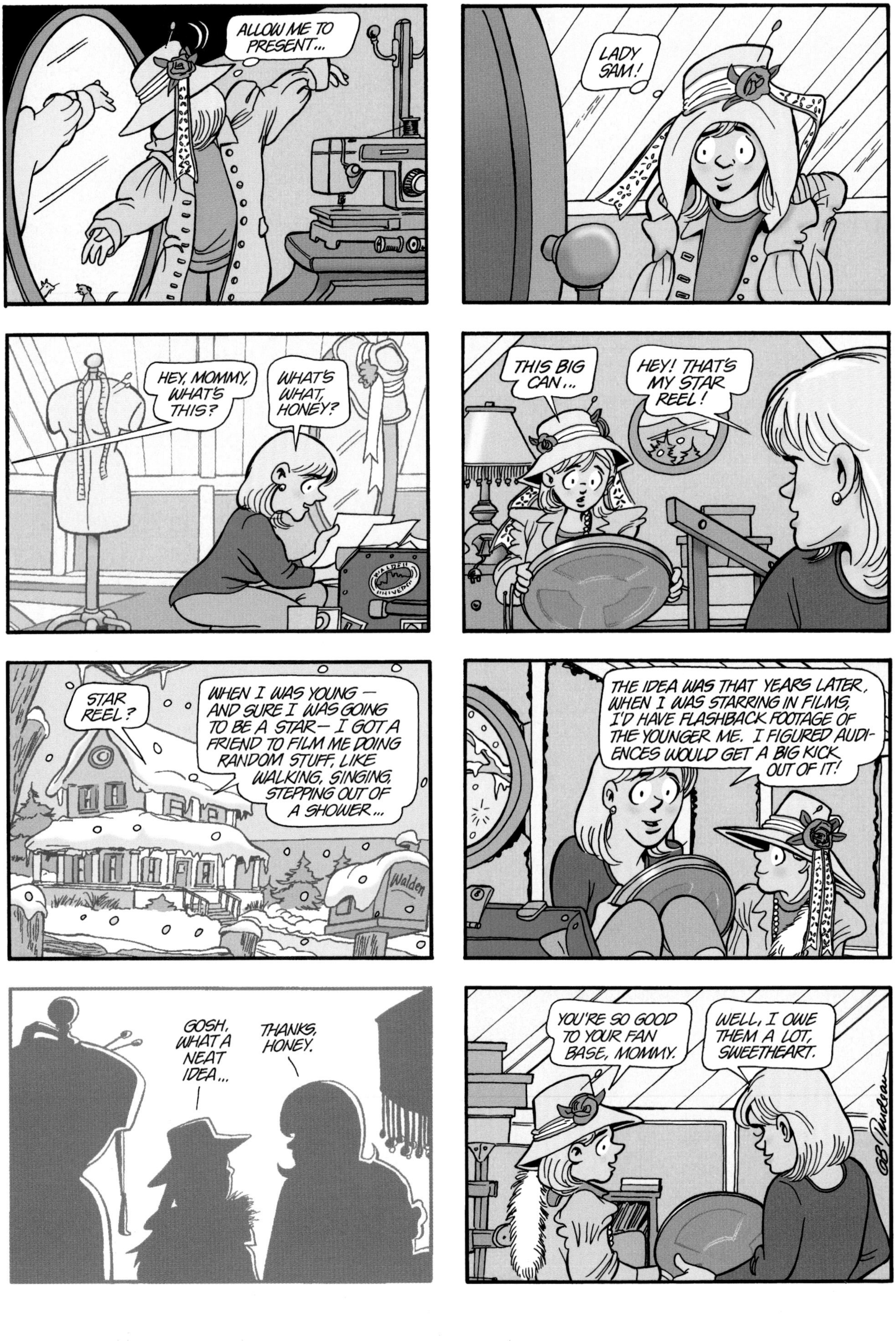
ALLOW ME TO PRESENT...
LADY SAM!
HEY, MOMMY, WHAT'S THIS?
WHAT'S WHAT, HONEY?
THIS BIG CAN...
HEY! THAT'S MY STAR REEL!
STAR REEL?
WHEN I WAS YOUNG — AND SURE I WAS GOING TO BE A STAR— I GOT A FRIEND TO FILM ME DOING RANDOM STUFF, LIKE WALKING, SINGING, STEPPING OUT OF A SHOWER...
Walden
THE IDEA WAS THAT YEARS LATER, WHEN I WAS STARRING IN FILMS, I'D HAVE FLASHBACK FOOTAGE OF THE YOUNGER ME. I FIGURED AUDIENCES WOULD GET A BIG KICK OUT OF IT!
GOSH, WHAT A NEAT IDEA...
THANKS, HONEY.
YOU'RE SO GOOD TO YOUR FAN BASE, MOMMY.
WELL, I OWE THEM A LOT, SWEETHEART.

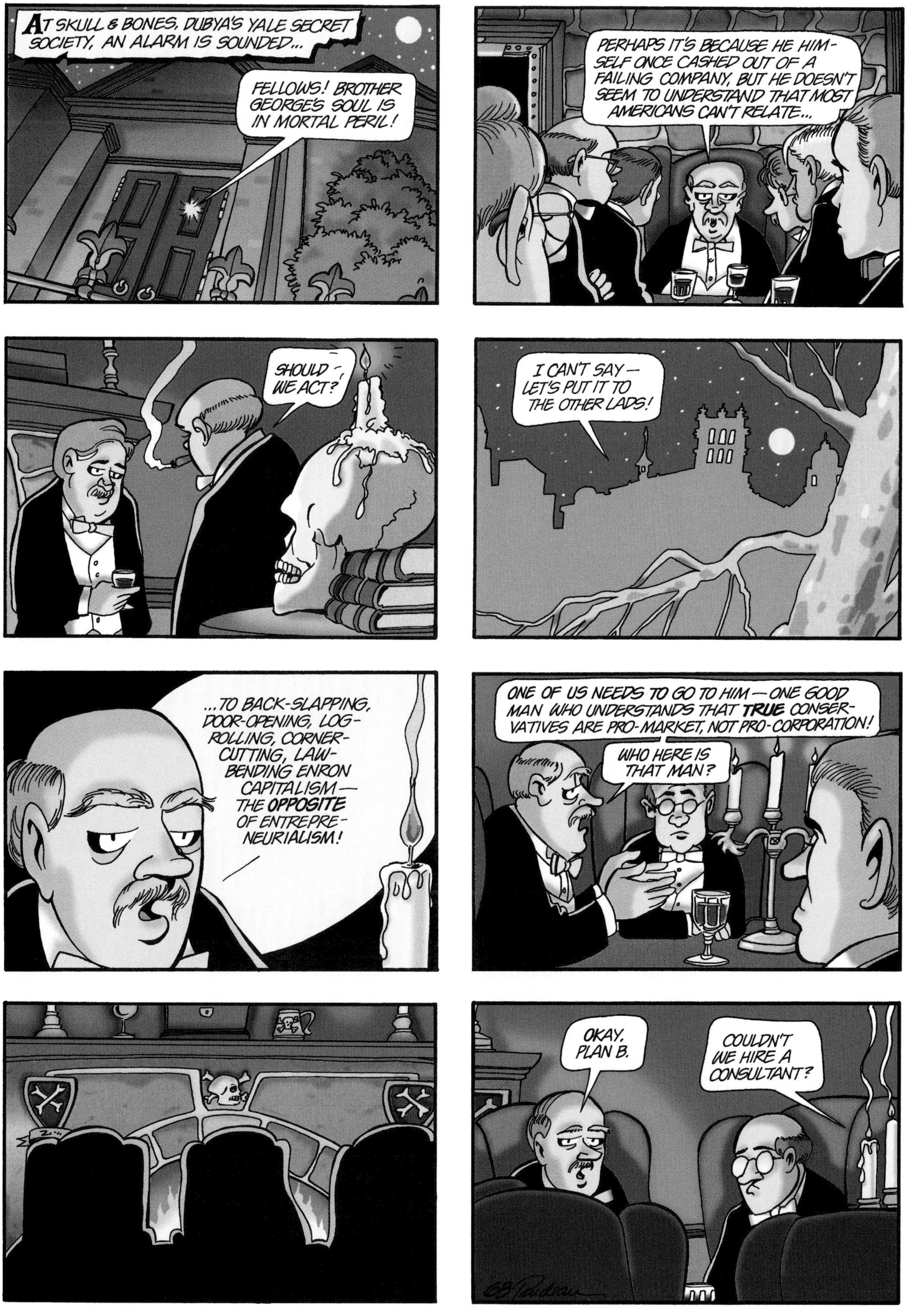
AT SKULL & BONES, DUBYA'S YALE SECRET SOCIETY, AN ALARM IS SOUNDED...
FELLOWS! BROTHER GEORGE'S SOUL IS IN MORTAL PERIL!
PERHAPS IT'S BECAUSE HE HIMSELF ONCE CASHED OUT OF A FAILING COMPANY, BUT HE DOESN'T SEEM TO UNDERSTAND THAT MOST AMERICANS CAN'T RELATE...
SHOULD WE ACT?
I CAN'T SAY — LET'S PUT IT TO THE OTHER LADS!
...TO BACK-SLAPPING, DOOR-OPENING, LOG-ROLLING, CORNER-CUTTING, LAW-BENDING ENRON CAPITALISM — THE OPPOSITE OF ENTREPRENEURIALISM!
ONE OF US NEEDS TO GO TO HIM — ONE GOOD MAN WHO UNDERSTANDS THAT TRUE CONSERVATIVES ARE PRO-MARKET, NOT PRO-CORPORATION!
WHO HERE IS THAT MAN?
OKAY. PLAN B.
COULDN'T WE HIRE A CONSULTANT?

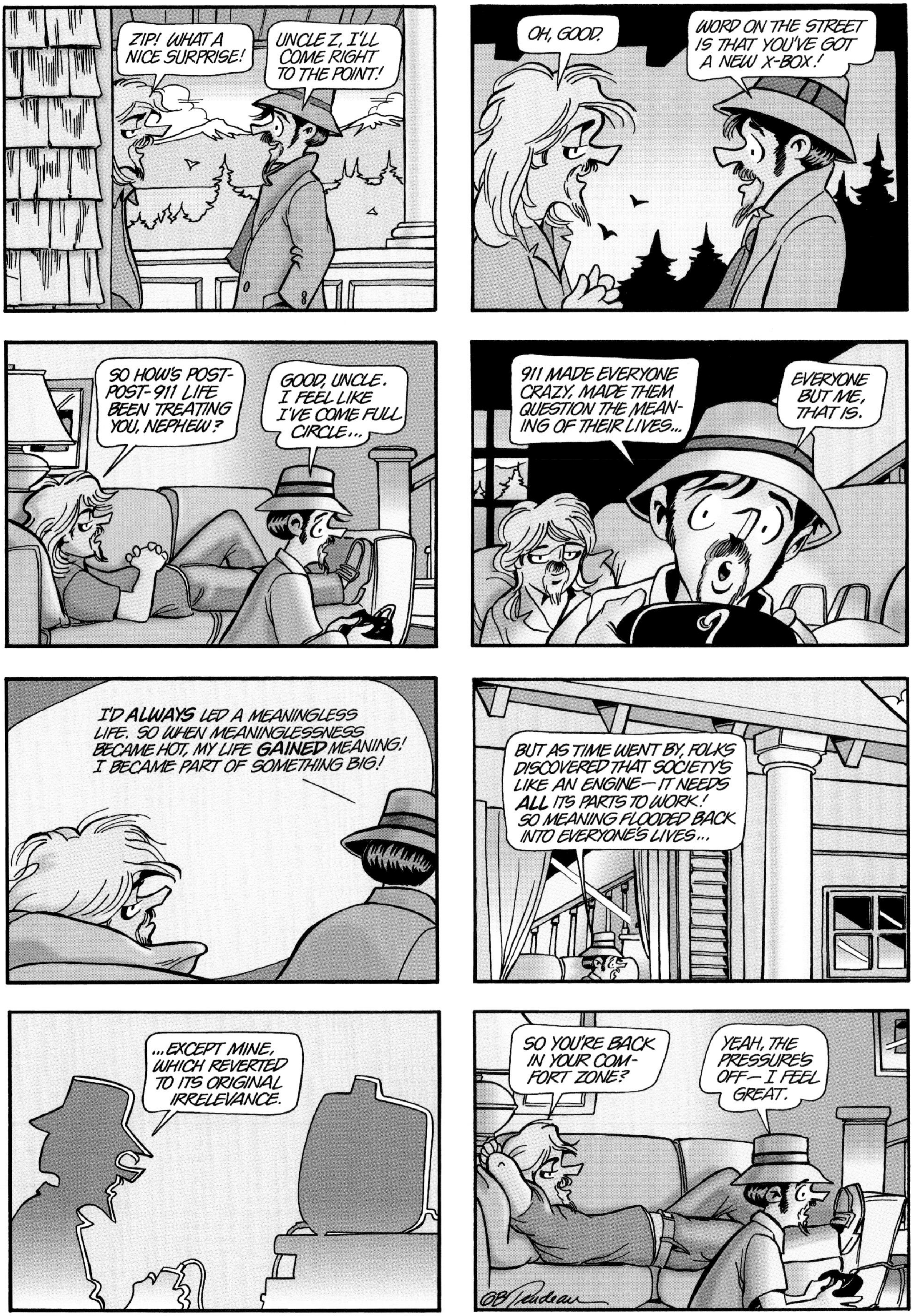

ZIP! WHAT A NICE SURPRISE!
UNCLE Z, I'LL COME RIGHT TO THE POINT!
OH, GOOD.
WORD ON THE STREET IS THAT YOU'VE GOT A NEW X-BOX!
SO HOW'S POST-POST-911 LIFE BEEN TREATING YOU, NEPHEW?
GOOD, UNCLE. I FEEL LIKE I'VE COME FULL CIRCLE...
911 MADE EVERYONE CRAZY. MADE THEM QUESTION THE MEANING OF THEIR LIVES...
EVERYONE BUT ME, THAT IS.
I'D ALWAYS LED A MEANINGLESS LIFE. SO WHEN MEANINGLESSNESS BECAME HOT, MY LIFE GAINED MEANING! I BECAME PART OF SOMETHING BIG!
BUT AS TIME WENT BY, FOLKS DISCOVERED THAT SOCIETY'S LIKE AN ENGINE—IT NEEDS ALL ITS PARTS TO WORK! SO MEANING FLOODED BACK INTO EVERYONE'S LIVES...
...EXCEPT MINE, WHICH REVERTED TO ITS ORIGINAL IRRELEVANCE.
SO YOU'RE BACK IN YOUR COMFORT ZONE?
YEAH, THE PRESSURE'S OFF—I FEEL GREAT.

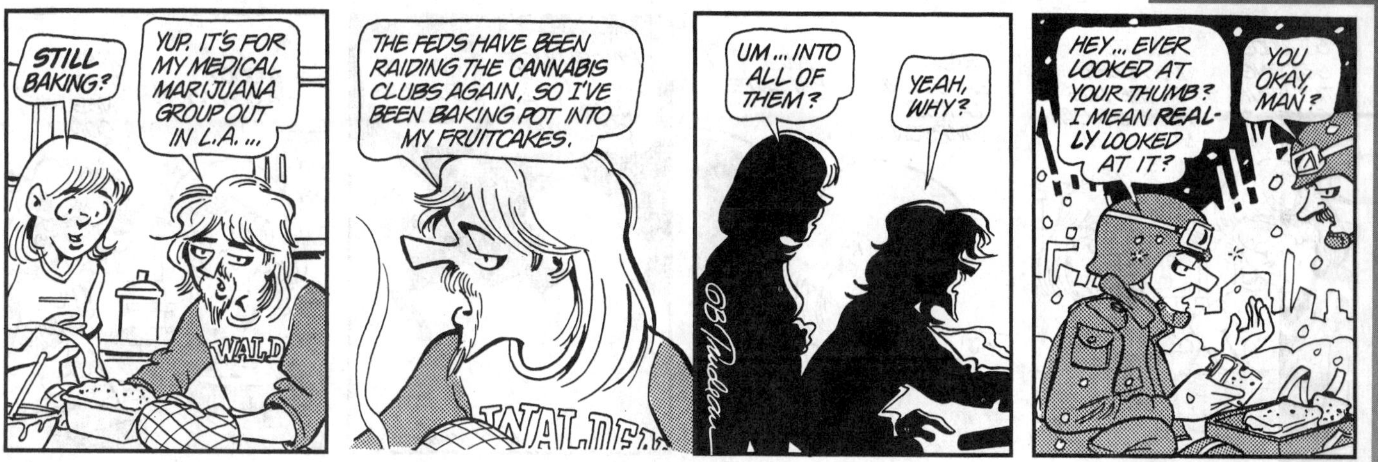
STILL BAKING?
YUP. IT'S FOR MY MEDICAL MARIJUANA GROUP OUT IN L.A. ...
THE FEDS HAVE BEEN RAIDING THE CANNABIS CLUBS AGAIN, SO I'VE BEEN BAKING POT INTO MY FRUITCAKES.
UM ... INTO ALL OF THEM?
YEAH, WHY?
HEY... EVER LOOKED AT YOUR THUMB? I MEAN REALLY LOOKED AT IT?
YOU OKAY, MAN?

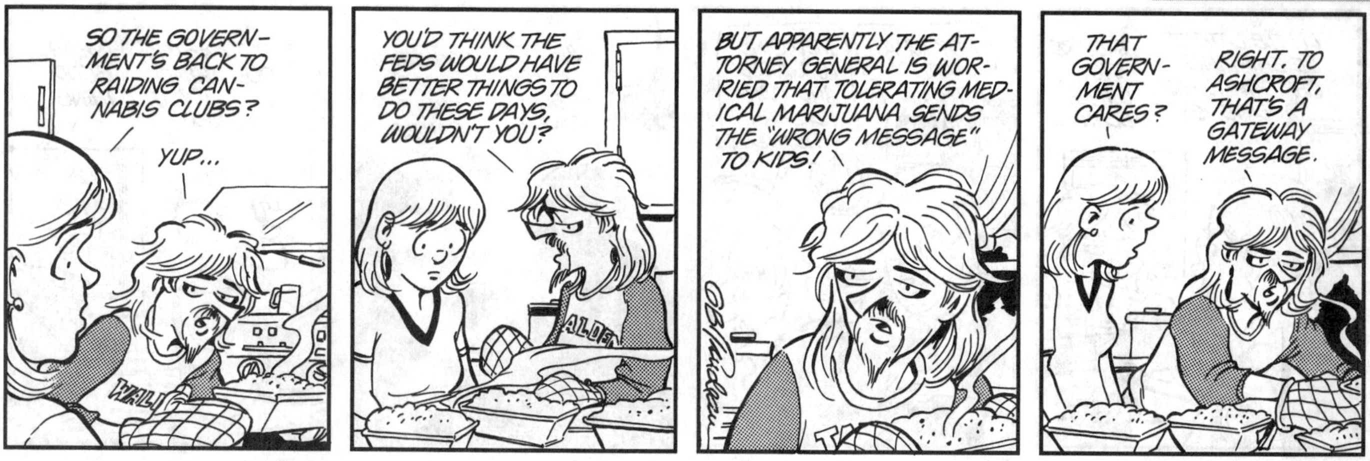
SO THE GOVERNMENT'S BACK TO RAIDING CANNABIS CLUBS?
YUP...
YOU'D THINK THE FEDS WOULD HAVE BETTER THINGS TO DO THESE DAYS, WOULDN'T YOU?
BUT APPARENTLY THE ATTORNEY GENERAL IS WORRIED THAT TOLERATING MEDICAL MARIJUANA SENDS THE "WRONG MESSAGE" TO KIDS!
THAT GOVERNMENT CARES?
RIGHT. TO ASHCROFT, THAT'S A GATEWAY MESSAGE.

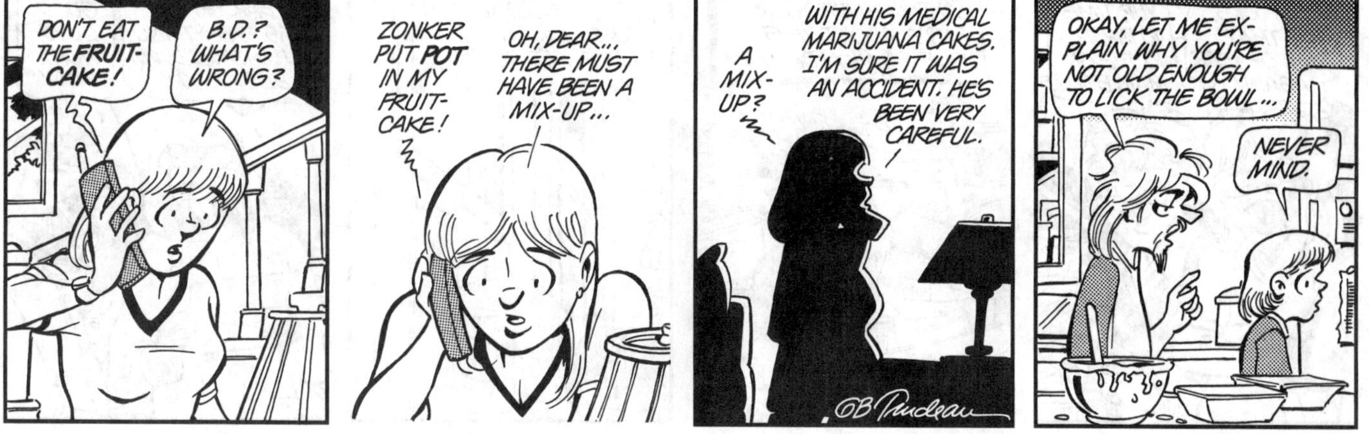
DON'T EAT THE FRUITCAKE!
B.D.? WHAT'S WRONG?
ZONKER PUT POT IN MY FRUITCAKE!
OH, DEAR... THERE MUST HAVE BEEN A MIX-UP...
A MIX-UP?
WITH HIS MEDICAL MARIJUANA CAKES. I'M SURE IT WAS AN ACCIDENT. HE'S BEEN VERY CAREFUL.
OKAY, LET ME EXPLAIN WHY YOU'RE NOT OLD ENOUGH TO LICK THE BOWL...
NEVER MIND.

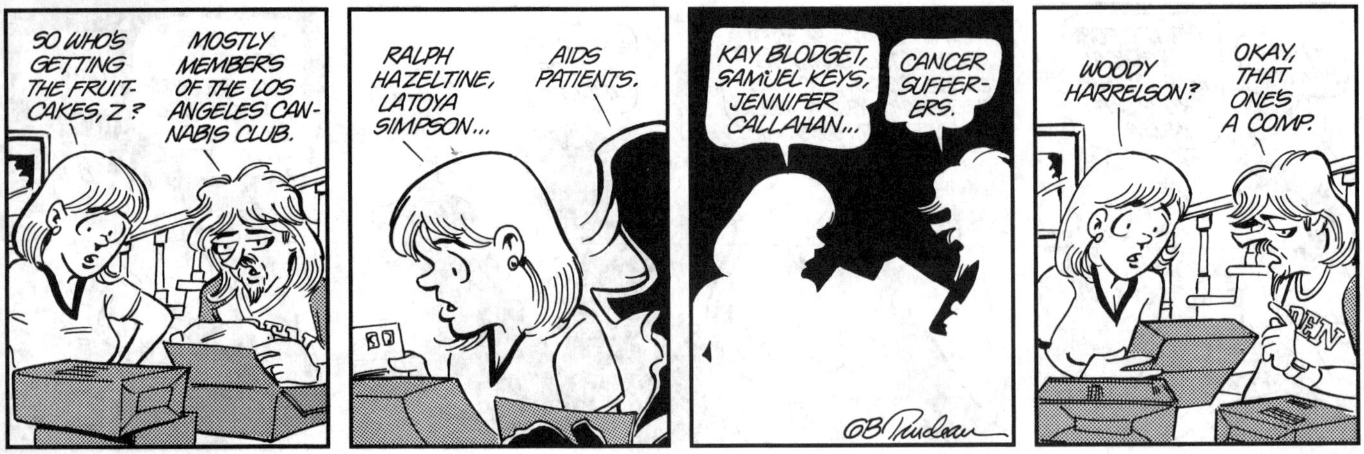
SO WHO'S GETTING THE FRUIT-CAKES, Z?
MOSTLY MEMBERS OF THE LOS ANGELES CAN-NABIS CLUB.
RALPH HAZELTINE, LATOYA SIMPSON...
AIDS PATIENTS.
KAY BLODGET, SAMUEL KEYS, JENNIFER CALLAHAN...
CANCER SUFFER-ERS.
WOODY HARRELSON?
OKAY, THAT ONE'S A COMP.

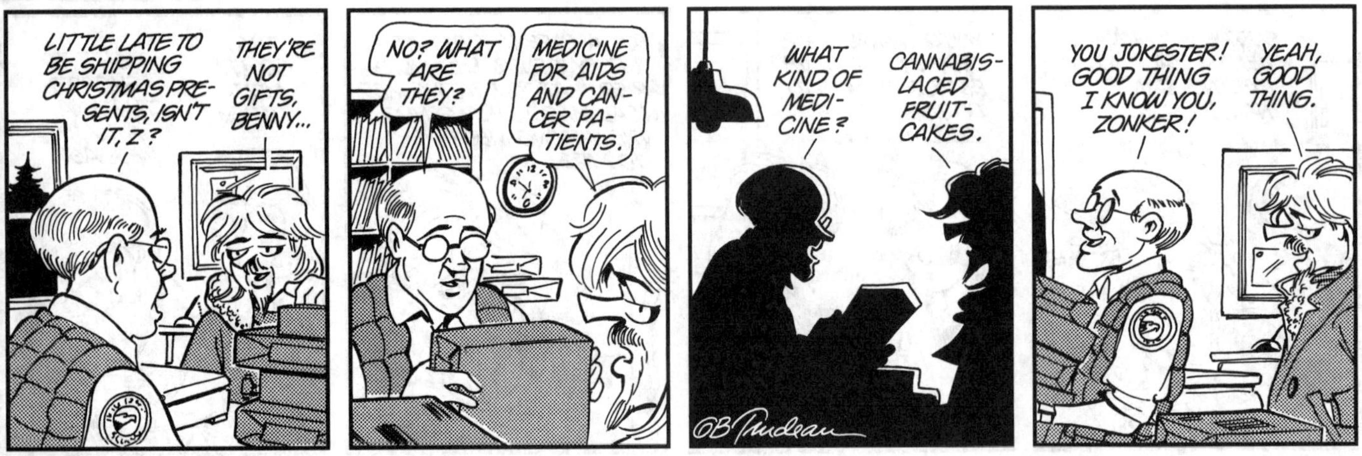
LITTLE LATE TO BE SHIPPING CHRISTMAS PRE-SENTS, ISN'T IT, Z?
THEY'RE NOT GIFTS, BENNY...
NO? WHAT ARE THEY?
MEDICINE FOR AIDS AND CAN-CER PA-TIENTS.
WHAT KIND OF MEDI-CINE?
CANNABIS-LACED FRUIT-CAKES.
YOU JOKESTER! GOOD THING I KNOW YOU, ZONKER!
YEAH, GOOD THING.

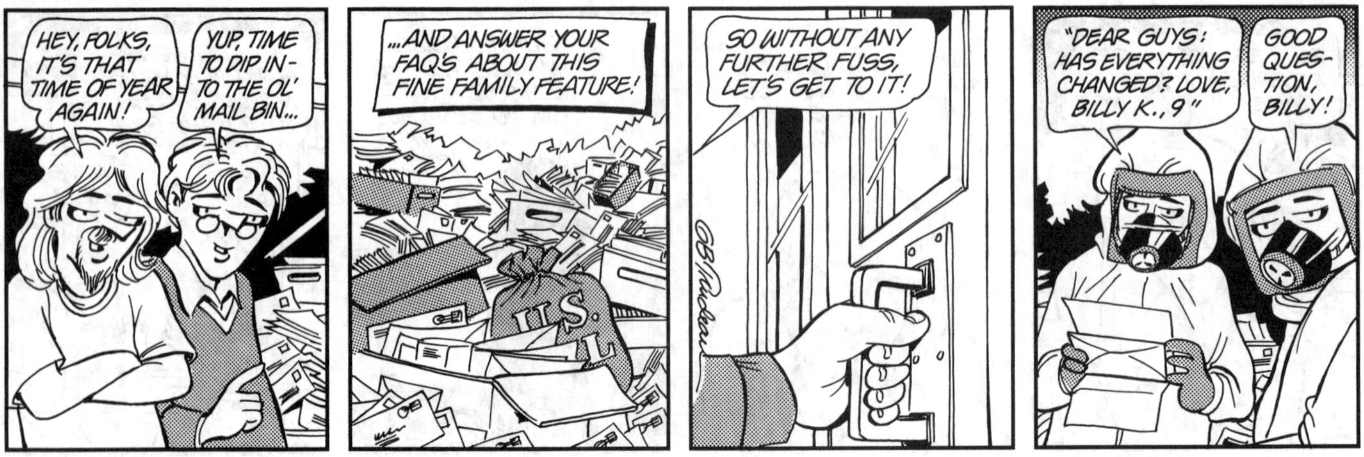
HEY, FOLKS, IT'S THAT TIME OF YEAR AGAIN!
YUP, TIME TO DIP IN-TO THE OL' MAIL BIN...
...AND ANSWER YOUR FAQ'S ABOUT THIS FINE FAMILY FEATURE!
U.S.
SO WITHOUT ANY FURTHER FUSS, LET'S GET TO IT!
"DEAR GUYS: HAS EVERYTHING CHANGED? LOVE, BILLY K., 9"
GOOD QUES-TION, BILLY!

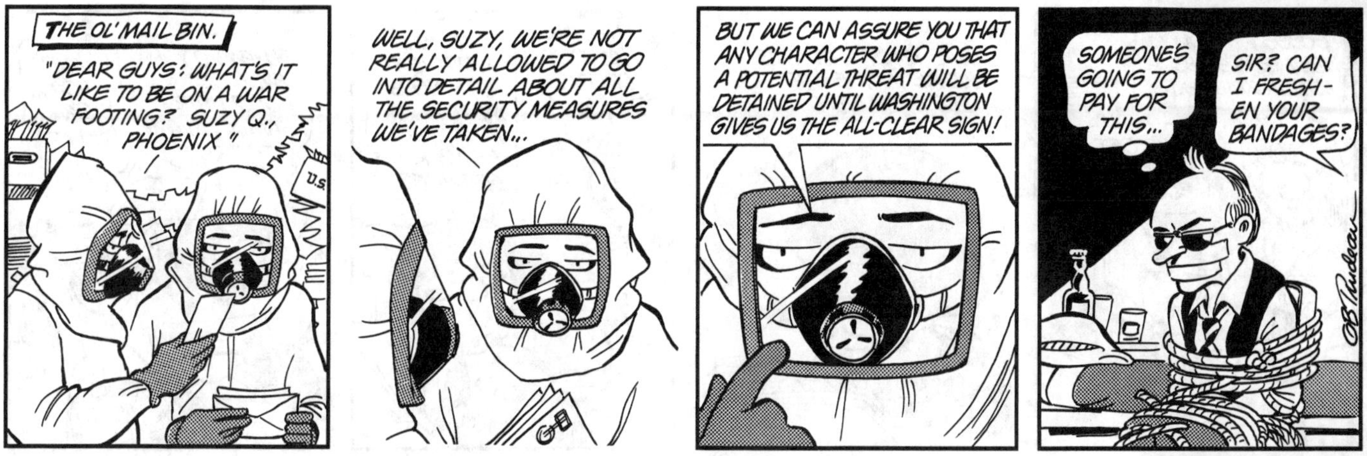
THE OL' MAIL BIN.
"DEAR GUYS: WHAT'S IT LIKE TO BE ON A WAR FOOTING? SUZY Q., PHOENIX"
WELL, SUZY, WE'RE NOT REALLY ALLOWED TO GO INTO DETAIL ABOUT ALL THE SECURITY MEASURES WE'VE TAKEN...
BUT WE CAN ASSURE YOU THAT ANY CHARACTER WHO POSES A POTENTIAL THREAT WILL BE DETAINED UNTIL WASHINGTON GIVES US THE ALL-CLEAR SIGN!
SOMEONE'S GOING TO PAY FOR THIS...
SIR? CAN I FRESH-EN YOUR BANDAGES?

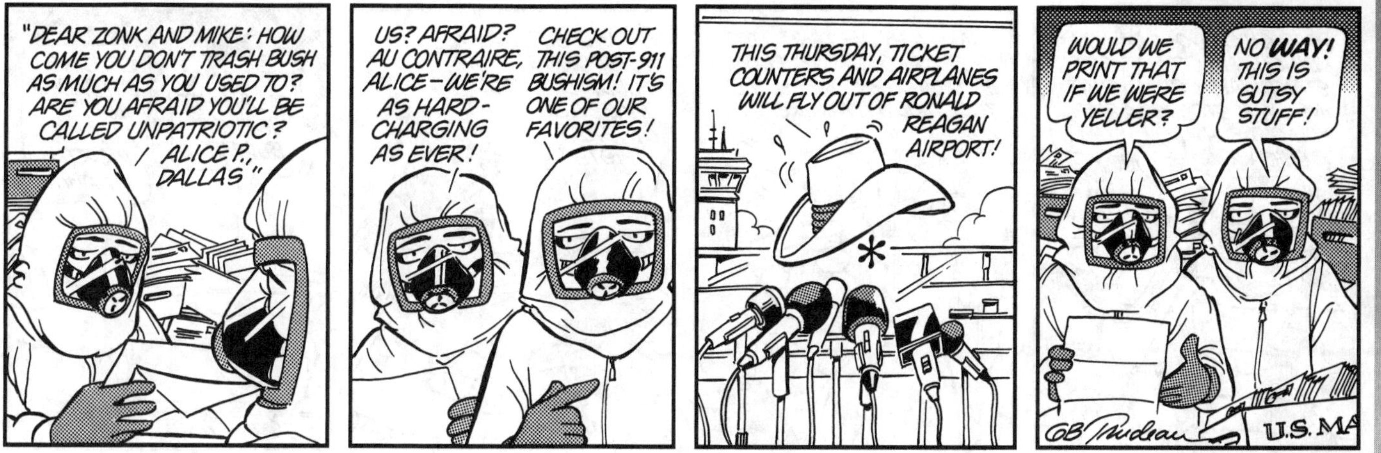
"DEAR ZONK AND MIKE: HOW COME YOU DON'T TRASH BUSH AS MUCH AS YOU USED TO? ARE YOU AFRAID YOU'LL BE CALLED UNPATRIOTIC? ALICE P., DALLAS"
US? AFRAID? AU CONTRAIRE, ALICE—WE'RE AS HARD-CHARGING AS EVER!
CHECK OUT THIS POST-911 BUSHISM! IT'S ONE OF OUR FAVORITES!
THIS THURSDAY, TICKET COUNTERS AND AIRPLANES WILL FLY OUT OF RONALD REAGAN AIRPORT!
WOULD WE PRINT THAT IF WE WERE YELLER?
NO WAY! THIS IS GUTSY STUFF!

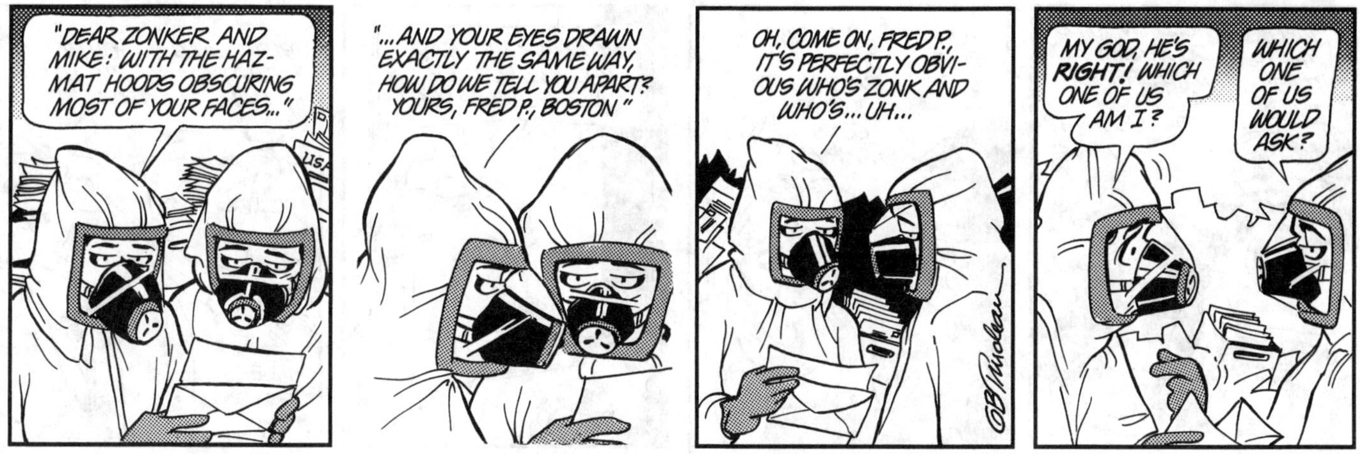
"DEAR ZONKER AND MIKE: WITH THE HAZ-MAT HOODS OBSCURING MOST OF YOUR FACES..."
"...AND YOUR EYES DRAWN EXACTLY THE SAME WAY, HOW DO WE TELL YOU APART? YOURS, FRED P., BOSTON"
OH, COME ON, FRED P., IT'S PERFECTLY OBVI-OUS WHO'S ZONK AND WHO'S... UH...
MY GOD, HE'S RIGHT! WHICH ONE OF US AM I?
WHICH ONE OF US WOULD ASK?

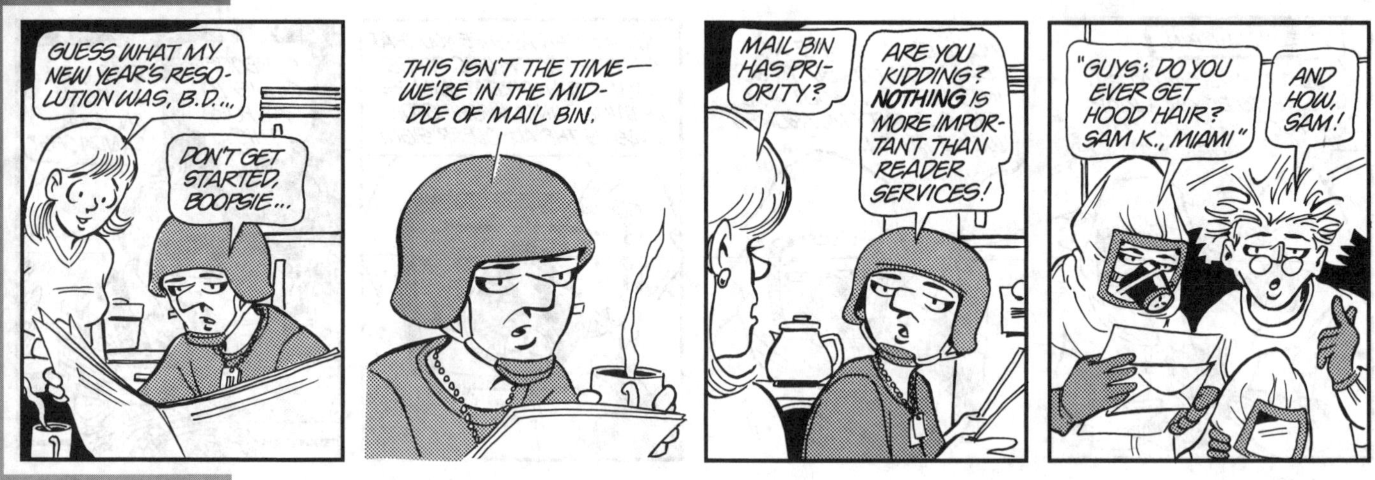
GUESS WHAT MY NEW YEAR'S RESOLUTION WAS, B.D....
DON'T GET STARTED, BOOPSIE...
THIS ISN'T THE TIME— WE'RE IN THE MIDDLE OF MAIL BIN.
MAIL BIN HAS PRIORITY?
ARE YOU KIDDING? **NOTHING** IS MORE IMPORTANT THAN READER SERVICES!
"GUYS: DO YOU EVER GET HOOD HAIR? SAM K., MIAMI"
AND HOW, SAM!

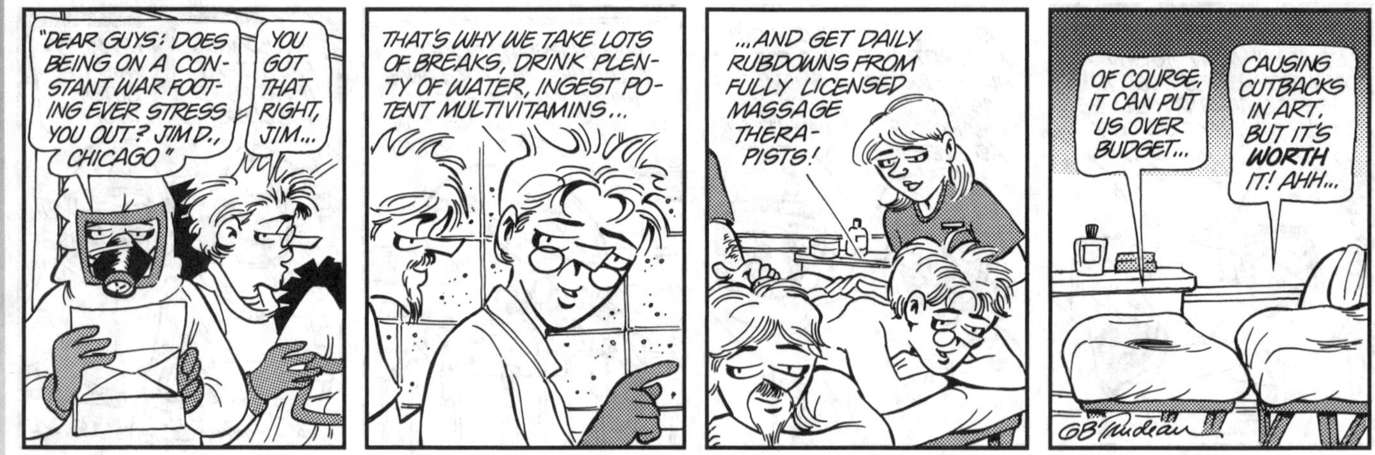
"DEAR GUYS: DOES BEING ON A CONSTANT WAR FOOTING EVER STRESS YOU OUT? JIM D., CHICAGO"
YOU GOT THAT RIGHT, JIM...
THAT'S WHY WE TAKE LOTS OF BREAKS, DRINK PLENTY OF WATER, INGEST POTENT MULTIVITAMINS...
...AND GET DAILY RUBDOWNS FROM FULLY LICENSED MASSAGE THERAPISTS!
OF COURSE, IT CAN PUT US OVER BUDGET...
CAUSING CUTBACKS IN ART, BUT IT'S **WORTH** IT! AHH...

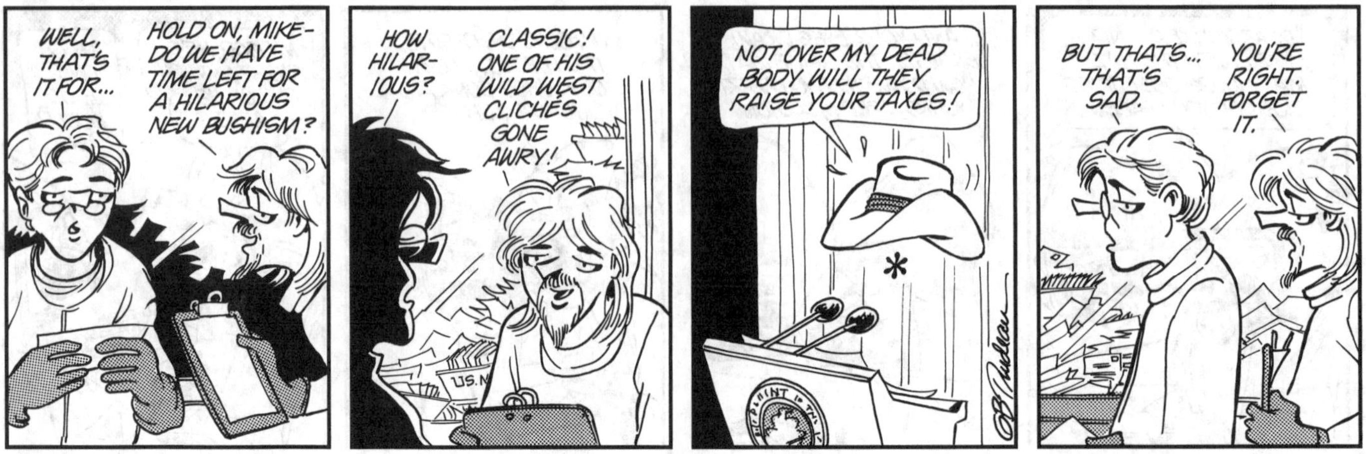
WELL, THAT'S IT FOR...
HOLD ON, MIKE—DO WE HAVE TIME LEFT FOR A HILARIOUS NEW BUSHISM?
HOW HILARIOUS?
CLASSIC! ONE OF HIS WILD WEST CLICHÉS GONE AWRY!
NOT OVER MY DEAD BODY WILL THEY RAISE YOUR TAXES!
BUT THAT'S... THAT'S SAD.
YOU'RE RIGHT. FORGET IT.

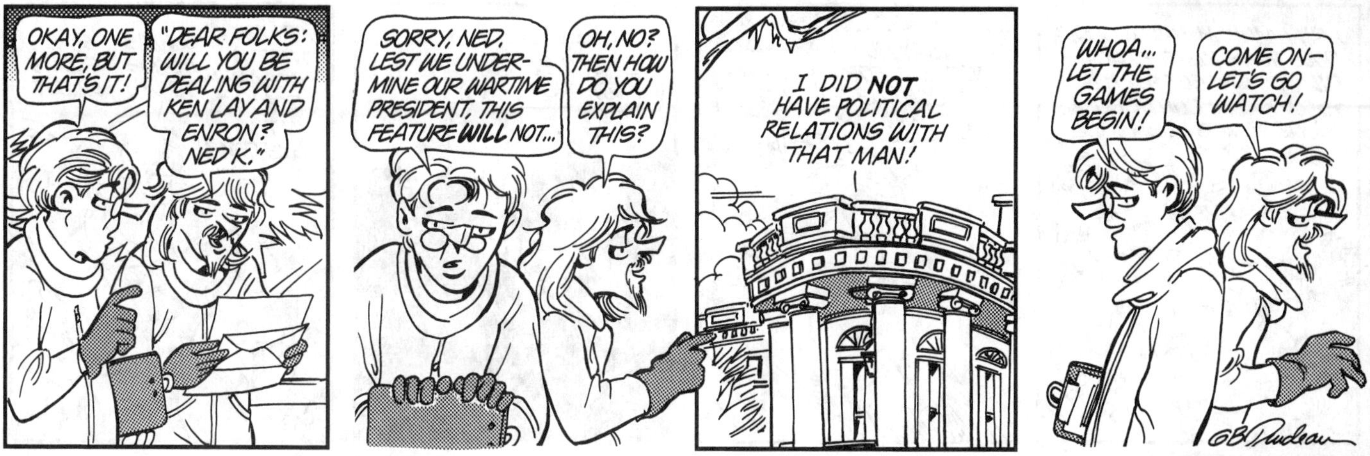
OKAY, ONE MORE, BUT THAT'S IT!
"DEAR FOLKS: WILL YOU BE DEALING WITH KEN LAY AND ENRON? NED K."
SORRY, NED. LEST WE UNDERMINE OUR WARTIME PRESIDENT, THIS FEATURE **WILL** NOT...
OH, NO? THEN HOW DO YOU EXPLAIN THIS?
I DID **NOT** HAVE POLITICAL RELATIONS WITH THAT MAN!
WHOA... LET THE GAMES BEGIN!
COME ON— LET'S GO WATCH!

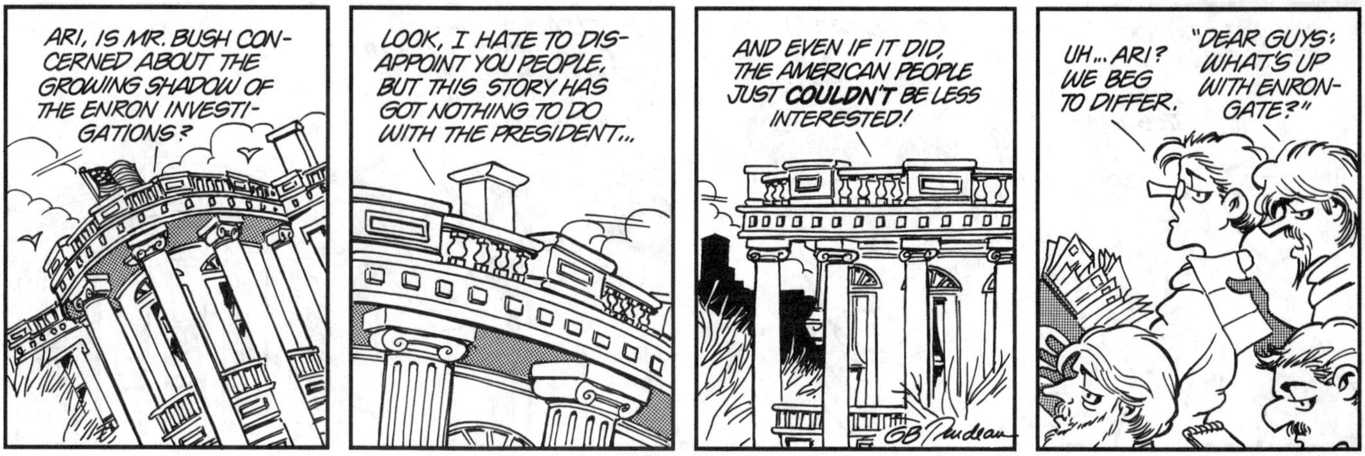
ARI, IS MR. BUSH CONCERNED ABOUT THE GROWING SHADOW OF THE ENRON INVESTIGATIONS?
LOOK, I HATE TO DISAPPOINT YOU PEOPLE, BUT THIS STORY HAS GOT NOTHING TO DO WITH THE PRESIDENT...
AND EVEN IF IT DID, THE AMERICAN PEOPLE JUST **COULDN'T** BE LESS INTERESTED!
UH... ARI? WE BEG TO DIFFER.
"DEAR GUYS: WHAT'S UP WITH ENRONGATE?"

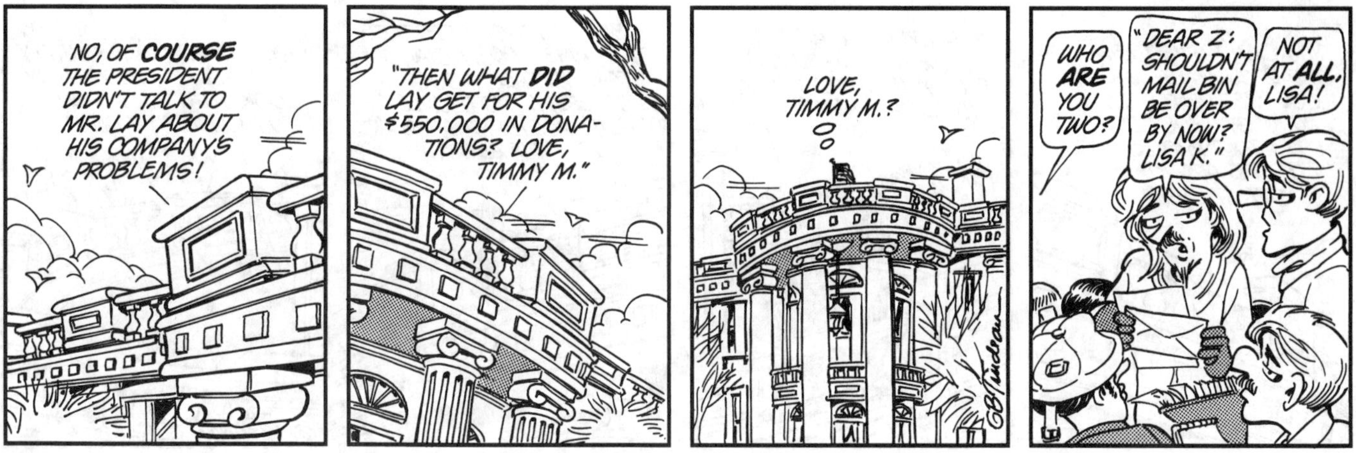
NO, OF **COURSE** THE PRESIDENT DIDN'T TALK TO MR. LAY ABOUT HIS COMPANY'S PROBLEMS!
"THEN WHAT **DID** LAY GET FOR HIS $550,000 IN DONATIONS? LOVE, TIMMY M."
LOVE, TIMMY M.?
WHO **ARE** YOU TWO?
"DEAR Z: SHOULDN'T MAIL BIN BE OVER BY NOW? LISA K."
NOT AT **ALL**, LISA!

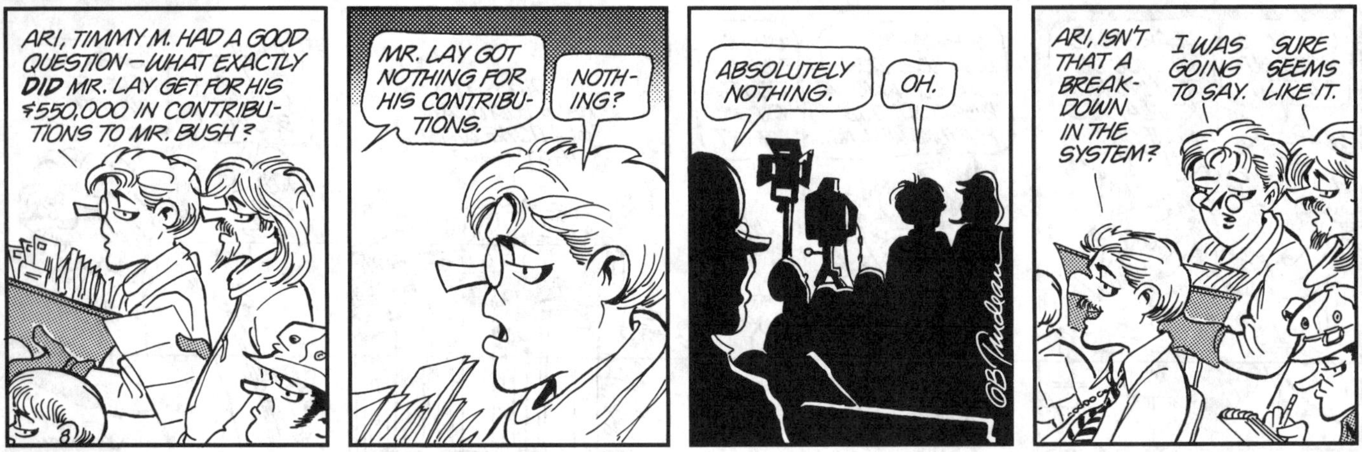
ARI, TIMMY M. HAD A GOOD QUESTION—WHAT EXACTLY **DID** MR. LAY GET FOR HIS $550,000 IN CONTRIBUTIONS TO MR. BUSH?
MR. LAY GOT NOTHING FOR HIS CONTRIBUTIONS.
NOTHING?
ABSOLUTELY NOTHING.
OH.
ARI, ISN'T THAT A BREAKDOWN IN THE SYSTEM?
I WAS GOING TO SAY.
SURE SEEMS LIKE IT.

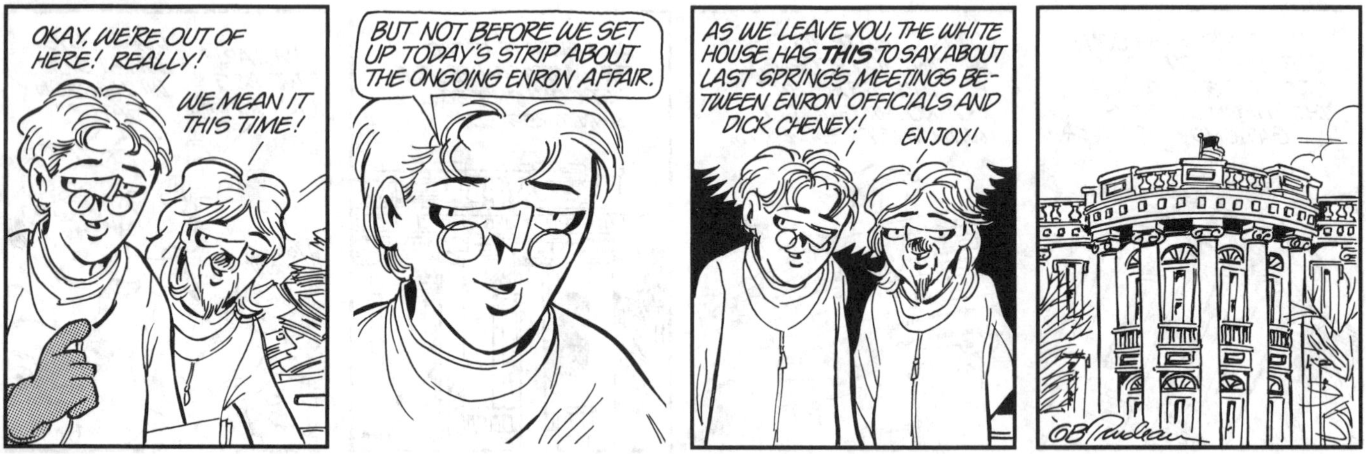
OKAY, WE'RE OUT OF HERE! REALLY!
WE MEAN IT THIS TIME!
BUT NOT BEFORE WE SET UP TODAY'S STRIP ABOUT THE ONGOING ENRON AFFAIR.
AS WE LEAVE YOU, THE WHITE HOUSE HAS **THIS** TO SAY ABOUT LAST SPRING'S MEETINGS BETWEEN ENRON OFFICIALS AND DICK CHENEY!
ENJOY!

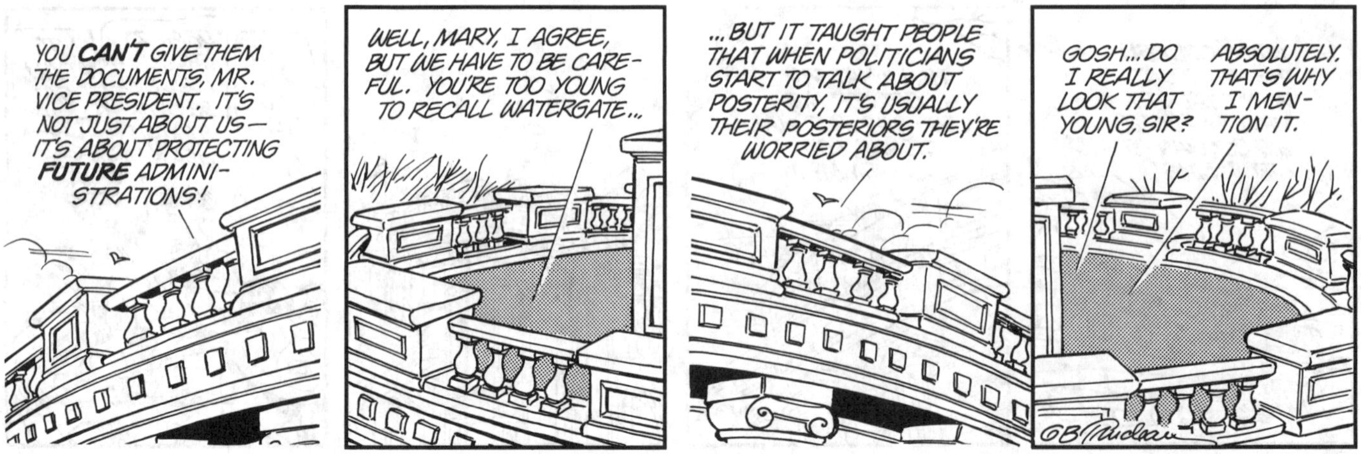
YOU **CAN'T** GIVE THEM THE DOCUMENTS, MR. VICE PRESIDENT. IT'S NOT JUST ABOUT US—IT'S ABOUT PROTECTING **FUTURE** ADMINISTRATIONS!
WELL, MARY, I AGREE, BUT WE HAVE TO BE CAREFUL. YOU'RE TOO YOUNG TO RECALL WATERGATE...
...BUT IT TAUGHT PEOPLE THAT WHEN POLITICIANS START TO TALK ABOUT POSTERITY, IT'S USUALLY THEIR POSTERIORS THEY'RE WORRIED ABOUT.
GOSH... DO I REALLY LOOK THAT YOUNG, SIR?
ABSOLUTELY. THAT'S WHY I MENTION IT.

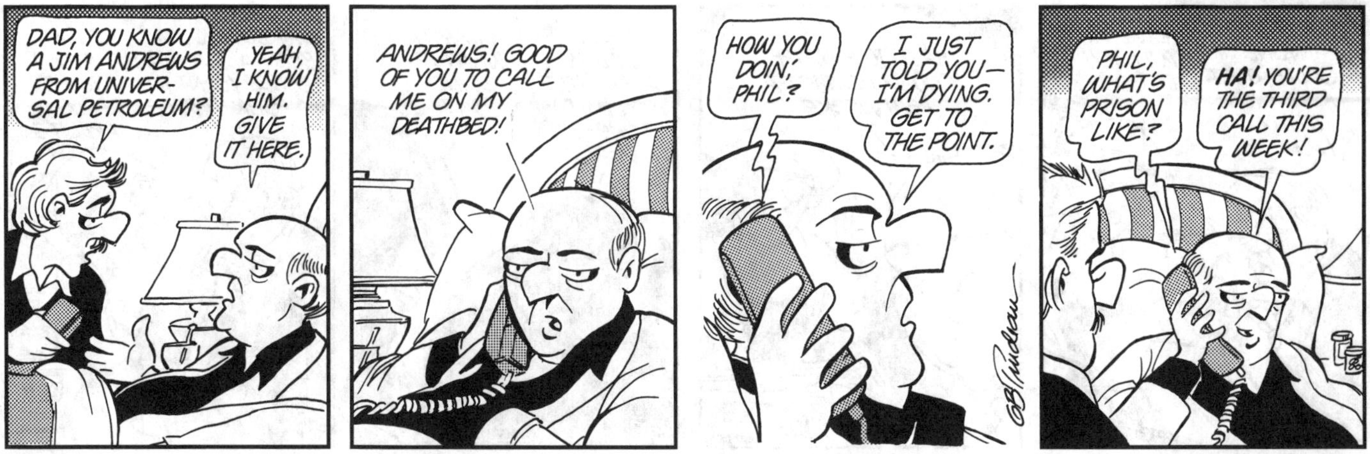
DAD, YOU KNOW A JIM ANDREWS FROM UNIVERSAL PETROLEUM?
YEAH, I KNOW HIM. GIVE IT HERE.
ANDREWS! GOOD OF YOU TO CALL ME ON MY DEATHBED!
HOW YOU DOIN', PHIL?
I JUST TOLD YOU— I'M DYING. GET TO THE POINT.
PHIL, WHAT'S PRISON LIKE?
HA! YOU'RE THE THIRD CALL THIS WEEK!

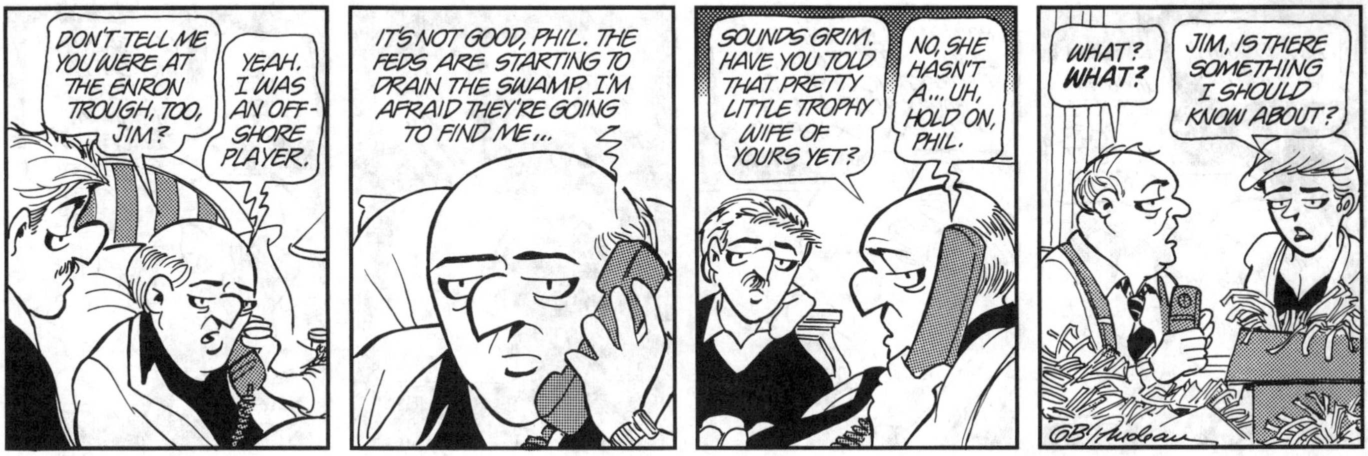
DON'T TELL ME YOU WERE AT THE ENRON TROUGH, TOO, JIM?
YEAH. I WAS AN OFFSHORE PLAYER.
IT'S NOT GOOD, PHIL. THE FEDS ARE STARTING TO DRAIN THE SWAMP. I'M AFRAID THEY'RE GOING TO FIND ME...
SOUNDS GRIM. HAVE YOU TOLD THAT PRETTY LITTLE TROPHY WIFE OF YOURS YET?
NO, SHE HASN'T A... UH, HOLD ON, PHIL.
WHAT? WHAT?
JIM, IS THERE SOMETHING I SHOULD KNOW ABOUT?

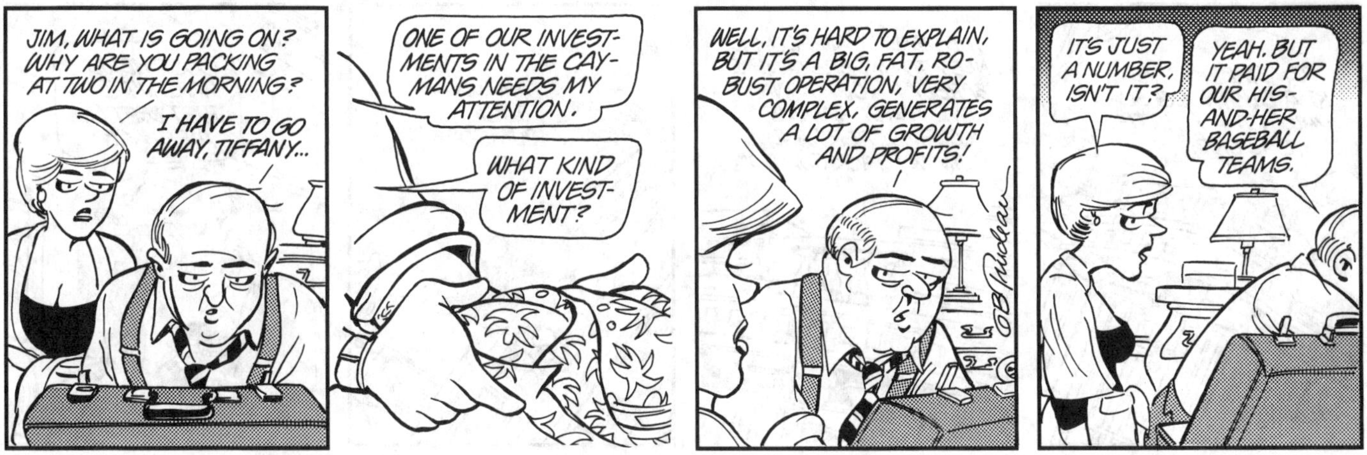
JIM, WHAT IS GOING ON? WHY ARE YOU PACKING AT TWO IN THE MORNING?
I HAVE TO GO AWAY, TIFFANY...
ONE OF OUR INVESTMENTS IN THE CAYMANS NEEDS MY ATTENTION.
WHAT KIND OF INVESTMENT?
WELL, IT'S HARD TO EXPLAIN, BUT IT'S A BIG, FAT, ROBUST OPERATION, VERY COMPLEX, GENERATES A LOT OF GROWTH AND PROFITS!
IT'S JUST A NUMBER, ISN'T IT?
YEAH. BUT IT PAID FOR OUR HIS-AND-HER BASEBALL TEAMS.

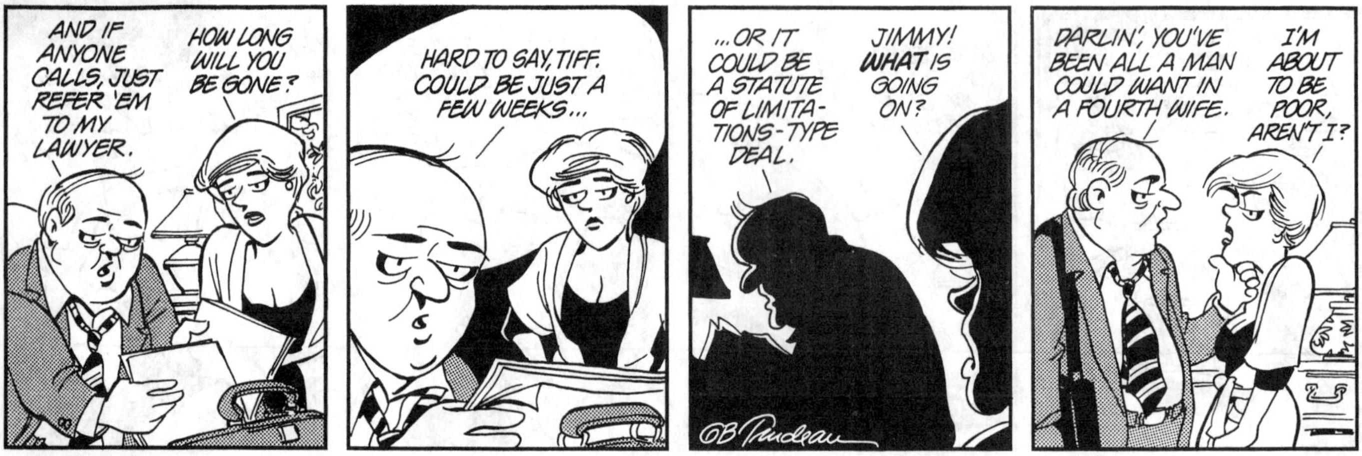
AND IF ANYONE CALLS, JUST REFER 'EM TO MY LAWYER.
HOW LONG WILL YOU BE GONE?
HARD TO SAY, TIFF. COULD BE JUST A FEW WEEKS...
...OR IT COULD BE A STATUTE OF LIMITATIONS-TYPE DEAL.
JIMMY! **WHAT** IS GOING ON?
DARLIN', YOU'VE BEEN ALL A MAN COULD WANT IN A FOURTH WIFE.
I'M ABOUT TO BE POOR, AREN'T I?
GB Trudeau

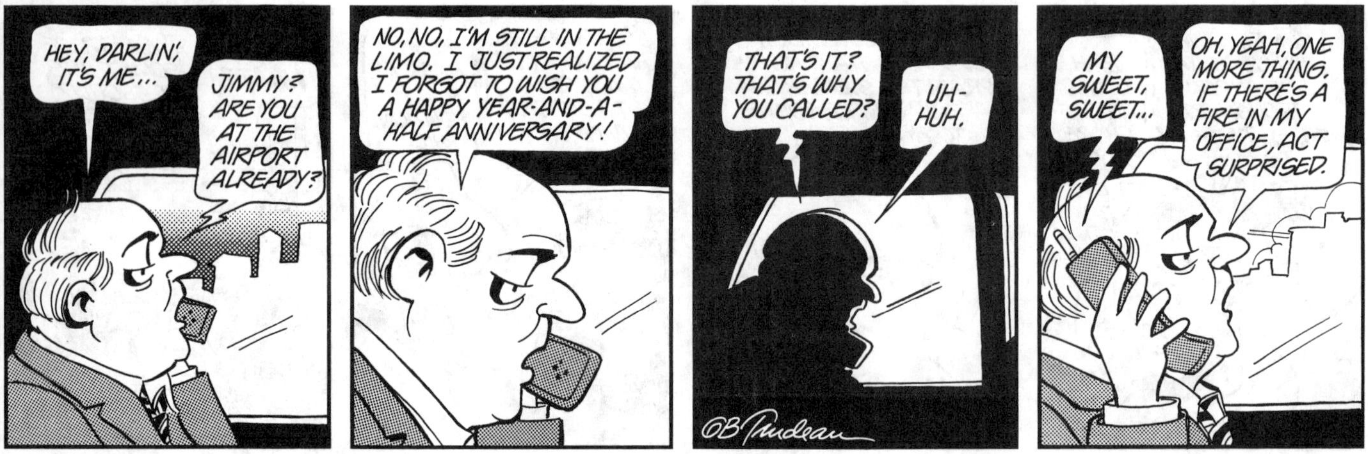
HEY, DARLIN', IT'S ME...
JIMMY? ARE YOU AT THE AIRPORT ALREADY?
NO, NO, I'M STILL IN THE LIMO. I JUST REALIZED I FORGOT TO WISH YOU A HAPPY YEAR-AND-A-HALF ANNIVERSARY!
THAT'S IT? THAT'S WHY YOU CALLED?
UH-HUH.
MY SWEET, SWEET...
OH, YEAH, ONE MORE THING. IF THERE'S A FIRE IN MY OFFICE, ACT SURPRISED.
GB Trudeau

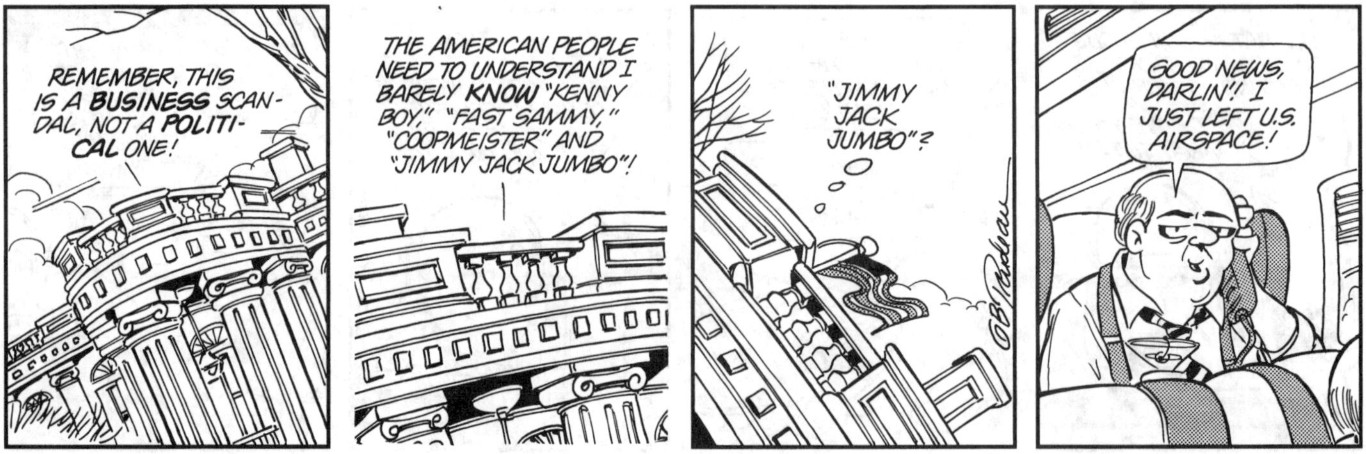
REMEMBER, THIS IS A **BUSINESS** SCANDAL, NOT A **POLITICAL** ONE!
THE AMERICAN PEOPLE NEED TO UNDERSTAND I BARELY **KNOW** "KENNY BOY," "FAST SAMMY," "COOPMEISTER" AND "JIMMY JACK JUMBO"!
"JIMMY JACK JUMBO"?
GB Trudeau
GOOD NEWS, DARLIN'! I JUST LEFT U.S. AIRSPACE!

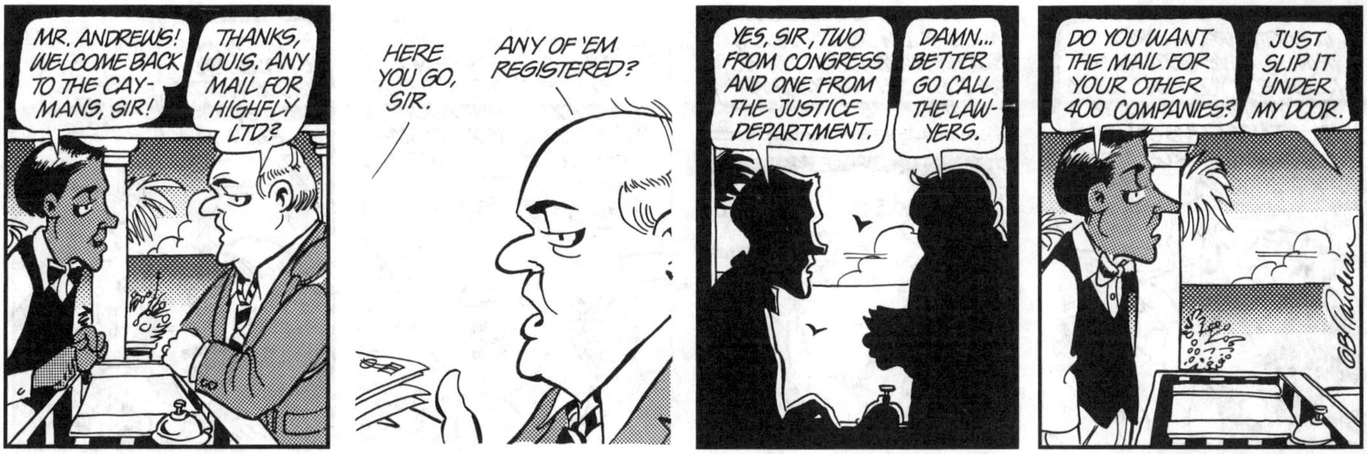
MR. ANDREWS! WELCOME BACK TO THE CAY-MANS, SIR!
THANKS, LOUIS. ANY MAIL FOR HIGHFLY LTD?
HERE YOU GO, SIR.
ANY OF 'EM REGISTERED?
YES, SIR, TWO FROM CONGRESS AND ONE FROM THE JUSTICE DEPARTMENT.
DAMN... BETTER GO CALL THE LAW-YERS.
DO YOU WANT THE MAIL FOR YOUR OTHER 400 COMPANIES?
JUST SLIP IT UNDER MY DOOR.

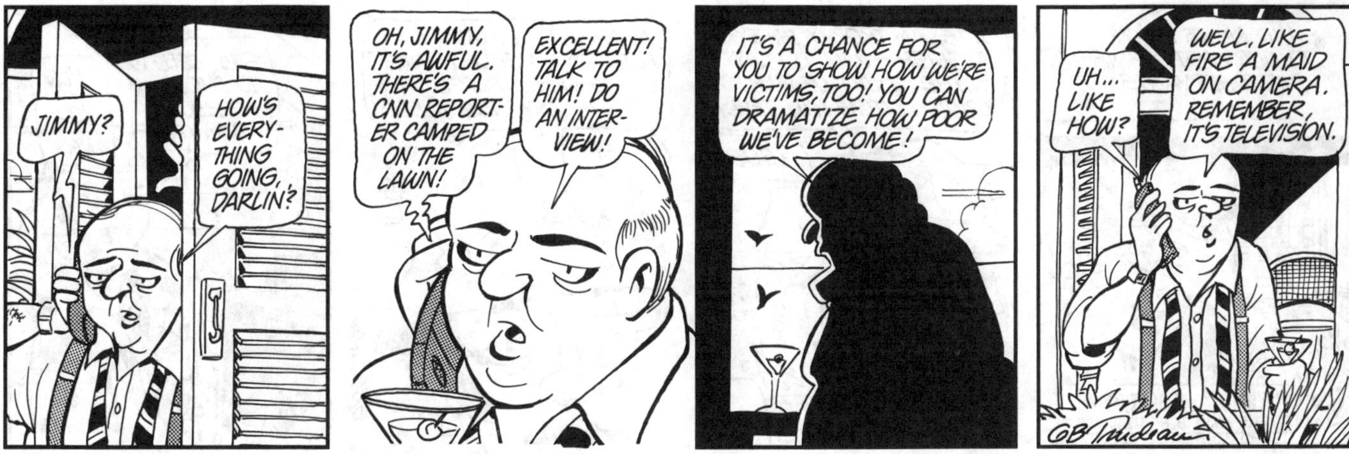
JIMMY?
HOW'S EVERY-THING GOING, DARLIN'?
OH, JIMMY, IT'S AWFUL. THERE'S A CNN REPORT-ER CAMPED ON THE LAWN!
EXCELLENT! TALK TO HIM! DO AN INTER-VIEW!
IT'S A CHANCE FOR YOU TO SHOW HOW WE'RE VICTIMS, TOO! YOU CAN DRAMATIZE HOW POOR WE'VE BECOME!
UH... LIKE HOW?
WELL, LIKE FIRE A MAID ON CAMERA. REMEMBER, IT'S TELEVISION.

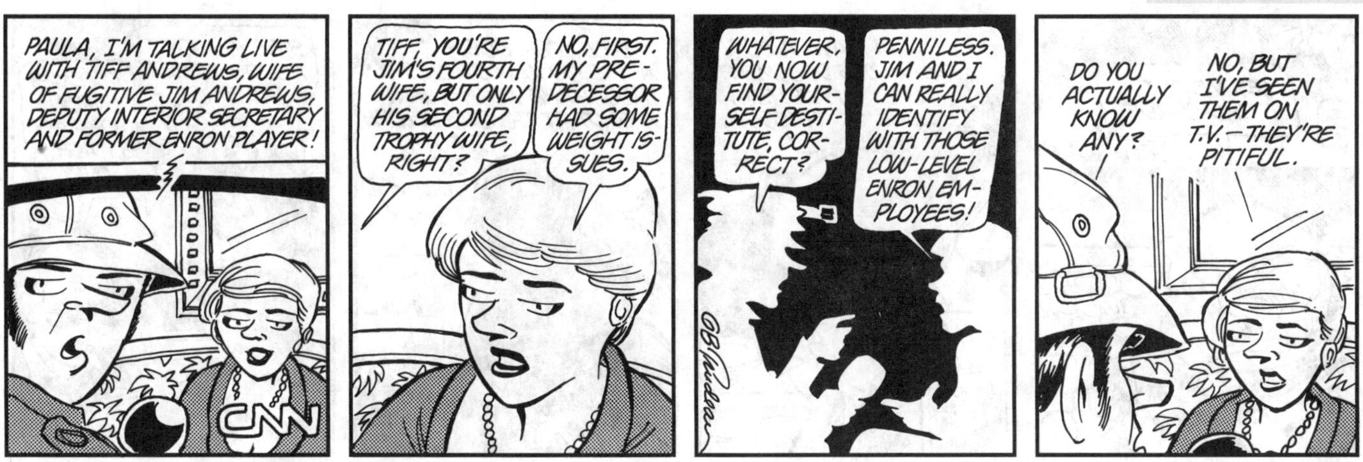
PAULA, I'M TALKING LIVE WITH TIFF ANDREWS, WIFE OF FUGITIVE JIM ANDREWS, DEPUTY INTERIOR SECRETARY AND FORMER ENRON PLAYER!
CNN
TIFF, YOU'RE JIM'S FOURTH WIFE, BUT ONLY HIS SECOND TROPHY WIFE, RIGHT?
NO, FIRST. MY PRE-DECESSOR HAD SOME WEIGHT IS-SUES.
WHATEVER, YOU NOW FIND YOUR-SELF DESTI-TUTE, COR-RECT?
PENNILESS. JIM AND I CAN REALLY IDENTIFY WITH THOSE LOW-LEVEL ENRON EM-PLOYEES!
DO YOU ACTUALLY KNOW ANY?
NO, BUT I'VE SEEN THEM ON T.V.—THEY'RE PITIFUL.

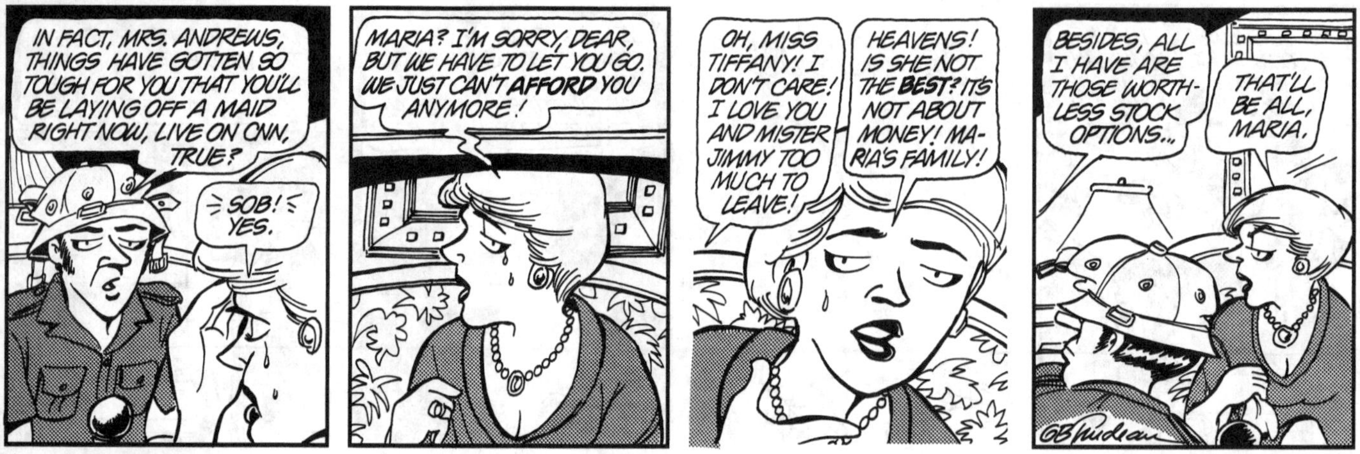
IN FACT, MRS. ANDREWS, THINGS HAVE GOTTEN SO TOUGH FOR YOU THAT YOU'LL BE LAYING OFF A MAID RIGHT NOW, LIVE ON CNN, TRUE?
SOB! YES.
MARIA? I'M SORRY, DEAR, BUT WE HAVE TO LET YOU GO. WE JUST CAN'T AFFORD YOU ANYMORE!
OH, MISS TIFFANY! I DON'T CARE! I LOVE YOU AND MISTER JIMMY TOO MUCH TO LEAVE!
HEAVENS! IS SHE NOT THE BEST? IT'S NOT ABOUT MONEY! MARIA'S FAMILY!
BESIDES, ALL I HAVE ARE THOSE WORTHLESS STOCK OPTIONS...
THAT'LL BE ALL, MARIA.
GB Trudeau

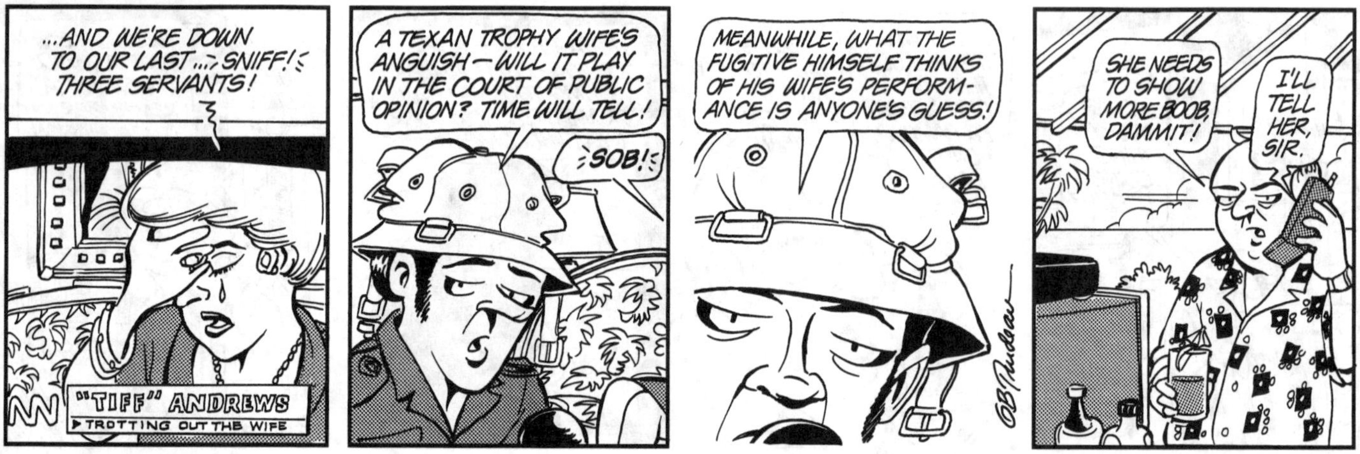
...AND WE'RE DOWN TO OUR LAST... SNIFF! THREE SERVANTS!
"TIFF" ANDREWS
TROTTING OUT THE WIFE
A TEXAN TROPHY WIFE'S ANGUISH — WILL IT PLAY IN THE COURT OF PUBLIC OPINION? TIME WILL TELL!
SOB!
MEANWHILE, WHAT THE FUGITIVE HIMSELF THINKS OF HIS WIFE'S PERFORMANCE IS ANYONE'S GUESS!
GB Trudeau
SHE NEEDS TO SHOW MORE BOOB, DAMMIT!
I'LL TELL HER, SIR.

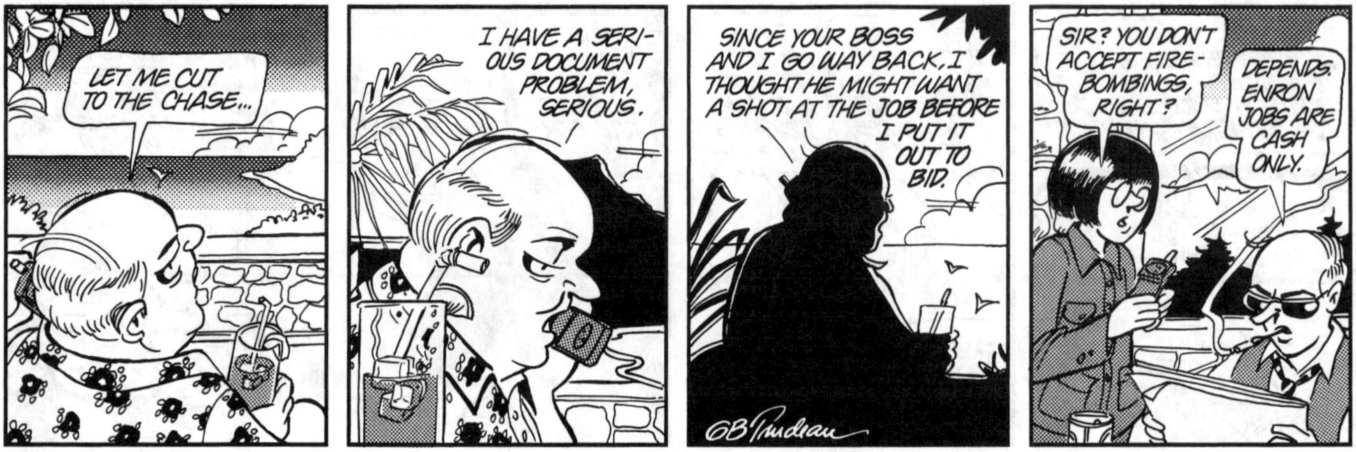
LET ME CUT TO THE CHASE...
I HAVE A SERIOUS DOCUMENT PROBLEM, SERIOUS.
SINCE YOUR BOSS AND I GO WAY BACK, I THOUGHT HE MIGHT WANT A SHOT AT THE JOB BEFORE I PUT IT OUT TO BID.
GB Trudeau
SIR? YOU DON'T ACCEPT FIRE-BOMBINGS, RIGHT?
DEPENDS. ENRON JOBS ARE CASH ONLY.

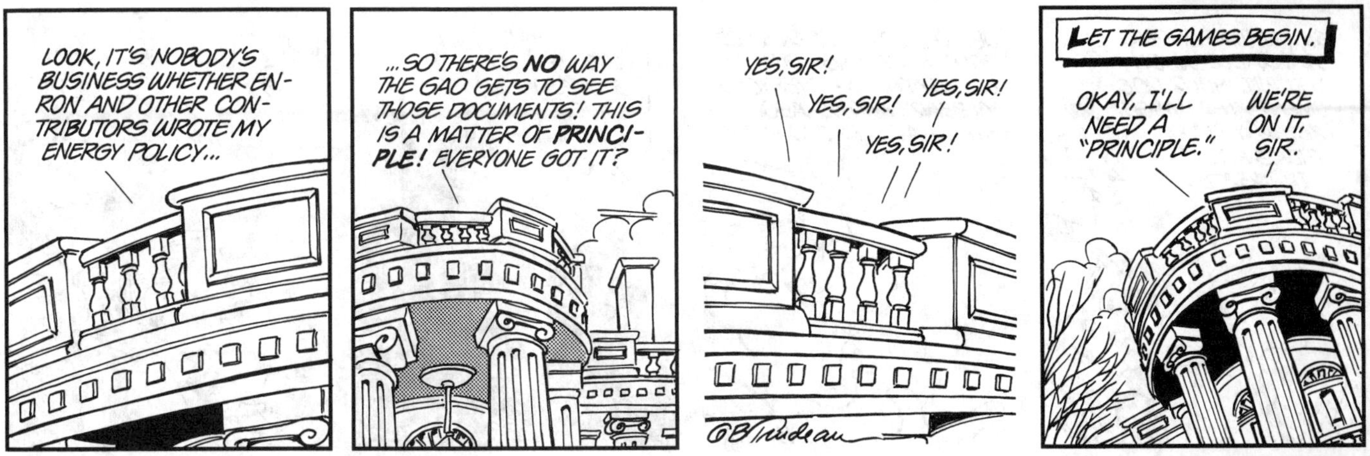
LOOK, IT'S NOBODY'S BUSINESS WHETHER ENRON AND OTHER CONTRIBUTORS WROTE MY ENERGY POLICY...
...SO THERE'S **NO** WAY THE GAO GETS TO SEE THOSE DOCUMENTS! THIS IS A MATTER OF **PRINCIPLE!** EVERYONE GOT IT?
YES, SIR!
YES, SIR!
YES, SIR!
YES, SIR!
©B Trudeau
LET THE GAMES BEGIN.
OKAY, I'LL NEED A "PRINCIPLE."
WE'RE ON IT, SIR.

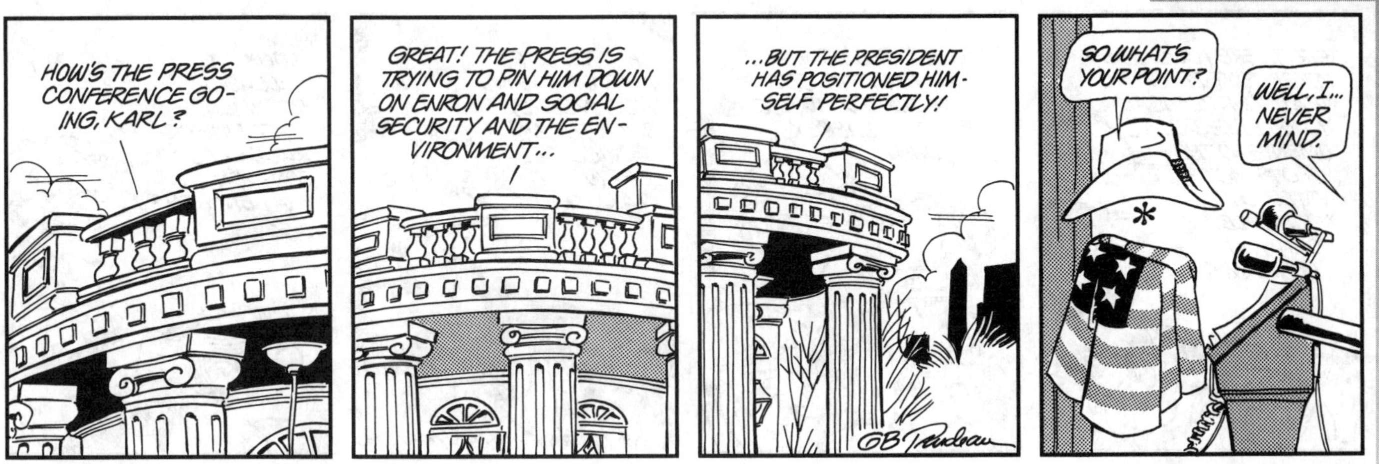
HOW'S THE PRESS CONFERENCE GOING, KARL?
GREAT! THE PRESS IS TRYING TO PIN HIM DOWN ON ENRON AND SOCIAL SECURITY AND THE ENVIRONMENT...
...BUT THE PRESIDENT HAS POSITIONED HIMSELF PERFECTLY!
©B Trudeau
SO WHAT'S YOUR POINT?
WELL, I... NEVER MIND.

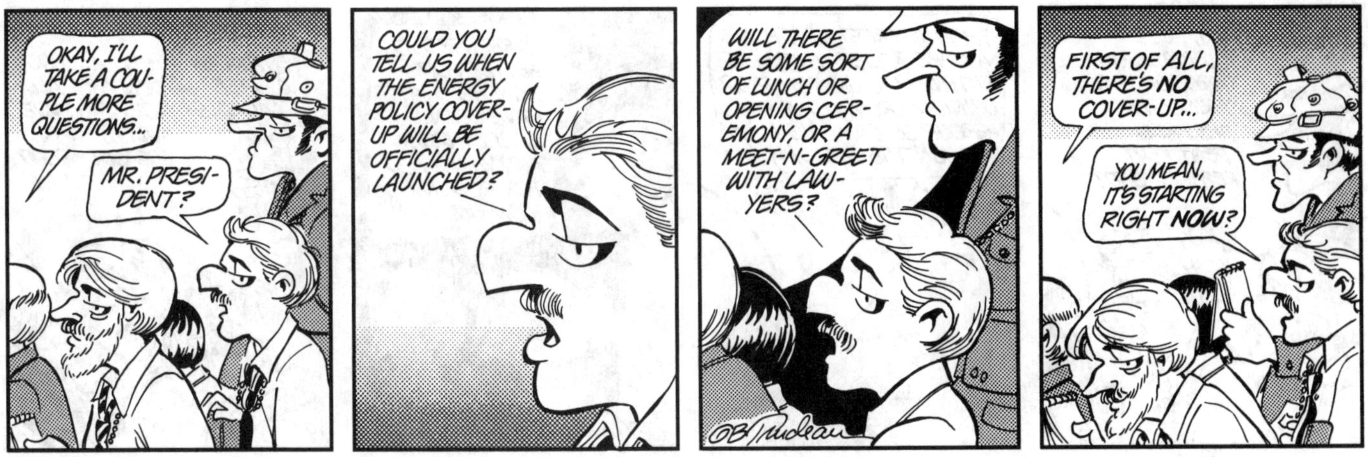
OKAY, I'LL TAKE A COUPLE MORE QUESTIONS...
MR. PRESIDENT?
COULD YOU TELL US WHEN THE ENERGY POLICY COVER-UP WILL BE OFFICIALLY LAUNCHED?
WILL THERE BE SOME SORT OF LUNCH OR OPENING CEREMONY, OR A MEET-N-GREET WITH LAWYERS?
©B Trudeau
FIRST OF ALL, THERE'S **NO** COVER-UP...
YOU MEAN, IT'S STARTING RIGHT **NOW**?

SIR, IT WAS UNDERSTANDABLE WHEN YOU WITHHELD DOCUMENTS THAT MIGHT REVEAL YOUR FATHER'S ROLE IN IRANGATE...
BUT WHY COVER UP ENRON'S ROLE IN WRITING YOUR ENERGY POLICY? EVERYONE ALREADY KNOWS ABOUT IT! WHAT'S LEFT TO HIDE?
LOTS OF STUFF! LIKE..., LIKE...
GB Trudeau
NICE TRY.
THANKS.

SIR, THERE HAVE BEEN PERSISTENT REPORTS THAT YOUR REFUSAL TO RELEASE DOCUMENTS TO THE GAO IS MOTIVATED BY "PRINCIPLE." CAN YOU CONFIRM?
YOU BET. THE PRINCIPLE IS MY RIGHT TO GET UNVARNISHED ADVICE FROM THE ENERGY LOBBY.
IF I RELEASE EMBARRASSING DOCUMENTS, THEN THE ONLY ADVICE I'LL GET WILL BE VARNISHED!
BUT...
GB Trudeau
LOOK! WE RELEASED DOCUMENTS THAT EMBARRASSED CLINTON! ISN'T THAT ENOUGH?
OH, RIGHT. SORRY.

ARI, COULD YOU WALK US THROUGH THE "PRINCIPLE" THE PRESIDENT KEPT REFERRING TO?
YES. THE PRESIDENT HAS A CORE BELIEF THAT HE'S ENTITLED TO UNVARNISHED OPINION FROM A DIVERSE GROUP OF CAMPAIGN CONTRIBUTORS.
HE REFUSES TO SETTLE FOR OPINIONS THAT HAVE BEEN SANDED DOWN AND VARNISHED FOR PUBLIC CONSUMPTION!
GB Trudeau
EVEN IF HE TAKES A SHELLACKING?
HEY! A VENEER OF CIVILITY, PLEASE!
YOU ALL HAVE A GOOD DAY.

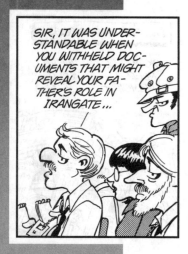

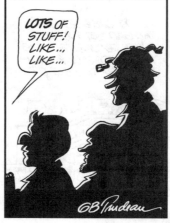

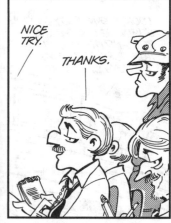

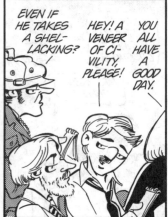

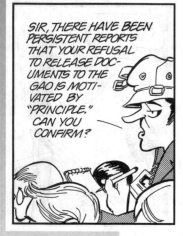

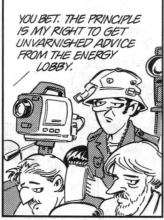

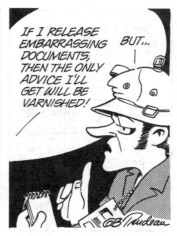

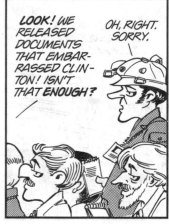

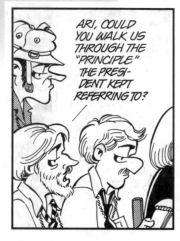

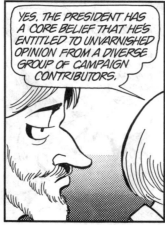

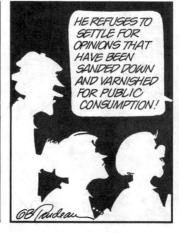

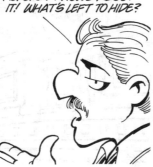

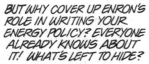

JIM, I'M TELLING YOU AS YOUR LAWYER, AS LONG AS THOSE FILES STILL EXIST, YOU ARE VERY VULNERABLE!
EDDY, RELAX, OKAY? IT'S UNDER CONTROL! TRUST ME... HOLD ON, I GOT ANOTHER CALL.
ANDREWS HERE.
I'M IN!
ABOUT TIME.

MOTHER, THE EAGLE HAS LANDED!
GOOD WORK, EAGLE...
PROCEED TO THE INNER OFFICE TO ACCESS THE MAIN SERVER.
I'M AL-READY IN THE INNER OFFICE.
HOW COULD YOU BE IN THE INNER OFFICE? I HAVEN'T EVEN TOLD YOU WHERE THE KEY IS YET!
KEY?
IT'S UNDER THE MAT.

OKAY, EAGLE, FIRST WE FIND THE POLITICAL FILES. GO TO THE HARD DRIVE AND PULL UP THE "DE-REG" FOLDER.
OKAY, NOW FIND A FILE CALLED "CHENEY"...
GOT IT!
CLAK! CLAK! CLAK!
GOT IT!
OKAY, OPEN IT UP. WHAT DO YOU SEE?
LOOKS LIKE UNVARNISHED POLITICAL ADVICE.
BINGO. DELETE IT.

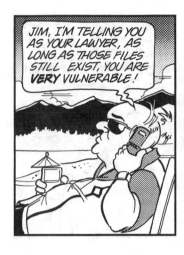

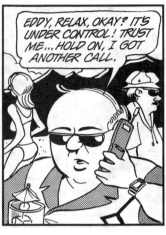

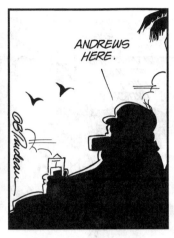

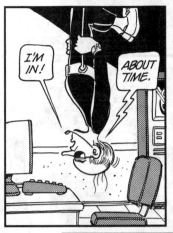

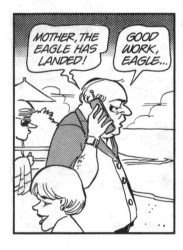

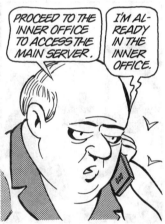

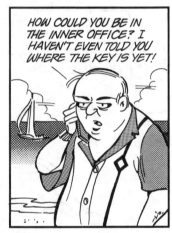

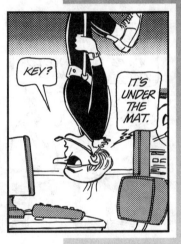

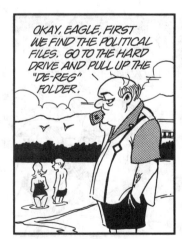

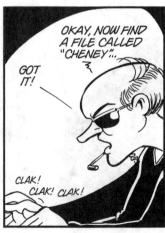

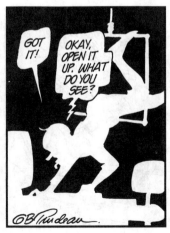

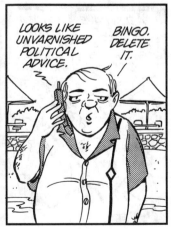

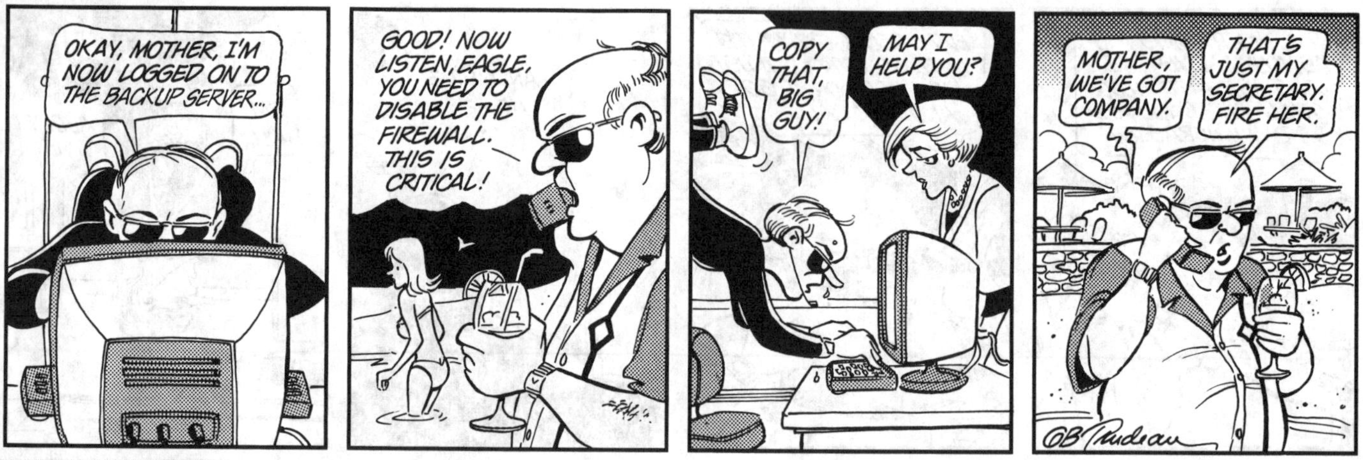
OKAY, MOTHER, I'M NOW LOGGED ON TO THE BACKUP SERVER...
GOOD! NOW LISTEN, EAGLE, YOU NEED TO DISABLE THE FIREWALL. THIS IS CRITICAL!
COPY THAT, BIG GUY!
MAY I HELP YOU?
MOTHER, WE'VE GOT COMPANY.
THAT'S JUST MY SECRETARY. FIRE HER.

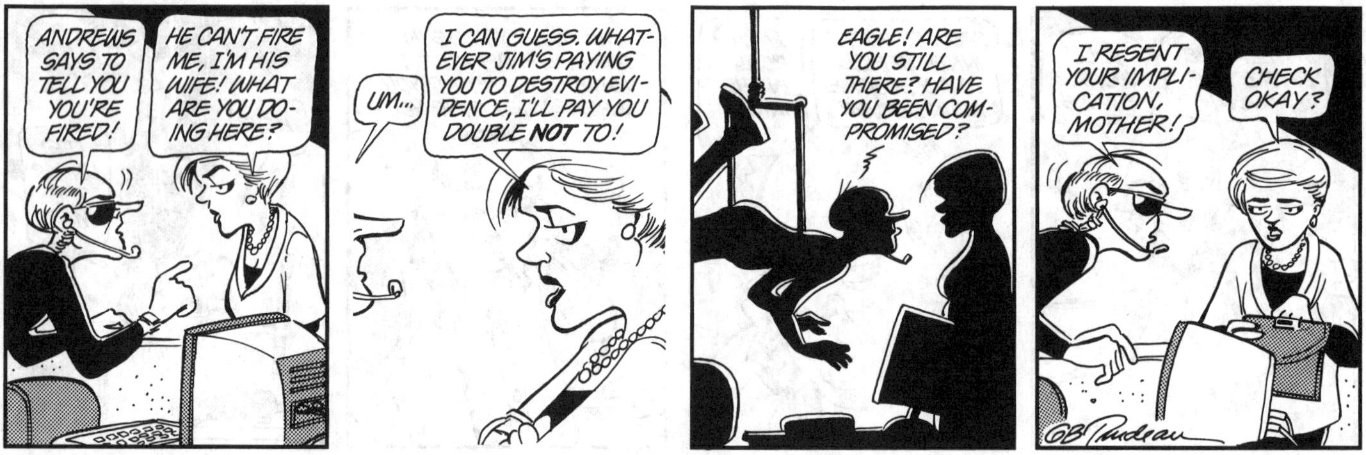
ANDREWS SAYS TO TELL YOU YOU'RE FIRED!
HE CAN'T FIRE ME, I'M HIS WIFE! WHAT ARE YOU DOING HERE?
UM...
I CAN GUESS. WHATEVER JIM'S PAYING YOU TO DESTROY EVIDENCE, I'LL PAY YOU DOUBLE NOT TO!
EAGLE! ARE YOU STILL THERE? HAVE YOU BEEN COMPROMISED?
I RESENT YOUR IMPLICATION, MOTHER!
CHECK OKAY?

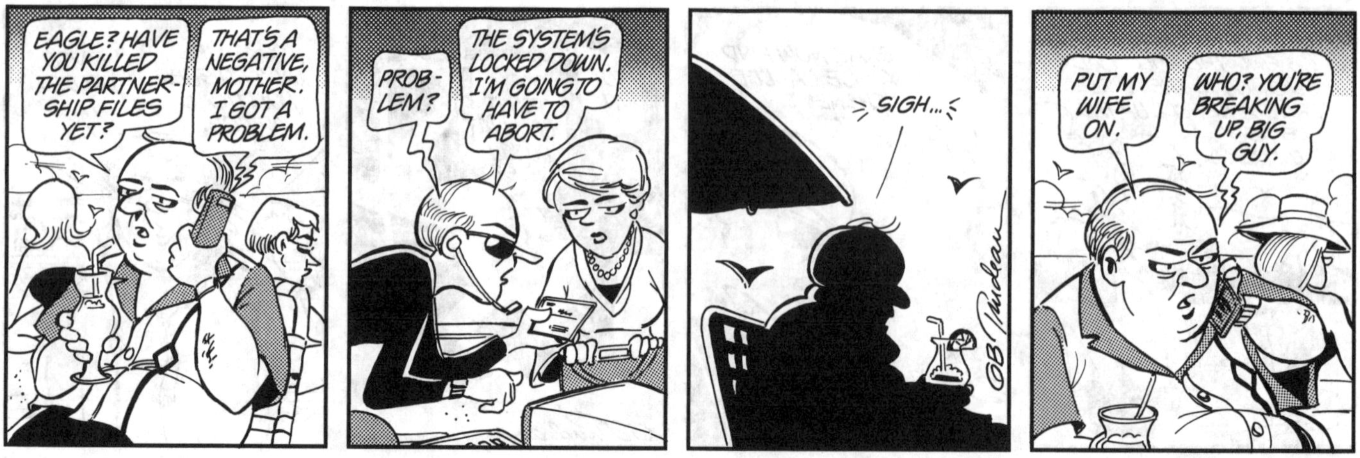
EAGLE? HAVE YOU KILLED THE PARTNERSHIP FILES YET?
THAT'S A NEGATIVE, MOTHER. I GOT A PROBLEM.
PROBLEM?
THE SYSTEM'S LOCKED DOWN. I'M GOING TO HAVE TO ABORT.
SIGH...
PUT MY WIFE ON.
WHO? YOU'RE BREAKING UP, BIG GUY.

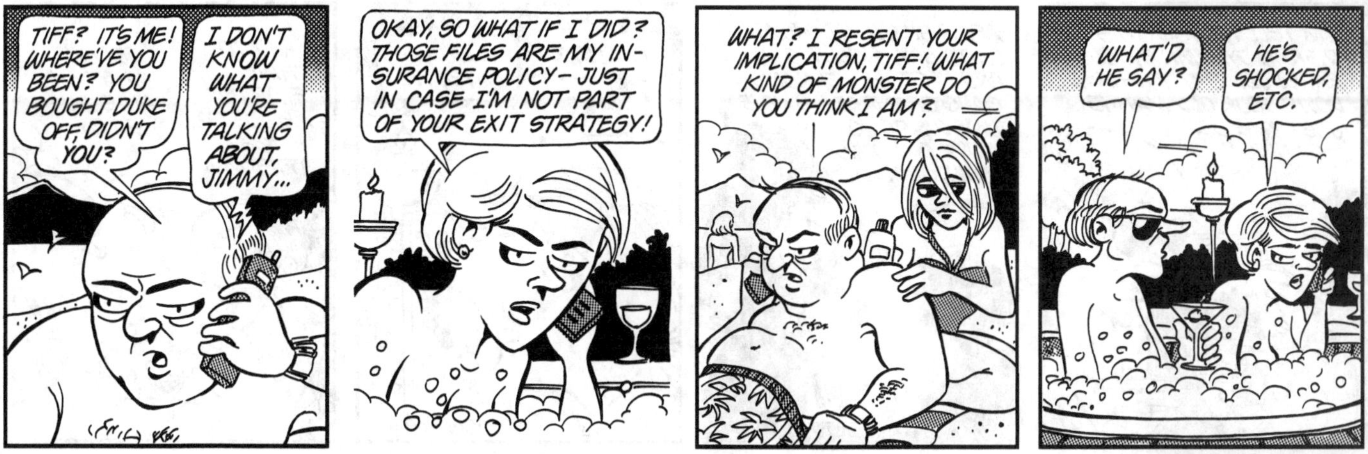
TIFF? IT'S ME! WHERE'VE YOU BEEN? YOU BOUGHT DUKE OFF, DIDN'T YOU?
I DON'T KNOW WHAT YOU'RE TALKING ABOUT, JIMMY...
OKAY, SO WHAT IF I DID? THOSE FILES ARE MY INSURANCE POLICY – JUST IN CASE I'M NOT PART OF YOUR EXIT STRATEGY!
WHAT? I RESENT YOUR IMPLICATION, TIFF! WHAT KIND OF MONSTER DO YOU THINK I AM?
WHAT'D HE SAY?
HE'S SHOCKED, ETC.

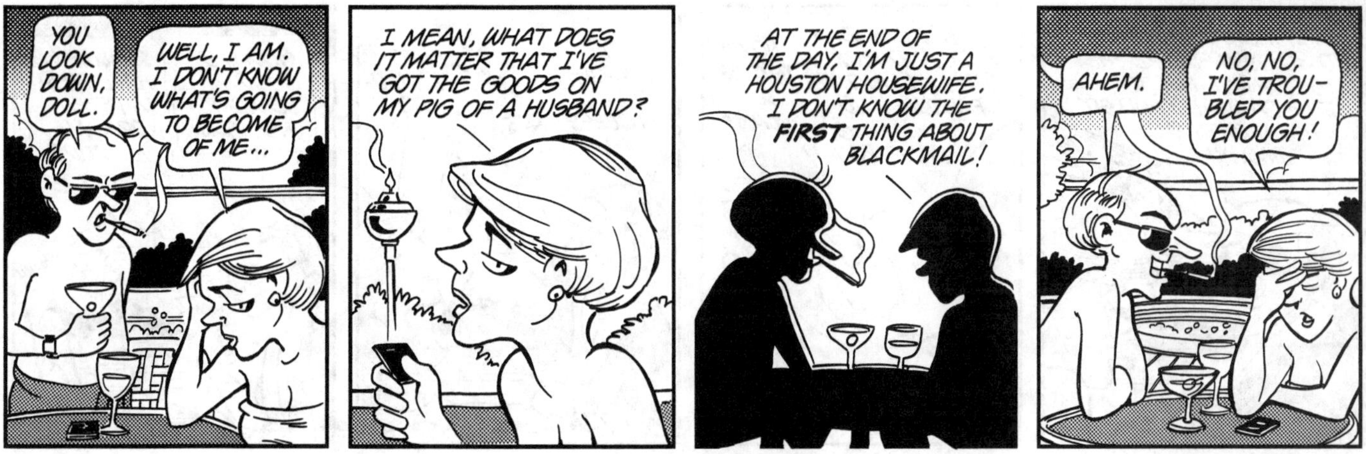
YOU LOOK DOWN, DOLL.
WELL, I AM. I DON'T KNOW WHAT'S GOING TO BECOME OF ME...
I MEAN, WHAT DOES IT MATTER THAT I'VE GOT THE GOODS ON MY PIG OF A HUSBAND?
AT THE END OF THE DAY, I'M JUST A HOUSTON HOUSEWIFE. I DON'T KNOW THE FIRST THING ABOUT BLACKMAIL!
AHEM.
NO, NO, I'VE TROUBLED YOU ENOUGH!

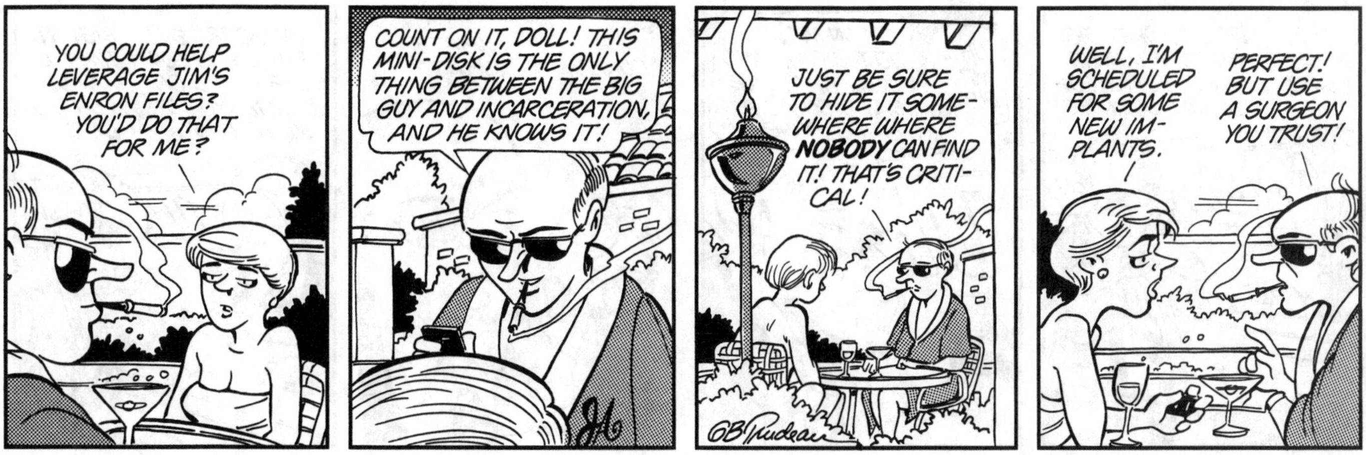
YOU COULD HELP LEVERAGE JIM'S ENRON FILES? YOU'D DO THAT FOR ME?
COUNT ON IT, DOLL! THIS MINI-DISK IS THE ONLY THING BETWEEN THE BIG GUY AND INCARCERATION, AND HE KNOWS IT!
JUST BE SURE TO HIDE IT SOMEWHERE WHERE NOBODY CAN FIND IT! THAT'S CRITICAL!
WELL, I'M SCHEDULED FOR SOME NEW IMPLANTS.
PERFECT! BUT USE A SURGEON YOU TRUST!

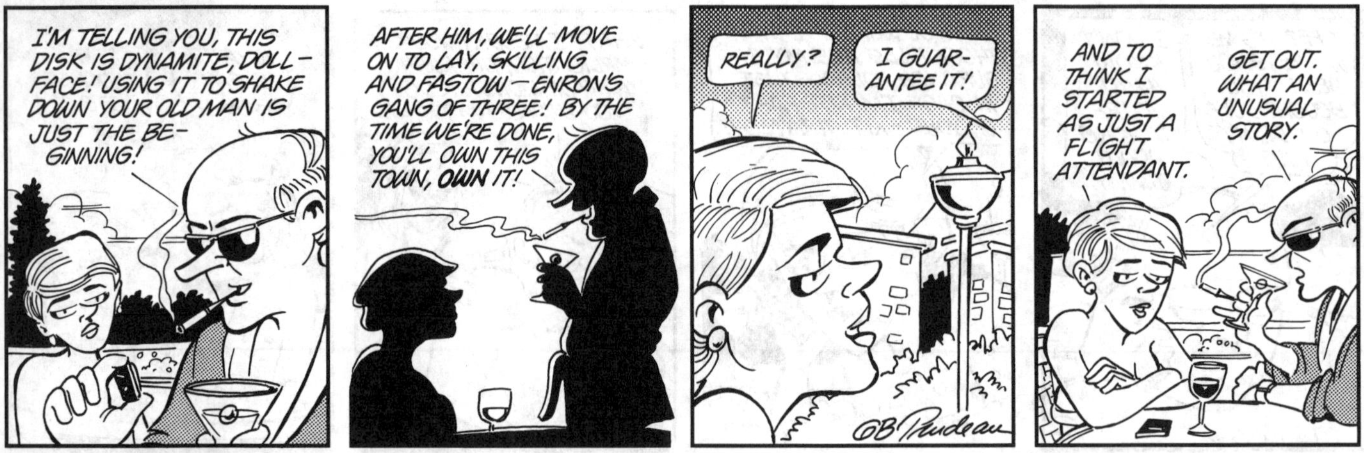
I'M TELLING YOU, THIS DISK IS DYNAMITE, DOLL-FACE! USING IT TO SHAKE DOWN YOUR OLD MAN IS JUST THE BE-GINNING!
AFTER HIM, WE'LL MOVE ON TO LAY, SKILLING AND FASTOW — ENRON'S GANG OF THREE! BY THE TIME WE'RE DONE, YOU'LL OWN THIS TOWN, OWN IT!
REALLY?
I GUAR-ANTEE IT!
GB Trudeau
AND TO THINK I STARTED AS JUST A FLIGHT ATTENDANT.
GET OUT. WHAT AN UNUSUAL STORY.

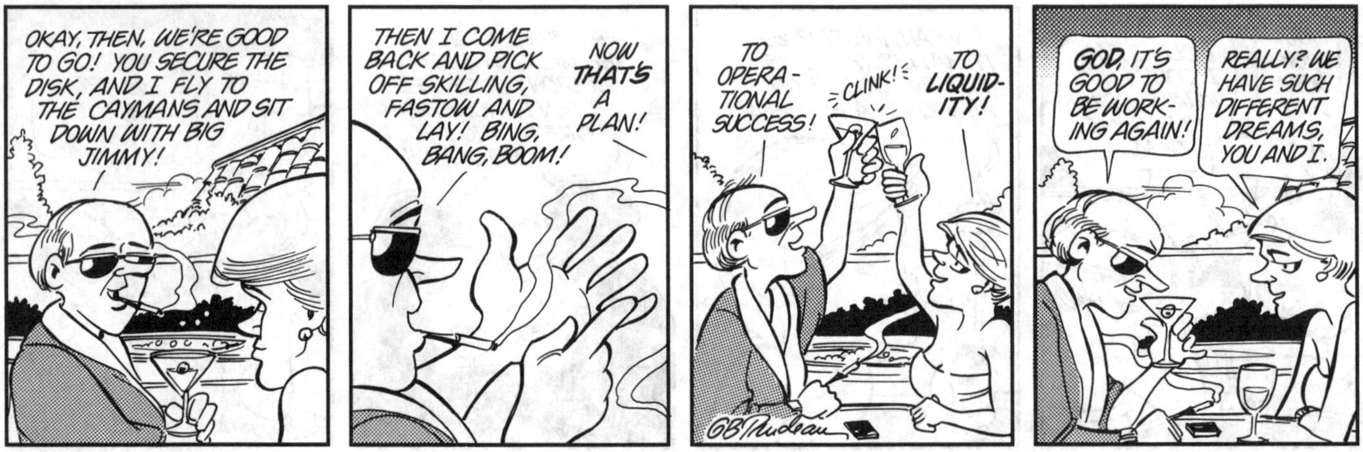
OKAY, THEN, WE'RE GOOD TO GO! YOU SECURE THE DISK, AND I FLY TO THE CAYMANS AND SIT DOWN WITH BIG JIMMY!
THEN I COME BACK AND PICK OFF SKILLING, FASTOW AND LAY! BING, BANG, BOOM!
NOW THAT'S A PLAN!
TO OPERA-TIONAL SUCCESS!
CLINK!
TO LIQUID-ITY!
GB Trudeau
GOD, IT'S GOOD TO BE WORK-ING AGAIN!
REALLY? WE HAVE SUCH DIFFERENT DREAMS, YOU AND I.

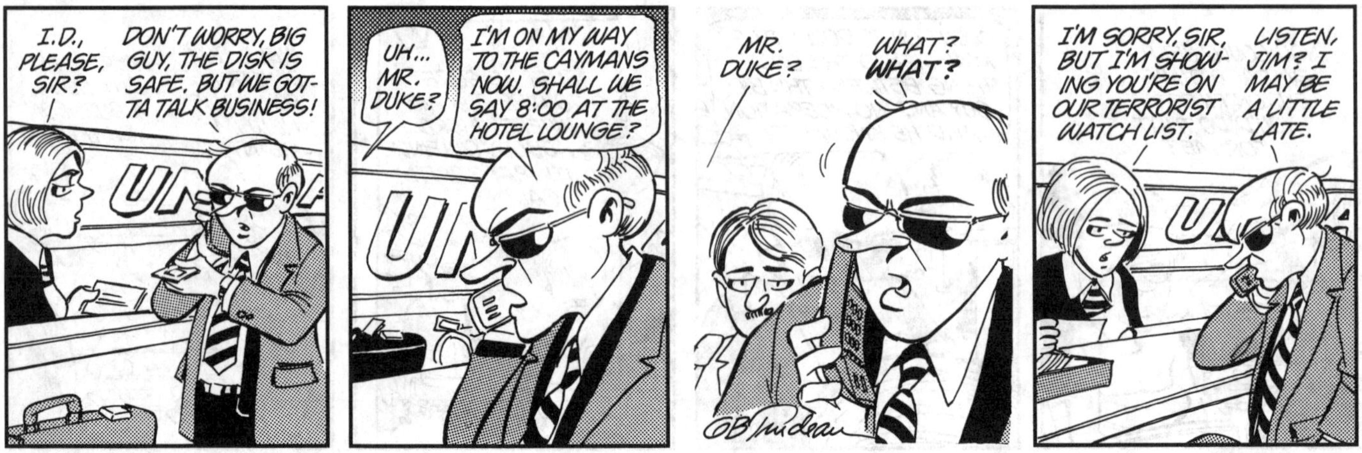
I.D., PLEASE, SIR?
DON'T WORRY, BIG GUY, THE DISK IS SAFE. BUT WE GOT-TA TALK BUSINESS!
UH... MR. DUKE?
I'M ON MY WAY TO THE CAYMANS NOW. SHALL WE SAY 8:00 AT THE HOTEL LOUNGE?
MR. DUKE?
WHAT? WHAT?
GB Trudeau
I'M SORRY, SIR, BUT I'M SHOW-ING YOU'RE ON OUR TERRORIST WATCH LIST.
LISTEN, JIM? I MAY BE A LITTLE LATE.

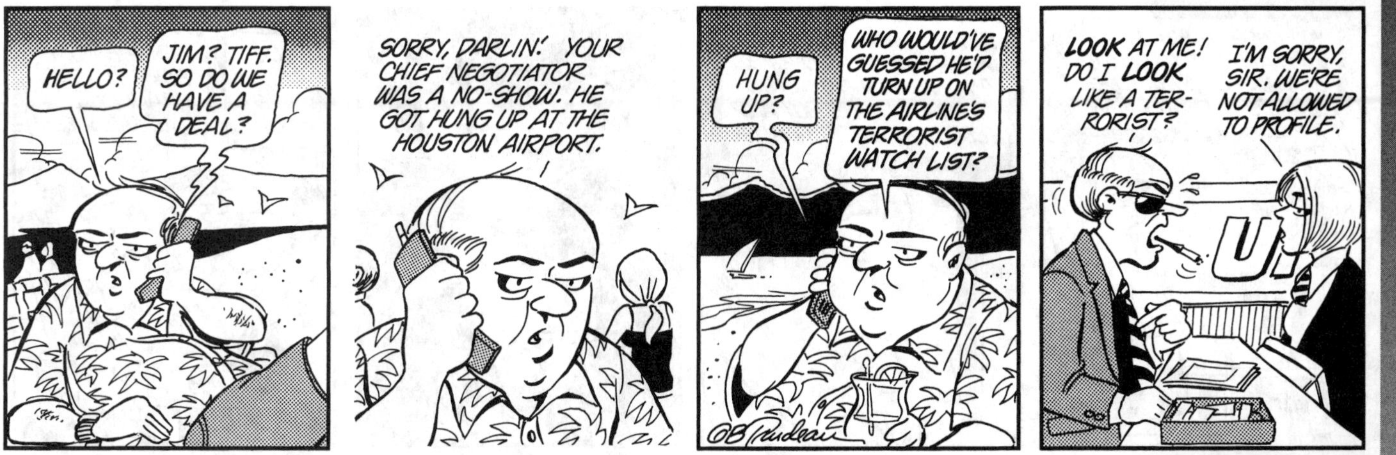
HELLO?
JIM? TIFF. SO DO WE HAVE A DEAL?
SORRY, DARLIN'. YOUR CHIEF NEGOTIATOR WAS A NO-SHOW. HE GOT HUNG UP AT THE HOUSTON AIRPORT.
HUNG UP?
WHO WOULD'VE GUESSED HE'D TURN UP ON THE AIRLINE'S TERRORIST WATCH LIST?
LOOK AT ME! DO I LOOK LIKE A TERRORIST?
I'M SORRY, SIR. WE'RE NOT ALLOWED TO PROFILE.
©B Trudeau

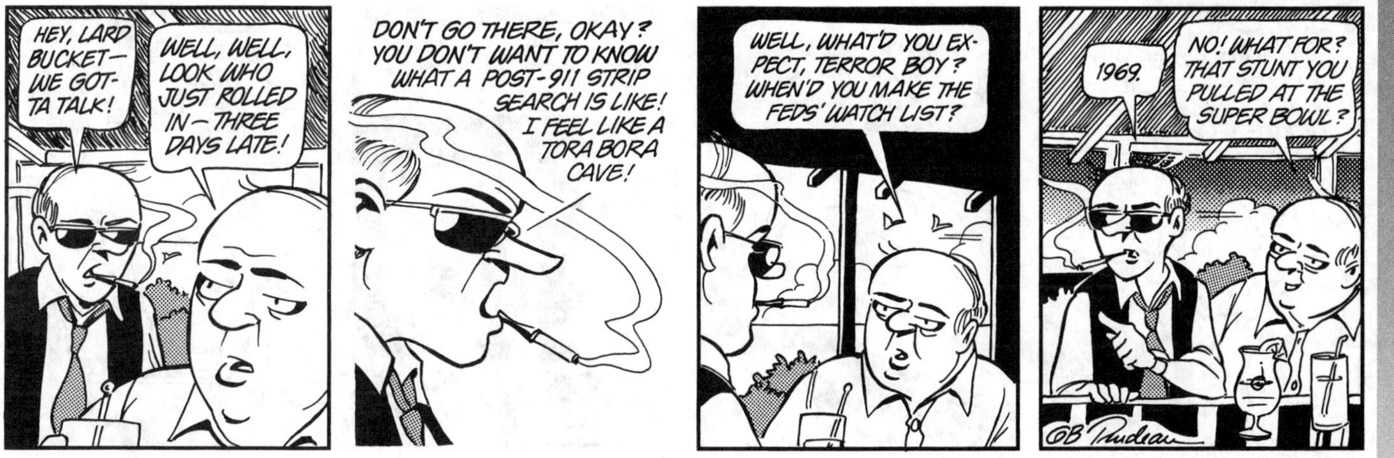
HEY, LARD BUCKET—WE GOTTA TALK!
WELL, WELL, LOOK WHO JUST ROLLED IN—THREE DAYS LATE!
DON'T GO THERE, OKAY? YOU DON'T WANT TO KNOW WHAT A POST-911 STRIP SEARCH IS LIKE! I FEEL LIKE A TORA BORA CAVE!
WELL, WHAT'D YOU EXPECT, TERROR BOY? WHEN'D YOU MAKE THE FEDS' WATCH LIST?
1969.
NO! WHAT FOR? THAT STUNT YOU PULLED AT THE SUPER BOWL?
©B Trudeau

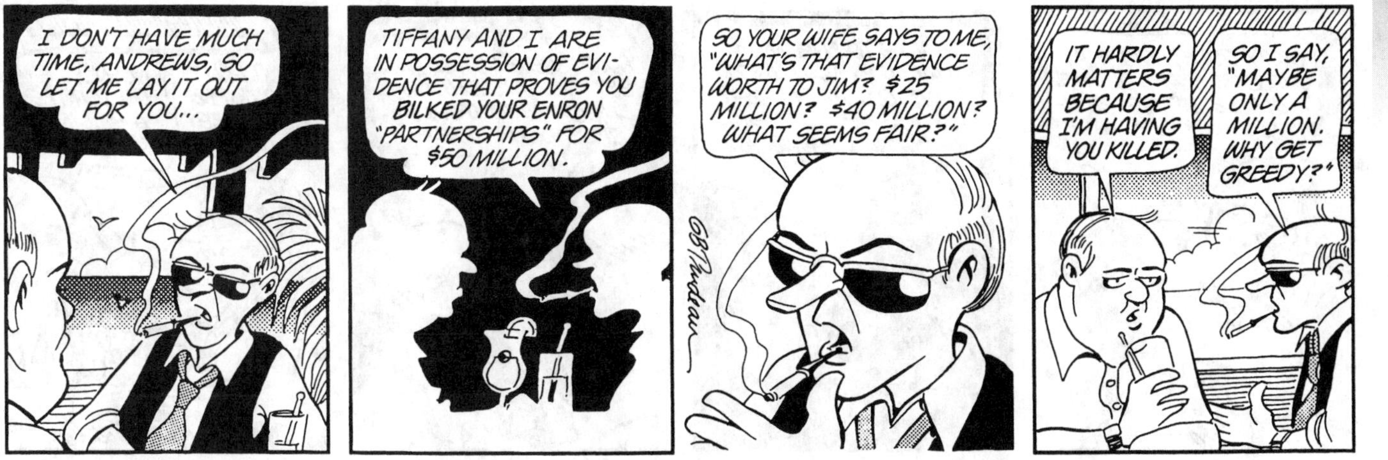
I DON'T HAVE MUCH TIME, ANDREWS, SO LET ME LAY IT OUT FOR YOU...
TIFFANY AND I ARE IN POSSESSION OF EVIDENCE THAT PROVES YOU BILKED YOUR ENRON "PARTNERSHIPS" FOR $50 MILLION.
SO YOUR WIFE SAYS TO ME, "WHAT'S THAT EVIDENCE WORTH TO JIM? $25 MILLION? $40 MILLION? WHAT SEEMS FAIR?"
©B Trudeau
IT HARDLY MATTERS BECAUSE I'M HAVING YOU KILLED.
SO I SAY, "MAYBE ONLY A MILLION. WHY GET GREEDY?"

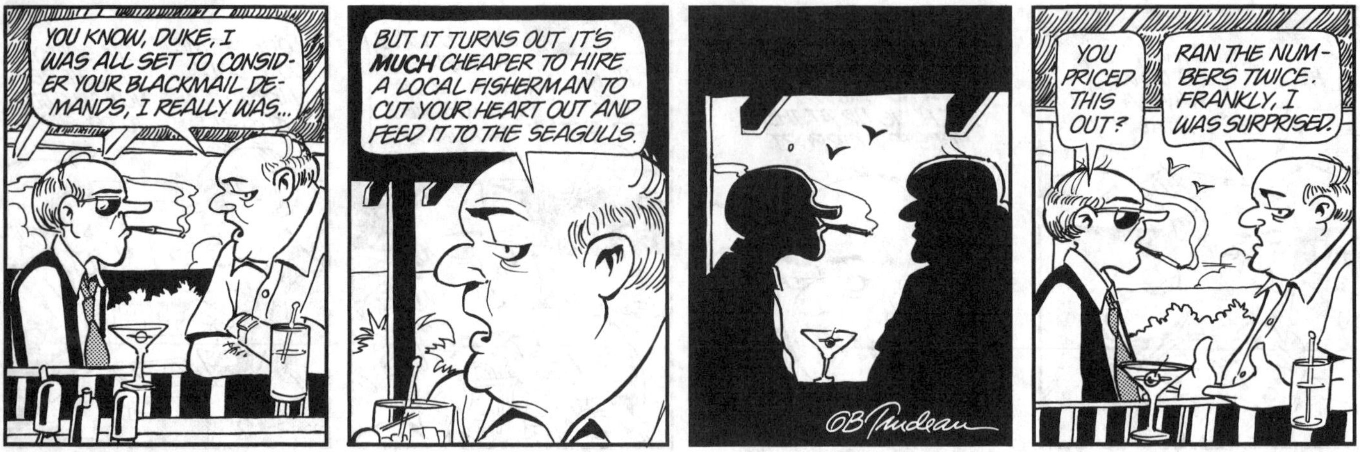
YOU KNOW, DUKE, I WAS ALL SET TO CONSIDER YOUR BLACKMAIL DEMANDS, I REALLY WAS...
BUT IT TURNS OUT IT'S **MUCH** CHEAPER TO HIRE A LOCAL FISHERMAN TO CUT YOUR HEART OUT AND FEED IT TO THE SEAGULLS.
©B Trudeau
YOU PRICED THIS OUT?
RAN THE NUMBERS TWICE. FRANKLY, I WAS SURPRISED.

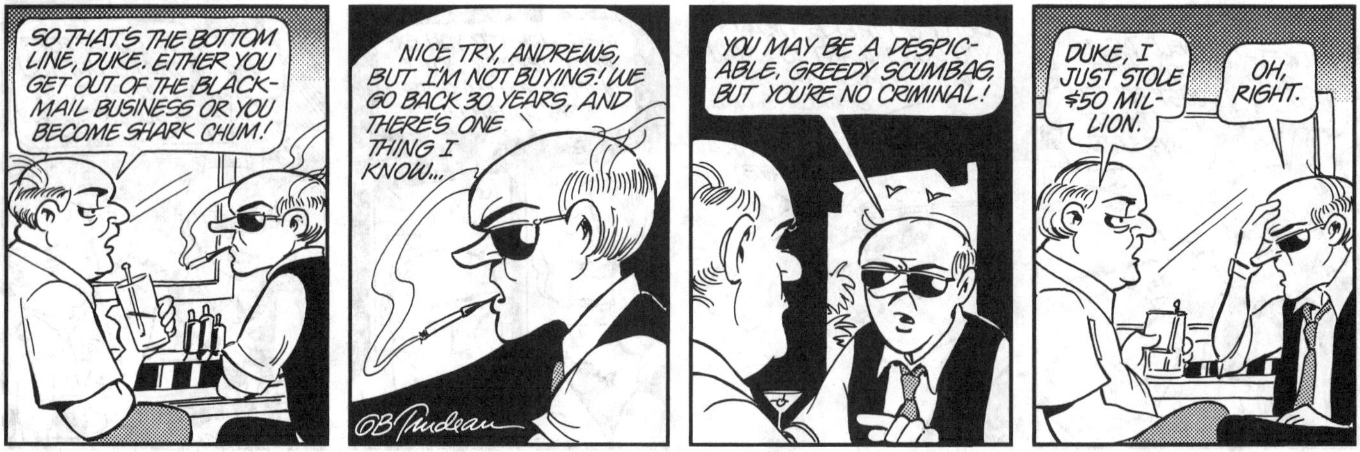
SO THAT'S THE BOTTOM LINE, DUKE. EITHER YOU GET OUT OF THE BLACKMAIL BUSINESS OR YOU BECOME SHARK CHUM!
NICE TRY, ANDREWS, BUT I'M NOT BUYING! WE GO BACK 30 YEARS, AND THERE'S ONE THING I KNOW...
©B Trudeau
YOU MAY BE A DESPICABLE, GREEDY SCUMBAG, BUT YOU'RE NO CRIMINAL!
DUKE, I JUST STOLE $50 MILLION.
OH, RIGHT.

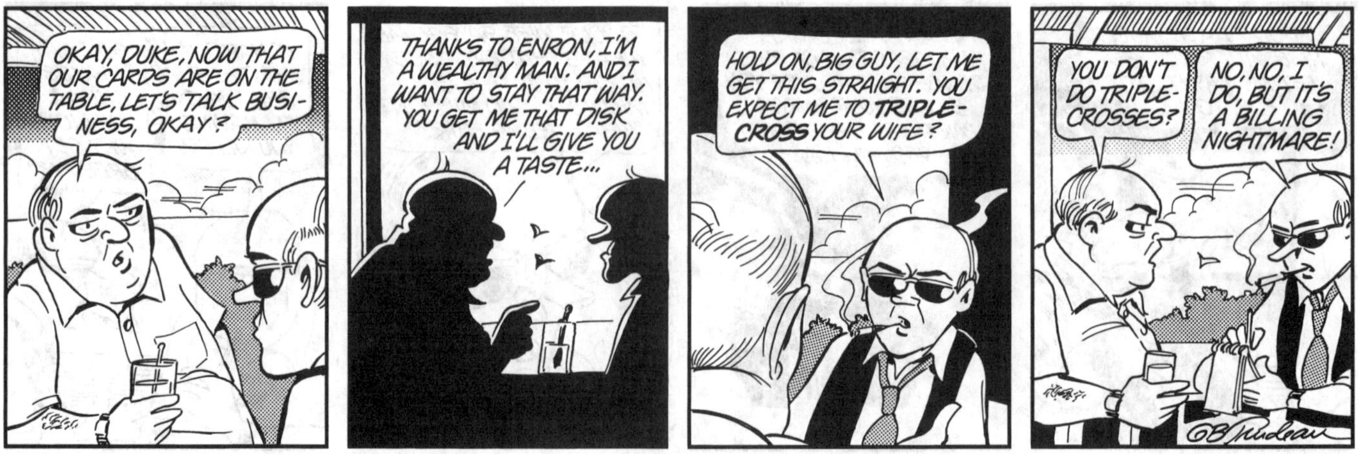
OKAY, DUKE, NOW THAT OUR CARDS ARE ON THE TABLE, LET'S TALK BUSINESS, OKAY?
THANKS TO ENRON, I'M A WEALTHY MAN. AND I WANT TO STAY THAT WAY. YOU GET ME THAT DISK AND I'LL GIVE YOU A TASTE...
HOLD ON, BIG GUY, LET ME GET THIS STRAIGHT. YOU EXPECT ME TO **TRIPLE-CROSS** YOUR WIFE?
YOU DON'T DO TRIPLE-CROSSES?
NO, NO, I DO, BUT IT'S A BILLING NIGHTMARE!
©B Trudeau

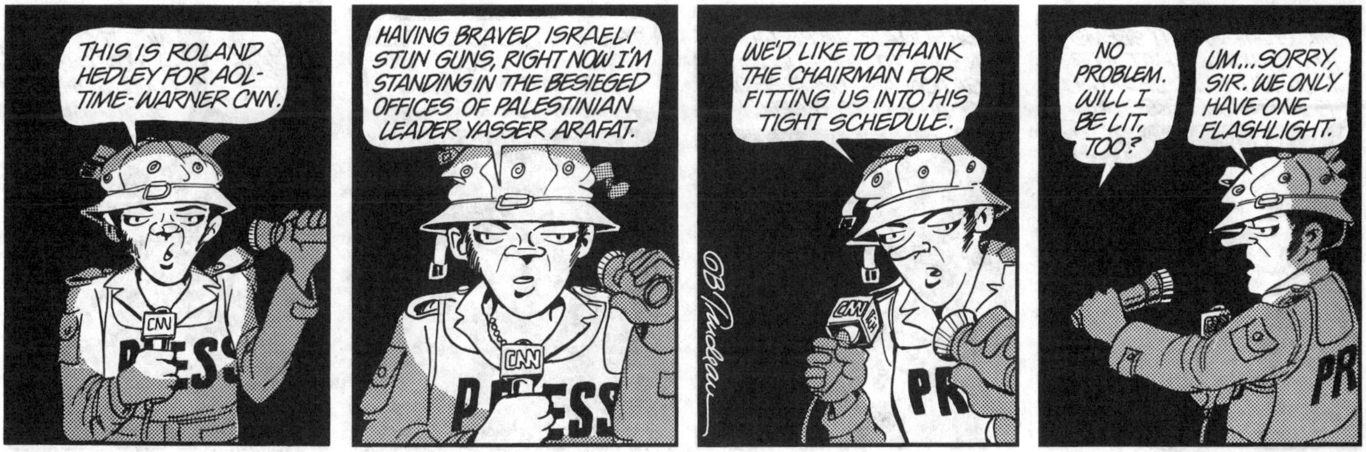
THIS IS ROLAND HEDLEY FOR AOL-TIME-WARNER CNN.
HAVING BRAVED ISRAELI STUN GUNS, RIGHT NOW I'M STANDING IN THE BESIEGED OFFICES OF PALESTINIAN LEADER YASSER ARAFAT.
WE'D LIKE TO THANK THE CHAIRMAN FOR FITTING US INTO HIS TIGHT SCHEDULE.
NO PROBLEM. WILL I BE LIT, TOO?
UM... SORRY, SIR. WE ONLY HAVE ONE FLASHLIGHT.

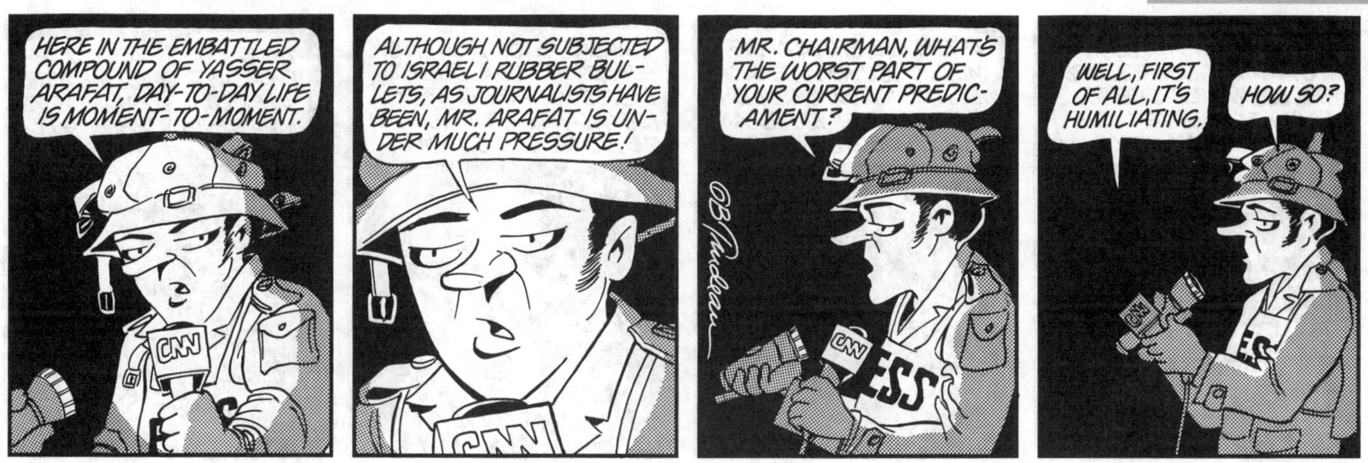
HERE IN THE EMBATTLED COMPOUND OF YASSER ARAFAT, DAY-TO-DAY LIFE IS MOMENT-TO-MOMENT.
ALTHOUGH NOT SUBJECTED TO ISRAELI RUBBER BULLETS, AS JOURNALISTS HAVE BEEN, MR. ARAFAT IS UNDER MUCH PRESSURE!
MR. CHAIRMAN, WHAT'S THE WORST PART OF YOUR CURRENT PREDICAMENT?
WELL, FIRST OF ALL, IT'S HUMILIATING.
HOW SO?

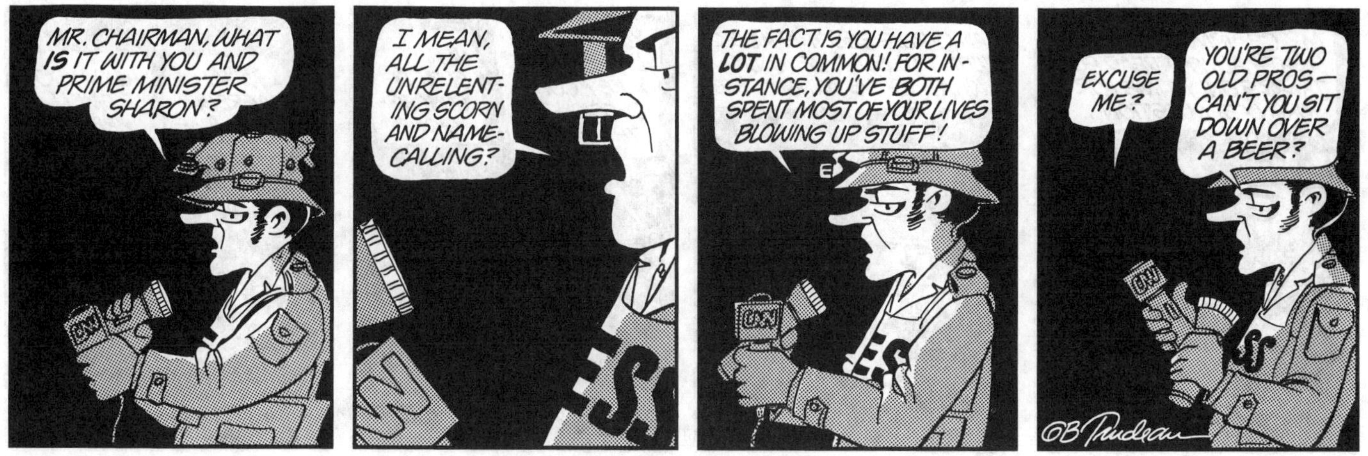
MR. CHAIRMAN, WHAT IS IT WITH YOU AND PRIME MINISTER SHARON?
I MEAN, ALL THE UNRELENTING SCORN AND NAME-CALLING?
THE FACT IS YOU HAVE A LOT IN COMMON! FOR INSTANCE, YOU'VE BOTH SPENT MOST OF YOUR LIVES BLOWING UP STUFF!
EXCUSE ME?
YOU'RE TWO OLD PROS — CAN'T YOU SIT DOWN OVER A BEER?

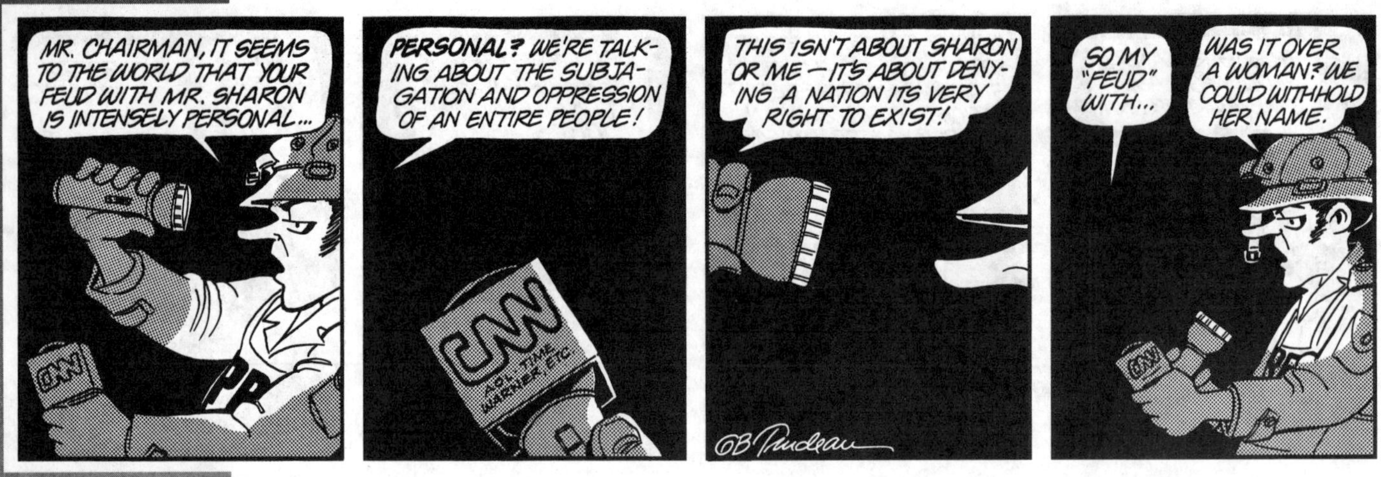
MR. CHAIRMAN, IT SEEMS TO THE WORLD THAT YOUR FEUD WITH MR. SHARON IS INTENSELY PERSONAL...
PERSONAL? WE'RE TALKING ABOUT THE SUBJAGATION AND OPPRESSION OF AN ENTIRE PEOPLE!
CNN
AOL TIME WARNER ETC.
THIS ISN'T ABOUT SHARON OR ME — IT'S ABOUT DENYING A NATION ITS VERY RIGHT TO EXIST!
SO MY "FEUD" WITH...
WAS IT OVER A WOMAN? WE COULD WITHHOLD HER NAME.

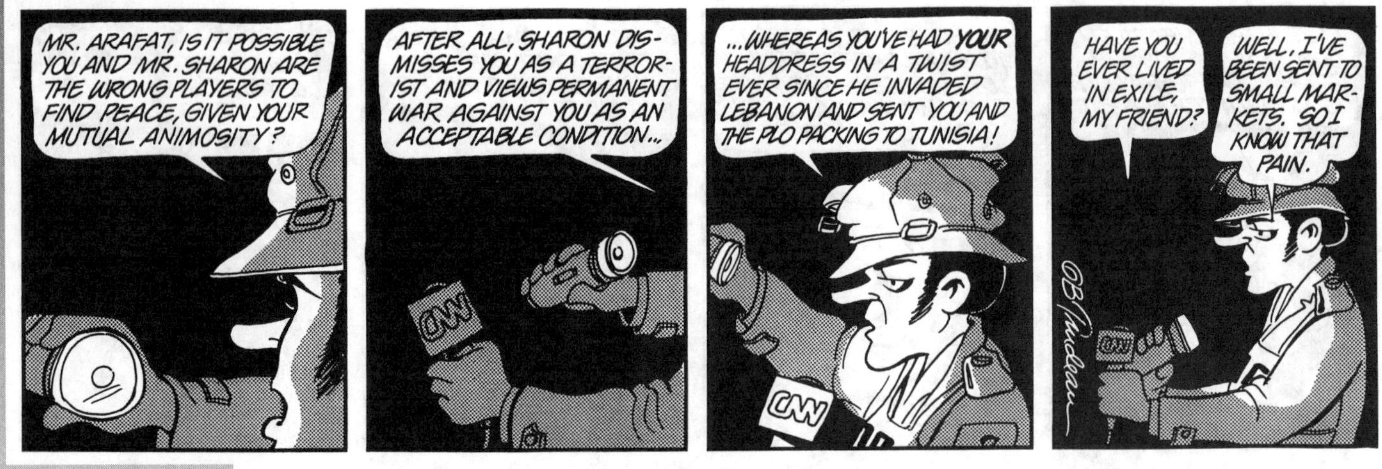
MR. ARAFAT, IS IT POSSIBLE YOU AND MR. SHARON ARE THE WRONG PLAYERS TO FIND PEACE, GIVEN YOUR MUTUAL ANIMOSITY?
AFTER ALL, SHARON DISMISSES YOU AS A TERRORIST AND VIEWS PERMANENT WAR AGAINST YOU AS AN ACCEPTABLE CONDITION...
...WHEREAS YOU'VE HAD YOUR HEADDRESS IN A TWIST EVER SINCE HE INVADED LEBANON AND SENT YOU AND THE PLO PACKING TO TUNISIA!
HAVE YOU EVER LIVED IN EXILE, MY FRIEND?
WELL, I'VE BEEN SENT TO SMALL MARKETS. SO I KNOW THAT PAIN.

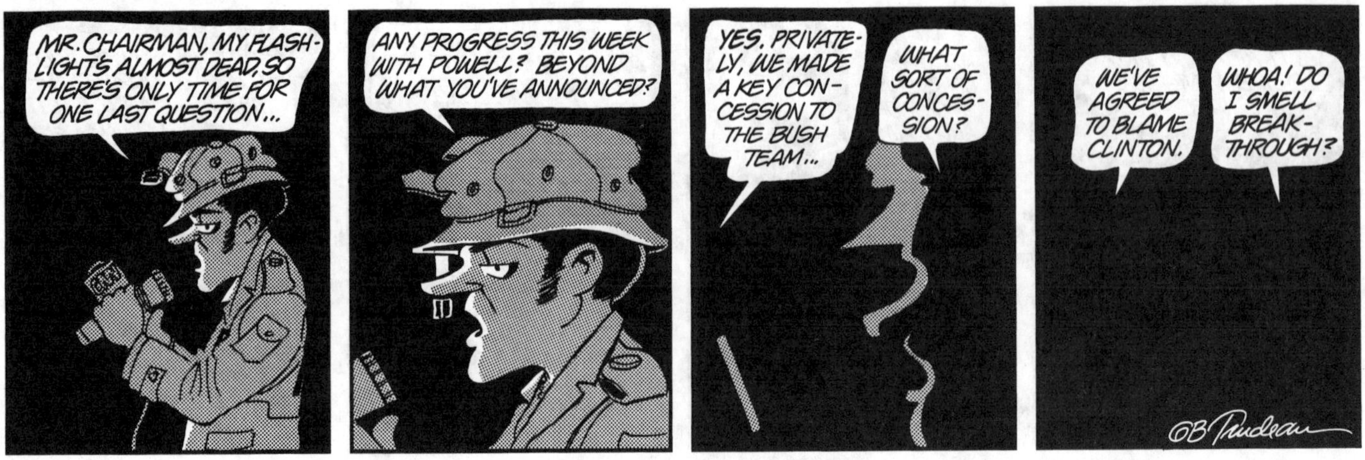
MR. CHAIRMAN, MY FLASHLIGHT'S ALMOST DEAD, SO THERE'S ONLY TIME FOR ONE LAST QUESTION...
ANY PROGRESS THIS WEEK WITH POWELL? BEYOND WHAT YOU'VE ANNOUNCED?
YES. PRIVATELY, WE MADE A KEY CONCESSION TO THE BUSH TEAM...
WHAT SORT OF CONCESSION?
WE'VE AGREED TO BLAME CLINTON.
WHOA! DO I SMELL BREAKTHROUGH?

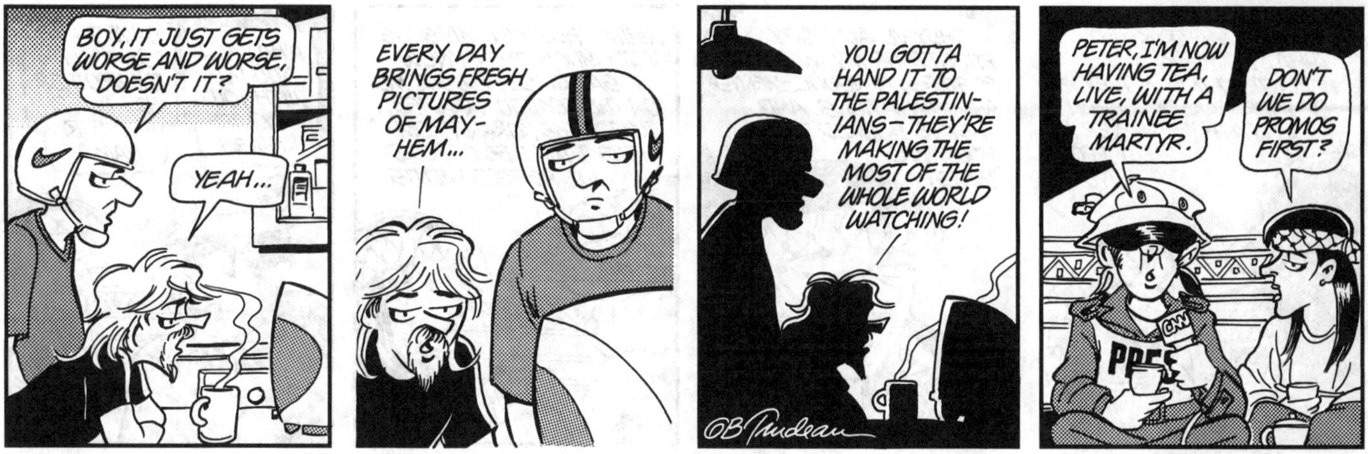
BOY, IT JUST GETS WORSE AND WORSE, DOESN'T IT?
YEAH...
EVERY DAY BRINGS FRESH PICTURES OF MAYHEM...
YOU GOTTA HAND IT TO THE PALESTINIANS—THEY'RE MAKING THE MOST OF THE WHOLE WORLD WATCHING!
©B Trudeau
PETER, I'M NOW HAVING TEA, LIVE, WITH A TRAINEE MARTYR.
DON'T WE DO PROMOS FIRST?
PRESS
CNN

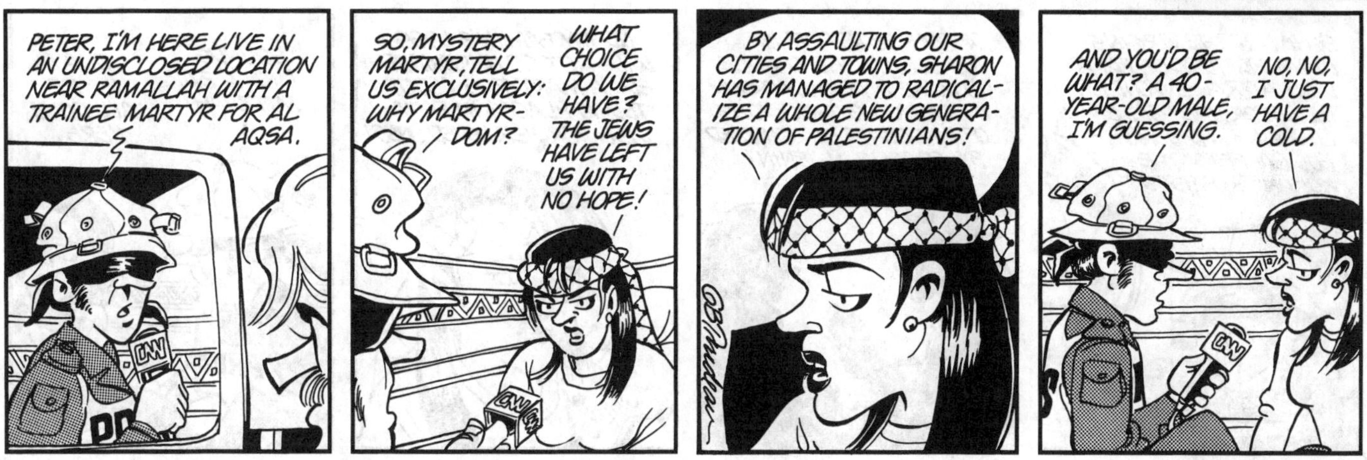
PETER, I'M HERE LIVE IN AN UNDISCLOSED LOCATION NEAR RAMALLAH WITH A TRAINEE MARTYR FOR AL AQSA.
SO, MYSTERY MARTYR, TELL US EXCLUSIVELY: WHY MARTYRDOM?
WHAT CHOICE DO WE HAVE? THE JEWS HAVE LEFT US WITH NO HOPE!
BY ASSAULTING OUR CITIES AND TOWNS, SHARON HAS MANAGED TO RADICALIZE A WHOLE NEW GENERATION OF PALESTINIANS!
AND YOU'D BE WHAT? A 40-YEAR-OLD MALE, I'M GUESSING.
NO, NO, I JUST HAVE A COLD.
CNN

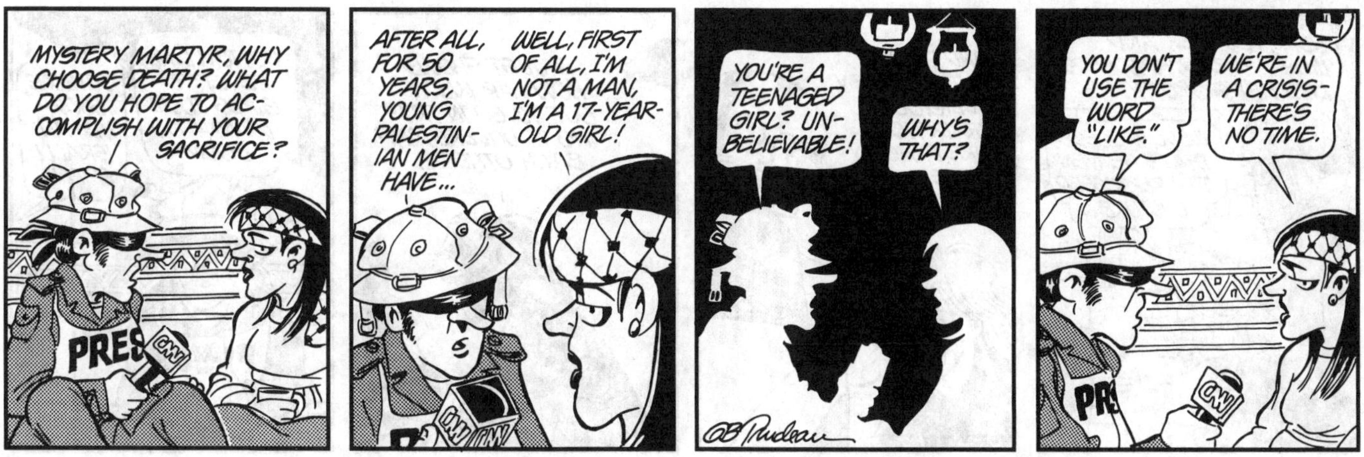
MYSTERY MARTYR, WHY CHOOSE DEATH? WHAT DO YOU HOPE TO ACCOMPLISH WITH YOUR SACRIFICE?
PRESS
AFTER ALL, FOR 50 YEARS, YOUNG PALESTINIAN MEN HAVE...
WELL, FIRST OF ALL, I'M NOT A MAN, I'M A 17-YEAR-OLD GIRL!
YOU'RE A TEENAGED GIRL? UNBELIEVABLE!
WHY'S THAT?
©B Trudeau
YOU DON'T USE THE WORD "LIKE."
WE'RE IN A CRISIS—THERE'S NO TIME.
CNN

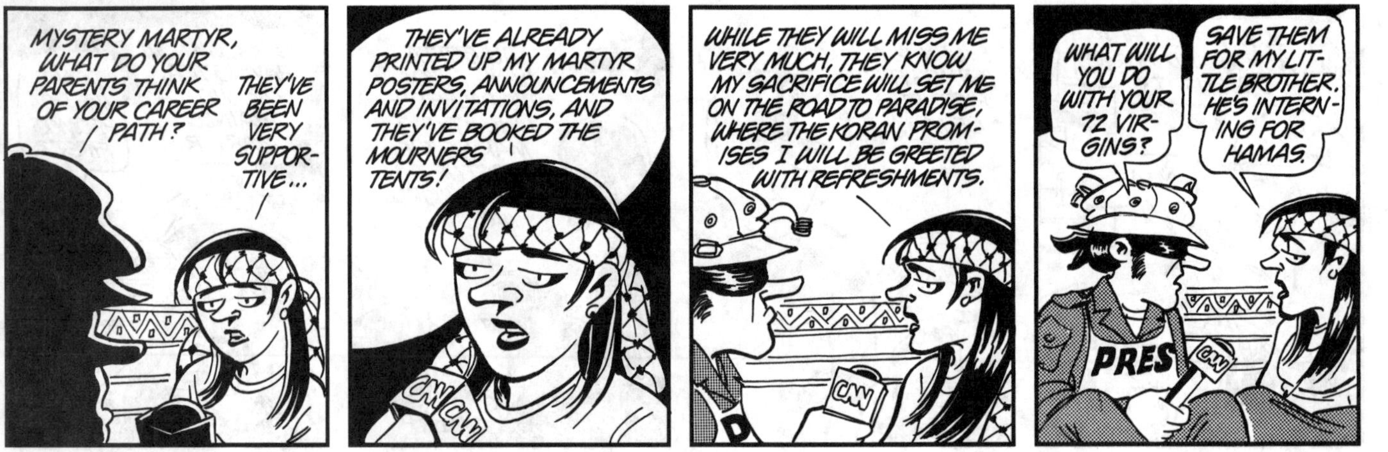
MYSTERY MARTYR, WHAT DO YOUR PARENTS THINK OF YOUR CAREER PATH?
THEY'VE BEEN VERY SUPPORTIVE...
THEY'VE ALREADY PRINTED UP MY MARTYR POSTERS, ANNOUNCEMENTS AND INVITATIONS, AND THEY'VE BOOKED THE MOURNERS TENTS!
WHILE THEY WILL MISS ME VERY MUCH, THEY KNOW MY SACRIFICE WILL SET ME ON THE ROAD TO PARADISE, WHERE THE KORAN PROMISES I WILL BE GREETED WITH REFRESHMENTS.
WHAT WILL YOU DO WITH YOUR 72 VIRGINS?
SAVE THEM FOR MY LITTLE BROTHER. HE'S INTERNING FOR HAMAS.
PRES

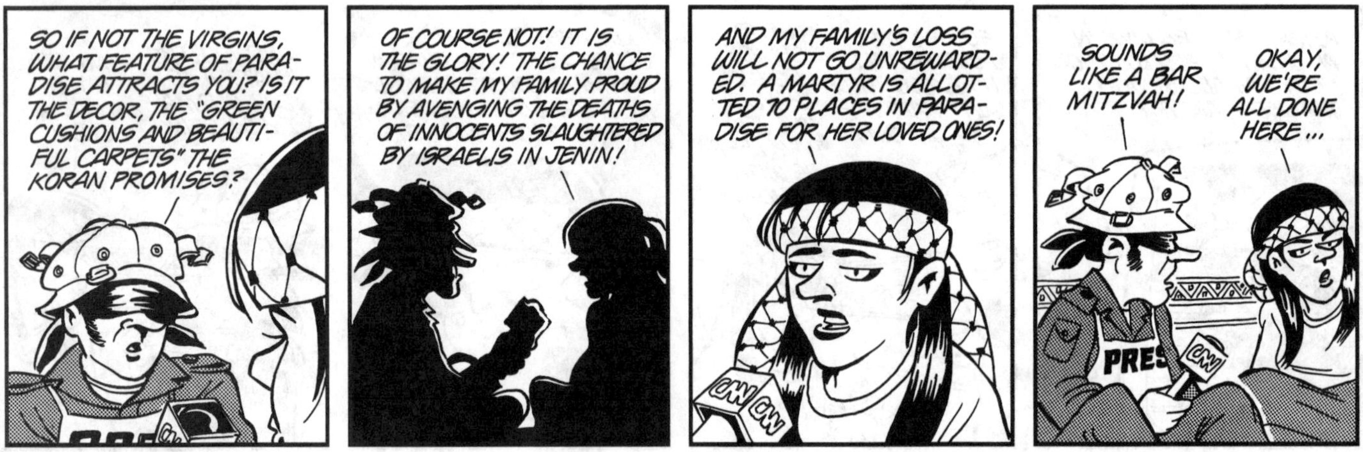
SO IF NOT THE VIRGINS, WHAT FEATURE OF PARADISE ATTRACTS YOU? IS IT THE DECOR, THE "GREEN CUSHIONS AND BEAUTIFUL CARPETS" THE KORAN PROMISES?
OF COURSE NOT! IT IS THE GLORY! THE CHANCE TO MAKE MY FAMILY PROUD BY AVENGING THE DEATHS OF INNOCENTS SLAUGHTERED BY ISRAELIS IN JENIN!
AND MY FAMILY'S LOSS WILL NOT GO UNREWARDED. A MARTYR IS ALLOTTED 70 PLACES IN PARADISE FOR HER LOVED ONES!
SOUNDS LIKE A BAR MITZVAH!
OKAY, WE'RE ALL DONE HERE...
PRES

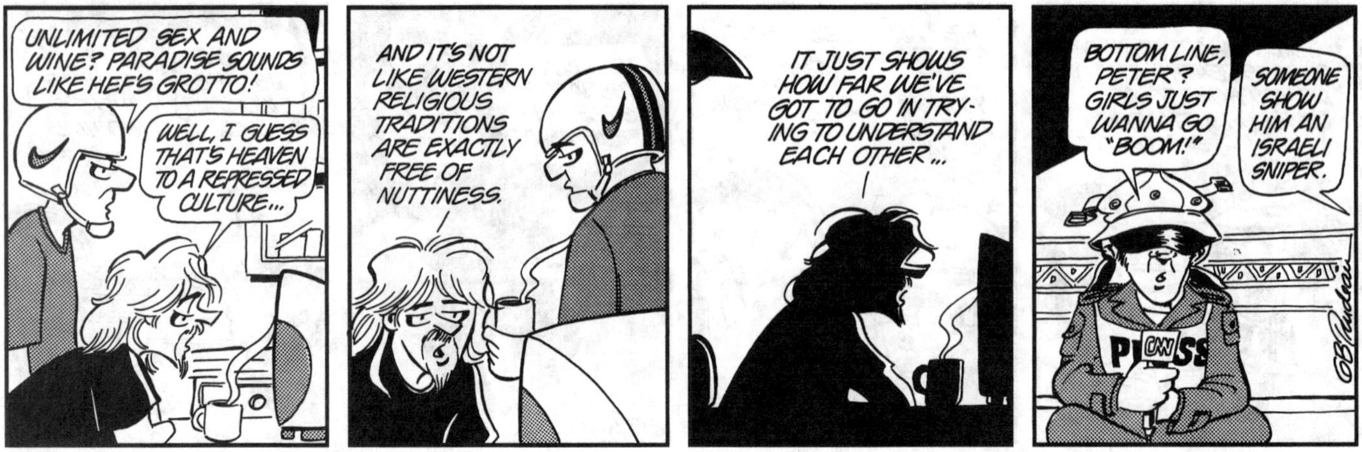
UNLIMITED SEX AND WINE? PARADISE SOUNDS LIKE HEF'S GROTTO!
WELL, I GUESS THAT'S HEAVEN TO A REPRESSED CULTURE...
AND IT'S NOT LIKE WESTERN RELIGIOUS TRADITIONS ARE EXACTLY FREE OF NUTTINESS.
IT JUST SHOWS HOW FAR WE'VE GOT TO GO IN TRYING TO UNDERSTAND EACH OTHER...
BOTTOM LINE, PETER? GIRLS JUST WANNA GO "BOOM!"
SOMEONE SHOW HIM AN ISRAELI SNIPER.
PRESS

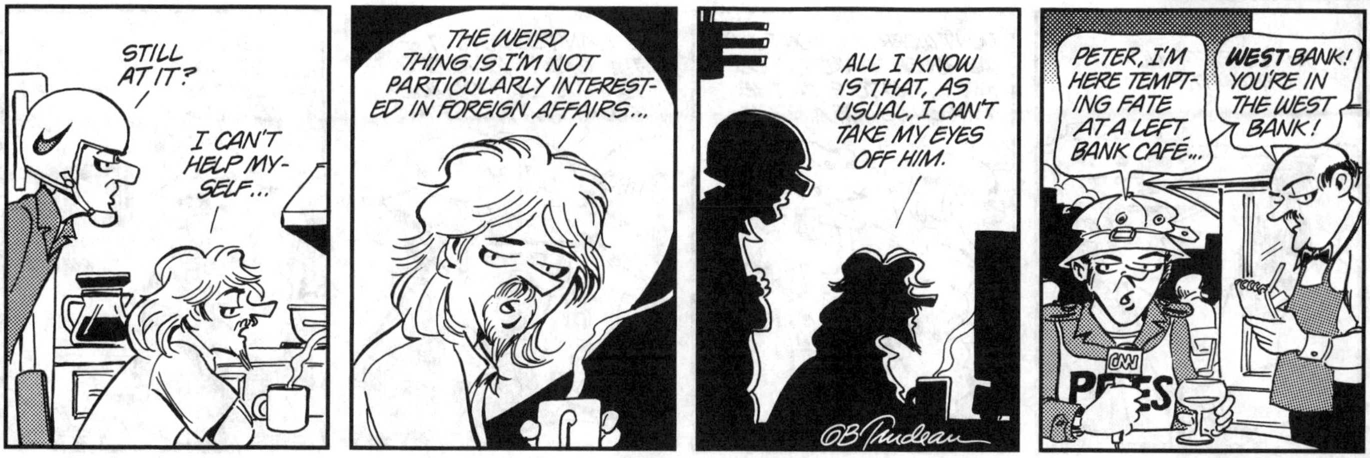
STILL AT IT?
I CAN'T HELP MY-SELF...
THE WEIRD THING IS I'M NOT PARTICULARLY INTEREST-ED IN FOREIGN AFFAIRS...
ALL I KNOW IS THAT, AS USUAL, I CAN'T TAKE MY EYES OFF HIM.
PETER, I'M HERE TEMPT-ING FATE AT A LEFT BANK CAFÉ...
WEST BANK! YOU'RE IN THE WEST BANK!
PRESS

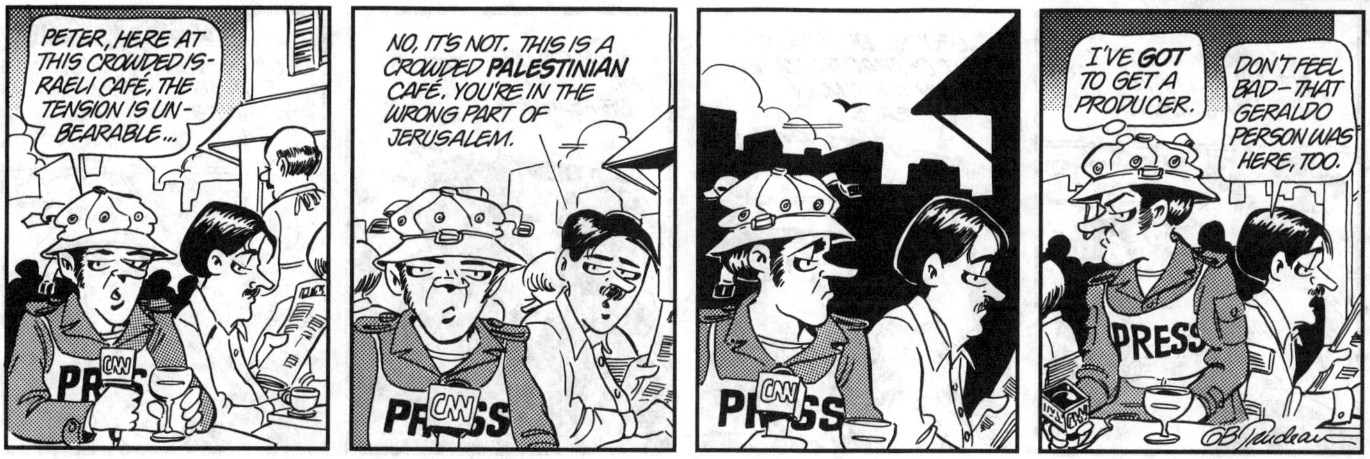
PETER, HERE AT THIS CROWDED IS-RAELI CAFÉ, THE TENSION IS UN-BEARABLE...
NO, IT'S NOT. THIS IS A CROWDED PALESTINIAN CAFÉ. YOU'RE IN THE WRONG PART OF JERUSALEM.
I'VE GOT TO GET A PRODUCER.
DON'T FEEL BAD—THAT GERALDO PERSON WAS HERE, TOO.
PRESS

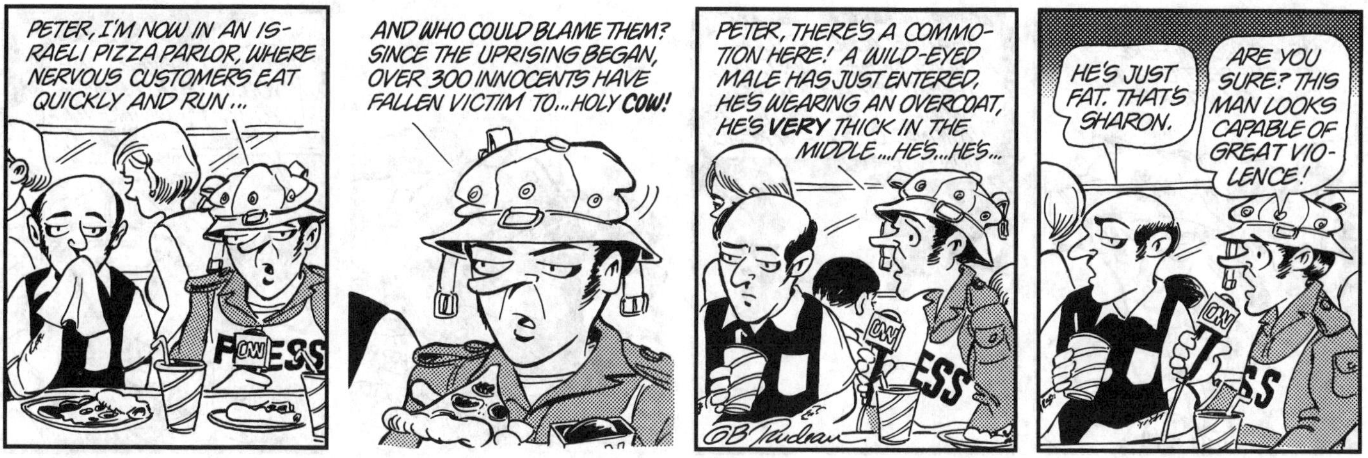
PETER, I'M NOW IN AN IS-RAELI PIZZA PARLOR, WHERE NERVOUS CUSTOMERS EAT QUICKLY AND RUN...
AND WHO COULD BLAME THEM? SINCE THE UPRISING BEGAN, OVER 300 INNOCENTS HAVE FALLEN VICTIM TO...HOLY COW!
PETER, THERE'S A COMMO-TION HERE! A WILD-EYED MALE HAS JUST ENTERED, HE'S WEARING AN OVERCOAT, HE'S VERY THICK IN THE MIDDLE...HE'S...HE'S...
HE'S JUST FAT. THAT'S SHARON.
ARE YOU SURE? THIS MAN LOOKS CAPABLE OF GREAT VIO-LENCE!
PRESS

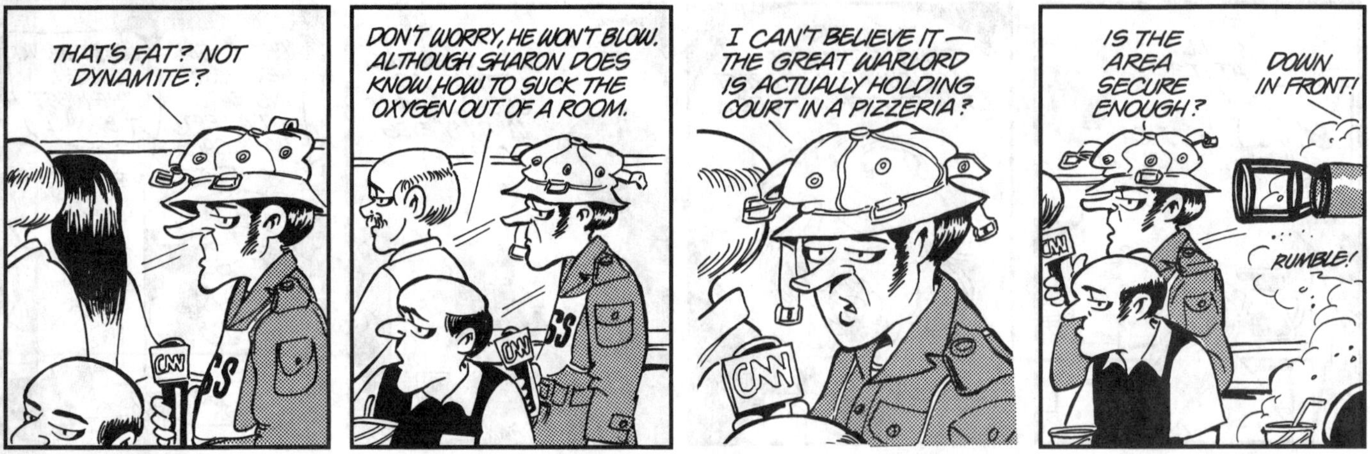
THAT'S FAT? NOT DYNAMITE?
DON'T WORRY, HE WON'T BLOW. ALTHOUGH SHARON DOES KNOW HOW TO SUCK THE OXYGEN OUT OF A ROOM.
I CAN'T BELIEVE IT — THE GREAT WARLORD IS ACTUALLY HOLDING COURT IN A PIZZERIA?
IS THE AREA SECURE ENOUGH?
DOWN IN FRONT!
RUMBLE!

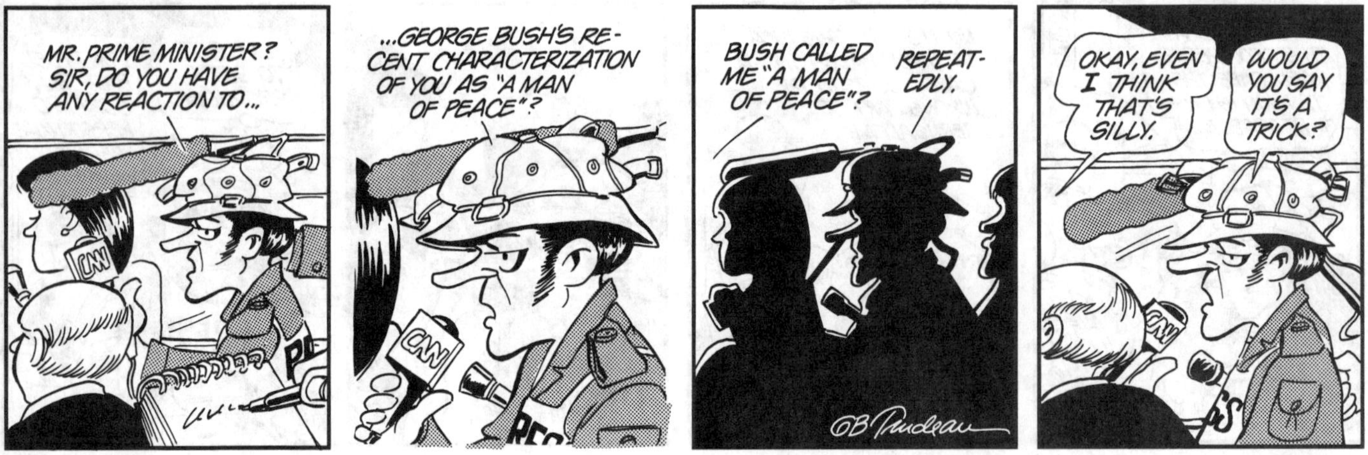
MR. PRIME MINISTER? SIR, DO YOU HAVE ANY REACTION TO...
...GEORGE BUSH'S RECENT CHARACTERIZATION OF YOU AS "A MAN OF PEACE"?
BUSH CALLED ME "A MAN OF PEACE"?
REPEATEDLY.
OKAY, EVEN I THINK THAT'S SILLY.
WOULD YOU SAY IT'S A TRICK?

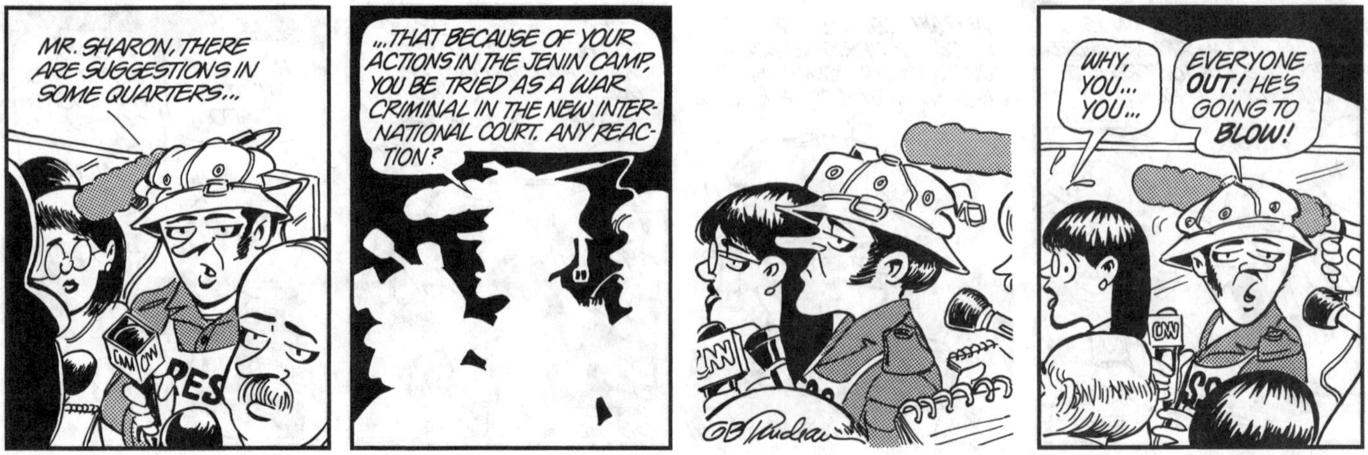
MR. SHARON, THERE ARE SUGGESTIONS IN SOME QUARTERS...
...THAT BECAUSE OF YOUR ACTIONS IN THE JENIN CAMP, YOU BE TRIED AS A WAR CRIMINAL IN THE NEW INTERNATIONAL COURT. ANY REACTION?
WHY, YOU... YOU...
EVERYONE OUT! HE'S GOING TO BLOW!

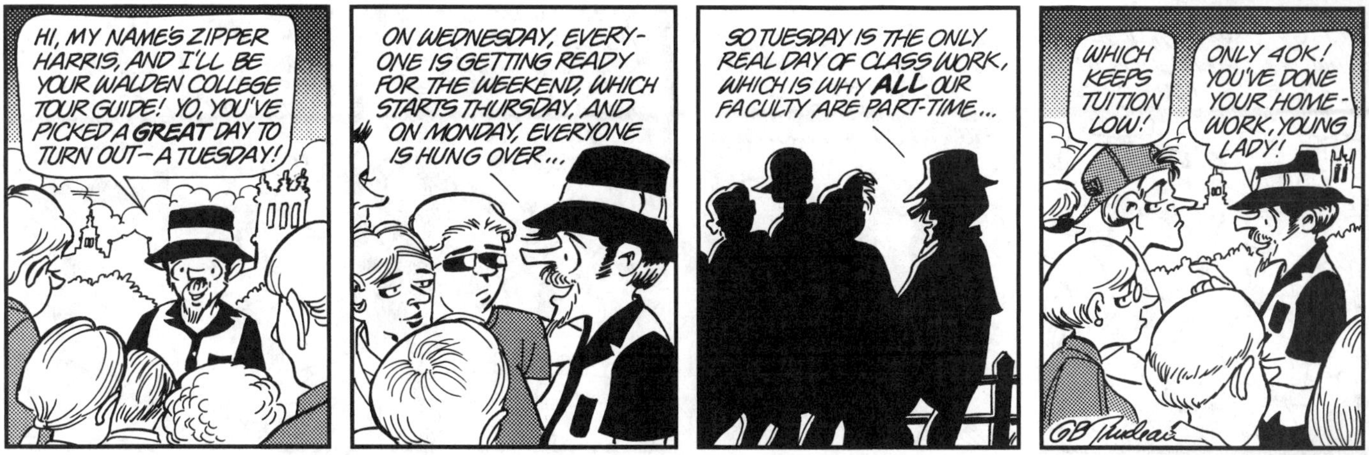
HI, MY NAME'S ZIPPER HARRIS, AND I'LL BE YOUR WALDEN COLLEGE TOUR GUIDE! YO, YOU'VE PICKED A **GREAT** DAY TO TURN OUT—A TUESDAY!
ON WEDNESDAY, EVERYONE IS GETTING READY FOR THE WEEKEND, WHICH STARTS THURSDAY, AND ON MONDAY, EVERYONE IS HUNG OVER...
SO TUESDAY IS THE ONLY REAL DAY OF CLASS WORK, WHICH IS WHY **ALL** OUR FACULTY ARE PART-TIME...
WHICH KEEPS TUITION LOW!
ONLY 40K! YOU'VE DONE YOUR HOMEWORK, YOUNG LADY!
GB Trudeau

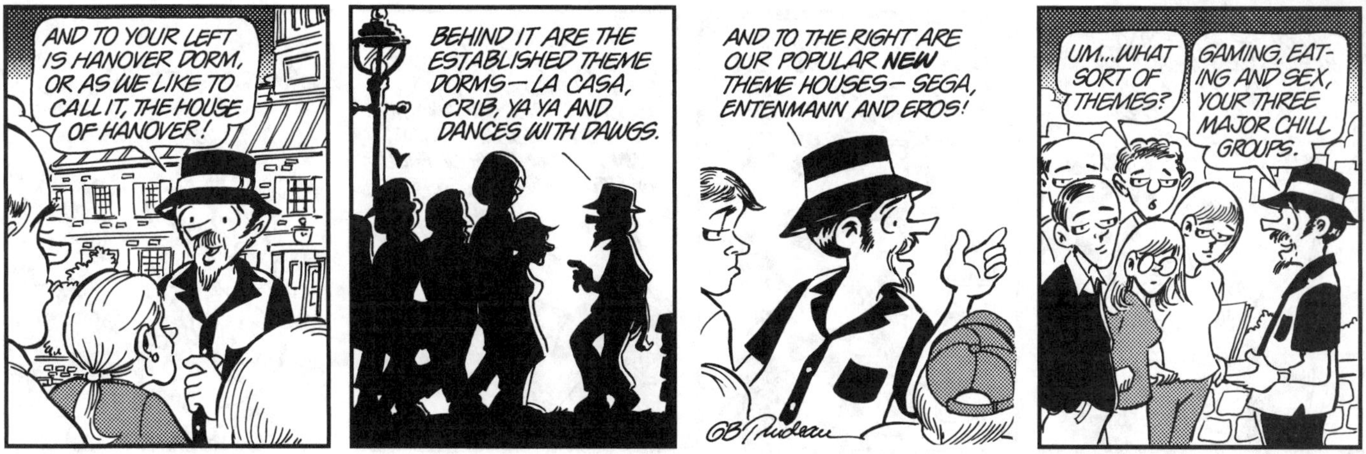
AND TO YOUR LEFT IS HANOVER DORM, OR AS WE LIKE TO CALL IT, THE HOUSE OF HANOVER!
BEHIND IT ARE THE ESTABLISHED THEME DORMS—LA CASA, CRIB, YA YA AND DANCES WITH DAWGS.
AND TO THE RIGHT ARE OUR POPULAR **NEW** THEME HOUSES—SEGA, ENTENMANN AND EROS!
GB Trudeau
UM...WHAT SORT OF THEMES?
GAMING, EATING AND SEX, YOUR THREE MAJOR CHILL GROUPS.

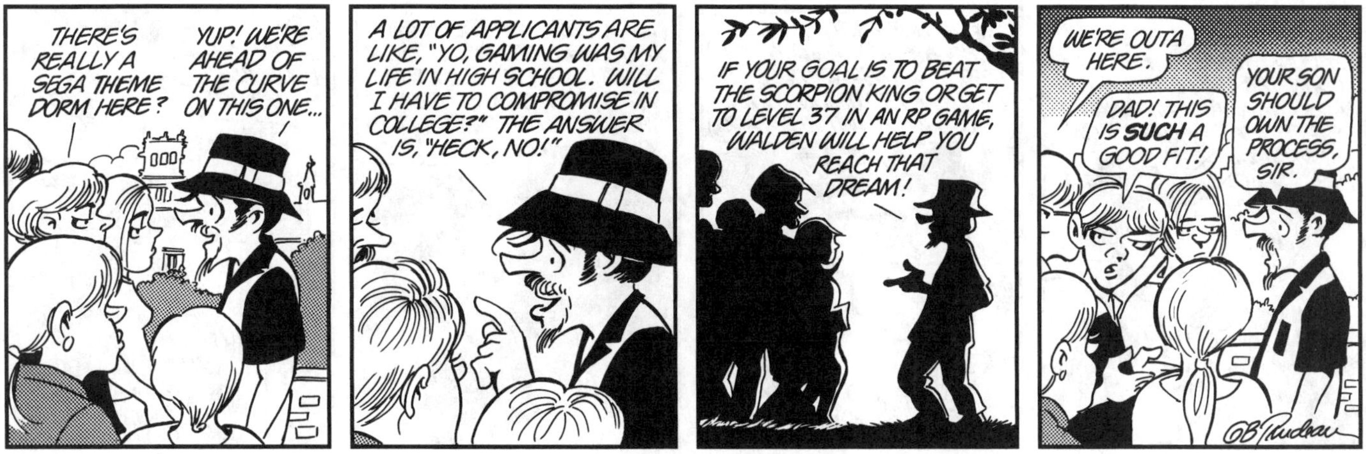
THERE'S REALLY A SEGA THEME DORM HERE?
YUP! WE'RE AHEAD OF THE CURVE ON THIS ONE...
A LOT OF APPLICANTS ARE LIKE, "YO, GAMING WAS MY LIFE IN HIGH SCHOOL. WILL I HAVE TO COMPROMISE IN COLLEGE?" THE ANSWER IS, "HECK, NO!"
IF YOUR GOAL IS TO BEAT THE SCORPION KING OR GET TO LEVEL 37 IN AN RP GAME, WALDEN WILL HELP YOU REACH THAT DREAM!
WE'RE OUTA HERE.
DAD! THIS IS **SUCH** A GOOD FIT!
YOUR SON SHOULD OWN THE PROCESS, SIR.
GB Trudeau

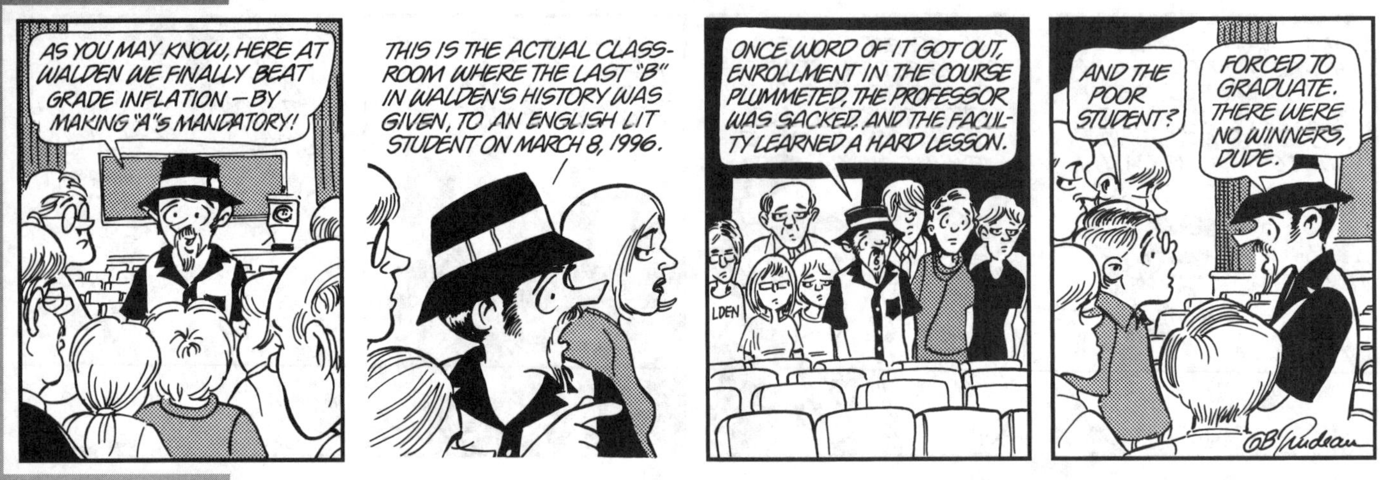
AS YOU MAY KNOW, HERE AT WALDEN WE FINALLY BEAT GRADE INFLATION — BY MAKING "A"s MANDATORY!
THIS IS THE ACTUAL CLASSROOM WHERE THE LAST "B" IN WALDEN'S HISTORY WAS GIVEN, TO AN ENGLISH LIT STUDENT ON MARCH 8, 1996.
ONCE WORD OF IT GOT OUT, ENROLLMENT IN THE COURSE PLUMMETED, THE PROFESSOR WAS SACKED, AND THE FACULTY LEARNED A HARD LESSON.
AND THE POOR STUDENT?
FORCED TO GRADUATE. THERE WERE NO WINNERS, DUDE.
GB Trudeau

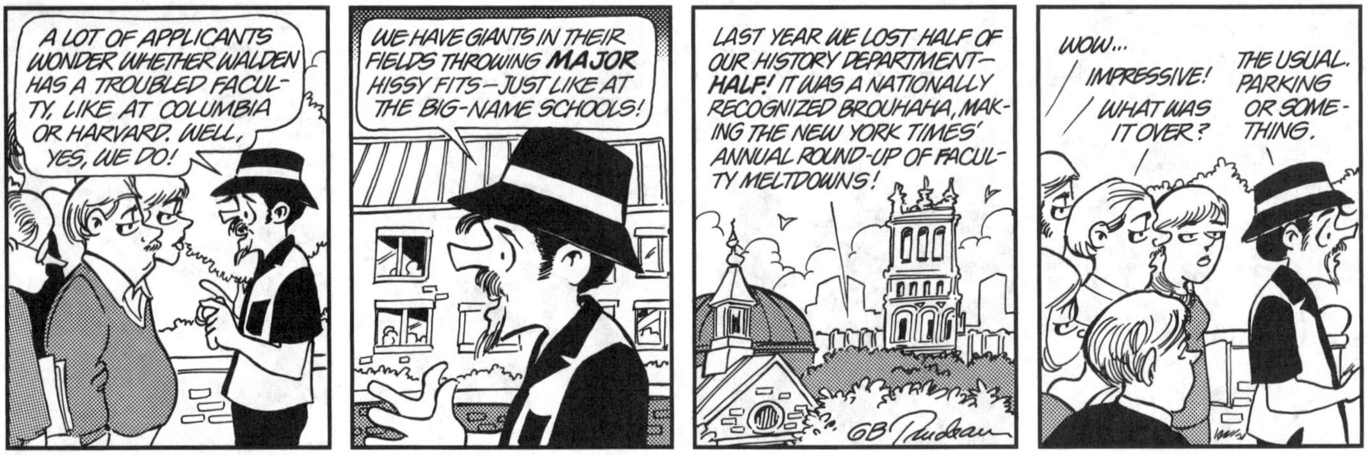
A LOT OF APPLICANTS WONDER WHETHER WALDEN HAS A TROUBLED FACULTY, LIKE AT COLUMBIA OR HARVARD. WELL, YES, WE DO!
WE HAVE GIANTS IN THEIR FIELDS THROWING MAJOR HISSY FITS — JUST LIKE AT THE BIG-NAME SCHOOLS!
LAST YEAR WE LOST HALF OF OUR HISTORY DEPARTMENT — HALF! IT WAS A NATIONALLY RECOGNIZED BROUHAHA, MAKING THE NEW YORK TIMES' ANNUAL ROUND-UP OF FACULTY MELTDOWNS!
GB Trudeau
WOW...
IMPRESSIVE!
WHAT WAS IT OVER?
THE USUAL. PARKING OR SOMETHING.

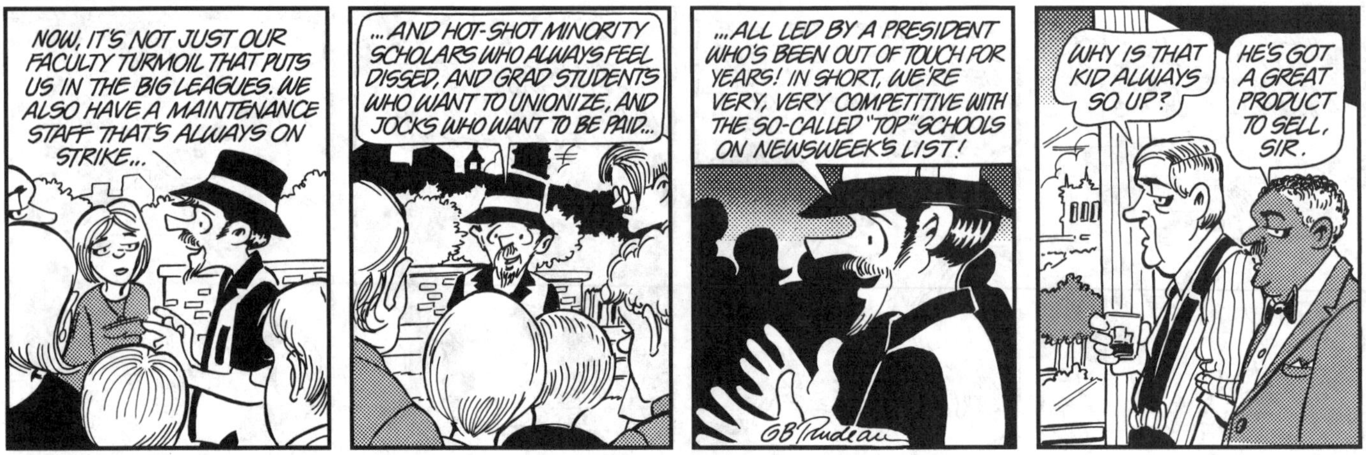
NOW, IT'S NOT JUST OUR FACULTY TURMOIL THAT PUTS US IN THE BIG LEAGUES. WE ALSO HAVE A MAINTENANCE STAFF THAT'S ALWAYS ON STRIKE...
...AND HOT-SHOT MINORITY SCHOLARS WHO ALWAYS FEEL DISSED, AND GRAD STUDENTS WHO WANT TO UNIONIZE, AND JOCKS WHO WANT TO BE PAID...
...ALL LED BY A PRESIDENT WHO'S BEEN OUT OF TOUCH FOR YEARS! IN SHORT, WE'RE VERY, VERY COMPETITIVE WITH THE SO-CALLED "TOP" SCHOOLS ON NEWSWEEK'S LIST!
GB Trudeau
WHY IS THAT KID ALWAYS SO UP?
HE'S GOT A GREAT PRODUCT TO SELL, SIR.

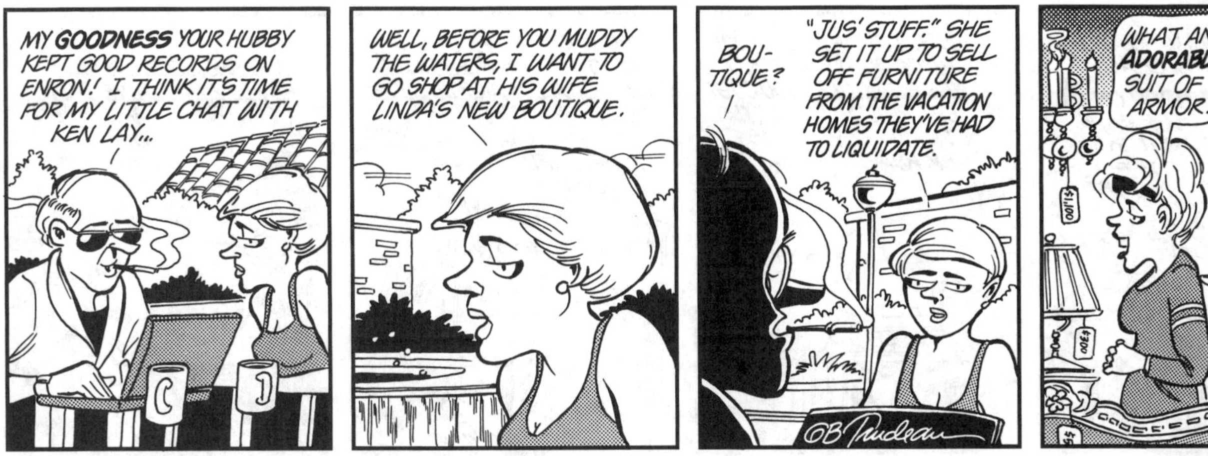
MY GOODNESS YOUR HUBBY KEPT GOOD RECORDS ON ENRON! I THINK IT'S TIME FOR MY LITTLE CHAT WITH KEN LAY...
WELL, BEFORE YOU MUDDY THE WATERS, I WANT TO GO SHOP AT HIS WIFE LINDA'S NEW BOUTIQUE.
BOUTIQUE?
"JUS' STUFF." SHE SET IT UP TO SELL OFF FURNITURE FROM THE VACATION HOMES THEY'VE HAD TO LIQUIDATE.
WHAT AN ADORABLE SUIT OF ARMOR!
ISN'T IT? IT'S FROM KEN'S WALK-IN HUMIDOR.

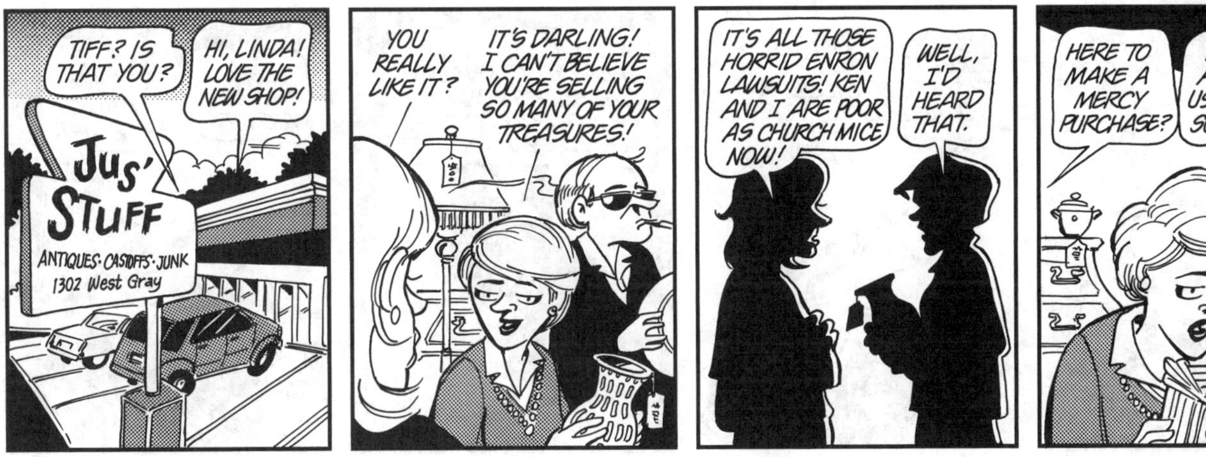
TIFF? IS THAT YOU?
HI, LINDA! LOVE THE NEW SHOP!
JUS' STUFF
ANTIQUES · CASTOFFS · JUNK
1302 West Gray
YOU REALLY LIKE IT?
IT'S DARLING! I CAN'T BELIEVE YOU'RE SELLING SO MANY OF YOUR TREASURES!
IT'S ALL THOSE HORRID ENRON LAWSUITS! KEN AND I ARE POOR AS CHURCH MICE NOW!
WELL, I'D HEARD THAT.
HERE TO MAKE A MERCY PURCHASE?
NO, NO. I ACTUALLY USED TO COVET SOME OF THIS.

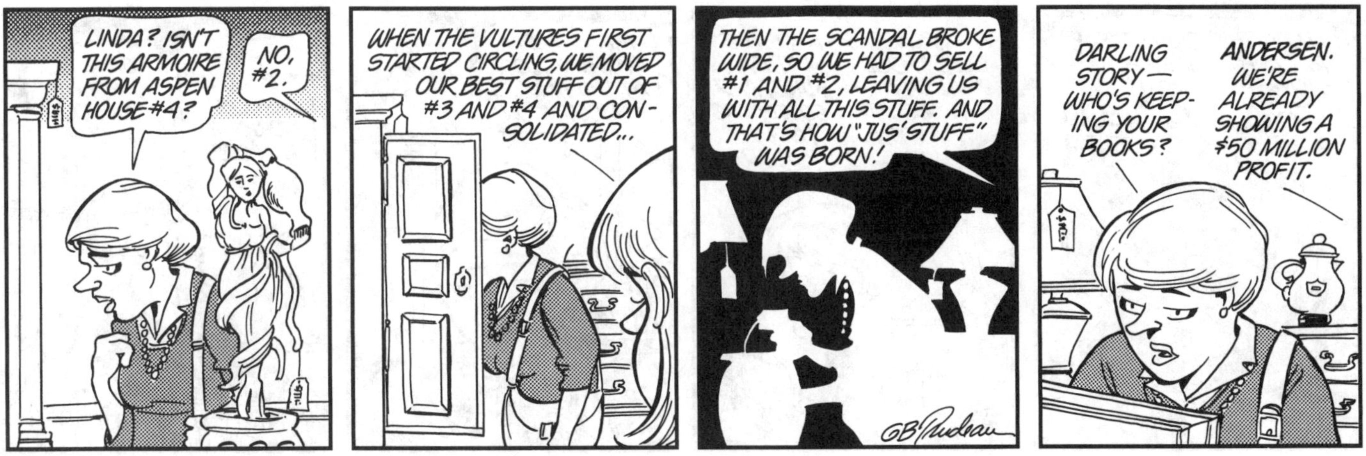
LINDA? ISN'T THIS ARMOIRE FROM ASPEN HOUSE #4?
NO, #2.
WHEN THE VULTURES FIRST STARTED CIRCLING, WE MOVED OUR BEST STUFF OUT OF #3 AND #4 AND CONSOLIDATED...
THEN THE SCANDAL BROKE WIDE, SO WE HAD TO SELL #1 AND #2, LEAVING US WITH ALL THIS STUFF. AND THAT'S HOW "JUS' STUFF" WAS BORN!
DARLING STORY — WHO'S KEEPING YOUR BOOKS?
ANDERSEN. WE'RE ALREADY SHOWING A $50 MILLION PROFIT.

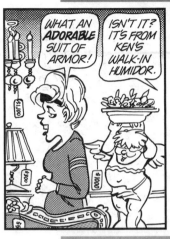

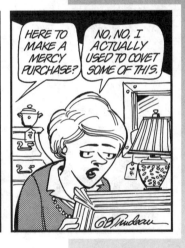

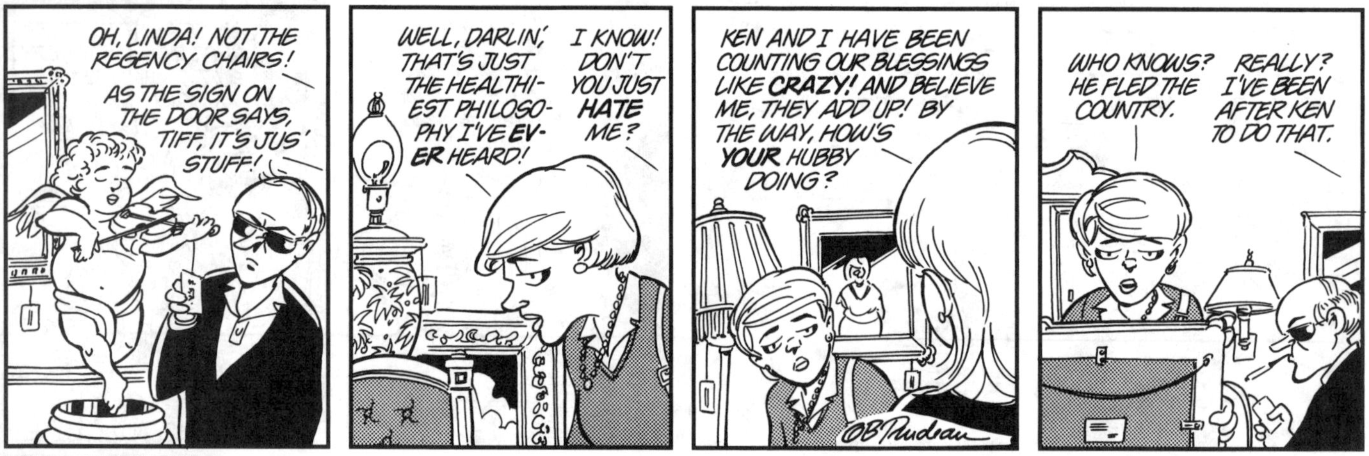
OH, LINDA! NOT THE REGENCY CHAIRS!
AS THE SIGN ON THE DOOR SAYS, TIFF, IT'S JUS' STUFF!
WELL, DARLIN', THAT'S JUST THE HEALTHIEST PHILOSOPHY I'VE EVER HEARD!
I KNOW! DON'T YOU JUST HATE ME?
KEN AND I HAVE BEEN COUNTING OUR BLESSINGS LIKE CRAZY! AND BELIEVE ME, THEY ADD UP! BY THE WAY, HOW'S YOUR HUBBY DOING?
WHO KNOWS? HE FLED THE COUNTRY.
REALLY? I'VE BEEN AFTER KEN TO DO THAT.

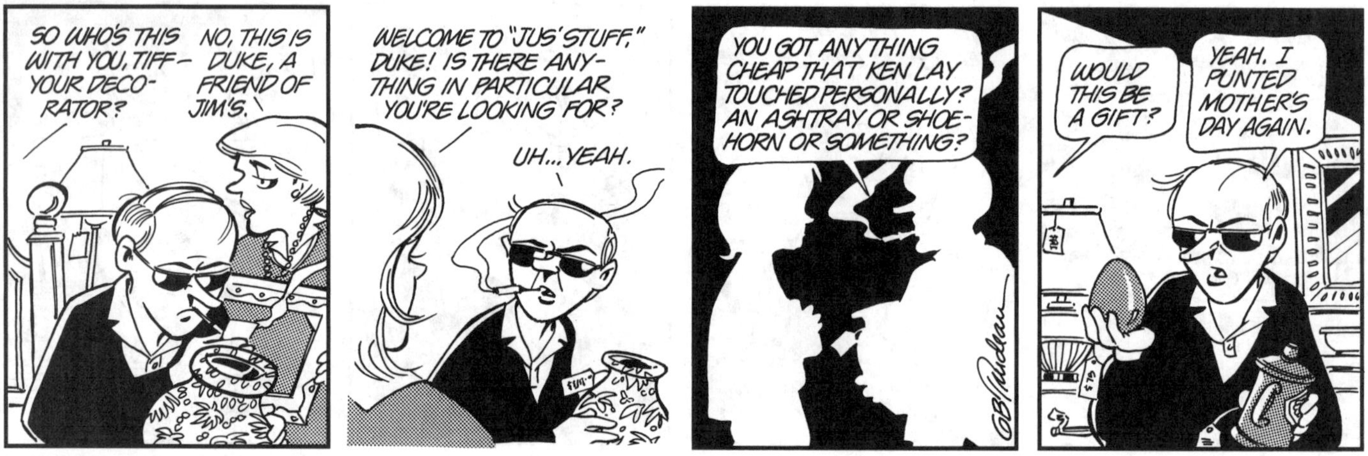
SO WHO'S THIS WITH YOU, TIFF– YOUR DECORATOR?
NO, THIS IS DUKE, A FRIEND OF JIM'S.
WELCOME TO "JUS' STUFF," DUKE! IS THERE ANYTHING IN PARTICULAR YOU'RE LOOKING FOR?
UH... YEAH.
YOU GOT ANYTHING CHEAP THAT KEN LAY TOUCHED PERSONALLY? AN ASHTRAY OR SHOEHORN OR SOMETHING?
WOULD THIS BE A GIFT?
YEAH. I PUNTED MOTHER'S DAY AGAIN.

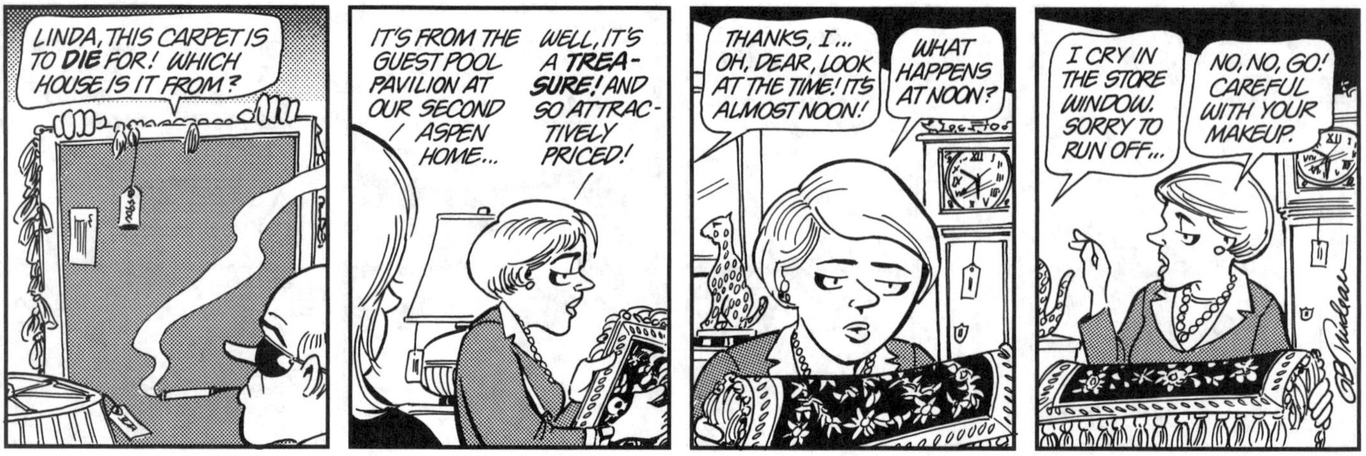
LINDA, THIS CARPET IS TO DIE FOR! WHICH HOUSE IS IT FROM?
IT'S FROM THE GUEST POOL PAVILION AT OUR SECOND ASPEN HOME...
WELL, IT'S A TREASURE! AND SO ATTRACTIVELY PRICED!
THANKS, I... OH, DEAR, LOOK AT THE TIME! IT'S ALMOST NOON!
WHAT HAPPENS AT NOON?
I CRY IN THE STORE WINDOW. SORRY TO RUN OFF...
NO, NO, GO! CAREFUL WITH YOUR MAKEUP.

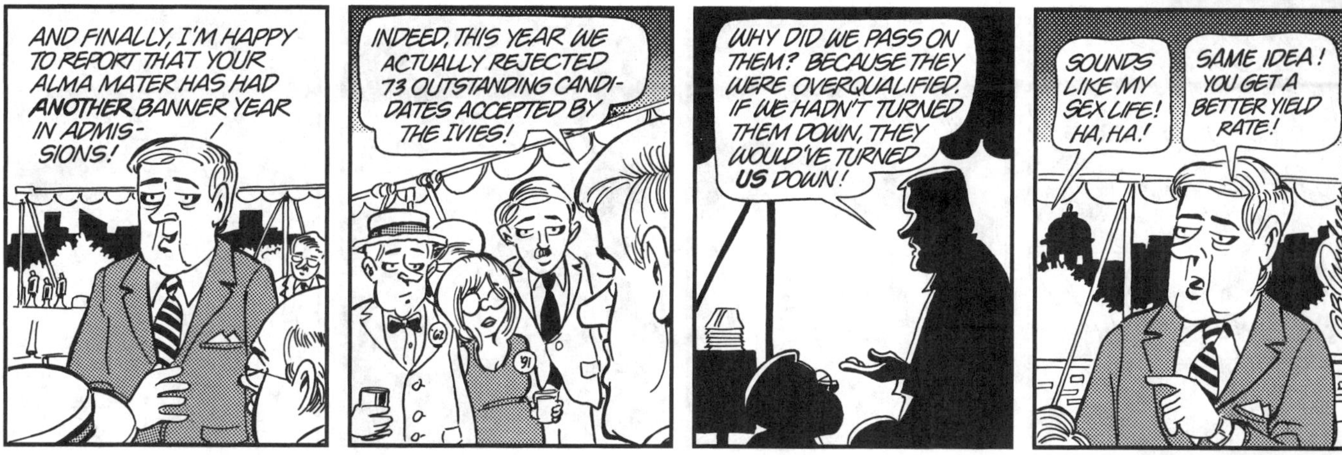
AND FINALLY, I'M HAPPY TO REPORT THAT YOUR ALMA MATER HAS HAD **ANOTHER** BANNER YEAR IN ADMIS-SIONS!
INDEED, THIS YEAR WE ACTUALLY REJECTED 73 OUTSTANDING CANDI-DATES ACCEPTED BY THE IVIES!
WHY DID WE PASS ON THEM? BECAUSE THEY WERE OVERQUALIFIED. IF WE HADN'T TURNED THEM DOWN, THEY WOULD'VE TURNED **US** DOWN!
SOUNDS LIKE MY SEX LIFE! HA, HA!
SAME IDEA! YOU GET A BETTER YIELD RATE!

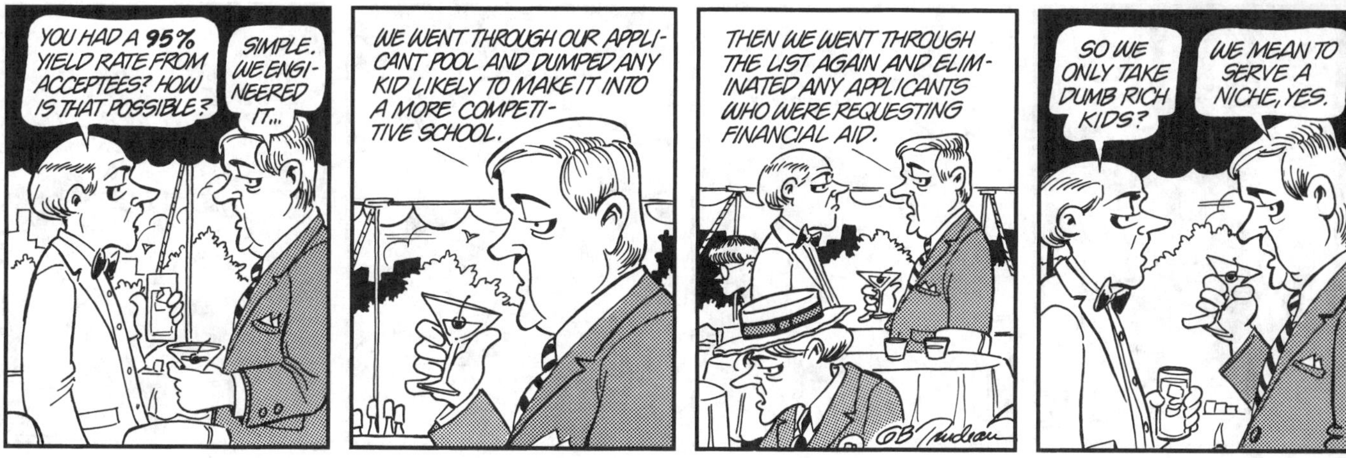
YOU HAD A **95%** YIELD RATE FROM ACCEPTEES? HOW IS THAT POSSIBLE?
SIMPLE. WE ENGI-NEERED IT...
WE WENT THROUGH OUR APPLI-CANT POOL AND DUMPED ANY KID LIKELY TO MAKE IT INTO A MORE COMPETI-TIVE SCHOOL.
THEN WE WENT THROUGH THE LIST AGAIN AND ELIM-INATED ANY APPLICANTS WHO WERE REQUESTING FINANCIAL AID.
SO WE ONLY TAKE DUMB RICH KIDS?
WE MEAN TO SERVE A NICHE, YES.

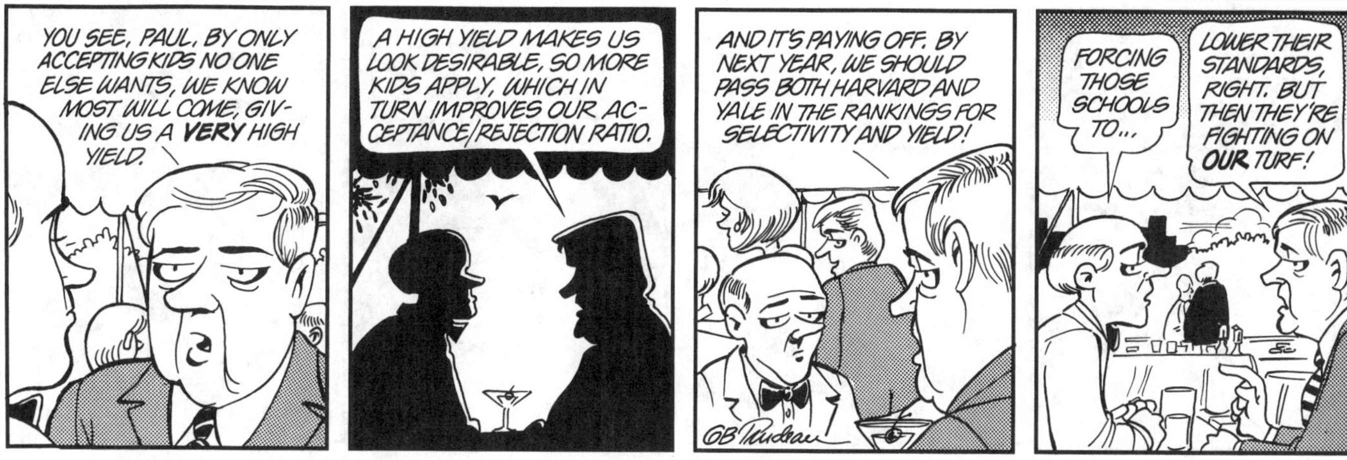
YOU SEE, PAUL, BY ONLY ACCEPTING KIDS NO ONE ELSE WANTS, WE KNOW MOST WILL COME, GIV-ING US A **VERY** HIGH YIELD.
A HIGH YIELD MAKES US LOOK DESIRABLE, SO MORE KIDS APPLY, WHICH IN TURN IMPROVES OUR AC-CEPTANCE/REJECTION RATIO.
AND IT'S PAYING OFF. BY NEXT YEAR, WE SHOULD PASS BOTH HARVARD AND YALE IN THE RANKINGS FOR SELECTIVITY AND YIELD!
FORCING THOSE SCHOOLS TO...
LOWER THEIR STANDARDS, RIGHT. BUT THEN THEY'RE FIGHTING ON **OUR** TURF!

SO WE DON'T OFFER SCHOLARSHIPS AT ALL ANYMORE?
WE CAN'T AFFORD THEM—EXCEPT FOR THE JOCKS.
TO KEEP UP APPEARANCES WE DO OFFER ONE NON-ATHLETIC SCHOLARSHIP, BUT IT GOES TO A LEGACY.
LEGACY?
LEGACY?
YUP! MY UNCLE ZONK HELD IT FOR 12 YEARS!

SO HOW WAS **YOUR** COLLEGE APPLICATION PROCESS?
BRUTAL. THE WORST.
WALDEN WAS MY FIRST CHOICE, OF COURSE, BUT I WAS BOMBARDED WITH LETTERS FROM OTHER SCHOOLS...
I SPENT THE WHOLE YEAR WORRIED **SICK** THAT ONE OF THEM WOULD SNAP ME UP!
UM... I THINK YOU HAVE TO APPLY.
NO, NO, THESE BOYS WERE ALL OVER ME!

WELL, WELL! YOU'RE OUR SCHOLARSHIP BOY, AREN'T YOU, SON?
YES, SIR! ZIPPER HARRIS!
AND HOW LONG HAVE YOU BEEN AT THE COLLEGE, MR. HARRIS?
THREE YEARS, SIR!
THREE YEARS?
SOMETHING LIKE THAT.
I HOPE BY NOW YOU'RE...
AFRAID NOT, SIR! STILL A FRESHMAN!

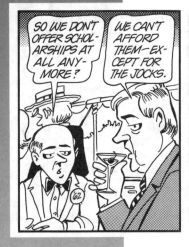

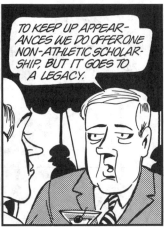

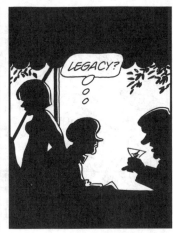

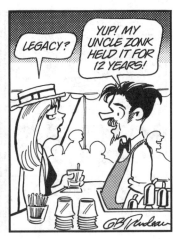

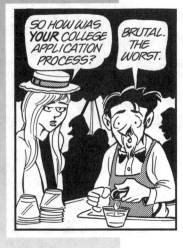

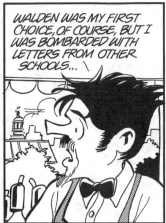

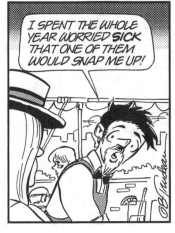

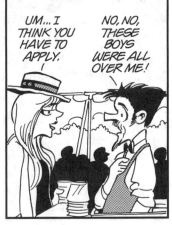

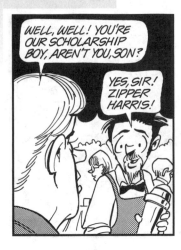

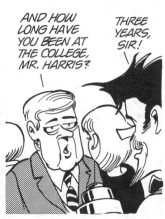

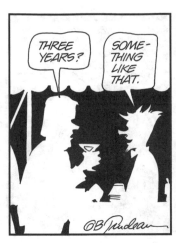

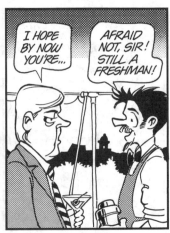

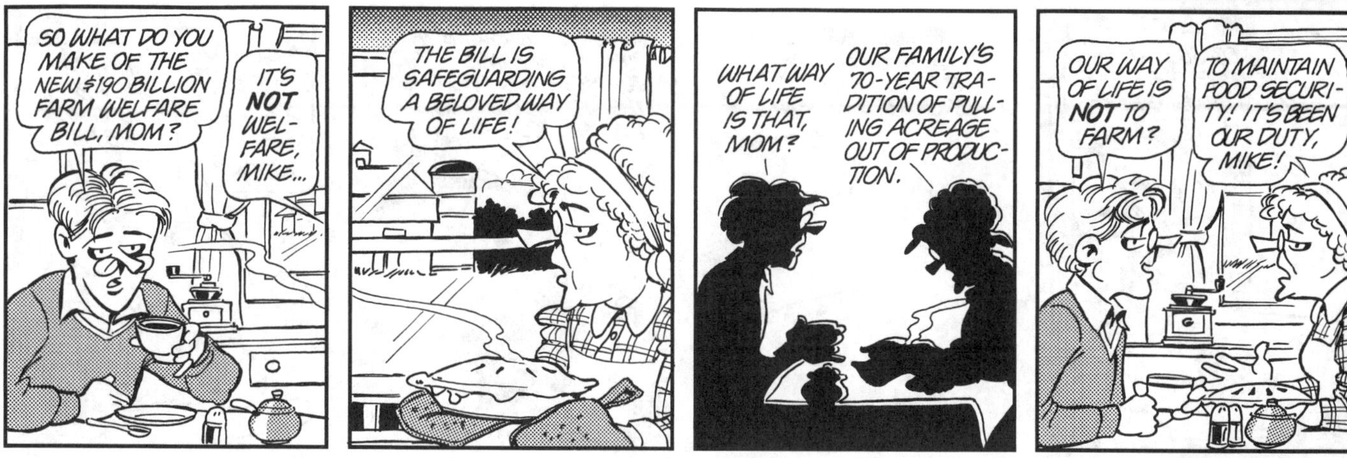
SO WHAT DO YOU MAKE OF THE NEW $190 BILLION FARM WELFARE BILL, MOM?
IT'S **NOT** WELFARE, MIKE...
THE BILL IS SAFEGUARDING A BELOVED WAY OF LIFE!
WHAT WAY OF LIFE IS THAT, MOM?
OUR FAMILY'S 70-YEAR TRADITION OF PULLING ACREAGE OUT OF PRODUCTION.
OUR WAY OF LIFE IS **NOT** TO FARM?
TO MAINTAIN FOOD SECURITY! IT'S BEEN OUR DUTY, MIKE!

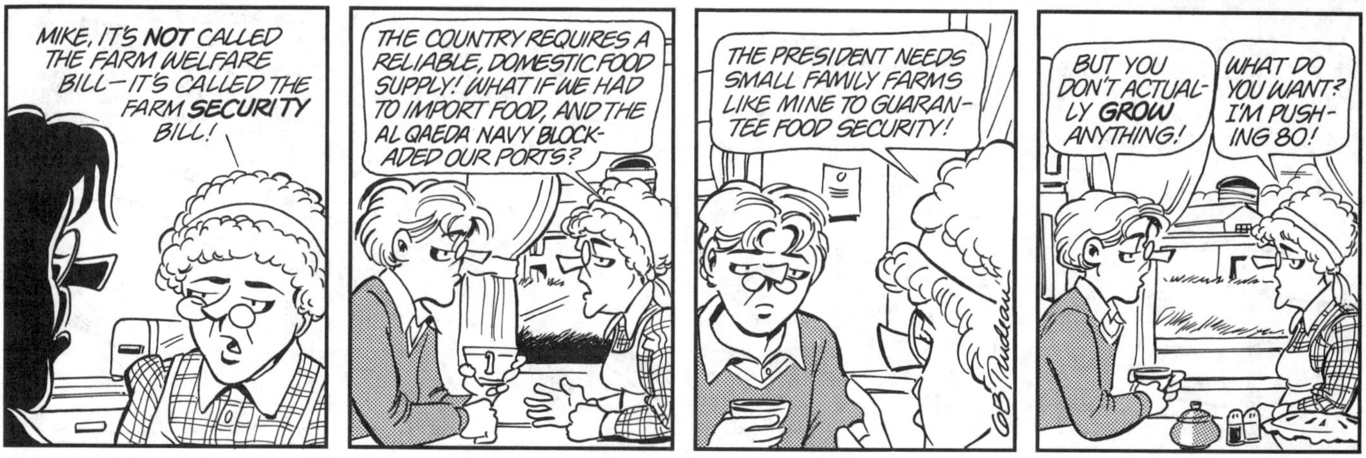
MIKE, IT'S **NOT** CALLED THE FARM WELFARE BILL—IT'S CALLED THE FARM **SECURITY** BILL!
THE COUNTRY REQUIRES A RELIABLE, DOMESTIC FOOD SUPPLY! WHAT IF WE HAD TO IMPORT FOOD, AND THE AL QAEDA NAVY BLOCKADED OUR PORTS?
THE PRESIDENT NEEDS SMALL FAMILY FARMS LIKE MINE TO GUARANTEE FOOD SECURITY!
BUT YOU DON'T ACTUALLY **GROW** ANYTHING!
WHAT DO YOU WANT? I'M PUSHING 80!

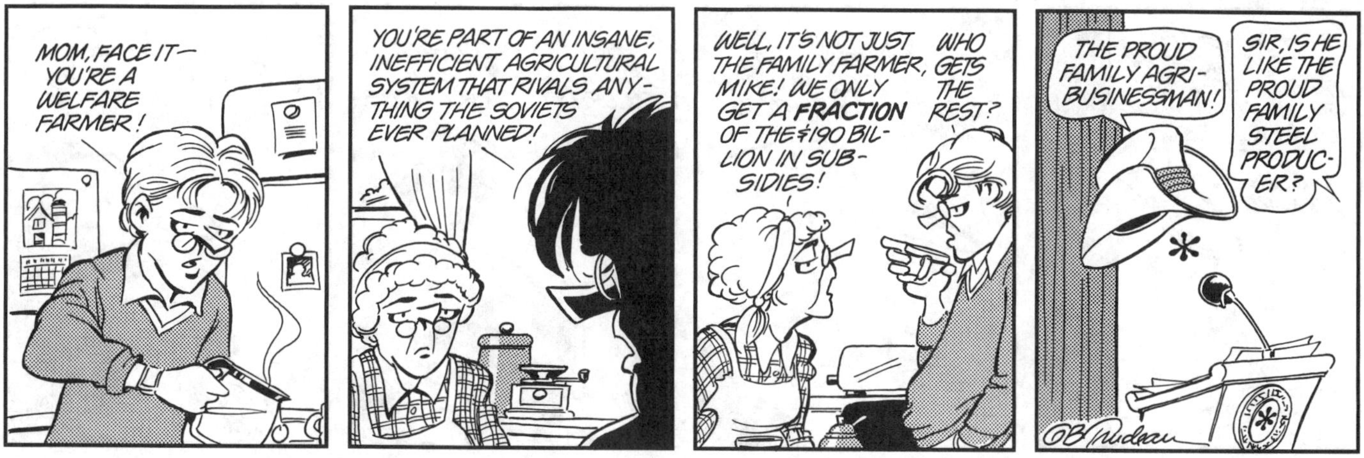
MOM, FACE IT—YOU'RE A WELFARE FARMER!
YOU'RE PART OF AN INSANE, INEFFICIENT AGRICULTURAL SYSTEM THAT RIVALS ANYTHING THE SOVIETS EVER PLANNED!
WELL, IT'S NOT JUST THE FAMILY FARMER, MIKE! WE ONLY GET A **FRACTION** OF THE $190 BILLION IN SUBSIDIES!
WHO GETS THE REST?
THE PROUD FAMILY AGRIBUSINESSMAN!
SIR, IS HE LIKE THE PROUD FAMILY STEEL PRODUCER?

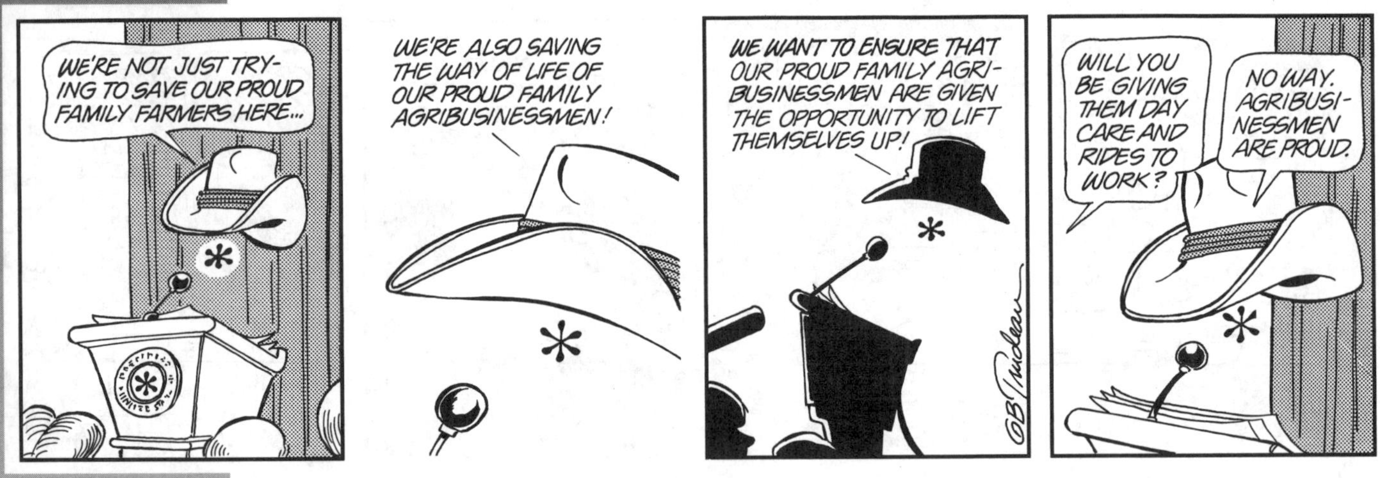
WE'RE NOT JUST TRYING TO SAVE OUR PROUD FAMILY FARMERS HERE...
WE'RE ALSO SAVING THE WAY OF LIFE OF OUR PROUD FAMILY AGRIBUSINESSMEN!
WE WANT TO ENSURE THAT OUR PROUD FAMILY AGRIBUSINESSMEN ARE GIVEN THE OPPORTUNITY TO LIFT THEMSELVES UP!
©B. Trudeau
WILL YOU BE GIVING THEM DAY CARE AND RIDES TO WORK?
NO WAY. AGRIBUSINESSMEN ARE PROUD.

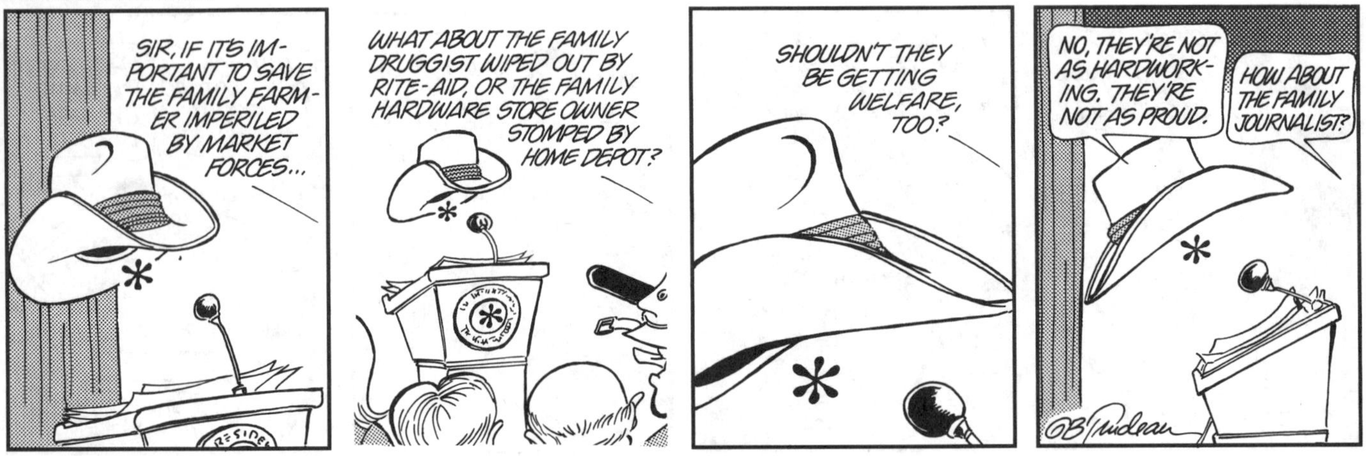
SIR, IF IT'S IMPORTANT TO SAVE THE FAMILY FARMER IMPERILED BY MARKET FORCES...
WHAT ABOUT THE FAMILY DRUGGIST WIPED OUT BY RITE-AID, OR THE FAMILY HARDWARE STORE OWNER STOMPED BY HOME DEPOT?
SHOULDN'T THEY BE GETTING WELFARE, TOO?
NO, THEY'RE NOT AS HARDWORKING. THEY'RE NOT AS PROUD.
HOW ABOUT THE FAMILY JOURNALIST?
©B. Trudeau

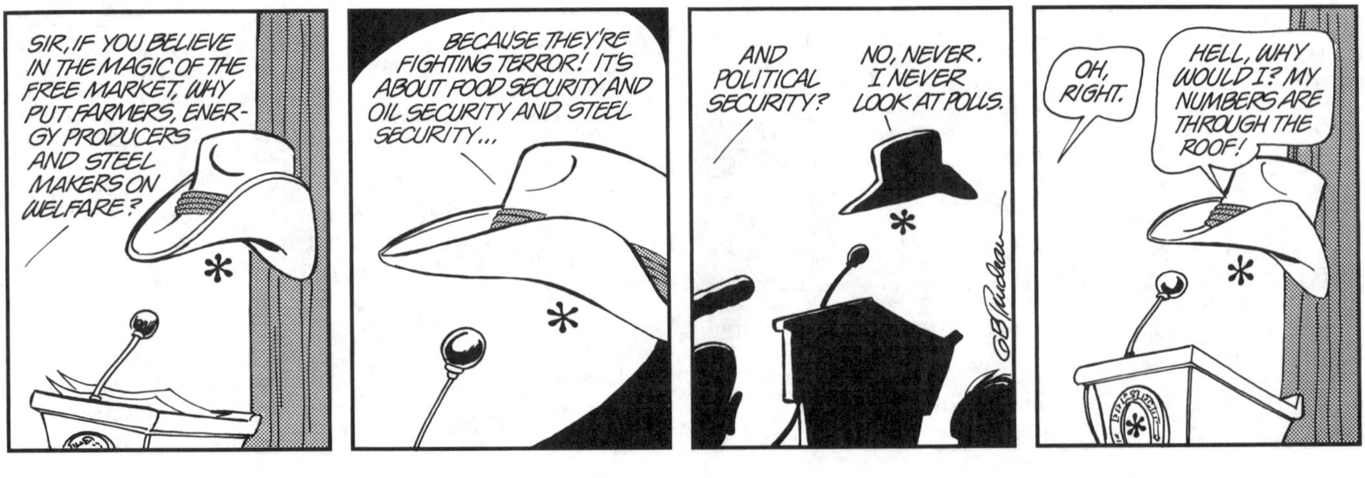
SIR, IF YOU BELIEVE IN THE MAGIC OF THE FREE MARKET, WHY PUT FARMERS, ENERGY PRODUCERS AND STEEL MAKERS ON WELFARE?
BECAUSE THEY'RE FIGHTING TERROR! IT'S ABOUT FOOD SECURITY AND OIL SECURITY AND STEEL SECURITY...
AND POLITICAL SECURITY?
NO, NEVER. I NEVER LOOK AT POLLS.
©B. Trudeau
OH, RIGHT.
HELL, WHY WOULD I? MY NUMBERS ARE THROUGH THE ROOF!

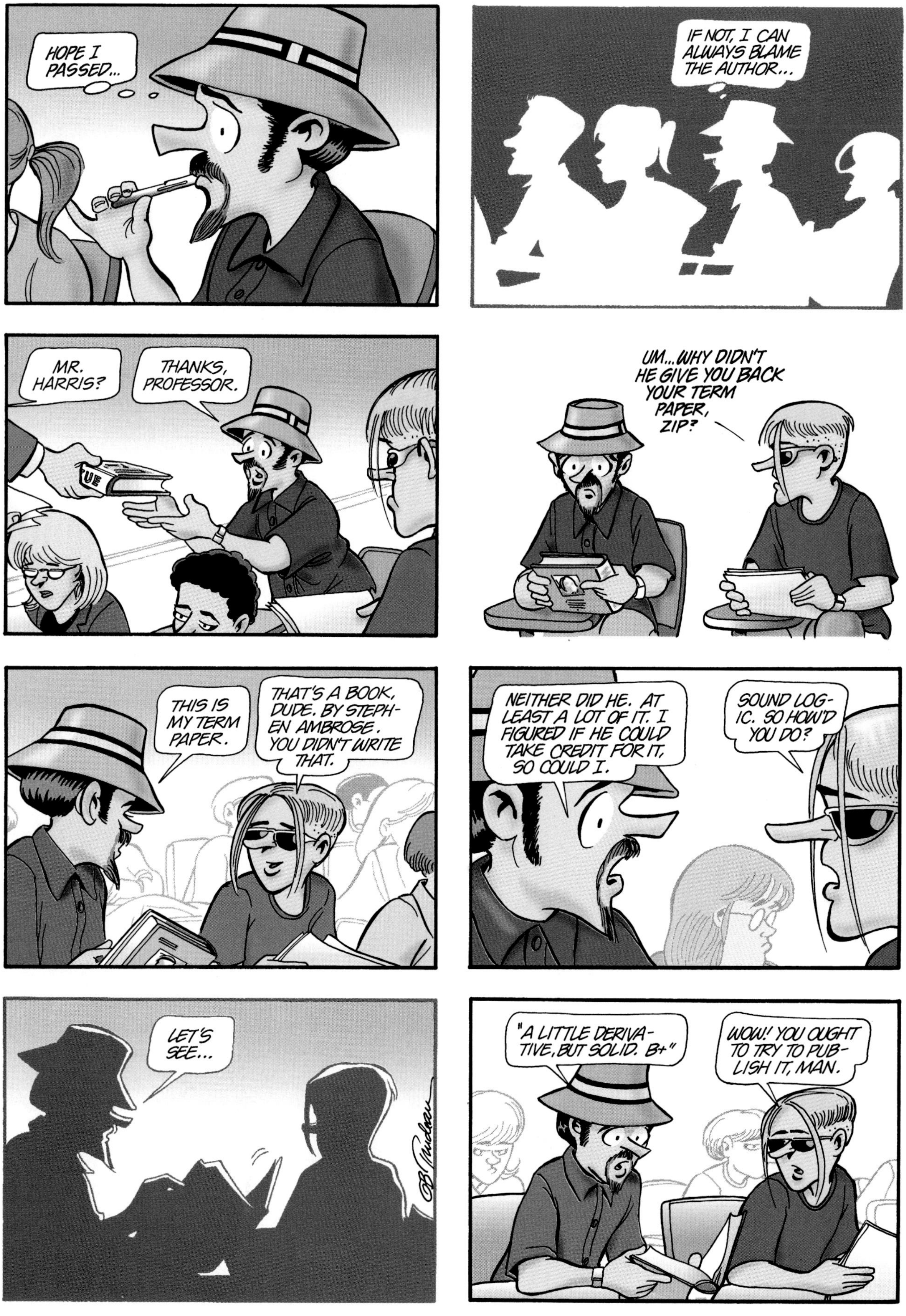
HOPE I PASSED...
IF NOT, I CAN ALWAYS BLAME THE AUTHOR...
MR. HARRIS?
THANKS, PROFESSOR.
UM...WHY DIDN'T HE GIVE YOU BACK YOUR TERM PAPER, ZIP?
THIS IS MY TERM PAPER.
THAT'S A BOOK, DUDE. BY STEPH-EN AMBROSE. YOU DIDN'T WRITE THAT.
NEITHER DID HE. AT LEAST A LOT OF IT. I FIGURED IF HE COULD TAKE CREDIT FOR IT, SO COULD I.
SOUND LOG-IC. SO HOW'D YOU DO?
LET'S SEE...
"A LITTLE DERIVA-TIVE, BUT SOLID. B+"
WOW! YOU OUGHT TO TRY TO PUB-LISH IT, MAN.

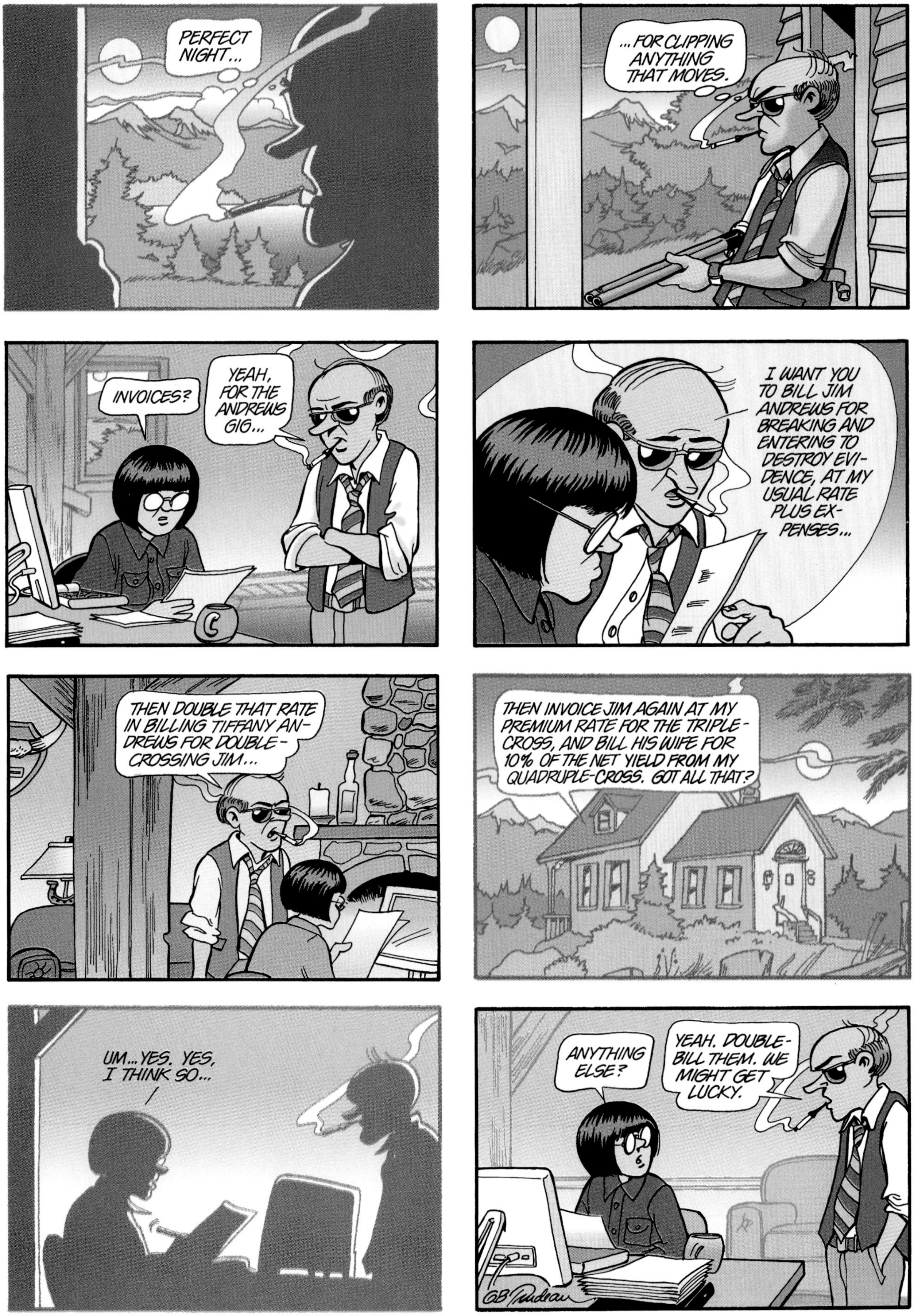
PERFECT NIGHT...
...FOR CLIPPING ANYTHING THAT MOVES.
INVOICES?
YEAH, FOR THE ANDREWS GIG...
I WANT YOU TO BILL JIM ANDREWS FOR BREAKING AND ENTERING TO DESTROY EVIDENCE, AT MY USUAL RATE PLUS EXPENSES...
THEN DOUBLE THAT RATE IN BILLING TIFFANY ANDREWS FOR DOUBLE-CROSSING JIM...
THEN INVOICE JIM AGAIN AT MY PREMIUM RATE FOR THE TRIPLE-CROSS, AND BILL HIS WIFE FOR 10% OF THE NET YIELD FROM MY QUADRUPLE-CROSS. GOT ALL THAT?
UM...YES. YES, I THINK SO...
ANYTHING ELSE?
YEAH. DOUBLE-BILL THEM. WE MIGHT GET LUCKY.
©B Trudeau

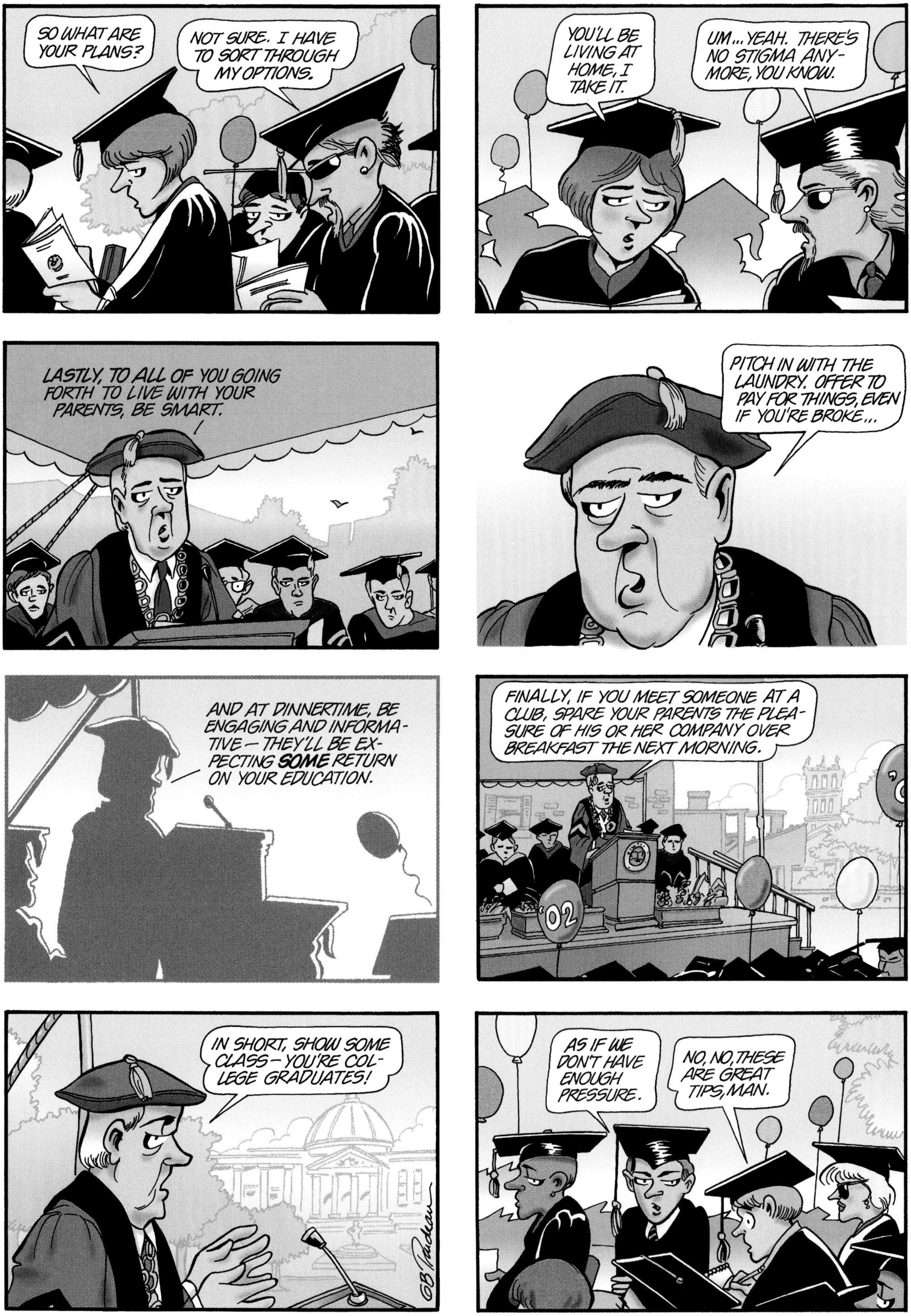
SO WHAT ARE YOUR PLANS?
NOT SURE. I HAVE TO SORT THROUGH MY OPTIONS.
YOU'LL BE LIVING AT HOME, I TAKE IT.
UM... YEAH. THERE'S NO STIGMA ANYMORE, YOU KNOW.
LASTLY, TO ALL OF YOU GOING FORTH TO LIVE WITH YOUR PARENTS, BE SMART.
PITCH IN WITH THE LAUNDRY. OFFER TO PAY FOR THINGS, EVEN IF YOU'RE BROKE...
AND AT DINNERTIME, BE ENGAGING AND INFORMATIVE — THEY'LL BE EXPECTING SOME RETURN ON YOUR EDUCATION.
FINALLY, IF YOU MEET SOMEONE AT A CLUB, SPARE YOUR PARENTS THE PLEASURE OF HIS OR HER COMPANY OVER BREAKFAST THE NEXT MORNING.
'02
IN SHORT, SHOW SOME CLASS — YOU'RE COLLEGE GRADUATES!
AS IF WE DON'T HAVE ENOUGH PRESSURE.
NO, NO, THESE ARE GREAT TIPS, MAN.

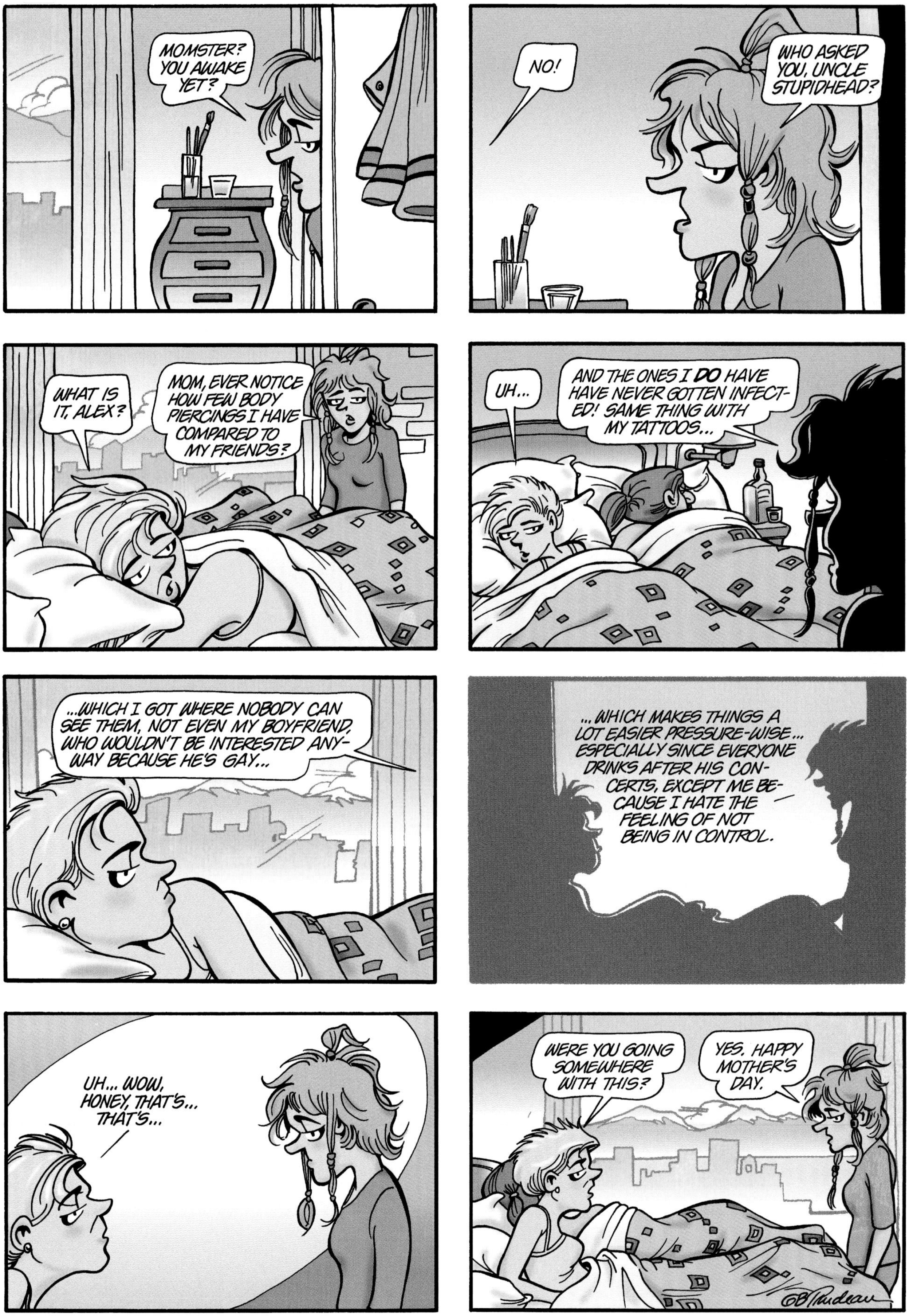
MOMSTER? YOU AWAKE YET?
NO!
WHO ASKED YOU, UNCLE STUPIDHEAD?
WHAT IS IT, ALEX?
MOM, EVER NOTICE HOW FEW BODY PIERCINGS I HAVE COMPARED TO MY FRIENDS?
UH...
AND THE ONES I **DO** HAVE HAVE NEVER GOTTEN INFECTED! SAME THING WITH MY TATTOOS...
...WHICH I GOT WHERE NOBODY CAN SEE THEM, NOT EVEN MY BOYFRIEND, WHO WOULDN'T BE INTERESTED ANYWAY BECAUSE HE'S GAY...
...WHICH MAKES THINGS A LOT EASIER PRESSURE-WISE... ESPECIALLY SINCE EVERYONE DRINKS AFTER HIS CONCERTS, EXCEPT ME BECAUSE I HATE THE FEELING OF NOT BEING IN CONTROL.
UH... WOW, HONEY, THAT'S... THAT'S...
WERE YOU GOING SOMEWHERE WITH THIS?
YES. HAPPY MOTHER'S DAY.
©B Trudeau

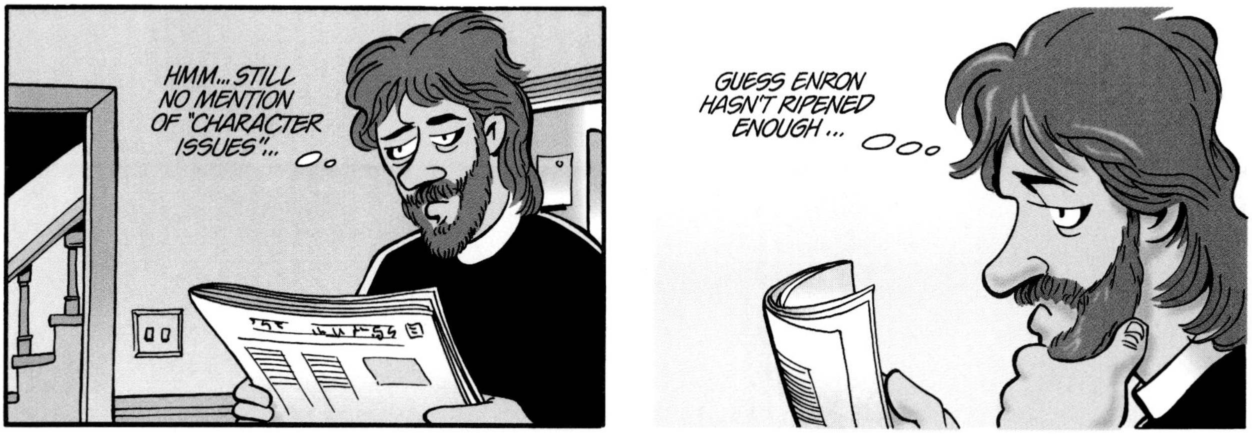
HMM... STILL NO MENTION OF "CHARACTER ISSUES"...
GUESS ENRON HASN'T RIPENED ENOUGH...

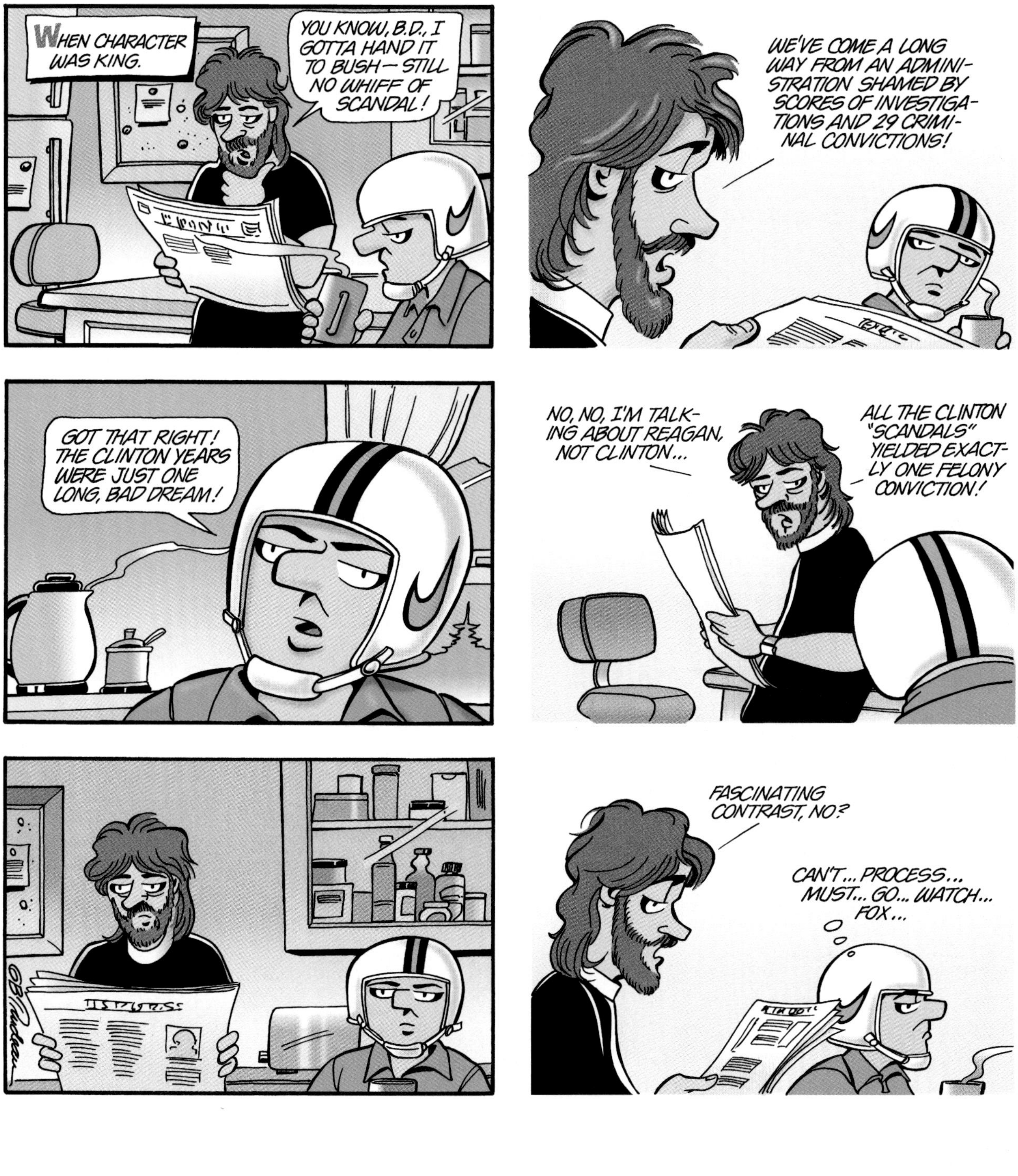
WHEN CHARACTER WAS KING.
YOU KNOW, B.D., I GOTTA HAND IT TO BUSH — STILL NO WHIFF OF SCANDAL!
WE'VE COME A LONG WAY FROM AN ADMINISTRATION SHAMED BY SCORES OF INVESTIGATIONS AND 29 CRIMINAL CONVICTIONS!
GOT THAT RIGHT! THE CLINTON YEARS WERE JUST ONE LONG, BAD DREAM!
NO, NO, I'M TALKING ABOUT REAGAN, NOT CLINTON...
ALL THE CLINTON "SCANDALS" YIELDED EXACTLY ONE FELONY CONVICTION!
FASCINATING CONTRAST, NO?
CAN'T... PROCESS... MUST... GO... WATCH... FOX...

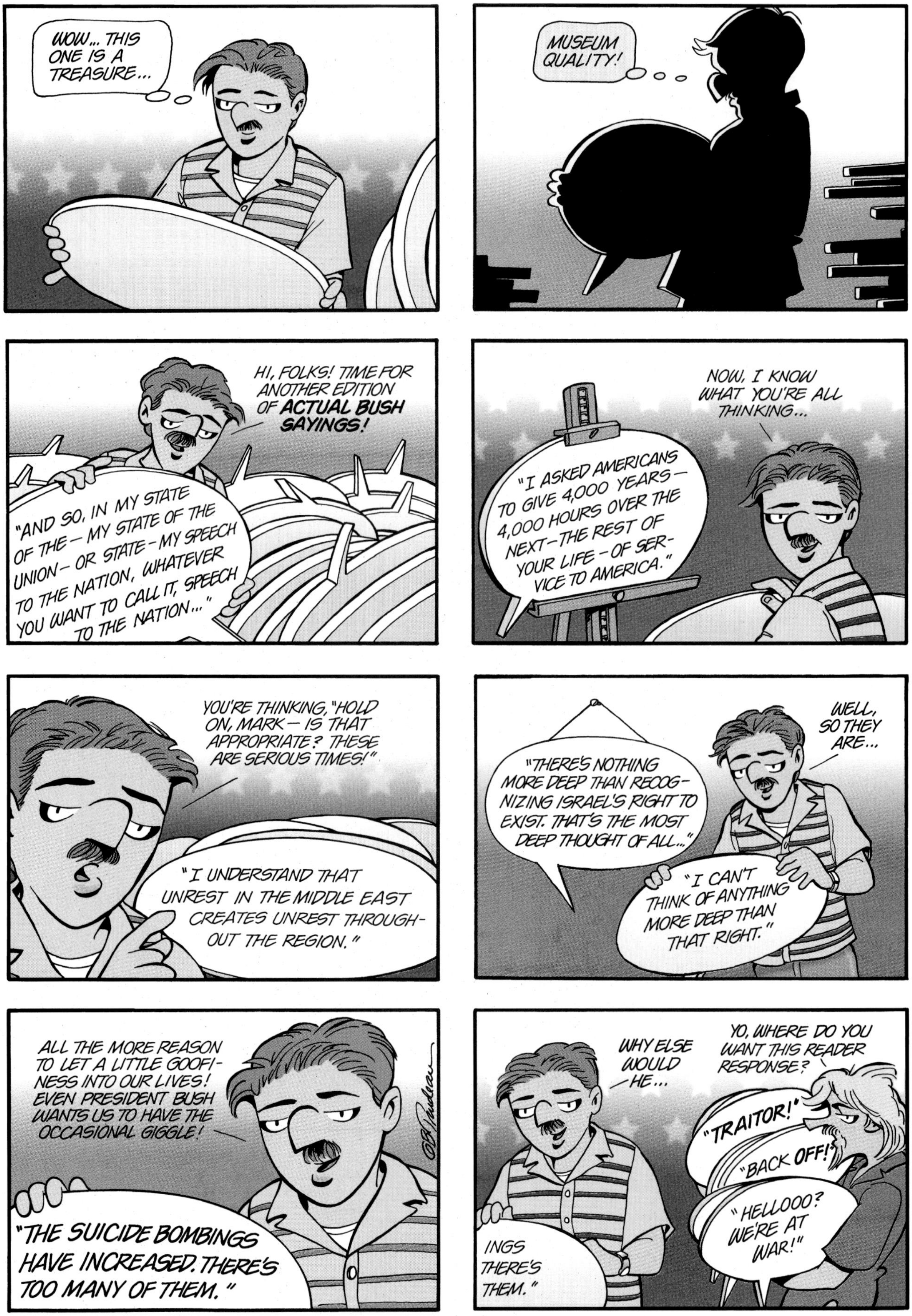
WOW... THIS ONE IS A TREASURE...
MUSEUM QUALITY!
HI, FOLKS! TIME FOR ANOTHER EDITION OF ACTUAL BUSH SAYINGS!
"AND SO, IN MY STATE OF THE— MY STATE OF THE UNION— OR STATE— MY SPEECH TO THE NATION, WHATEVER YOU WANT TO CALL IT, SPEECH TO THE NATION..."
NOW, I KNOW WHAT YOU'RE ALL THINKING...
"I ASKED AMERICANS TO GIVE 4,000 YEARS— 4,000 HOURS OVER THE NEXT— THE REST OF YOUR LIFE— OF SERVICE TO AMERICA."
YOU'RE THINKING, "HOLD ON, MARK— IS THAT APPROPRIATE? THESE ARE SERIOUS TIMES!"
"I UNDERSTAND THAT UNREST IN THE MIDDLE EAST CREATES UNREST THROUGHOUT THE REGION."
WELL, SO THEY ARE...
"THERE'S NOTHING MORE DEEP THAN RECOGNIZING ISRAEL'S RIGHT TO EXIST. THAT'S THE MOST DEEP THOUGHT OF ALL..."
"I CAN'T THINK OF ANYTHING MORE DEEP THAN THAT RIGHT."
ALL THE MORE REASON TO LET A LITTLE GOOFINESS INTO OUR LIVES! EVEN PRESIDENT BUSH WANTS US TO HAVE THE OCCASIONAL GIGGLE!
"THE SUICIDE BOMBINGS HAVE INCREASED. THERE'S TOO MANY OF THEM."
WHY ELSE WOULD HE...
INGS THERE'S THEM."
YO, WHERE DO YOU WANT THIS READER RESPONSE?
"TRAITOR!"
"BACK OFF!"
"HELLOOO? WE'RE AT WAR!"

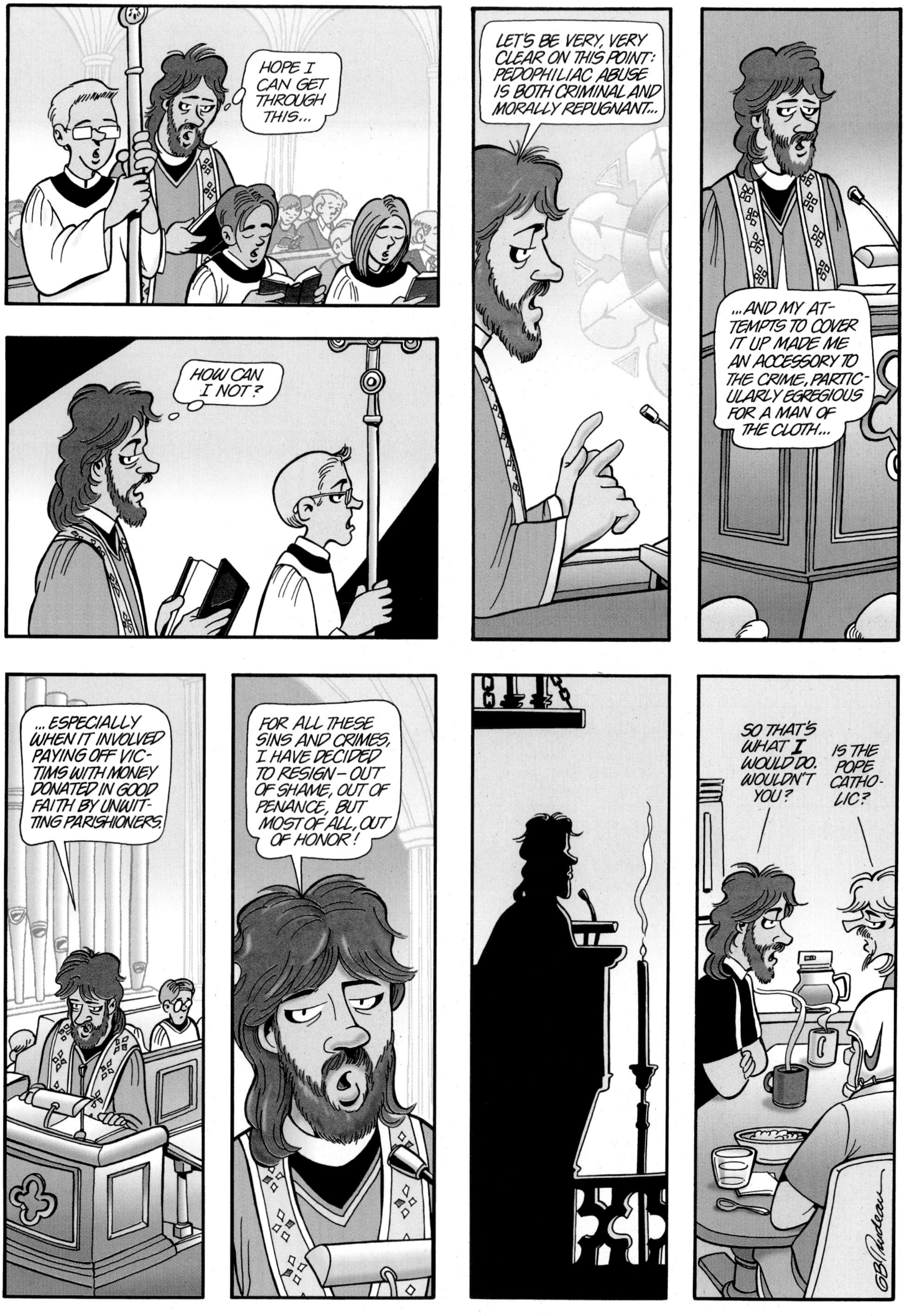
HOPE I CAN GET THROUGH THIS...
HOW CAN I NOT?
LET'S BE VERY, VERY CLEAR ON THIS POINT: PEDOPHILIAC ABUSE IS BOTH CRIMINAL AND MORALLY REPUGNANT...
...AND MY ATTEMPTS TO COVER IT UP MADE ME AN ACCESSORY TO THE CRIME, PARTICULARLY EGREGIOUS FOR A MAN OF THE CLOTH...
...ESPECIALLY WHEN IT INVOLVED PAYING OFF VICTIMS WITH MONEY DONATED IN GOOD FAITH BY UNWITTING PARISHIONERS.
FOR ALL THESE SINS AND CRIMES, I HAVE DECIDED TO RESIGN – OUT OF SHAME, OUT OF PENANCE, BUT MOST OF ALL, OUT OF HONOR!
SO THAT'S WHAT **I** WOULD DO. WOULDN'T YOU?
IS THE POPE CATHOLIC?
©B.Trudeau

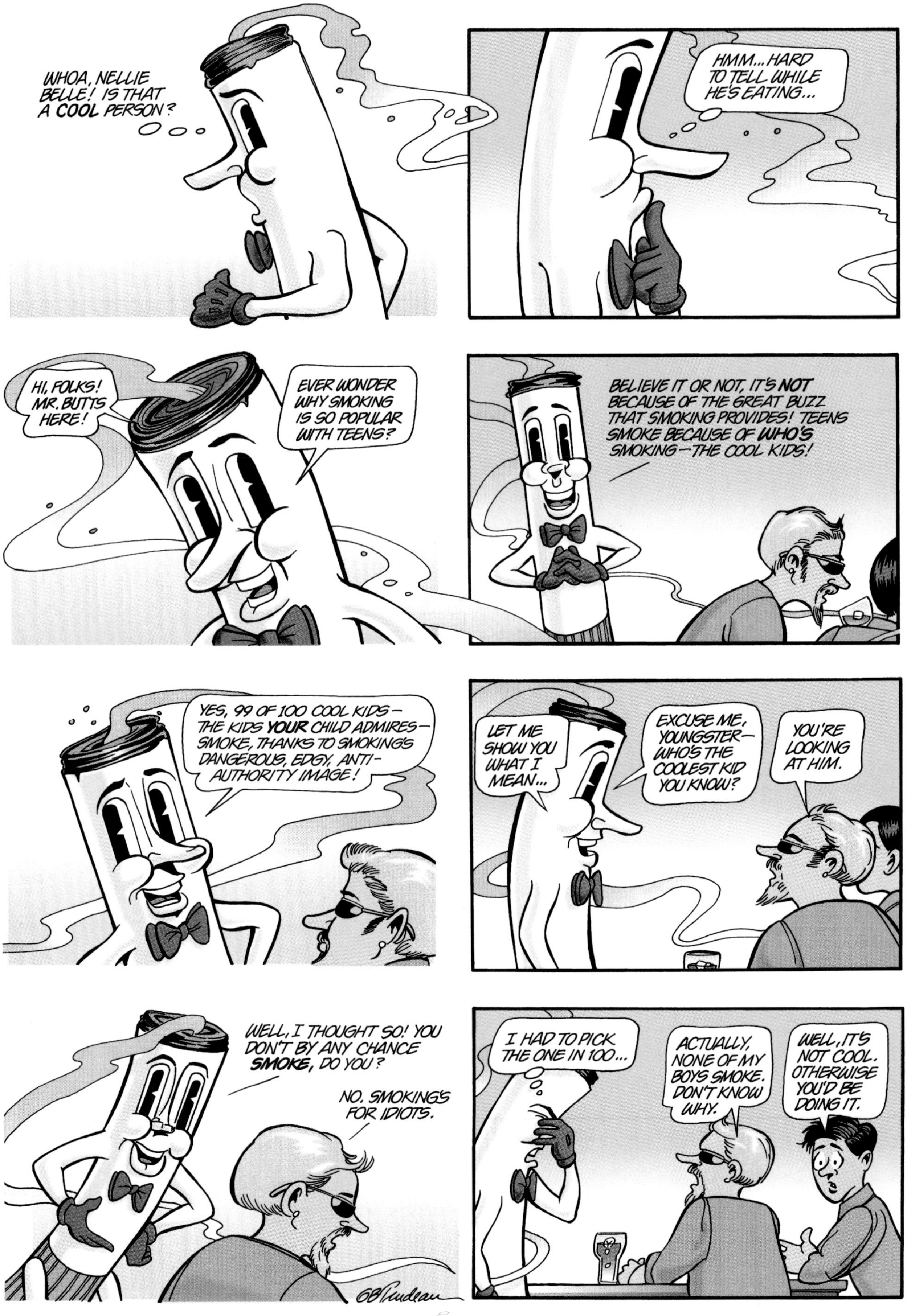
WHOA, NELLIE BELLE! IS THAT A COOL PERSON?
HMM... HARD TO TELL WHILE HE'S EATING...
HI, FOLKS! MR. BUTTS HERE!
EVER WONDER WHY SMOKING IS SO POPULAR WITH TEENS?
BELIEVE IT OR NOT, IT'S NOT BECAUSE OF THE GREAT BUZZ THAT SMOKING PROVIDES! TEENS SMOKE BECAUSE OF WHO'S SMOKING—THE COOL KIDS!
YES, 99 OF 100 COOL KIDS—THE KIDS YOUR CHILD ADMIRES—SMOKE, THANKS TO SMOKING'S DANGEROUS, EDGY, ANTI-AUTHORITY IMAGE!
LET ME SHOW YOU WHAT I MEAN...
EXCUSE ME, YOUNGSTER—WHO'S THE COOLEST KID YOU KNOW?
YOU'RE LOOKING AT HIM.
WELL, I THOUGHT SO! YOU DON'T BY ANY CHANCE SMOKE, DO YOU?
NO. SMOKING'S FOR IDIOTS.
I HAD TO PICK THE ONE IN 100...
ACTUALLY, NONE OF MY BOYS SMOKE. DON'T KNOW WHY.
WELL, IT'S NOT COOL. OTHERWISE YOU'D BE DOING IT.
GBTrudeau

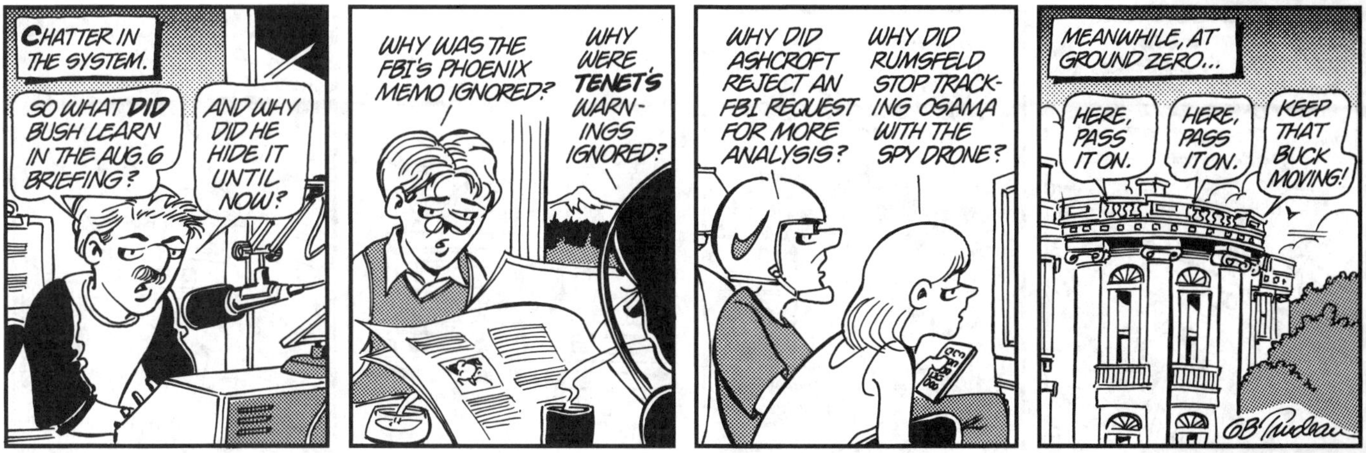
CHATTER IN THE SYSTEM.
SO WHAT DID BUSH LEARN IN THE AUG. 6 BRIEFING?
AND WHY DID HE HIDE IT UNTIL NOW?
WHY WAS THE FBI'S PHOENIX MEMO IGNORED?
WHY WERE TENET'S WARNINGS IGNORED?
WHY DID ASHCROFT REJECT AN FBI REQUEST FOR MORE ANALYSIS?
WHY DID RUMSFELD STOP TRACKING OSAMA WITH THE SPY DRONE?
MEANWHILE, AT GROUND ZERO...
HERE, PASS IT ON.
HERE, PASS IT ON.
KEEP THAT BUCK MOVING!
GB Trudeau

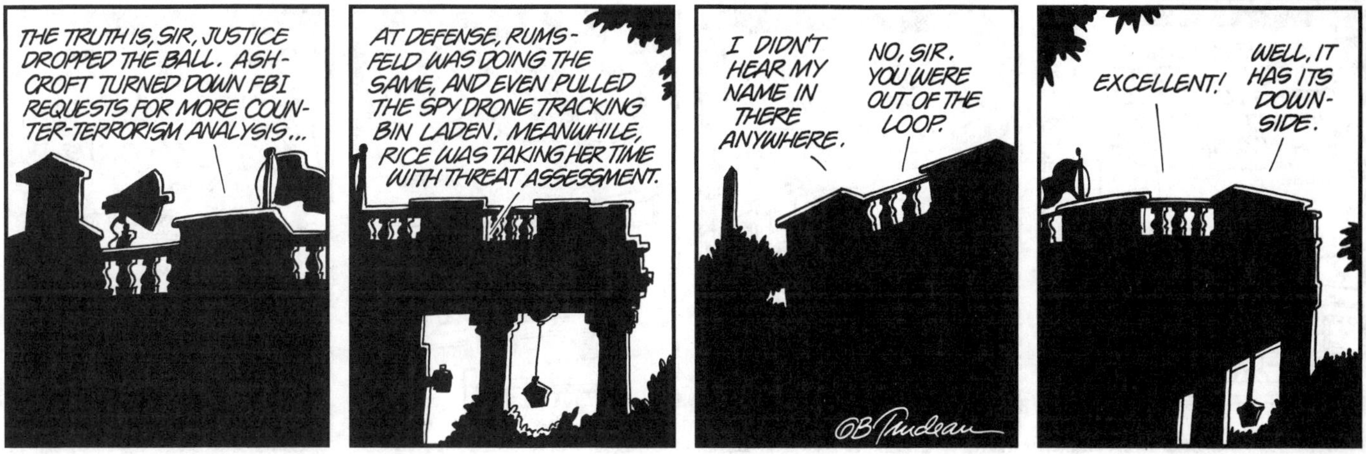
THE TRUTH IS, SIR, JUSTICE DROPPED THE BALL. ASHCROFT TURNED DOWN FBI REQUESTS FOR MORE COUNTER-TERRORISM ANALYSIS...
AT DEFENSE, RUMSFELD WAS DOING THE SAME, AND EVEN PULLED THE SPY DRONE TRACKING BIN LADEN. MEANWHILE, RICE WAS TAKING HER TIME WITH THREAT ASSESSMENT.
I DIDN'T HEAR MY NAME IN THERE ANYWHERE.
NO, SIR. YOU WERE OUT OF THE LOOP.
GB Trudeau
EXCELLENT!
WELL, IT HAS ITS DOWNSIDE.

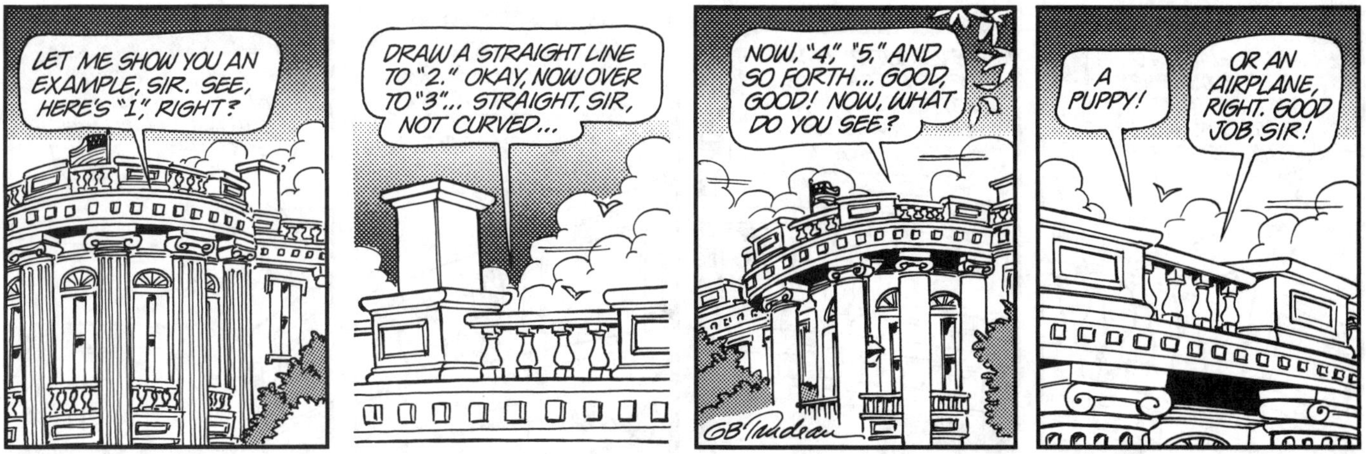
LET ME SHOW YOU AN EXAMPLE, SIR. SEE, HERE'S "1," RIGHT?
DRAW A STRAIGHT LINE TO "2." OKAY, NOW OVER TO "3"... STRAIGHT, SIR, NOT CURVED...
NOW, "4," "5," AND SO FORTH... GOOD, GOOD! NOW, WHAT DO YOU SEE?
GB Trudeau
A PUPPY!
OR AN AIRPLANE, RIGHT. GOOD JOB, SIR!

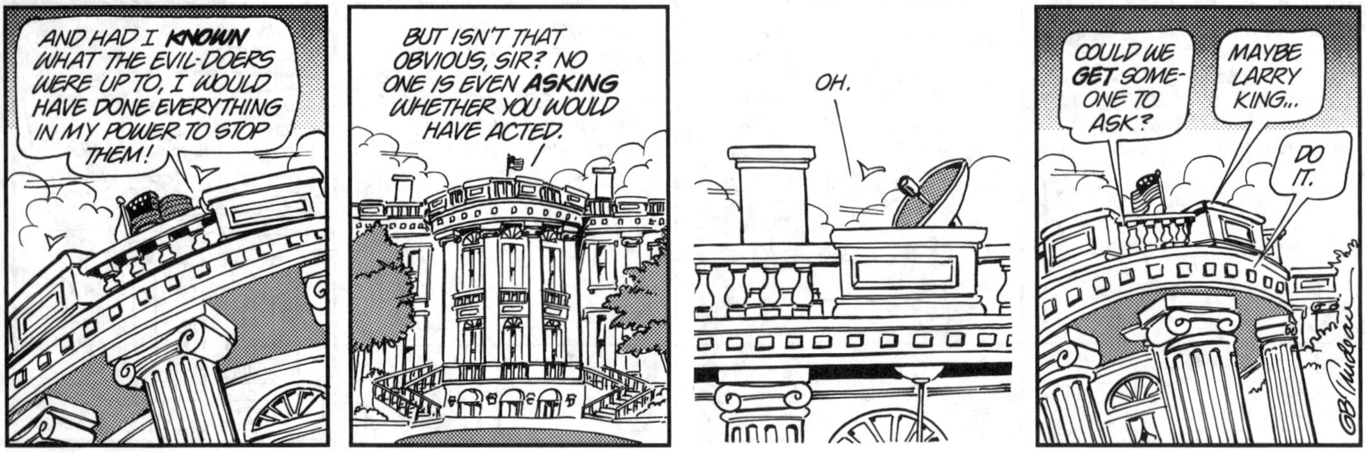
AND HAD I **KNOWN** WHAT THE EVIL-DOERS WERE UP TO, I WOULD HAVE DONE EVERYTHING IN MY POWER TO STOP THEM!
BUT ISN'T THAT OBVIOUS, SIR? NO ONE IS EVEN **ASKING** WHETHER YOU WOULD HAVE ACTED.
OH.
COULD WE **GET** SOME-ONE TO ASK?
MAYBE LARRY KING...
DO IT.

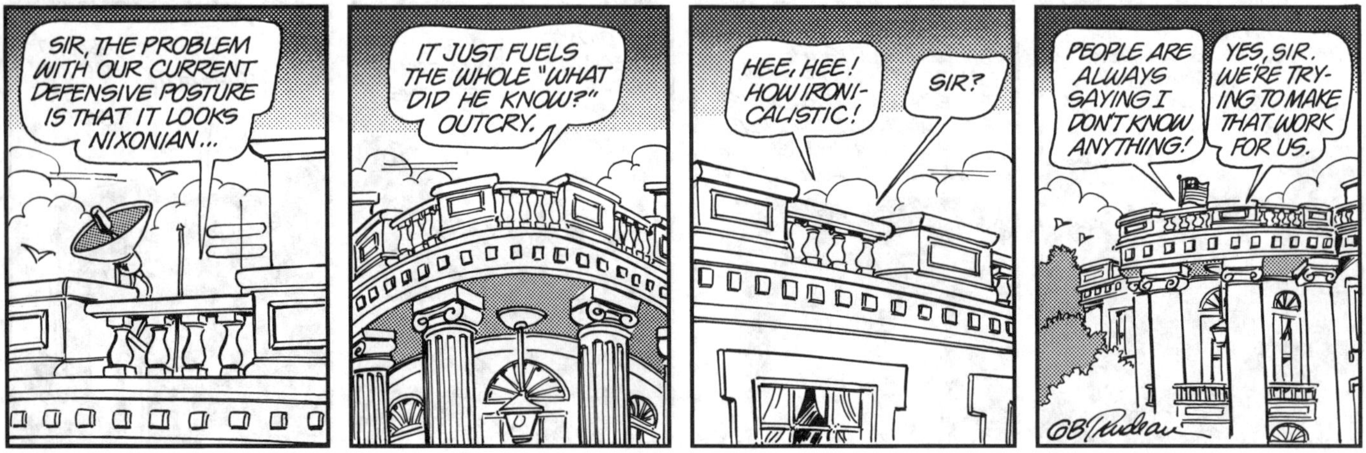
SIR, THE PROBLEM WITH OUR CURRENT DEFENSIVE POSTURE IS THAT IT LOOKS NIXONIAN...
IT JUST FUELS THE WHOLE "WHAT DID HE KNOW?" OUTCRY.
HEE, HEE! HOW IRONI-CALISTIC!
SIR?
PEOPLE ARE ALWAYS SAYING I DON'T KNOW ANYTHING!
YES, SIR. WE'RE TRY-ING TO MAKE THAT WORK FOR US.

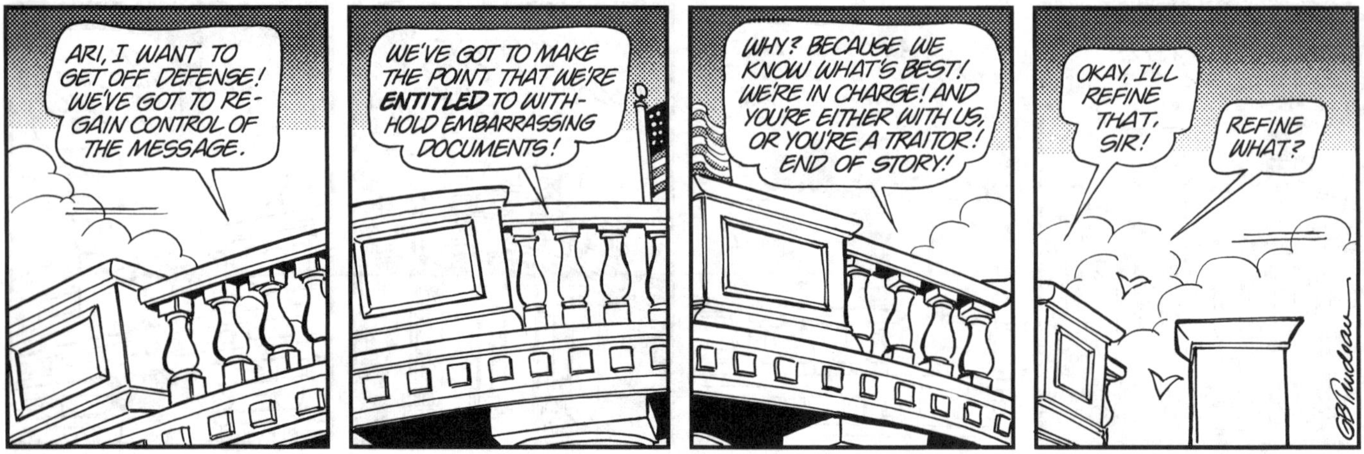
ARI, I WANT TO GET OFF DEFENSE! WE'VE GOT TO RE-GAIN CONTROL OF THE MESSAGE.
WE'VE GOT TO MAKE THE POINT THAT WE'RE **ENTITLED** TO WITH-HOLD EMBARRASSING DOCUMENTS!
WHY? BECAUSE WE KNOW WHAT'S BEST! WE'RE IN CHARGE! AND YOU'RE EITHER WITH US, OR YOU'RE A TRAITOR! END OF STORY!
OKAY, I'LL REFINE THAT, SIR!
REFINE WHAT?

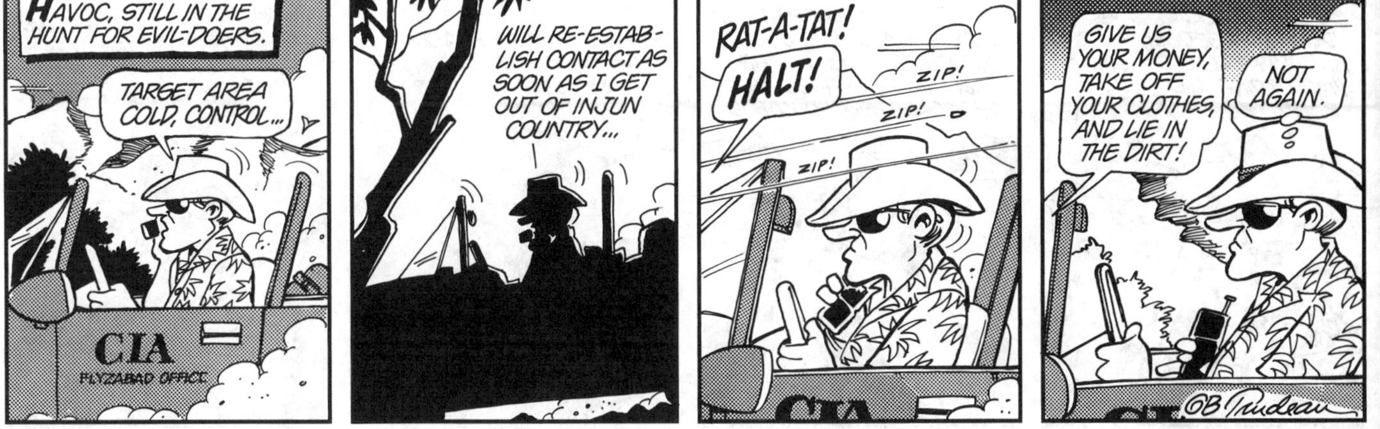
HAVOC, STILL IN THE HUNT FOR EVIL-DOERS.
TARGET AREA COLD, CONTROL...
CIA
FLYZABAD OFFICE
WILL RE-ESTABLISH CONTACT AS SOON AS I GET OUT OF INJUN COUNTRY...
RAT-A-TAT!
HALT!
ZIP!
ZIP!
ZIP!
GIVE US YOUR MONEY, TAKE OFF YOUR CLOTHES, AND LIE IN THE DIRT!
NOT AGAIN.

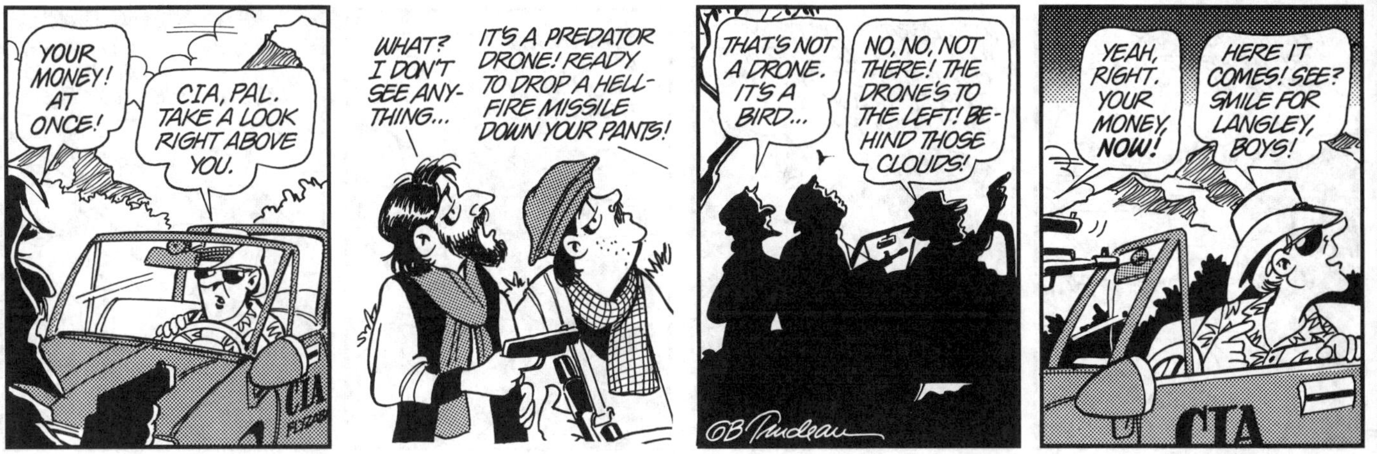
YOUR MONEY! AT ONCE!
CIA, PAL. TAKE A LOOK RIGHT ABOVE YOU.
WHAT? I DON'T SEE ANYTHING...
IT'S A PREDATOR DRONE! READY TO DROP A HELLFIRE MISSILE DOWN YOUR PANTS!
THAT'S NOT A DRONE. IT'S A BIRD...
NO, NO, NOT THERE! THE DRONE'S TO THE LEFT! BEHIND THOSE CLOUDS!
YEAH, RIGHT. YOUR MONEY, NOW!
HERE IT COMES! SEE? SMILE FOR LANGLEY, BOYS!
CIA

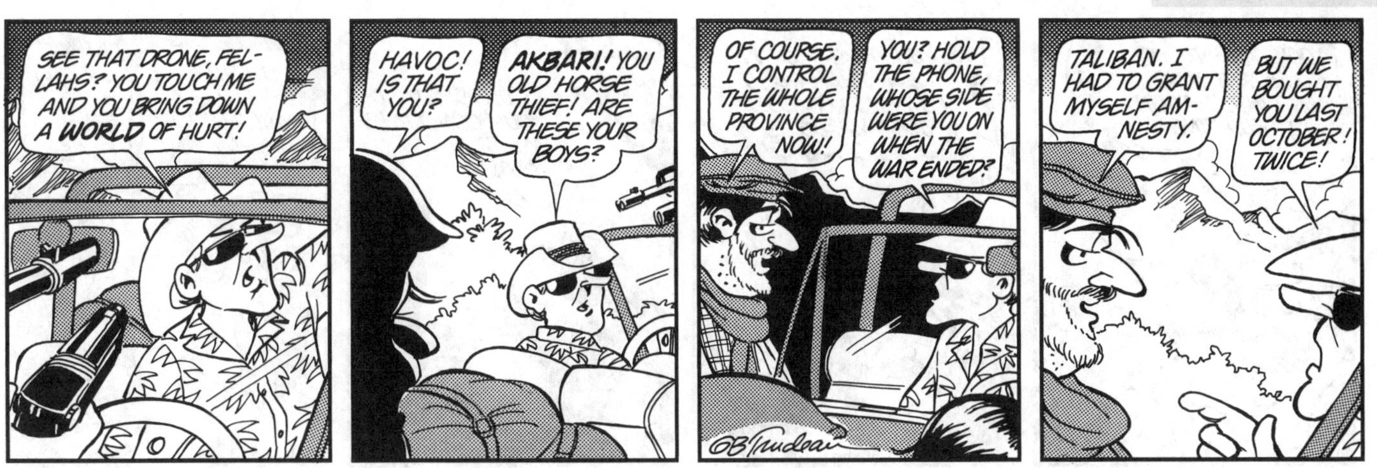
SEE THAT DRONE, FELLAHS? YOU TOUCH ME AND YOU BRING DOWN A WORLD OF HURT!
HAVOC! IS THAT YOU?
AKBARI! YOU OLD HORSE THIEF! ARE THESE YOUR BOYS?
OF COURSE. I CONTROL THE WHOLE PROVINCE NOW!
YOU? HOLD THE PHONE. WHOSE SIDE WERE YOU ON WHEN THE WAR ENDED?
TALIBAN. I HAD TO GRANT MYSELF AMNESTY.
BUT WE BOUGHT YOU LAST OCTOBER! TWICE!

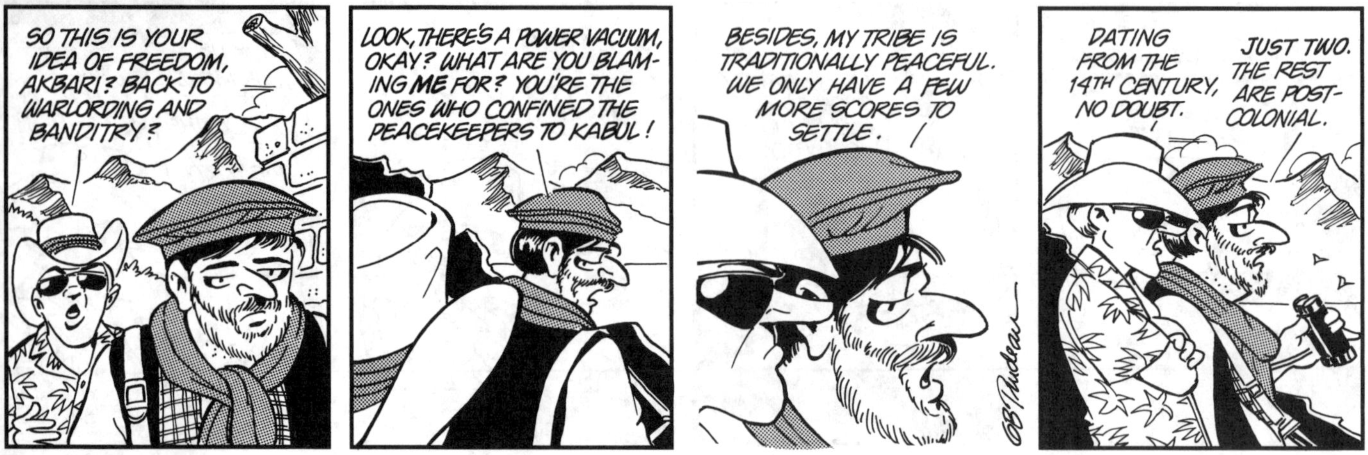
SO THIS IS YOUR IDEA OF FREEDOM, AKBARI? BACK TO WARLORDING AND BANDITRY?
LOOK, THERE'S A POWER VACUUM, OKAY? WHAT ARE YOU BLAMING ME FOR? YOU'RE THE ONES WHO CONFINED THE PEACEKEEPERS TO KABUL!
BESIDES, MY TRIBE IS TRADITIONALLY PEACEFUL. WE ONLY HAVE A FEW MORE SCORES TO SETTLE.
DATING FROM THE 14TH CENTURY, NO DOUBT.
JUST TWO. THE REST ARE POST-COLONIAL.

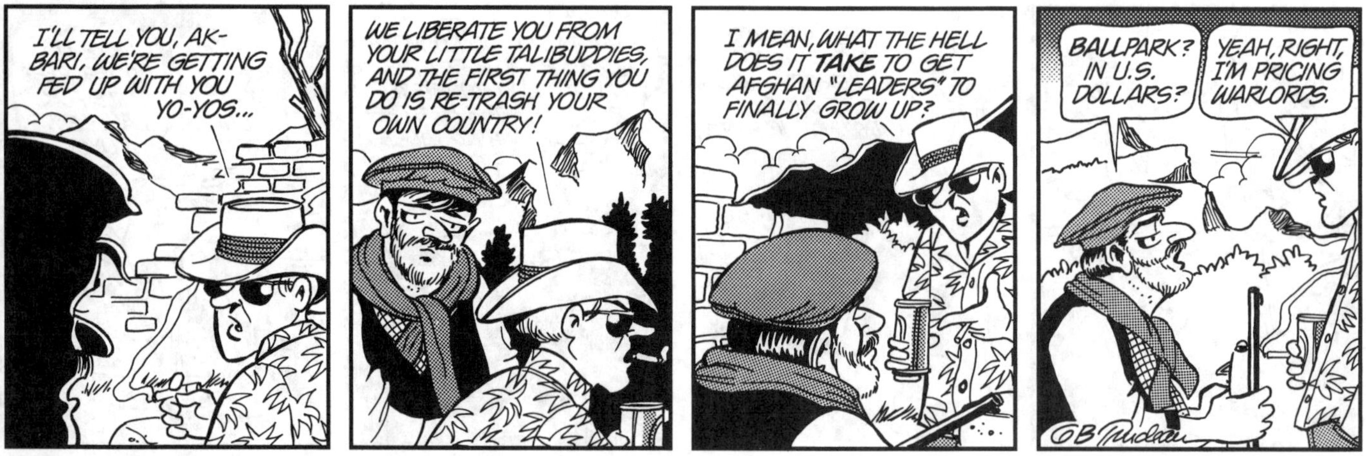
I'LL TELL YOU, AKBARI, WE'RE GETTING FED UP WITH YOU YO-YOS...
WE LIBERATE YOU FROM YOUR LITTLE TALIBUDDIES, AND THE FIRST THING YOU DO IS RE-TRASH YOUR OWN COUNTRY!
I MEAN, WHAT THE HELL DOES IT TAKE TO GET AFGHAN "LEADERS" TO FINALLY GROW UP?
BALLPARK? IN U.S. DOLLARS?
YEAH, RIGHT, I'M PRICING WARLORDS.

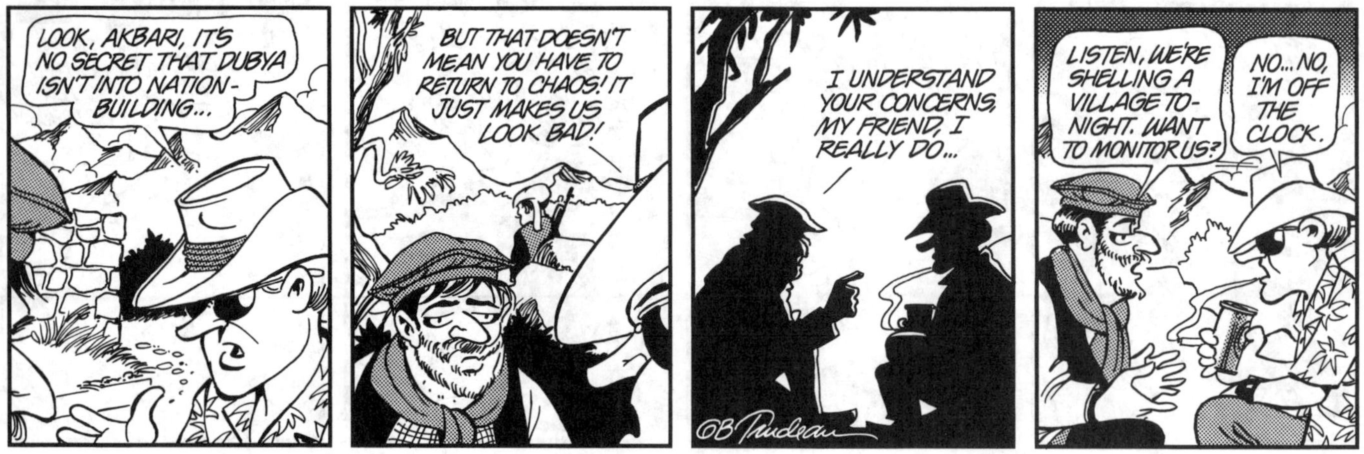
LOOK, AKBARI, IT'S NO SECRET THAT DUBYA ISN'T INTO NATION-BUILDING...
BUT THAT DOESN'T MEAN YOU HAVE TO RETURN TO CHAOS! IT JUST MAKES US LOOK BAD!
I UNDERSTAND YOUR CONCERNS, MY FRIEND, I REALLY DO...
LISTEN, WE'RE SHELLING A VILLAGE TONIGHT. WANT TO MONITOR US?
NO... NO, I'M OFF THE CLOCK.

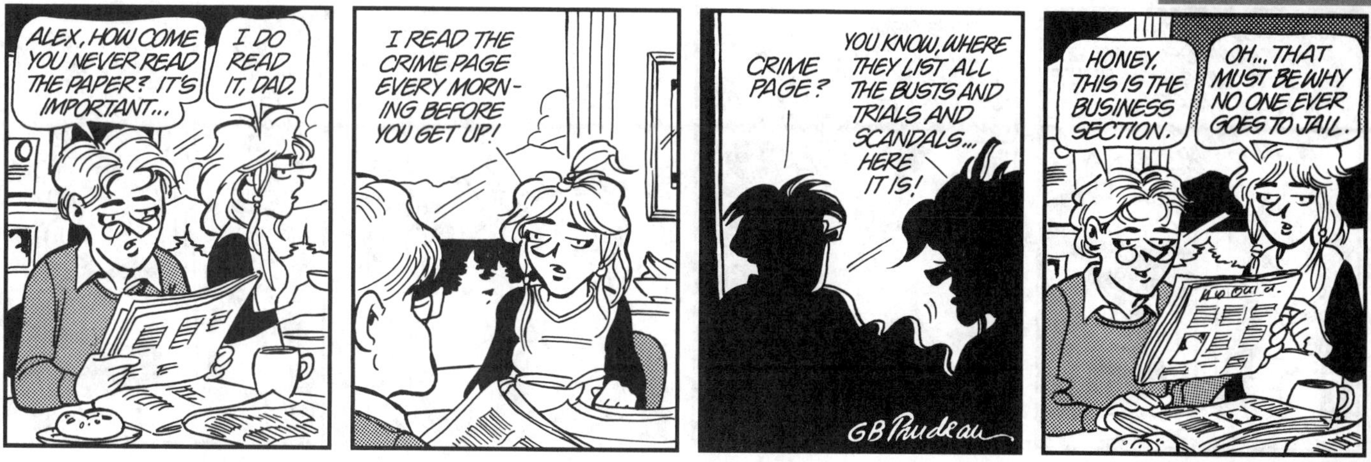
ALEX, HOW COME YOU NEVER READ THE PAPER? IT'S IMPORTANT...
I DO READ IT, DAD.
I READ THE CRIME PAGE EVERY MORNING BEFORE YOU GET UP!
CRIME PAGE?
YOU KNOW, WHERE THEY LIST ALL THE BUSTS AND TRIALS AND SCANDALS... HERE IT IS!
HONEY, THIS IS THE BUSINESS SECTION.
OH... THAT MUST BE WHY NO ONE EVER GOES TO JAIL.
GB Trudeau

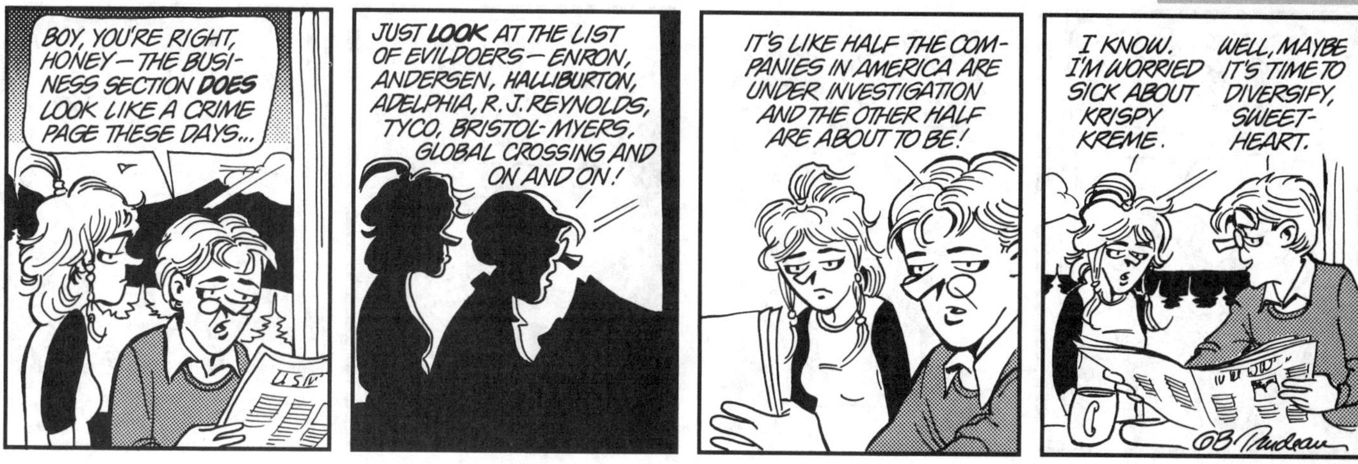
BOY, YOU'RE RIGHT, HONEY — THE BUSINESS SECTION DOES LOOK LIKE A CRIME PAGE THESE DAYS...
JUST LOOK AT THE LIST OF EVILDOERS — ENRON, ANDERSEN, HALLIBURTON, ADELPHIA, R.J. REYNOLDS, TYCO, BRISTOL-MYERS, GLOBAL CROSSING AND ON AND ON!
IT'S LIKE HALF THE COMPANIES IN AMERICA ARE UNDER INVESTIGATION AND THE OTHER HALF ARE ABOUT TO BE!
I KNOW. I'M WORRIED SICK ABOUT KRISPY KREME.
WELL, MAYBE IT'S TIME TO DIVERSIFY, SWEETHEART.
GB Trudeau

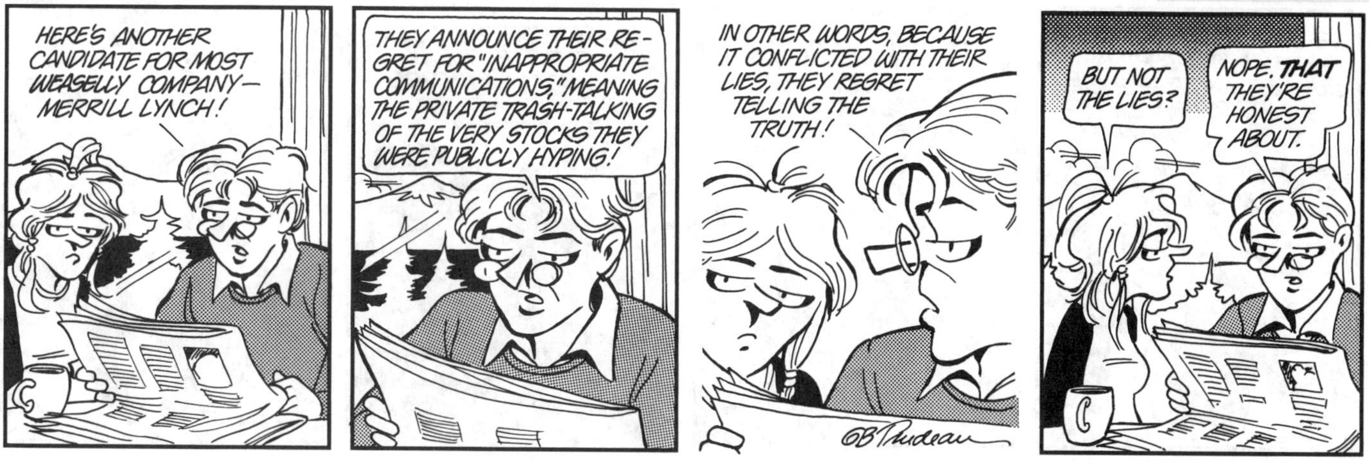
HERE'S ANOTHER CANDIDATE FOR MOST WEASELLY COMPANY — MERRILL LYNCH!
THEY ANNOUNCE THEIR REGRET FOR "INAPPROPRIATE COMMUNICATIONS," MEANING THE PRIVATE TRASH-TALKING OF THE VERY STOCKS THEY WERE PUBLICLY HYPING!
IN OTHER WORDS, BECAUSE IT CONFLICTED WITH THEIR LIES, THEY REGRET TELLING THE TRUTH!
BUT NOT THE LIES?
NOPE. THAT THEY'RE HONEST ABOUT.
GB Trudeau

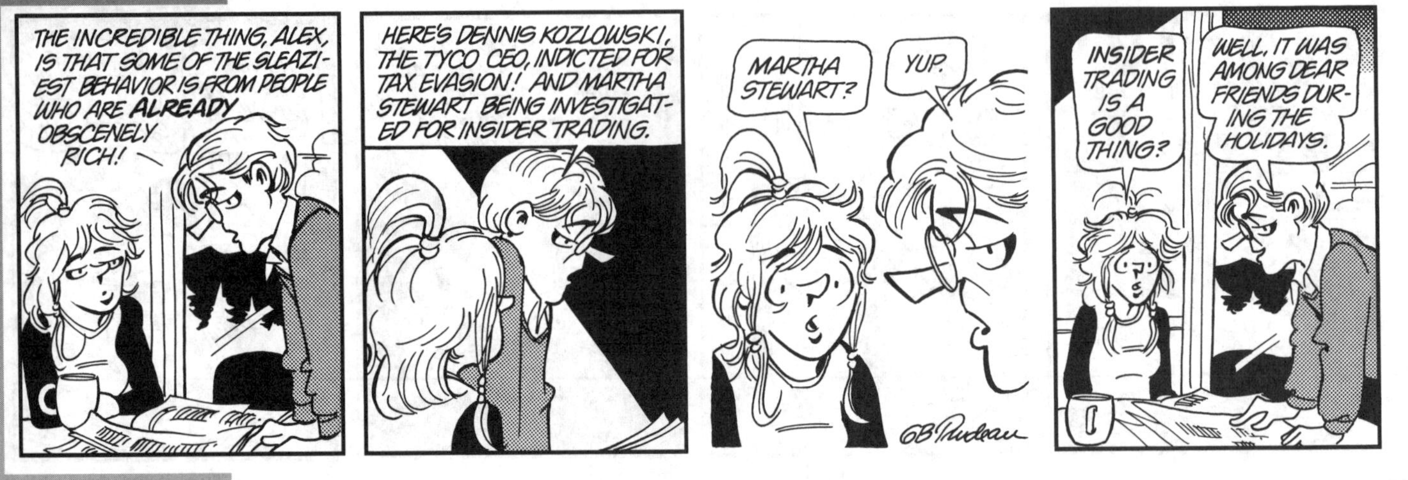
THE INCREDIBLE THING, ALEX, IS THAT SOME OF THE SLEAZIEST BEHAVIOR IS FROM PEOPLE WHO ARE ALREADY OBSCENELY RICH!
HERE'S DENNIS KOZLOWSKI, THE TYCO CEO, INDICTED FOR TAX EVASION! AND MARTHA STEWART BEING INVESTIGATED FOR INSIDER TRADING.
MARTHA STEWART?
YUP.
INSIDER TRADING IS A GOOD THING?
WELL, IT WAS AMONG DEAR FRIENDS DURING THE HOLIDAYS.
GBTrudeau

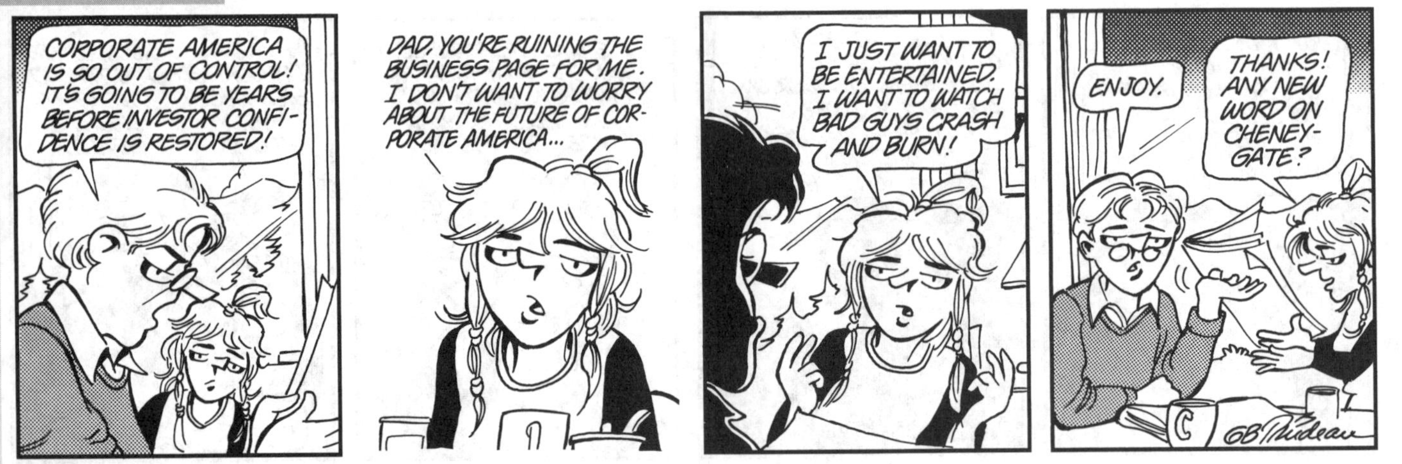
CORPORATE AMERICA IS SO OUT OF CONTROL! IT'S GOING TO BE YEARS BEFORE INVESTOR CONFIDENCE IS RESTORED!
DAD, YOU'RE RUINING THE BUSINESS PAGE FOR ME. I DON'T WANT TO WORRY ABOUT THE FUTURE OF CORPORATE AMERICA...
I JUST WANT TO BE ENTERTAINED. I WANT TO WATCH BAD GUYS CRASH AND BURN!
ENJOY.
THANKS! ANY NEW WORD ON CHENEY-GATE?
GBTrudeau

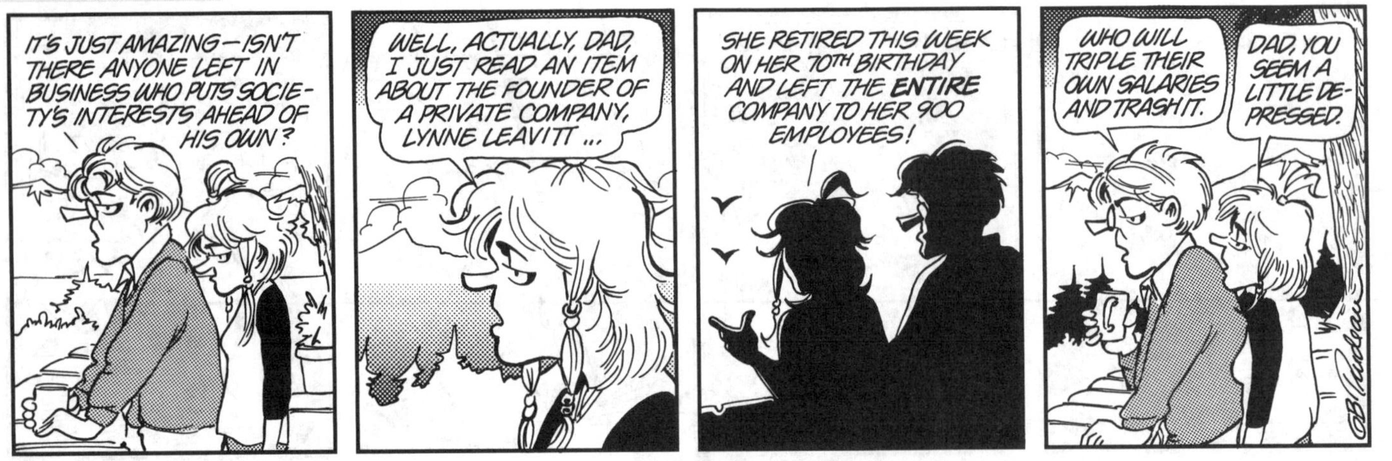
IT'S JUST AMAZING—ISN'T THERE ANYONE LEFT IN BUSINESS WHO PUTS SOCIETY'S INTERESTS AHEAD OF HIS OWN?
WELL, ACTUALLY, DAD, I JUST READ AN ITEM ABOUT THE FOUNDER OF A PRIVATE COMPANY, LYNNE LEAVITT ...
SHE RETIRED THIS WEEK ON HER 70TH BIRTHDAY AND LEFT THE ENTIRE COMPANY TO HER 900 EMPLOYEES!
WHO WILL TRIPLE THEIR OWN SALARIES AND TRASH IT.
DAD, YOU SEEM A LITTLE DEPRESSED.
GBTrudeau